Race,
Politics,
and
Culture

Recent Titles in
Contributions in Afro-American and African Studies
Series Advisers: John W. Blassingame and Henry Louis Gates, Jr.

Philanthropy and Jim Crow in American Social Science
John H. Stanfield

Israel in the Black American Perspective
Robert G. Weisbord and Richard Kazarian, Jr.

African Culture: The Rhythms of Unity
Molefi Kete Asante and Kariamu Welsh Asante, editors

Writing "Independent" History: African Historiography, 1960–1980
Caroline Neale

More Than Drumming: Essays on African and Afro-Latin American
Music and Musicians
Irene V. Jackson, editor

More Than Dancing: Essays on Afro-American Music and Musicians
Irene V. Jackson, editor

Sterling A. Brown: Building the Black Aesthetic Tradition
Joanne V. Gabbin

Amalgamation!: Race, Sex, and Rhetoric in the Nineteenth-Century
American Novel
James Kinney

Black Theatre in the 1960s and 1970s: A Historical-Critical Analysis
of the Movement
Mance Williams

An Old Creed for the New South: Proslavery Ideology and
Historiography, 1865–1918
John David Smith

Wilson Harris and the Modern Tradition: A New Architecture
of the World
Sandra E. Drake

Portrait of an Expatriate: William Gardner Smith, Writer
LeRoy S. Hodges, Jr.

RACE, POLITICS, AND CULTURE

CRITICAL ESSAYS ON THE RADICALISM OF THE 1960s

Edited by
ADOLPH REED, JR.

CONTRIBUTIONS IN AFRO-AMERICAN AND
AFRICAN STUDIES, NUMBER 95

GREENWOOD PRESS
NEW YORK • WESTPORT, CONNECTICUT • LONDON

Library of Congress Cataloging-in-Publication Data

Main entry under title:

Race, politics, and culture.

(Contributions in Afro-American and African studies, ISSN 0069-9624 ; no. 95)
  Bibliography: p.
  Includes index.
  1. Afro-Americans—Politics and government—Addresses, essays, lectures. 2. United States—Politics and government—1961–1963—Addresses, essays, lectures.
3. United States—Politics and government—1963–1969—Addresses, essays, lectures. 4. Radicalism—United States—History—20th century—Addresses, essays, lectures. I. Reed, Adolph, 1947–   . II. Series.
E185.615.R213 1986   305.8′00973   85-27162

ISBN 0-313-24480-4 (lib. bdg. : alk. paper)

Library of Congress Catalog Card Number: 85-27162
ISBN: 0-313-24480-4
ISSN: 0069-9624

First published in 1986

Greenwood Press, Inc.
88 Post Road West
Westport, Connecticut 06881

Printed in the United States of America

♾

The paper used in this book complies with the Permanent Paper Standard issued by the National Information Standards Organization (Z39.48-1984).

10 9 8 7 6 5 4 3 2 1

For my parents,
my son Touré,
and the spirit of Herbert Marcuse

To articulate the past historically does not mean to recognize it "the way it really was." It means to seize hold of a memory as it flashes up at a moment of danger. . . . In every era the attempt must be made to wrest tradition away from a conformism that is about to overpower it. . . . Only that historian will have the gift of fanning the spark of hope in the past who is firmly convinced that *even the dead* will not be safe from the enemy if he wins. And this enemy has not ceased to be victorious.

—Walter Benjamin, "Theses on the Philosophy of History"

Contents

INTRODUCTION
Adolph Reed, Jr.   3

Part I: Black Political and Cultural Radicalism   **11**

1 Ideology and Politics: Their Status in Afro-American
  Social Theory
  Alex Willingham   13

2 Cultural Nationalism in the 1960s: Politics and Poetry
  Jennifer Jordan   29

3 The "Black Revolution" and the Reconstitution
  of Domination
  Adolph Reed, Jr.   61

Part II: New Left Politics and Counterculture   **97**

4 Culture, Politics, and "Lifestyle" in the 1960s
  David Gross   99

5 Paths to Failure: The Dialectics of Organization and
  Ideology in the New Left
  Andrew Feenberg   119

6 The Medical Committee for Human Rights: A Case
  Study in the Self-Liquidation of the New Left
  Rhonda Kotelchuk and Howard Levy   145

Part III: Critical Theory and the Changing Social Context of Activism   **181**

7 The Modern Service State: Public Power in America
   from the New Deal to the New Beginning
   Timothy W. Luke   183

8 Rationalization and the Family
   Joel Kovel   207

9 The Future of Capitalism
   Paul Piccone   227

Part IV: What's Left?: An Exchange   **245**

BIBLIOGRAPHICAL NOTE   275

INDEX   279

ABOUT THE CONTRIBUTORS   285

Race,
Politics,
and
Culture

Introduction

Russell Jacoby has argued that a peculiar, amnestic principle increasingly constrains American life, militating against development of critical thinking. "Social amnesia," as Jacoby calls it, is enmeshed with reification, the spurious presentation of the "human and social relationships of society as natural—and—unchangeable—relations between things."[1] To the consciousness formed under those circumstances the dominant viewpoint of the present is taken as "neutral and absolute truth, outside—not inside—history."[2] The past, therefore, is reduced to positive (as similarity) or negative (as deviation) affirmation of whatever currently exists. To the social amnesiacs past and present appear as discontinuous, and thus practically irrelevant to each other, or the past flounces around as a Mardi-Gras image: this week's banalities adorned by replicas of obsolete artifacts; in either case only a reified present seems to organize life.

Popular culture offers perhaps clearest illustration of the quietistic consequences of the obliteration of historical consciousness. On the one hand, films such as *Reds* or *Return of the Secaucus Seven* deauthorize the principle of opposition by locking it within the past perfect tense; radicalism and idealism were appropriate stances "back then" because unfairness *had* existed, and, besides, the activists inhabited a naive world that did not yet understand the futility of idealism. On the other hand, the television "docudrama" proceeds from a formula that reads back into the past even the most historically specific attitudes and behaviors of the present; black freedmen or Shogun warriors interact among their fellows through a distinctly mass capitalist discourse of psychobabble and human relations engineering. In both cases a hollow past is pasted together only to validate the present.

Not even so recent a past as the 1960s is immune. Now that the postwar baby boom has settled into maturity, at least two forms of amnestic decay suffuse reflection on its youthful activism. In one, the political and/social movements and personalities prominent during that period are hypostatized as "the Sixties." The critiques and visions articulated by those movements and the self-understandings of participants in them are melded with styles of hair and clothing into a single, time-bound image. Thus classified, this image requires little further rumination; "the Sixties" constitute another "back then," worthy of note only as a curio piece that underscores the natural order of the present. By the latter 1970s the stage was set for a where-are-they-now popular journalism in which activist relics enter the spotlight to acknowledge the image's obsolescence. With a kitschy irony born of cynicism, the mass media have paraded a string of God-that-failed (or God-that-succeeded) revelations by old movement symbols, a characteristically sensational kind of mass culture show trial.

So, we saw Rennie Davis traipsing around behind a pudgy, improbable guru and Abbie Hoffman exposing himself in the pages of *People* and *Viva* to reassure us that his underground tour—inspired by flight from a prison term for selling cocaine—had shown him balance in the "heartland of America" and a new awakening on the horizon. Jerry Rubin, lauding the "inner revolution," was equally sanguine about the lessons of his meandering journey within, announcing that he could now revel in his ever-youthful, evanescent Self—which thereupon became a stockbroker/consultant. Bob Dylan resurfaced as a fundamentalist Christian gospel singer; Mike Klonsky lingers as a de facto agent of whatever faction rules in China; and the FBI—four years before the Nyack, New York, Brinks robbery—proclaimed the Weather Underground to be no longer even worthy of prosecution. Obituaries of Marcuse, Sartre, and Paul Goodman were written also as obituaries of opposition. At the same time, on the other side of Du Bois's veil, Eldridge Cleaver—ever the media creature—returned to America as a latter-day Cold Warrior, holy roller, advocate of wife-beating (a mellowing of his earlier defense of rape?), and designer of pornographic pants. Huey Newton's name came to evoke suspicions of drug-dealing, murder, and extortion, and Bobby Seale was showcased as a nightclub comedian and cookbook author. H. Rap Brown returned to public view as a Muslim small businessman, consuming his time in prayer to Allah, Martin Luther King became a holiday and a postage stamp, a meal ticket for his widow and hobby for Stevie Wonder. In each case the message rings clear; opposition is the property of the image of "the Sixties," and it is, therefore, like bell-bottom pants, dashikis, and long hair, no longer appropriate.

A second variant of amnesia concerning recent movements is more complex, in part because it is frequently well intentioned. Toward the end of the 1970s a number of social scientists undertook in different ways to assess the impact of black activism on American political life. Even though those scholars' dispositions generally have been sympathetic, the structuralist and empiricist orientation of their accounts, by collapsing the intentions and outcomes of activism, have vitiated what they would vindicate. These accounts demonstrate that the Civil Rights and Black Power movements ensued in more thorough integration of blacks into the negotiating arena of electoral pluralism. To that extent this scholarship has helped to establish a solid picture of the outcomes of activism, principal among them enhancement of the position of blacks as a legitimate constituency to be factored into the steering calculus of the pluralist system. However, this outcome is taken as if it were the objective that stimulated activism in the first place. Suppressed in historical memory is the ambiguous, yet global, vision that gave those movements the heroic character through which they sustained themselves. These interpretations, therefore, sabotage the historical integrity of activism by forgetting its moments of transcendence, its openness to alternative possibility. They represent Civil Rights and Black Power activism as strategic behavior grounded entirely on pluralist rationality as a structuring principle.

The effects of that representation undermine even the best intentions. Retrospective reading of the objectives of those movements as rational pluralism suppresses the moments of opposition constituted in them both as utopian vision and programmatic radicalism. No matter how fleeting or marginal the oppositional tendencies in black activism were, they existed as discrete options among a number of embedded possibilities in contention to steer the movement's articulation. The reductionism inherent to structuralist and empiricist readings inclines toward a victor's history; once Civil Rights and Black Power activism are reduced to their outcomes, what remains of their genesis is only an objectified tale of the linear unfolding of the present arrangements.

So it is that James Button, in an empirically useful account, simply assumes the urban uprisings of the 1960s to have been politically cognizant expressions of discontent with urban blacks' position in the pluralist queue. Following this assumption, which he recycles from the collective wisdom of theorists of collective violence, Button invests urban disorders with responsibility for "performing attention-getting and catalytic functions on behalf of the partisans of violence."[3] That is, even the most explicit quotidian repudiation of the current order becomes a de facto affirmation of its inescapable hegemony. Similarly, Doug McAdam is so much concerned with the movement's structural antecedents and empirical trace materials (e.g., number of demonstrations, demographic characteristics of initiating agents) that he never actually discusses what he calls the "black movement" as a dynamic entity at all. As a result he rewrites the trajectory of more than two generations of black activism to yield a story of the working out of an invariant strategy of interest-group articulation. His account so tightly binds that activity to the imputed goal of expanded pluralist participation that he concludes, preposterously, that the "movement" declined primarily because it ventured too far from the "limited-reform goals" and postures required to retain support from powerful white entrenched elites.[4] In other words, deviation from the regnant pluralist calculus of dominance and subordination is hopeless and, for McAdam, unthinkable.

Ironically, this scholarship draws much of its inspiration from the Marxist-structuralist interpretation proposed by Piven and Cloward, whose account—although much more sophisticated than McAdam's— also is disposed to explain activism in terms of its structural coordinates and by-products. Because their focus is elsewhere, these authors abstract away from the internal dynamics of the Civil Rights movement, and as a result they reduce the movement's goals to a least common denominator, the objectives of the liberal-reform tendencies that ultimately won the struggle for hegemony over the civil rights agenda.[5] This reduction, filtered through their structural determinism, leads Piven and Cloward to characterize the political negation constituted by black activism as "defiance"—a notion connected with demands for positional adjustment in pluralist queueing—rather than opposition.[6] Although it is hardly their intention, Piven and Cloward thereby reduce activism categorically to an epiphenomenon of the prevailing system of governance.

A partial exception to this structuralist reductionism is Robert Smith's discussion of the role of the Black Power movement as an agency for facilitating pluralist integration. Smith, unlike the others, acknowledges the existence of different tendencies in the movement. However, he then retroactively vests each of those tendencies with a substantive purpose of advancing pluralist participation. All roads lead to the New Deal coalition.[7] Significantly, he cites Bayard Rustin's well-known 1965 *Commentary* article to illustrate the empirical transmutation of Black Power radicalism into interest-group politics. The reference forgets that Rustin was not *documenting* a shift "From Protest to Politics"; he was a partisan, lobbying for a particular—and very much controversial—point of view within the Civil Rights movement. Rustin's point of view became fully dominant eventually, but not until the 1970s and as the outcome of an accretion of political choices made in response to arrays of concrete options posed by dynamics operative in and on the movement. Smith's rendition glosses the controversy surrounding each step in the march toward pluralism. By discussing the radical elements only in terms of their immanent functionality for pluralist integration—which can become most significant only ex post facto, once integration has occurred—but not also in relation to their intentional stance of opposition, Smith's interpretation forgets an important and problematic motif in the transformation he describes. To the extent that he disconnects that transformation from a contest of tendencies within the movement, he surrounds the development toward interest-group liberalism with an aura of inevitability. Like Button in intelligently describing substantive outcomes of the movement and like McAdam and Piven and Cloward in carefully relating those outcomes to movement characteristics, Smith shares with all the others an interpretive bias that reads the contingency out of past activism. So, while popular culture dispatches post-Cold War activism to the clothes bins of obsolete fashion, social scientists pacify it through reconstructions that eliminate its internal tensions and foregone possibilities as excess baggage. The one approach suppresses the historical specificity of "the Sixties' " social movements by reifying their pastness; the other flattens those movements' lived history until it appears only as an embryo of an inexorable present. Both careful, sympathetic scholarship and cynical popular culture sanctify the present by amnestically eradicating its morphological origin.

The contributions to this volume, while generally accepting the premise that 1960s radicalism dissolved into pluralist politics and mass consumption culture, come together around a common perception that that dissolution was neither natural, inevitable, nor desirable. Rather, a thread that unites this collection is the desire to shed light on the dialectic of internal tensions and external pressures that eventuated in passage of black, counterculture and other New Left movements from critical opposition to new styles of interest-group politics and new consumer markets. Emerging from the collection as a totality is a view that connects the various currents of upheaval in "the Sixties" both with one another and with forces that simultaneously were reshaping the American social order in ways often opaque to but reinforced by the activists themselves. The picture thus presented is one of the erosion of oppositional content as a result of choices exercised (and rejected) within a universe of options structured by the developmental logic of post-World War II institutions.

Our project shares with structural accounts recognition of the need to situate the movements in relation to the social order in which they were articulated. Luke analyzes the development of the clientelistic "service state" as an integrative mechanism in the modern United States. Kovel examines the impact of capitalist rationalization on individual and family life, especially in the post-World War II period, and he suggests a basis for relating that impact to the problems and options that the New Left perceived for itself. Piccone provides a global critique of the logic of capitalist social administration since the New Deal and connects 1960s activism with a crisis of administrative rationality. The other authors as well are sensitive to the historical or "conjunctural" specificity of the activist motion.

Unlike structuralist readings, however, this volume concentrates its focus on the movements themselves. Willingham examines ideological variants of black radicalism in relation to persisting issues of social theory and practical politics among Afro-Americans. Jordan provides a thoroughgoing internal critique of black cultural nationalism, based mainly on historically grounded close reading of that movement's literary texts as well as its political tracts. My contribution reconstructs the interaction of institutional and theoretical characteristics of black activism—radical and liberal—that undermined its oppositional content. Similarly, Feenberg unravels the interplay of organizational, theoretical, and ideological forces that drove the white New Left. Gross examines the assumptions and styles of counterculture radicalism and relates them critically to operating principles of the mass-consumption culture against which radicals defined themselves. Kotelchuk and Levy, in the mode of a critical phenomenology, excavate the natural history of a single movement organization that was an arena for all the major ideological tendencies of post-Cold War activism—from Civil Rights liberalism through Maoist death agonies.

At the same time that this volume's insistence on critique of activism's internal dynamics distinguishes it from structuralist renditions, the authors' general acknowledgment that 1960s radicalism failed as an emancipatory politics sets this collection apart from another body of recent literature on the various components of the New Left. At the end of the 1970s and into the early 1980s reflection on 1960s activism attained a certain topicality, and a number of interesting, generally cogent reconstructions appeared in response to the vogue.[8] Yet most of these volumes (Gitlin's is a welcome exception) are dominated by a cheery, positive thinking that obscures the problematic fact that Vietnam era radicalism—black or white—was unable to survive as coherent political opposition. Several of these volumes, e.g., those by Evans and Case and Taylor, offer valuable critical histories of given currents of 1960s activism. Each identifies weaknesses, misunderstandings, and contradictions existing in the movement in its heyday. However, each assures that those activist streams opened new vistas for emancipatory social intervention and that they minimally have "enriched the heritage of the left and contributed towards visions of the future."[9] Despite these assurances, the fact remains that by the middle of the 1970s no signs of an oppositional political movement could be observed in the United States. The marginalized left's standard explanations—cooptation, repression—are hardly more than excuses. All opposition movements must face those obstacles, by definition. The ultimate sources of decline must be sought within the movements themselves. Through that search this volume seeks also to overcome the disparity between saccharine prognostication and bleak reality.

This project began with a symposium at Howard University on "Race, Politics and Culture in the Sixties and Beyond" at which most of the volume's contributors participated. That symposium provided a setting for a unique dialogue among a group of black and white intellectuals, all veterans of the motion in the 1960s, exploring systematically the dynamics that underlay the rise and passage of 1960s activism. Several of the contributions to this collection began as papers given at that gathering. Current versions reflect, inter alia, incorporation of insights produced by our interaction. A flavor of that interaction is presented here in a general exchange among contributors on the demise of radicalism.

The spirit of this volume accepts as an initial premise and problem the decline of political opposition in the 1970s and 1980s; to that extent it also proceeds from an assumption of the ultimate failure of new left activism (including black radicalism), inasmuch as institutionalization of an emancipatory force in America was one of the left's major objectives. The premise that activism failed, however, should not be read as belittling either the heroic sacrifices made by individuals or the actual successes of their movements, e.g., the destruction of racial segregation as a social system, the opening of pluralist politics to clienteles that previously had been excluded, and the articulation of feminist voices that have cracked the shell of givenness securing male dominance. Nor should that premise be taken even to hint at repudiation of opposition or resignation to the current order of things. Rather, the heroism of Viola Liuzzo, James Chaney, Fannie Lou Hamer, and the many less-well-known others who gave greatly of themselves in striving to actualize transcendent visions in the various movements of the 1960s is honored here not with sanctimony or hollow celebration but with a refusal to abandon the emancipatory project that evoked heroic effort in the first place. Indeed, those movements can be judged to have failed only in the context of the unrealized possibilities that they had opened. In recovering the sources of their failure, therefore, this collection pays homage to them by striving to remember opposition as a real historical possibility.

NOTES

1. Russell Jacoby, *Social Amnesia: A Critique of Conformist Psychology from Adler to Laing* (Boston, 1975), p. 4.

2. Ibid., p. 2.

3. James W. Button, *Black Violence: Political Impact of the 1960s Riots* (Prince-

ton, 1978), p. 162. Button's account is characteristic of literature on the urban uprisings in its overly rationalistic reading in of strategic political motivations. A far more interesting and, I believe, accurate interpretation of the self-understanding of participants appears in Hajime Tada, "The Ghetto Riots As Celebrations of Communitas," senior essay, Department of Political Science, Yale University, 1983.

4. Doug McAdam, *Political Processes and the Development of Black Insurgency, 1930–1970* (Chicago, 1982), p. 228.

5. Frances Fox Piven and Richard A. Cloward, *Poor People's Movements: Why They Succeed, How They Fail* (New York, 1977), p. 181 passim.

6. This aspect of the focus on defiance as a critical category is most apparent in Piven and Cloward's discussion of the Welfare Rights movement in ibid., pp. 264ff.

7. Robert Smith, "Black Power and the Transformation from Protest to Politics," *Political Science Quarterly* 96 (Fall, 1981), pp. 431–443.

8. Among the best of these are: Sara Evans, *Personal Politics: The Roots of Women's Liberation in the Civil Rights Movement and the New Left* (New York, 1979); Todd Gitlin's masterful study, *The Whole World Is Watching!: Mass Media in the Making and Unmaking of the New Left* (Berkeley, 1980); Wini Breines, *Community and Organization in the New Left, 1962–1968* (Amherst, Mass., 1982); Clayborne Carson, *In Struggle: SNCC and the Black Awakening of the 1960s* (Cambridge, 1981); John Case and Rosemary C. R. Taylor, eds., *Co-ops, Communes and Collectives: Experiments in Social Change in the 1960s and 1970s* (New York, 1979), and Nigel Young, *An Infantile Disorder?: The Crisis and Decline of the New Left* (Boulder, Colo., 1977). Among the worst is Dick Cluster, ed., *They Should Have Served That Cup of Coffee: Seven Radicals Remember the Sixties* (Boston, 1979). This literature is discussed more systematically in a bibliographical note at the end of this volume.

9. David Moberg, "Experimenting with the Future: Alternative Institutions and American Socialism," in Case and Taylor, p. 303.

Part I

Black Political and
Cultural Radicalism

1

Ideology and Politics: Their Status in Afro-American Social Theory

ALEX WILLINGHAM

The great visibility accorded political struggle among black Americans over the 1960s has obscured the fact that these people still lack a compelling model of themselves, of their purposes in North American society, and of the kind of reasoning which can generate such a model. We see this among political activists when we examine recent controversies over a "race" or a "class" interpretation of the black community, the call to join traditional African customs, the attempts to prevent the rise of a "nationalism" within the black community, the effort to implant "scientific" analysis, or the vain search for a glorious black history which has no present and for which nobody has demonstrated a need. The result has been a failure to develop a radical politics which can make unambiguous demands on the American state.

The times seem much like they were in the Age of Washington when social initiative passed from the hands of blacks into those of southern and national spokesmen and industrial activists. Yet today, as the corrective changes from the Civil Rights movement have been given such wide attention, it has been difficult to keep persistent theoretical problems in focus and to resolve them. The basis for a militant, self-confident critical assessment of American society was severely modified with the removal of racial segregation. Thus to discuss the problem of ideology and politics, even in terms of the remote future of the black community, challenges us to a new description of contemporary social structure, accounting for extensive changes and estimating limits. In order to see the relationship between that structure and theoretical problems, it will be useful to relate present trends to those prevalent during the previous "age."

ssumption is that, as a matter of principle, the general
irectly confronted by social institutions and adjusts ac-
urvival criterion.[1] We can call this the most elemental
dividual social action. In the prior historical epoch (circa
hen those adjustments took the form of subordination be-
veloping walls of racial segregation, individual leaders took
it u₊ ₂mselves to articulate a "theory" to affirm the adjustment.
In another epoch, the postsegregation era in which we are now, another adjustment is occurring, also of massive proportions, and, returning to form, other spokesmen are attempting to articulate this motion. Now as then those responsible for the ideology, while they may
be condemned for many valid reasons, do stand close to actual changes
that people are going through. Today the general black population seems
to be readjusting after the upheavals of the Civil Rights era.

On the face of it these are commonplace remarks with which many
would agree. Yet today we seldom hear an effort made to say who is
supporting the adjustments and how that group should be approached
theoretically. If we were to speculate, we might conclude that they are
the proverbial cultural or revolutionary nationalists, the new commu-
nists, the scientific socialists or the Pan-Africanists. We would be in
error in each case. The problem of this essay is to discuss why this
question has been so seldom asked or meaningfully answered. In the
process it will be necessary to characterize the malaise which has undermined the critical forces in the black community and foisted on them
a style of analysis which is escapist. It is my hope that by so doing we
can push political discussion beyond mere ideological debate and restore to it both a capacity to criticize social practice and the potential to
engender, among black people, a receptive response to progressive
politics. So while we may agree pro forma with the need to define the
social character of the post-Civil Rights black community, it should be
remembered that this has special importance for those unhappy with
the beast.

THE RISE OF A NEW ELITE

In order to identify those elites who are more intimately connected
with mass adjustments, their politicking, and their ideology, we can
take a hint from a process of analysis used by Frantz Fanon in his
evaluation of revolutionary Algeria.[2] There he identifies a group of native politicians aligned with the cosmopolitan sector of the settler population and occupying privileged positions relative to the mass of natives. This group assimilates and functions according to the rationalist
thought criteria prevalent among the settler bourgeoisie. Such principles ultimately lead it to serve a dynamic nationalist function starting

from a class demand for larger participation in the present governing setup, a demand which becomes increasingly extreme, provoking "repression," expulsion, a resort to independent party organizing, suppression of the elitist party, and, finally, a resort to the mass party out of which a movement is generated to reclaim the territory and expel the settlers.

This little group of native liberals thus carry through a process which eventuates in a self-determining situation in which a people are now confronted with all the problems and opportunities of an independent social existence. While the particulars of Algeria do not apply to North America, the way in which Fanon conceptualized decolonization there is useful methodologically if we focus on the discrete phases of the process. Thus in terms of formal modeling, we can identify each phase, say what is positive or negative about it, the empirical indices which allow us to project the probability of proceeding beyond a given stage, the changing class dynamics of each phase (e.g., the extent to which the internal strata maintain traditional or customary loyalties), and how the character of either phase predisposes the general movement toward more or less humane ends. Generally speaking Fanon's model would judge the movement more humane the extent to which prior, received class configurations are dialectically resolved into a new "nation." [3]

In the Afro-American situation it is possible to apply Fanon's ideal type. We can identify an equivalent group of activists, relate them institutionally to cosmopolitan sectors of the American bourgeoisie, and chart the conflicts or tension between the two groups. In terms of such a process the Civil Rights movement can be understood in a historically specific sense. We find, however, that the Afro-American elite's function is less progressive than that imputed by the ideal type. Generally, the character of the struggle perpetuated by the black elites of North America never sets up a situation in which either that sector or any other in the black community could be transformed beyond its received social role—unless it be toward closer approximations of the authentic models of such roles prevalent in white society. Two mechanisms had accounted for such transformation in the ideal model: first, the generation, by the liberal activists, of absolute claims against the (settler) state—a condition forced on them by the nationalist demands of another more numerous stratum and concretized in a demand for the land, and, second, the total affirmation of violence which fastened a cover of seriousness onto the struggle and set a tough criterion of skepticism within which any compromise would be evaluated.

In the United States, on the contrary, the state was looked upon as an object to get into, and, as nearly as it was possible to have an "official" black position on political conflict, it was to be grounded in a so-called philosophy of nonviolence. The result was an incomplete "black" revolution considered peculiar to North America in which the largely homogeneous former slaves developed internal stratification and made peace with the American state.

A black status group then has come to occupy authoritative positions in America which leave them "more free" than during previous eras but closely tied and subordinate to the cosmopolitan sector of the American power elite. The major mechanism covering this tie is the Democratic party. The McGovern reforms were efforts to formalize a new status for this group of participants in the party. In other cases their strength comes from appointed positions in federal, state, and local governments as well as actual offices held in the U.S. Congress, the state houses, and local aldermanic councils. Indeed the group of big city mayors is just now probably one of the most glamorous political groups in the entire black world. The significance of these trends may inhere in the fact that probably none of these individuals would have any prominence were it not for politics (i.e., their actual cultural and economic work has been insignificant) giving credence to a charge by Booker T. Washington that "politics is parasitic." Still they exist as a going social force in contemporary America.

However, to identify this process and to point to its end result creates a serious problem of taxonomy: what name is to be given the new elite or its behavior?[4] It is fashionable these days, in some circles at least, to identify the above mentioned phenomenon and to condemn it as neo-colonialism. Thus Amiri Baraka has so concluded, in terms of his discussion of Kenneth Gibson, mayor of Newark, New Jersey:

Newark, New Jersey [is] a classic neo-colonial creation, where Black United Front of Blacks and Puerto Ricans moved through the late sixties to elect Kenneth Gibson black mayor. . . . Now some of the fruits born of the struggles of the sixties can be tasted in their bitterest aspect. These black faces in high places are simply objective agents of the rule of monopoly capitalism, as cold and as cynical as they have to be.[5]

Yet such neo-colonial analysis is fine only so far. To the extent that it affirms the need for criticism of the situation and of the antagonism there it is fine. Yet the analysis is misleading insofar as it implies that a "coherent" people stand juxtaposed to the new elite with a program of action that has been betrayed. Such might usually be the case in Third World situations where: 1) native culture can be distinguished from alien dominance and, perhaps, corruption, and 2) some kind of social independence has been experienced. In the case of the Afro-American there would be no need for a prefix on "colonialism."

At the very least we must start to focus on the continuity between the Age of Washington and the post-Civil Rights era. Certainly it is the Gibsons et al. who articulate the adjustment that the people have had to make. However, like Booker T. Washington modern elite ideology is directly linked to real, necessary living patterns and represents—and I see little reason to think this does not hold for the mass of black people—accurate depictions of some binding constraints of American life. Because the Civil Rights movement compromised too drastically on the rearrangement of American institutions of order, it failed to modify the real relationship of black people to them, and the black elite functions today in a situation in which the prior subordination of their constituency is accepted as a given.[6] Their honest articulation of this gives them a credibility not to be found among those who play on variations of "blacks should take the lead" slogans.[7] Indeed such clarion calls can only be considered threatening when viewed by the potential agents themselves. As was true of Washington, modern leadership ideology has the positive aspect of being thus "realistic."[8] Yet because the subordination of the black community was not engineered by the handiwork of an indigenous class, we get a paradox which allows this group to develop and accumulate a reservoir of sympathy. This paradox suggests the peculiar difficulty of applying traditional models to the situation.

To recapitulate: in order to develop a viable model to criticize the black situation it is necessary to have a conception of social structure covering American institutions and the black masses and elite activists. A black left (i.e., the group engaging in and acting on the actual criticism) is possible only as it is conceptualized outside the Holy Family. Certainly there will be a few reading this who will notice and be disappointed at a definition of the left based on status rather than ideas. Such caution is warranted, but two things justify the definition: one is the absence of an authentic black radical praxis comprehensive enough to withstand the needs of modern political analysis, and the other is the cooptation by liberalism, during the Civil Rights era, of the only black radical tradition available, i.e., Du Boisian protest. Certain dynamics of recent politics give further support to the status approach, however. For example, the uncomfortable suspicion persists that militant radicalization and criticism from the mid-1960s on is directly related to the status of the ideologues relative to the developing liberal establishment. As they have suffered personal exclusion, they have become disaffected with the Civil Rights settlement and open to radical ideas. These conditions set the context for a black left entity to develop. Increasing self-consciousness about this is the key to generating a new criticism capable of withstanding the many rationalizations which legitimate American society today.

We may treat the question of ideology and politics as two phases of the same problem. To those still concerned about removing the fetters from left forces in the black community—and this means first and foremost establishing a dependable basis for criticism—it means close attention must be given to both phases: 1) the subtle but pervasive difference between "ideology" and social analysis or theory, and 2) constraints imposed on radical politics by the new black experience which entails actual participation in authoritative U.S. institutions. Neither of these has been recognized as a problem previously even though historical changes have moved them to center stage now. Let us consider each in turn.

IDEOLOGY

Again the main problem here has to do with the capacity to distinguish between "ideology" and effective social theory. What we have seen in the past and especially in the evolution during the 1960s through Du Boisian protest, Black Power, black nationalism, Pan-Africanism, intercommunalism, or Marxism-Leninism is the tendency to select already defined ideology and stipulate the black theoretical task as one of taking it to the people. The consequence of such an effort is to focus attention away from direct analysis of social practice toward "study." The failure of recent activists to take a direct approach to social analysis (consequently settling for previously aggregated "ideologies") may result from their continued and perhaps unconscious reliance on a model of thought developed concurrently with the practical subordination of black people through racial segregation.

Thinkers like W. T. Fontaine and L. D. Reddick raised some criticisms of developing black thought in the late 1930s and charged that, in the black community itself, there were tendencies to do analysis already circumscribed by theoretical formulations.[9] A more direct statement of the tendency, albeit one that approved it, can be found in Gunnar Myrdal's classic work *American Dilemma*, written after the American pattern of race relations had been set. Of black thinking he said:

Negro thinking is almost completely determined by white opinions—negatively and positively. It develops as an answer to the popular theories prevalent among whites by which they rationalize their upholding of caste. In this sense it is a derivative, or secondary thinking. The Negroes do not formulate the issues to be debated; these are set for them by the dominant group. Negro thinking develops upon the presuppositions of white thinking. In its purest form it is a blunt denial and a refutation of white opinions.[10]

What is to be emphasized here is the withdrawal of the philosophic constraint from this peculiar kind of thought by virtue that its "presuppositions" are set outside of any self-conscious epistemology.[11] What it means is that for social theory to be meaningful for blacks (i.e., when done by black thinkers) it must answer a range of practical questions relevant to the world of immediate action or public policy. To the extent that such policy is developed by prejudicial reasoning then blacks have a special obligation to protest. C. Wright Mills isolated this as just one aspect of "political philosophy" and called it ideology.[12] I follow his usage although we cannot review all of his argument here. Suffice it to say that such ideology has as its fault the obscuring of basic criteria in terms of which the significance of practical questions is determined. Thus ideological work proceeds most smoothly when several other theoretical solutions can be taken for granted. Yet at least since the 1930s just such ideology has been supposed to have been the special black approach to political theory.

I conclude that in order to provide integrity to social criticism in the post-Civil Rights era it will be necessary to restore the philosophic constraint. Perhaps some modern theorists will rephrase the danger stated by Myrdal especially to supplement the racialist part implied in his phrase "presuppositions of white thinking." Consequently we may relate the earlier model to recent changes in analysis and account for the continuing tendency to fail to evaluate presuppositions even when they bear no relationship to the thought of American racists. In any case it seems well established that past analysis by and about black people justifies the need for careful scrutiny of any proposed theoretical innovations put forth.

A negative point needs to be made here. It is in answer to the query: what is the specific danger of a "black" ideology which is unaware of its presuppositions? The point: it certainly is not an inability to put forth logically consistent descriptions of social actions. In fact political analysis shares with other nonphilosophical modes of thought the drive for a systemic rendering of the real world. For example, in recent black analysis what was more systematic than Kawaida nationalism or revolutionary intercommunalism? It is interesting, though, that when one thinks of the litany of European theorists usually relied on to illustrate model social analysis, the unique virtue of political theory may be an inability or unwillingness to explain every facet of the phenomenon as one is sure to find in more "mystical" systems like Christianity or astrology.

Further, as political thinkers our efforts to persuade people to an ideology may be self-defeating by tapping, perhaps indirectly, a residue of faith in finality first embedded by the Judeo-Christian tradition (operationally brought to African people by missionaries in one form or another), a continuing source of strength for bourgeois society and a prop for self-alienation ever since merry England first proclaimed herself the workshop of the world. Such, I think, is the main consequence and danger of calling these ideologies "scientific" when in fact, like all social theory, they remain merely the not-too-successful efforts of a particular people in one epoch. Scientistic thought predisposes us to rush to accept as concrete what is nothing more than the product of our wishes.[13] If these are drawn from and set by the crass filth and unrelieved suffering that is American society today, then the function of the left ideologue is to reinforce the pattern of life prevalent in this country. Such primitivism must be overcome.

What is needed is an approach to social theory that is reflective, critical, and purposive. Even use of the word "ideology" should be curtailed in social discourse except as it is used—as I do below—as a term to "translate" prior theoretical conclusions or to cover rationalization of privilege. We should think instead in terms of critical social theory which, following Cruse, dialectically relates political, cultural, and economic matters into a theoretical form as they so interact in any specific social practice or in general behavioral systems. To paraphrase Plato: black ideologues must either become philosophers or remain the inadvertent purveyors of bourgeois reaction.

IDEOLOGY AND CRITICISM

I have argued that current social trends call attention to the rise of the black bourgeoisie complete with glamorous politicians, mass constituencies, and specific change ideologies. Their rise is as undeniable today as were those of yesteryear who amassed the material wherewithal to establish themselves as special among God's children and gave the Western world such slogans as "life, liberty, and property," "equality, fraternity, liberty," and "cast down your buckets where you are." This same combination of accumulation and political advancement characterized our modern bourgeois elite.

The character of the new criticism will be determined by the relationship of its practitioners to this bourgeoisie. Its personnel will include those who have not been included among, or saw fit to join, the reigning crowd. What ties the two factions of blacks irrevocably together is that we compete for the same constituency: the mass of black people. Those who miss this point and gaze off into a heaven of aracial revolutionary toiling masses are merely refusing to accept the real challenge and capitulating to reaction. The result is a bogus effort to separate what is really inseparable, namely the sustained rise of the black bourgeoisie and the series of defeats inflicted on the black left at least since the persecution of Paul Robeson. The consequence of ideologizing has been most pernicious and misunderstood in relation to this process. Thus instead of developing a strategy to meet the real situation we shift ideologies and pretend that that was the problem.

In terms of ideology the criticism has been that the new elite is "neo-colonialist." Yet for reasons noted above, the black bourgeoisie constantly complains about America, and the data they use—social welfare statistics—are the same ones that the would-be critics appeal to. In the long run the criticism will not clarify theoretical differences and reduces to a call by the black left that the elites go further and/or be sincere. The new critics are not sensitive enough to the changed character of the ideology of the new elite. Again a comparison to Washington is necessary because, since that gentleman's death, there has grown a myth that his was a philosophy resigned to satisfaction with Negro life. He was, it came to be said, "against change." Yet such an interpretation is strained at best.[14] The appropriate critique of Washington is precisely the image of change he had, a very practical one which called for the assimilation of the virtues of the American national bourgeoisie. American society during the Age of Washington was not a settled entity against which calls for change could be raised; rather it was at that time resettling itself and adjusting to new conditions. Everybody was for change. Thus in order to function critically against a change ideology a qualitative selection is necessary which calls for new data, claims and competes for definite constituencies, promulgates new models, and develops a fighting spirit vis-à-vis ascendant definitions of social ills. The new criticism in the black community suffers from an inability to transcend the categories of liberal ideology. Implicit in such a situation is an inadequate model of left praxis which is limited to sincerity and guided by a myth that there exists a quota of moral ideals which are accepted by all and only need application.

We do not get around this problem by selecting a new nonbourgeois ideology of "new communism," "antiimperalism," or by fanciful beliefs that America is falling under its own weight. On the contrary there must be a dialectical critique growing in contention with the specifics of the prior model, directly linked to mobilizing in relation to the present social structure and grounded in a comprehensive vision of a liberated individual or people. The resolution of the question of the relation of black people to a viable socialist movement in America is dependent on such analysis. Without it socialism merely becomes one more ideology to annoy people.

POLITICS

We can understand better the political obligations facing the new black left by tying its ideological and political changes to its increasing elimination from mainstream Civil Rights activity since about 1966 or about the time of Black Power. Since that time criticism has been tied to ideology selected in increasing isolation from the new electoral/administrative experience developing in the black community. Nor has such ideology fared well in gaining mass support. The new black elite is now distinguished both by an actual devolution of authority and a community base. They accepted the constraints of that authority and became legitimate participants in America in the name of black people generally. Those who rejected these constraints longed for a different settlement but have taken a roundabout route since 1966 to the confusion which descended in the mid-1970s and in which impotence has threatened to become a permanent condition of left criticism.

The relationship between these two sectors was wrought with interest in the last several years of the 1960s and early 1970s. When the left adhered to various makeshift racial pride-type ideologies, the black bourgeoisie rode chitterlings right into the Waldorf-Astoria to consolidate things with cosmopolitan America. Yet as the black militant posture has shifted to an ostensible antibourgeois stance it has come only to the social welfarism already monopolized by the black liberals. When the black left tried a sort of crypto-terrorist tactic ("off the pig"), it found itself resorting to the black liberals to negotiate their "demands" for amnesty or to shorten jail sentences. In 1972, desiring to meet in general session, the critics had to go to the liberals to call a National Black Political Convention.

In those places where confrontations have occurred we see the same pattern. In the black universities—from Southern University, Texas Southern, Jackson State, Orangeburg, Howard—the liberals are in smooth command and much more enlightened now about their roles; black studies programs are rapidly confirming the most dire predictions of Martin Kilson. The pragmatists control the labor unions. While all American liberals shout hosannah about the way the system worked to "free" Angela Davis, the black left was burdened with the painful reality that H. Rap Brown remained in jail and numerous others were exiled in Cuba, Tanzania, and such, while lives have been lost, and uncompensated for, from the university campuses to otherwise obscure apartments in Chicago. With all of this it is amazing that that same left would propagandize itself into locating the "left" and the "right" of the black community on the central committee of the African Liberation Support Committee! It was a tacit admission that they did not want to join the real battle and had conceded a war that never really was declared. In the face of it all we are supposed to turn to the latter-day Deweyites in the blue collar sector of America.

In terms of constituency the criticism has been that the black bourgeoisie has none. They lack, so it goes, a "mass base." Yet in terms of the one unambiguous index of support for leadership among blacks— the vote—liberals have taken the day in every case. The rallies, demonstrations, etc., called by the left have, on the contrary, been paltry by comparison. The failure to recognize this basic fact prompts two observations. First, the call for principled ideological debate did not correct earlier errors calling for "operational unity" or "unity without uniformity." Those slogans had obscured the fact that the assembled constituency was really accountable to the liberals. Yet the call for principled debate was naive by virtue that it promoted internecine conflict. Second, it is the critical sector which lacks a competitive base, and there seems little reason now not to expect that the black left would join any movement generated if it had a few people participating (and some media coverage). This seems certainly to be the case in the Boston school demonstration of 1974–1975. Long gone are the days when intraracial contentions were such that Washington was shouted off the speaker's podium or Malcolm was relegated to the role of spectator at the 1963 March on Washington! Thus the black bourgeoisie has a monopoly on the vote and enlivens any given protest demonstration through its selective participation. Such a situation is vivid testimony to the hegemony of this sector of the black community and to the squalor of the negro left.

Several specific tactics have been tried by the left to impact on the black community. We can identify the following five for discussion: 1) the forming of counterinstitutions, 2) the move to rejoin allegedly mass-based community institutions, 3) the tactic of "unity without uniformity," 4) the resort to incest, and 5) electoral competition. There are several others that we could identify including independent party organizing a la the Black Panther Party (BPP), continuing protest demonstrations, and specific campus movements including the demand for black studies. However, the character of the overall strategy can be illustrated by reference to the basic five.

The first tactic, that of building counterinstitutions, is symbolized by Malcolm X Liberation University (MXLU) in North Carolina. Other examples include the Center for Black Education and the Institute of the Black World, in Washington and Atlanta, respectively. Of all the tactics this one provides the most direct link with the Civil Rights dissidents because of the close relationship then between Owusu Sadaukai, who organized MXLU, and Stokely Carmichael and Willie Ricks, both of whom were on the Meredith march in 1966.[15] The counterinstitution tactic illustrates the danger of undialectical shifts among the black left. For in spite of the fact that confrontations had occurred at both A and T State and Duke universities, suggesting the limits of traditional black and white schools for significant social action, MXLU always stood as an entity whose authenticity was to be determined by the purity of its ideology rather than any engaged relationships with institutions in which blacks were actually being socialized. Thus the struggle for counterinstitutions directed attention away from adjustments people were forced to make on a daily basis. Political party building could be included here but there were few cases of that outside the BPP.

It was during the demise of the BPP, however, that we get an articulation of the second tactic: the return to mass-based black institutions. Huey Newton concluded that the Panthers had become isolated from the people. His correction for that problem was to have a Grand Return. He suggested two tactics: a focus on the American South and a return to the black church. Such a suggestion was useful insofar as it explicated the isolationism of the counterinstitution strategy. What it did not address was the problem of gaining support from the people in these institutions, nor the reactionary basis on which these institutions are maintained. The black preachers in the National Baptist Convention, the Roman Church, and, increasingly, the Nation of Islam illustrate the elites operative there, and none of them seems anxious to subordinate himself to secular politics.

The third tactic, closely related to the previous one, is that of "unity without uniformity." It is symbolized by the Pan-racial movements such as the Congress of African Peoples (Atlanta), the National Black Political conventions (Gary, Little Rock), and the first African Liberation Day (Washington, 1972). In one sense it might be seen as the corruption of the prior tactic of returning to the people, for in effect the return was used as a rationalization to form questionable coalitions with elite elements who claimed to have mass constituencies yet pursued reactionary politics. The experience under "unity without uniformity" certainly illustrates the relative ineffectiveness of the left in these coalitions, however.

A fourth tactic, incest, resembles the earlier counterinstitution strategy but can be distinguished from it both by the time and ideology involved. It focuses essentially on internal purification. Two striking examples are the purges in the BPP and the "principled ideological struggle" on the African Liberation Support Committee. What happens is the increasing circumscribing of political discussion to smaller factions. Such incest eventually developed in each of the other organizations formed under the "unity without uniformity" tactic, i.e., the Black Assembly or the NBPC and the Congress of African Peoples. To the extent that post-Civil Rights criticism aimed to make use of the most effective anticapitalist critique available (i.e., Marxism) there must be disappointment that such analysis has been so closely associated with black incest. It is in just such situations that political discussion can take on an increasing significance.

The final tactic is electoral competition. Here the left competes with the new black elite in direct challenge for public office. This tactic has not occurred too often where there is a real chance of winning. Two outstanding examples continue to be Bobby Seale's campaign in Oakland and the efforts of Baraka in Newark. The related tactic of nominating a candidate who has no chance of winning (historically associated with the Communist Party and the Socialist Workers Party) is not significant enough to be considered. In assessing the tactic of electoral competition the results are mixed. It is clearly important because such competition is a possible way of placing contrasting ideologies before the people and to get a "realistic" feel for the practical adjustments they have made. How effective either of the actual campaigns was is open to question. On the other hand, the electoral arena is a briar patch for the rabbits of the new black elite, and any oppositional candidate or party starts with a major disadvantage.

The future political behavior of the black left will be dependent on rethinking those past tactics. It seems to me that such rethinking should be disciplined by two concerns: first, that the black bourgeoisie not be allowed to monopolize the experiences now available to the black community for the first time, and second, that in the process of reversing this pattern structural situations be identified where "antibourgeois" analysis can be effectively generated in relation to the new adjustment patterns. In this regard the only solution is the development of a secular party instrument. It is the obligation of the black left to retrigger the Fanonist process and carry it through. To fall back, at this time, on unimaginative slogans, is, to paraphrase the opening paragraphs of the *Eighteenth Brumaire*, more farce than tragedy!

CONCLUSION

This then is the key problem suggested by the chapter title "Ideology and Politics." It suggests that, first, for all practical purposes the problem of the left among blacks has been the artificial separation of social criticism and politics and the limiting of discussion to a caricature of the former. Second, it calls our attention to the possibility that real politics is now a matter outside of such discussion having to do with the adjustment of the masses. From the Gary and Little Rock NBPCs, the Congress of African Peoples, the African Liberation Support Committee, etc., black political discussion has lost its capacity to be dangerous by disconnecting itself from the real adjustments of the people and occupying, instead, an incestuous world in which are manufactured a "left" and "right" bitterly in contention between themselves but impervious to living conditions except as these are filtered through Bureau of Labor Statistics data. When we speak of the problem of "ideology and politics" for the present or future of black people, it is this problem of separation which we must find a way to resolve and integrate.

A FINAL COMMENT ON OUR SOCIAL SCIENTISTS

Through it all we can only lament the cringing role of the social and political scientists in these changes. Their refusal to fulfill the promise of social analysis has had two consequences: 1) their own models of the world remain stagnant reflections of the social science developed by the white petty bourgeoisie, and 2) impassioned social criticism has passed increasingly to activists and poets and other literati of the black community whose ideologizing remains an embarrassing indication of their innocence of the constraints of political analysis. Withal because of the servility of the social scientists, academia stands even more in opposition to our people, contributing nothing nor giving respite from the reigning ideologues who take advantage of the splendid possibilities of our cultural ambiguity.

NOTES

1. Generally I use the term "social institutions" to cover three distinct forms of institutions—political, economic, and cultural—which may be isolated for purposes of analysis but which interact dialectically to create a given social situation. The epistemological basis for this procedure is in the work of Harold Cruse; see his *Crisis of the Negro Intellectual* (New York, 1967).

2. Frantz Fanon, *A Dying Colonialism* (New York, 1965), trans. by Haakon Chevalier with intro. by Adolfo Gilly. C. E. J. Hobsbawn, "Passionate Witness," *New York Review of Books* (February 22, 1973), 6–10, and Jack Woddis, *New Theories of Revolution* (New York, 1972).

3. The significance of class categories is tied to the productive relationships in modern capitalist society. Yet the advantages such a society maintains in relation to other societies (e.g., neocolonialism) depends on politically significant groups who may have no economically productive role. "Class" then is a trained use which, in these cases, may depend more on status or custom and have a different functional significance than is usually the case. I continue to use "class," though without any "scientific" pretentions, and consider it part of the broader problem of taxonomy.

4. If it is the outgrowth of prior historical trends, probably a bias this author would support, we might use black bourgeoisie as developed in E. Franklin Frazier, *Black Bourgeoisie: The Rise of a New Middle Class* (1957). Cf., however, the reservations stated in Oliver Cox, "Introduction," in Nathan Hare, *The Black Anglo-Saxons* (New York, 1965).

5. Imamu Amiri Baraka, "Newark Seven Years Later: ¡Unidad y Luncha!," *Monthly Review* (January, 1975), 16–24.

6. Alex Poinsett, "Class Patterns in Black Politics," *Ebony* 28 (August, 1973), 35ff.

7. The tendency is associated with Grace and James Boggs in their conception of the new American Revolution. Most recently it took the form of a slogan on black workers for the African Liberation Support Committee. See Abdul Alkalimat and Nelson Johnson, "Toward the Ideological Unity of the African

Liberation Support Committee: A Response to Criticisms of the A.L.S.C. Statement of Principles" (1974).

8. In contemporary circles of "scientific" analysts it might be called "materialist." Thus we could emphasize the actual impact of the adjustments on the daily lives of the people and exorcise attempts to make this just happy-go-lucky survivalism. However, the resort to so-called materialism among this group hardly reassures me that they will be able to grasp reality any better than Alice in Wonderland! In fact their application of the materialist method, in spite of numerous formal definitions, is consistent with the opening statement in chapter 11, verse 1 of the King James version of the Holy Bible. For help in locating this citation I am indebted to Rosa Lee Johnson and Viola Young.

9. W. T. Fontaine, "An Interpretation of Contemporary Negro Thought from the Standpoint of the Sociology of Knowledge," *Journal of Negro History* 25 (1940), 6–13, and " 'Social Determination' in the Writings of Negro Scholars," *American Journal of Sociology* 49 (January, 1944) 302–315; L. D. Reddick, "A New Interpretation for Negro History," *Journal of Negro History* 22 (1937), 17–28.

10. Gunnar Myrdal, *An American Dilemma* (New York, 1944).

11. Here I utilize some suggestions from Sheldon Wolin, *Politics and Vision: Continuity and Change in Western Political Theory* (Boston, 1960).

12. C. Wright Mills, *The Marxists* (New York, 1962), pp. 12–13.

13. Adolph Reed, Jr., "Scientistic Socialism: Notes on the New Afro-American Magic Marxism," *Endarch* 1 (Fall, 1974), 21–39.

14. See Louis R. Harlan, "The Secret Life of Booker T. Washington," *Journal of Southern History* 37 (August, 1971), 393–416; Judith Stein, " 'Of Mr. Booker T. Washington and Others': The Political Economy of Racism in the United States," *Science and Society* 38 (Winter, 1974–1975), 422–463.

15. Stokely Carmichael, *Stokely Speaks: Black Power Back to Pan-Africanism*, edited with an intro. by Ethel Minor (New York, 1971).

2

Cultural Nationalism in the 1960s: Politics and Poetry

JENNIFER JORDAN

The 1960s, for which all rebels and misfits secretly or openly yearn, was a time of turbulence and violence. It was a time when southern Black folks died to integrate into the American system, and significant numbers of Blacks, mostly from the North and the West, demonstrated that they would rather die than become a part of it. Yet the correlation of these two seemingly antagonistic impulses becomes obvious on examination. The stench of death and the terror of the South were central in the conversion of the Student Non-Violent Coordinating Committee (SNCC) into a nationalist organization. The sight of police dogs biting defenseless children, Bull Connor's red face scowling on the living room television set, and King's, and even Kennedy's, bloody finales, frozen on front pages and incessantly reenacted and rerun in black and white or even living color, made Elijah Muhammad seem promising, turned Malcolm into a saint and a prophet, and sent Black folks into the streets. The nationalism that resulted was a protean force that sheltered a number of divergent movements, the most prominent of which, according to James Turner, were the religious nationalism of the Nation of Islam, the Marxist revolutionary nationalism of the Black Panther Party, the economic nationalism of Black capitalism, the political nationalism of the Republic of New Africa, Pan-African nationalism, and cultural nationalism.[1] Turner's categories are useful for the purpose of discourse, but it is obvious that elements of one type often overlap others. The Nation of Islam, for instance, was once a stronghold of Black capitalism and a peculiar type of cultural nationalism. A certain type of cultural nationalism came to be almost synonymous with Pan-Africanism. Indeed, all the various movements, with perhaps the exception of Black _apitalism, which was really pure Americana, had to cope with the issue of cultural nationalism, if only because of the use of a particular type of dress or uniform, the presence of various rituals and artifacts which were used to decorate organizations and their activities, and the language which such organizations chose to express their view of the world.

Cultural nationalism has come to be identified with its most rigid adherents—those of an Africanist or pseudo-Africanist stripe—but an examination of the phenomenon will show that two types of cultural nationalism were evident in the latter half of the 1960s—one which was based on the culture produced by Black people in America; the other which looked back to traditional Africa or, at least, to an Africa as imagined by the twentieth-century Afro-American mind.

Afro-American cultural nationalism has probably existed as long as that hybrid creature, the Afro-American, has. It is the impetus that made Black people create the cakewalk, the slave's mocking reproduction of the ways of white folks. It is expressed in the works of Afro-American poets from Dunbar's "When Malindy Sings" to the folkloric expressions of Langston Hughes and Sterling Brown. Generally such nationalism was based on a partiality for those elements of the Afro-American culture of which Black people have always been the proudest—our music, from the blues and spirituals of slavery to the urban-produced sounds of jazz; the poetry and music of Black speech with its metaphor and rhythms; and the song of the body, the dance. Despite our powerlessness and our resultant oppression, our art has bloomed, and we have always been chauvinistic about it.

Cultural nationalism also has been a strong influence in Afro-American literature. Writers like Ellison and Baldwin have emphasized those elements of Black life that they felt worthy of praise and preservation. Baldwin's early writings reflect a romantic, almost masochistic glorification of the drama of the church and the "pathos" of the Black man in his "continuing despair of the goodness of the Lord."[2] There is romance, for Baldwin, in the tragic heroism, the endless adaptability, and the moral superiority of the victim. For Baldwin, our "past, this endless struggle to achieve and reveal and confirm a human identity, human authority, yet contains, for all its horror, something very beautiful."[3] Ellison, growing up as an isolated Black child in a relatively middle-class environment, found an "enviable" excitement and richness in the life led by poorer Black children whose folkways "seemed much more real than the Negro middle-class values which were taught in school."[4]

In the 1960s Afro-American cultural nationalism was best expressed by Larry Neal although it was very much a part of LeRoi Jones even after he became Imamu Amiri Baraka. Neal's work stresses the continuity of Black culture, or more specifically Black art, from the folklore of slavery to the creative output of the present. For him the blues singer becomes the essence of Black culture, "the bearer of the group's working myths, aspirations, and values." Neal's nationalism was most decidedly apolitical. The genius of Blackness, for him, resided in everybody from pimps to college presidents.[5]

This glorification of the cultural attainments of Afro-Americans tends to be a conservative force which grows out of a desire to see the Black man remain a distinct entity in the plastic and antihuman world called America. At the same time, however, this desire means the attempted maintenance of qualities and elements of Black life which are destructive to Black people or, at least, supportive of the system that oppresses them. From the beginning the religion, the music, the dance provided solace for Black people, channeled energy that could have been used in revolt; and the qualities praised by both Baldwin and Ellison are the same qualities that made the Black man a good slave. Ellison laments the possible passing of the Negro into history:

Our Negro situation is changing rapidly, but so much which we've gleaned through the harsh discipline of Negro American life is simply too precious to be lost. I speak of the faith, the patience, the humor, the sense of timing, rugged sense of life and the manner of expressing it which all go to define the American Negro. These are some of the things which we dare not fail to adapt to changed conditions lest we destroy ourselves. Times change but these possessions must endure forever—not simply because they define us as a group, but because they represent a further instance of man's triumph over chaos.[6]

Ellison not only sounds like Thomas Nelson Page eulogizing the good ole days of slavery but also fails to realize that we did not triumph over the chaos but adjusted to it, lamented about it, raged impotently against it. Larry Neal, who was instrumental in the Black Arts movement of the 1960s, makes an even more telling statement:

A revolution without a culture would destroy the very thing that now unites us, the very things we are trying to save along with our lives. That is the feeling and love-sense of the blues and other forms of Black music. The feeling of a James Brown or an Aretha Franklin. That is the feeling that unites us and makes it more possible for us to move and groove together, to do whatever is necessary to liberate ourselves. John Coltrane's music must unquestioningly be a part of any future revolutionary society.[7]

This insistence on the preservation of culture, even in a revolutionary situation, is typical of the intellectual and the aesthete, and Larry Neal was a thinker and an artist for whom art was as important as life. For him revolution had to be about blues *and* bread. Whatever happened in the process of liberation, he wanted to hold on to the soul feeling, the ironic combination of anguish and joy that grew out of our African-ness and the degradation of slavery, and that serves, despite Neal's wishful thinking, more as a palliative than as a force of liberation. Larry Neal wanted to conserve the tradition. To conserve. It is no wonder that the artist has such difficulty surviving revolutions and coexisting with the men of ideology and guns and economic plans.

The desire of the cultural nationalist to freeze Black people in time and to hold on to those things which are meaningful to all but the most alienated of Black intellectuals is understandable. A cultural conserva-tism is especially pronounced in those historical periods in which un-precedented numbers of Blacks enter the middle class, that great arena of assimilation and homogenization, for such periods create a fear of the disappearance of the race into the larger group, not necessarily the physical disappearance—miscegenation has not been a serious threat to Afro-American existence—but the disappearance of Blacks as a unique cultural group in America.

For if the events of history result in the assimilation of Blacks, there will be no realistic way to hold on to Black culture as we know it, no way to keep the blues except as some relic of a dead past, much as European classical music serves as a memorial to a Europe that no longer exists. The blues even today is a music which has become increasingly removed from its creative source, a music much loved by middle-class white youth who are evidently more blue than Black youth or who perhaps are merely nostalgic for the time when Black people were a little less threatening and the white man was the unquestioned master of his and our fate. I cannot accept Fanon's definition of the blues as a "type of jazz howl hiccupped by a poor misfortunate Negro," "trapped between five glasses of whiskey, the curse of his race, and the racial hatred of the white men."[8] We know that John Lee Hooker has more spirit than this description implies, that the blues is more than some self-pitying lament. However, as much as we might love John Lee, the plantation drudgery and the particular type of depredations that his particular Mississippi visited upon him no longer exist; and the present cannot reproduce his duplicate. Since culture does not remain static, the only way that the blues can remain vital is for it to be transformed by the present. Yet when Hendrix played it the only way that a young man of the 1960s could, given his place in history, the majority of Black people rejected him and his music. So maybe the blues will have to disappear or live on in our literature. There is no choice really. To try to hold on to it or to any cultural material which is no longer organic is to try to stop time.

However, Afro-American cultural nationalism on the part of the Black intelligentsia is not merely an act of preservation. Periods of integra-

tion, which cause middle-class Blacks to be both culturally and economically separated from the rest of Black people, also produce a great
deal of middle-class anxiety, guilt, and intense reidentification with the
group and its culture. Fanon remarked that African intellectuals suffered a similar anxiety which resulted in a desire "to shrink away from
that Western culture in which they all risked being swamped. Because
they realized they [were] in danger of losing their lives and thus becoming lost to their people, these men . . . relentlessly determined to
renew contact once more with the oldest and most pre-colonial springs
of life of their people."[9] When in America the affluence of the 1920s
produced for the first time a solid core of middle-class Blacks, young
intellectuals and artists of that class fervently reaffirmed their allegiance to the poorer majority. Jean Toomer in *Cane* sang of the South
and his aborted attempt to return to the soil and the folk, and Langston
Hughes and Sterling Brown looked to both the rural and urban masses
for inspiration and material. During the 1960s—with the passing of the
last possible civil rights laws, which said on paper we were Americans,
and with the establishment of the poverty program, which fattened the
pockets of the Black middle class—a similar phenomenon occurred. There
are striking similarities between Langston Hughes's "The Negro and
the Racial Mountain" and LeRoi Jones's "The Myth of a Negro Literature," both manifestos which insist that the richest source of Black
creativity resides in Black folklore. In addition, the psychological pain
that Langston Hughes suffered at having to choose between the middle class and anti-Black existence of his economically comfortable father
and the poverty of his mother and the rest of his people is apparent in
his autobiography, *The Big Sea*. The same anguish is evident in much
of the early writing of LeRoi Jones (Baraka). In *Tales* he writes, "I live
in Harlem with a baby shrew and suffer for my decadence which kept
me away so long. When I walk in the streets, the streets don't claim
me, and people look at me, knowing the strangeness of my manner,
and the objective stance from which I attempt to 'love' them."[10] They
both chose the folk and attempted/attempt to live with the contradictions of that choice.

Numerous intellectuals who saw nothing of value in a slave culture
made different choices. Richard Wright, whose poverty-stricken and
alienated existence prevented him from finding relief in a stable family
life and the cultural institutions of the Black South—the church and the
school—proclaims in *Black Boy*:

(After I had outlived the shocks of childhood, after the habit of reflection had
been born in me, I used to mull over the strange absence of real kindness in
Negroes, how unstable was our tenderness, how lacking in genuine passion
we were, how void of great hope, how timid our joy, how bare our traditions,

how hollow our memories, how lacking we were in those intangible sentiments that bind man to man, and how shallow was even our despair. . . .

(Whenever I thought of the essential bleakness of black life in America, I knew
that Negroes had never been allowed to catch the full spirit of Western civilization, that they lived somehow in it but not of it. And when I brooded upon
the cultural barrenness of black life, I wondered if clean positive tenderness,
love, honor, loyalty, and the capacity to remember were native with man . . .)[11]

In the 1940s Wright's solution to his inability to find sustenance in
Black life was the interracial life of the North and exile in Europe. However, for intellectual writers of the 1960s, who could find no haven in
a separate Black existence, in the desolate life of middle-class America,
or in European exile, there was traditional Africa, a pristine paradise
which could be as glorious as the imagination could make it. One could
become a Pan-Africanist and find respite in contemplating one's supposed descent from splendid African nobility rather than from despised American slaves. Of course, not all Pan-African cultural nationalism was based on a hatred of the Negro past. Other major impetuses
were a desire to resolve the contradictions of being both Black and
American, the cultural schizophrenia that Du Bois identified in *The Souls
of Black Folks*; the inviting mystique of an Africa that seemed to be freeing
itself; and the belief that Black people in America lived a colonialized
existence parallel to that of African nations. A good case can be made,
however, that much of the love of Africa was what Adolph Reed, Jr.,
called "a sublimated form of the black bourgeois and petit-bourgeois
flight from 'low-down' Afro-American cultural forms."[12]

Rather than talk about the beauty of the blues or the revolutionary
zeal of Nat Turner, the Africanist reveled in the glories of Egyptian
civilization and the heroism of Shaka. People left the Baptist church or
atheism and became aficionados of the Yoruba faith, and prided themselves on recognizing and owning authentic Kinte cloth and tie-dyed
African fabrics, bought at outrageous prices from Ashanti's Bazaar. Although Black people needed to rescue the retelling of all our past from
white tribal minds who pretended so-called civilization started with the
Greeks, a fixation on the past did not change the realities of contemporary America or Africa. It also became obvious that it takes more
than an African robe and a change of name to transform a Bernard into
a Kwame. In fact, the transformation proved to be an impossibility.
One positive note: at least the pure Africanist did not claim to be a
revolutionary.

Those who did not have the energy to try to recapture the reality of
the African past or found that past unproductive for their purposes

created an Africa out of whole cloth or patchwork. Ron Karenga and his Kawaida doctrine supposedly took elements from Africa and used them to recreate an Afro-American culture. Culture to Karenga included mythology, history, social organization, political organization, economic organization, creative motif, and ethos. The mythology of this new Afro-American culture probably rose full-blown from Karenga's head. It is difficult to say since it was never defined. At least he did not swear to have seen some vision while riding on the freeway in sunny California. The social organization consisted of Karenga as almost deified head, various followers, one of whom called Karenga "the leader of this era," who had "saved" him and shown him "the Path of Blackness,"[13] and a system of polygamy whose female participants were to prove their femininity by "being submissive."[14] Political organization was left conveniently undefined. Economics consisted of a warmed-up version of "Buy Black." Ethos was simple: man, or maybe just the members of US, were God,[15] and Jesus was a psychotic white boy.[16] Life was to be governed by the famous Nguzu Saba or Seven Principles: Umoja (unity), Ujamaa (cooperative economics), Kujichagulia (self-determination, which consisted only of the ability "to define ourselves, name ourselves, and speak for ourselves"), Ujima (collective work and responsibility or the building and maintenance of Black businesses and the sharing of profits), Nia (purpose or community control), Kuumba (creativity), and Imani (faith in one's teacher, in the people, and in the "righteousness of the struggle").[17] Karenga might have been quietly forgotten or at least remembered in some footnote as the man connected somehow with the death of two Panthers, but LeRoi Jones discovered him and, like Saul on the road to Damascus, came home with a new name and a new mission in life.

For quite a while cultural nationalism gave voice to the idea of some violent revolution. However, a careful examination of its use of the word "revolution," a much misused term during the 1960s, and the actuality of the political and social practices of cultural nationalism show it to be conservative, if not reactionary in nature.

There were many who felt that a cultural program, divorced from any kind of political or economic action, could be revolutionary. If Negroes could be made into Black people, America would either have to change or be destroyed[18]; and white America's reaction to "Black Is Beautiful" and the desire for Black Studies programs was so vehement that large numbers of Blacks were convinced that what they were asking for was indeed "revolutionary." Interestingly enough, Fanon noted a similar response to the African intellectual's rejection of white culture on the part of the European settlers, a response that convinced the African intellectual that he was on the right path to liberation.[19] The difference between European and American societies, however, is the seemingly endless ability of America to convert and subvert elements of change.

The conflict that arose between those who felt that economics and politics were central to liberation and the cultural nationalist who felt that the cultural battle had to be won before one made political moves reached a level of acrimony that resulted in violence. Karenga's rationalization for his complete political inaction, however, was that a violent revolution would work only if a "revolution to win the minds of the people" was successful.[20] The first task, however, was to convert oneself from a dead Negro to a nationalist, an endeavor that took a lifetime.[21] Economics was not important because the race question "ruled out economics."[22] Karenga makes clear in his *Quotable Karenga* that the members of US belonged "first to the Black community, second to the American society. The community is the group who share values; a society takes care of goods and services."[23] Except for some rather vague talk about cooperative economics, it was obvious that Karenga saw nothing terribly wrong with how goods and services were being provided by the larger "society."

Baraka instituted a group similar to US called Black Community Development (BCD) in Newark in 1968.[24] At the time he perceived politics, art, and religion as equally influential components of culture. In Baraka's mind, however, the purpose of politics was to create a world that was conducive to the Black man's culture, a place where one could create art and practice one's religion.[25] Obviously, if one can accomplish this goal without any major upheaval of the larger society, then political action becomes unnecessary. Baraka's analysis becomes highly questionable with the recognition that art and religion are not crucial issues in the discontent that Blacks in America feel.

Besides their basic conservatism on the political and economic level, the adherents of cultural nationalism suffered another fatal flaw—an astonishing lack of understanding of how culture works. Although Karenga and Baraka talked about culture consisting of politics, economics, art, and various other ingredients, an examination of the structures of BCD and US shows that other than some very superficial changes, such as clothing, a smattering of Swahili, the introduction of some Islamic influences into BCD, and the use of a great deal of pageantry and ritual, there were no real and lasting cultural changes taking place. There also seemed to be the strange belief that the word was the deed, perhaps some atavistic remembrance of the power of Nommo, the African "life force which produces all life, which influences things in the shape of the word."[26] For Karenga and Baraka seemed to believe that all they had to do was to invent a world on paper and it would be so. Cultural nationalists were always tossing about the names of Fanon, Sekou Touré, and Cabral, but nobody evidently read any of their books, which address themselves to the issue of creating culture in a vacuum rather than in conjunction with a political and social struggle.[27] Fanon speaks of the need for the more advanced of the people to sway the larger group by making "existing structures" progressive. He condemns those who, instead of using their "theoretical knowledge to the service of the people," make plans and then try to force the people into that plan.[28]

Karenga and Baraka were prolific makers of plans, but there was very little chance of their forcing them on the people. As leaders of cult groups who in reality were isolated from the larger community, their actual influence on the majority of Black people was negligible. Baraka's group, BCD, at its height had 150 people—100 men and 50 women.[29] However, Karenga, Baraka, and Haki Madhubuti (Don L. Lee) were widely sought on the college lecture circuit and managed to have a broad, if momentary, influence on Black college students. In many large cities and university towns, one could find cultural nationalist groups which gave verbal allegiance to the Nguzu Saba.

An analysis of cultural nationalism, both the Afro-American version and the Pan-African variety, makes clear that its middle-class and intellectual adherents were motivated to shape a separatist ideology by a wide variety of reasons. However, like other types of nationalists their refusal to claim allegiance to the American system was given added impetus by the general deterioration of American life and the awareness of the villainous role America was playing in Vietnam and other Third World countries. To integrate into America meant to share in its guilt and to lose the moral superiority that the Black man could claim as simple victim. So in the late 1960s the question that Baldwin asked in *The Fire Next Time*—"Do I really *want* to be integrated into a burning house?"[30]—still had to be answered. Baldwin's answer was that Black people had to help save America because they had no other home and because there was an inextricable bond between Black and white Americans. Baraka's reply was "NEGRO STAY OUT! Because now, when Charles is uptight all over the world, and will of course ask the black lackeys to help him out, it is high time the black man began to make use of the Tonto-syndrome, i.e., leave the Lone Ranger to his own devices, and his own kind of death."[31] Furthermore, Baraka did not support the idea that Black people can merely claim to be helpless victims. The following statement is very definitely addressed to the Black middle class: "All you Negroes making 'good livings' now, do you know what the fruits of your labor are being used for? Usually your labors contribute heavily to the murders of nonwhite peoples all over the globe."[32] Baraka's answer meant joining forces with people of color all over the world to destroy America. He later changed his mind about the cooperative efforts with other than African peoples (and then changed it again), but the idea of the destruction of America remained integral to the cultural nationalist scenario. What was to happen to Afro-America, "deep in the belly of the whale" as nationalists liked to say, was a question nobody answered aloud. One well-known adherent of Pan-Africanism casually offered up all 22 million of us as kamikazes, cannon fodder for Mother Africa. Whatever the nationalists' final solution, America's culpability on a domestic and international level made joining forces with it a highly unattractive proposition.

Even on a cultural level America offered nothing but dilution and mediocrity. Racial separation seemed a blessing that had maintained the strength and integrity of Black art and music,[33] and integration meant "Radio City Music Hall . . . the insipidities of television . . . , the impossibility of becoming a man in a place that doesn't demand manhood any more—in fact, a place where manhood has become a kind of alien grace."[34]

During the latter part of the 1960s, cultural nationalism seemed to hold sway over the other nationalist movements. A great deal of its prominence can be attributed to the fact that there were no real concrete political issues with which to galvanize Black people. The poverty program and then the white backlash of the Nixon years had silenced the Black middle class. The war issue for the most part was seen as the province of the white left, although Vietnam and the disproportionate number of dead Black soldiers were always part of the nationalist rhetoric. The threatening, adventurist challenge to the system by the Black Panthers was resulting in a heavy toll in prison sentences and deaths. What seemed like paranoia about government spying but what turned out to be a good understanding of reality was creating havoc, not only through the resultant individual psychological tension but also through fratricidal conflicts. Genocide seemed very real to the nationalist world, the fear of it permeating the literature and graphic art of the time. Cultural nationalism became that middle place between violent rebellion and acquiescence, a place where one could escape death and prison but still shout out one's defiance. In the tumult of the 1960s, cultural nationalism was a stable, even warm, place to be for the disenchanted who found existential living impossible.

Antonin J. Liehm, in *The Politics of Culture*, examines an interestingly similar dominance of culture over politics in Czechoslovakia. He speaks of the past German domination over the Czech people, a domination which prevented the formation of an aristocracy, the traditional—at least in Liehm's mind—creators of culture. Because of this cultural vacuum, contemporary Czech artists/intellectuals entered modern politics with an intense concern about the formation and revitalization of Czech language and culture. The intellectuals and writers became the "spiritual" and "political" elite—the aristocracy. After the Russians squashed the 1960s rebellion, cultural issues became even more dominant. Says Liehm, "Whenever people are deprived of political rights, whenever a society lacks a functioning political system commensurate with its level of development, then culture takes over the role normally played by politics. And culture continues to perform political tasks until normal political processes are restored."[35]

There was a tremendous proliferation of Black art during the 1960s, surpassing the output—at least in quantity—of the Harlem Renaissance. Cultural workshops, offering courses in writing, photography, and graphic arts, sprang up in every major city in the country. New York alone had seven, among them the Umbra workshop, founded by Tom Dent, Calvin Hernton, and David Henderson, and the Black Arts Repertory and School, founded by Baraka (Baraka later established the Spirit House Movers in Newark). The organizers of OBAC (Organization of Black American Culture) included Hoyt Fuller, editor of the now-defunct *Negro Digest/Black World*, which along with *Nommo* provided publishing outlets for OBAC writers. In California the Watts Writers Workshop included Quincy Troupe, Stanley Crouch, and Jayne Cortez. The variety and wide dispersement of these cultural institutions are deceiving. If one examines the members of the workshops, the editorial boards of journals like *Umbra*, *Black World*, *Nommo*, *Journal of Black Poetry*, *Soulbook*, *Dialogue*, *Black Expressions*, the *Black Collegian*, and *Black Books Bulletin*, and the contributors to these journals, one can discern that there existed, with the aid of the jet plane and money from Black Studies programs, a network of writers and critics who, though limited in number, cooperated with and reacted to one another on a national level. These same writers and critics, influenced by the desire to set up permanent institutions, were instrumental in developing a number of presses: Broadside Press (Detroit), Jihad (Newark), Free Black Press of California, Black Dialogue Press (New York), Journal of Black Poetry Press (California), and Third World Press (Chicago).[36] Of all the literary genres, poetry was undoubtedly the strongest, with a resurgence of interest in the drama; and of all the writers, the poets were the strongest advocates of the Black Aesthetic.

"Black Aesthetic," which should be a system by which to judge what good Black literature is, has become a term like "nationalism"—much used and poorly defined. Part of the problem is that when the young cultural nationalists used the term they wanted to apply it only to the works of those who shared their ideology; everybody else wrote Negro art. The only critic prominently associated with the Black Aesthetic movement who has addressed himself to a critical approach that is useful in analyzing all of Black literature is Stephen Henderson who, in his *Understanding the New Black Poetry*, explores the literature at the point where it diverges from the rest of American literature, the point where the written literature, although sharing in elements of European, American, and past Afro-American literature, converges with the folklore of Black people. Henderson does an excellent job of examining the special uses that Black poetry makes of Black speech and Black music. His theory of saturation, which is an attempt to measure the extent that a writer's work is reflective in theme and structure of the Black experience,[37] is necessarily vague and does not take into account the growth of the Black middle class and the general massification of culture which makes it increasingly difficult to define what the real Black experience is. Black people at one point in time were bound to the soil, and their folklores reflected that. The younger writers of the 1960s obviously thought the Black experience meant Chicago and New York. Yet Henderson is saying that no matter how removed experientially one may be from participation in either the rural or urban Black life, which by implication is the life of poor Blacks who constitute the majority of Black people, one must share in the race memory and history of Black people in order to be a Black writer, must somehow reflect what it means to have been the only people in America to have been legal slaves and second-class citizens.[38] Henderson, however, does not really answer the question of what to do with poetry, like some of Dunbar's standard English verse, which is not Black in theme, structure, or saturation.

The cultural nationalists of the 1960s saw the Black Aesthetic as a means of measuring a writer's ideological commitment. There was a general refusal or inability to define what specifically the Black Aesthetic was, but there was agreement on a number of requirements. First of all, Black writing was to be addressed only to Black people and was to be a functional art. Haki Madhubuti's definition of what was functional was so broad that it encompassed every work of art ever done by any human being. Functional art to him was art that served a purpose—created some emotion, was incorporated into dance, moved an individual to action.[39] However, most of the nationalist critics felt that to be functional, art had to serve a specific social purpose. There were some general purposes that were often mentioned in the critical material of the period. Black art should:

1. reveal the decadence of white culture and expose the white man as the oppressor of Black people;
2. reaffirm the beauty of Black culture and history (obviously whether one meant Afro-American, African, or both cultures depended on one's definition of cultural nationalism);
3. create new and positive images; make Blackness, both the word and the concept, mean beauty;

4. make Black people conscious of the nature of their racial oppression and expose the self-defeating tendencies that have resulted from that oppression;

5. give Black people political and social direction (the proper direction varied from artist to artist).[40]

Most critics of a cultural nationalist persuasion did not insist on any specific form or language, but there was much talk about the necessity of couching the poetry in a language that was readily accessible to the larger Black community.[41] Carolyn Rodgers, nationalist poet and critic, was the most adamant of all the artists about the question of language. She called for the use of Black language, by which she evidently meant the urban language of poor Black folks, and insisted that Black poetry ignore grammatical sentences and "European" structures (something e. e. cummings had done rather well much earlier).[42] She also was presumptuous enough to criticize the language of Gwendolyn Brooks (ah, the folly of youth) and to complain about the un-Black diction of Kereopetse (Willie) Kgositsile, whose native tongue and language of creation is the African language, Tswana (how much Blacker can you get?).[43]

The whole argument about the use of Black language versus standard English becomes an irrelevant issue when one recognizes that the majority of the cultural nationalist poets were highly literate people, college graduates writing for a college audience. We saw too often the rather patronizing and inadequate attempts of middle-class Blacks to capture a "Black language." Pearl Cleage Lomax's "schemin" is a perfect example:

> i used to be dreamin'
> and schemin' bout you
> all the time.
> didn't a day go by
> but i wadn't
> trying' to work a root
> or two on you. . . .
>
> cause I'd be sayin charms
> to make you mine
> and scatterin' dust the way
> I knew you'd pass
> schemin' back!
> And I ain't talking about no
> abra-kadabra shit either.
> I'm talkin' about real magic
> that works—really works.
> i know.
> just look at you.[44]

The inconsistencies in language are obvious (varying spellings for "ing," the strange "wadn't," the conflicting phonetics of "ta" and "you," the inconsistent use of "I used to be" and "I'd be"). Basically the spirit of the poem is false. By the end of the poem, the poet has dropped all pretenses of a Black ghetto language. However, even the champion of Black speech, Miss Rodgers, comes in for a rather pointed critique by Haki Madhubuti, who sounds like a proponent of New Criticism, as he carefully picks apart Miss Rodgers's "misuses of language."[45] Even if the poetry had been perfect in its reproduction of Black urban language, it wouldn't have mattered; the average college student who constituted the major audience for the poetry of the 1960s never would have noticed.

Of all the poets, Haki Madhubuti and Imamu Amiri Baraka seemed most aware of the problem of actually reaching the masses of Black people. Both artists were and are extremely media-conscious, and Haki constantly addressed the problem of competing with the seductive powers of television. By the time he wrote *Dynamite Voices* he had convinced himself that Black poetry, a la Don L. Lee and the Last Poets, had become competitive with Black music.[46] Such a belief was an illusion. Although Haki probably sold more poetry than any poet, white or Black, during the 1960s, the written or spoken word is no match for the pervasive and massive influence of television, radio, and film, especially if the object of one's propaganda is Black people, whose reading material leans toward the likes of *Jet* and the dream book.[47]

The needless imbroglio over the language question was only part of the problem, for although the Black Aesthetic freed Black writers from the *New York Times* and white critics, it subjected them to a new Black establishment whose restrictions were even more rigid. Baraka excommunicated a number of people from the race in a speech at Rockland Park in January, 1969: "The Negro artist who is not a nationalist at this late date is a white artist, even without knowing it. He is creating death snacks, for and out of dead stuff. What he does will not matter."[48] The net result was that there was a tremendous amount of imitation of both Baraka and Haki, as well as a great deal of dissembling and confusion on the part of Black poets who wanted to be published and dutifully tried to adhere to an ideology that they did not understand or did not believe. Haki points out the contradictions in the poetry of Nikki Giovanni, who had gotten the party line confused and whose contradictions became more evident the more she published.[49] She went rather rapidly from "nigger can you kill?" to the idea that motherhood was revolutionary.

Despite the obvious confusion resulting from numerous interpretations of the goals of the Black Aesthetic, the idea that the writer had a special role to guide and direct the masses was one that had firm hold on the consciousness of the younger writers. It is no new idea. Richard Wright in 1937 believed that Black writers had a "moral duty" to replace both the Negro church and the Negro middle class as leaders of the masses of Black people. His rhetoric, if not his ideology, is surprisingly close to that of the cultural nationalists of the 1960s. The writer is to "create values by which his race is to struggle, live, and die."[50] He is to become the high priest, and the connection of culture with religion probably grew out of that time when religion so permeated the life of man that it was inseparable from every act that he performed, and the artist himself has always perpetuated the idea that his gift was some mystical power bestowed upon him, his artistry a calling from God or fate to which he merely responded. Even in a supposedly atheistic society the connection between culture and religion persists. Liehm, in his discussion of Czech society and culture, says, "No society . . . can get along without the kind of 'religion' represented by culture. It is 'religious' in the sense that like religion, culture is a constant reminder of tradition, history, memory, a criterion of values, a touchstone of morality and character in the individual and in society, a keeper of the sacred flame."[51] In the 1960s the writers and the critics made cultural nationalism the religion, and, as Stephen Henderson points out, the poets became the "profoundest preachers."[52]

Of all the writers of the period, Baraka took the idea of poet as spiritual leader most seriously and proceeded to try to actualize that concept in a most concrete fashion. He had dabbled in Islam and the Yoruba religions in New York, received instruction in Islam (the Hanafi version) in Newark, and studied Christianity, Zen, and Buddhism in the 1950s.[53] Upon establishing Spirit House in Newark in 1968, he became Imamu (poet/priest) Amiri (warrior/leader) Baraka (blessing or blessed of God),[54] holder of the awesome powers of both the secular and religious thrones for a small group of followers of the Kawaida religion. He proclaims in *In Our Terribleness*, "I am a vessel, a black priest interpreting / the present and the future for my people . . . — Allah speaks in and thru me now . . . / Rays of God plunged thru us all-uh / bids me raise myself to tell you / Look! / Listen! / I am in an ecstasy a swoon in actual touch with everything."[55]

It was not religion in the formal sense, however, that made Baraka a high priest/magician. It was his art, particularly his poetry, whose purpose was to "evoke the divine" and bring man into touch with the holy and the invisible, which in Baraka's mind, was "more real than the visible world." The artist/priest's tools—"words, the signs, the symbols, the artifacts"—were "magic things."[56] The message was cultural nationalism and the goal restoration of the Black man to his supposedly lofty former place in the universe.

Baraka did not discourage religiosity and fanaticism; he told his fol-

lowers instead that they should have "simple faith, like church people
. . . hard rock emotional faith in what we are doing. The same way
grandmamma used to weep and wring her hands believing in Jeez-us,
that deep deep connection with the purest energy, that is what the
nationalist must have."[57] There is throughout the writings of Baraka a
rejection of rationality and a reliance upon the spirit, upon feeling. In
"Poetry and Karma," he says, "The intellectual is sorely limited. It does
not get to the wellsprings of knowledge, it is a corny 'activity' actually.
It fits slower beings, but the subtlest and surest knowledge is what
Hegel thought of as intuition. The intimacies of the Spirit."[58] By rely-
ing on feeling, the heart, and by becoming virtuous, the Black man,
according to Baraka, will reinherit the earth. For in Baraka's mythology, the Black man was the first man to walk the earth, was at one
time in and of the whole universe, and is now "the universal energy
transforming itself."[59] This romantic view of sensation and emotion,
this mysticism, is very much akin to the Senghorian Negritude that
proclaims that the essence of the African mind is "intuitive reason,
. . . sentient reason . . . which expresses itself emotionally, through
that self-surrender, that coalescence of subject and object; through myth,
by which I mean the archetypal images of the collective Soul, above all
through primordial rhythms, synchronized with those of the cos-
mos."[60] In other words, the Black man does not think in a European
manner, does not merely perceive objects but becomes one with those
objects. He is natural man completely in tune with the rest of the universe. Taking those qualities which the white man has considered the
proof of Black inferiority—so-called irrationality, emotionalism—Senghor and Baraka divest them of negative connotations and make them
virtues. Senghor is concerned about the issue of Black equality and
humanity. Baraka's position is that the Black man has a natural superiority.

In his poetry Baraka makes much use of African images and symbols, but he does not, as does Haki Madhubuti, find it necessary to
deprecate Afro-American culture. There is a skillful interweaving of both
Africa and Afro-America, but ultimately his folk hero is the street nigger. Baraka has, since the beginning, been a rather romantic Afro-
American cultural nationalist, almost chauvinistically so. A writer whose
caustic wit and intense irony is interlaced with an irrepressible streak
of sentimentality, Baraka in *Dead Lecturer* (1964) even manages to pro-
claim the heroism of Mantan Moreland, Buckwheat, and Willie Best,
the Stepin Fetchit of his day.[61] Despite his sentimentality and an early
obscurantism, Baraka has always effectively used Black urban folklore.
The blues is a central force in his first book of poetry, *Preface to a Twenty
Volume Suicide Note*, and he later plays the dozens on Johnson and his

mama with an obscene finesse rarely seen in print.[62] Even after he becomes involved in Kawaida, the emphasis is still on Afro-America, which, according to Baraka, has "a special way into the struggle, and perhaps a special role, as the second largest and richest Afrikan nation in the world."[63]

True to the Black Aesthetic and his expressed sentiments, Baraka appears to direct much of his later poetry to the average Black man in the city and courts him with gentle proddings and high praise in a form that takes its shape from the sermon and the jazz solo, preacher's voice and saxophone both starting off gently and reaching a crescendo that ends in no words but a talking in tongues, a screeching cacophony that still has rhythm. The form is still in an experimental stage in "Sermon for Maturity" in *Nation Time* (pp. 13–20). By the time he writes *In Our Terribleness*, he has perfected the form by adding the coda, the resolution that exists in both the jazz solo and the sermon and that is a softer sound, a reinforcement of the message without the emotionalism. The message in *In Our Terribleness* is what all sermons are about: the coming of the Kingdom. However, Baraka's kingdom is to be an urban paradise where Black people can be as fly and free and wild as ever and at the same time become virtuous rulers not only of America but the world and the universe (an irreconcilable paradox if I ever saw one). Baraka says, "Our style will remain."

Weaving his words in between Fundi's photographic images, softened shots of inner city scenes, Baraka turns the world upside down with urban speech that has always moved in opposition to standard English. Baraka expands the language by sometimes using both the Black and standard meaning. "Terrible" means "out-of-sight," "fantastic," but also "capable of producing terror, awe." Also, not only is the language reversed; so are the images. Next to a picture of a brother with a red hat and a flashing razor, Baraka writes, "The red hat is a magic hat, the razor a sword flasher." Those things which evoke shame and/or fear in the Black and white middle class take on supernatural significance, become powerful and positive. There is a picture of a working man with an apron on, a toothpick in his mouth, Langston Hughes's Simple, really. Baraka makes him a wizard, that toothpick an African swagger stick which sprays light, a magician's wand. Those pastimes which most Black people still enjoy but which carry in the middle-class world the stigma of being stereotypic talents of the happy darky receive attention and an added dimension:

> You can dance nigger I know it
> Dance on to freedom
> You can sing nigger sing

Sing about your rare movement
in space
Grow you pierced the clouds of
animal ignorance.

Baraka finds pride in the idea that Black people can supposedly run
faster and play ball better than anybody in the world. Even Jim Brown
and Muhammad Ali get a good word. Baraka sounds like Baldwin when
he says, "Our terribleness is our survival as beautiful beings, anywhere," and in lines that are reminiscent of Sterling Brown's "Strong
Men" he praises our adaptability and our ability to find humor in our
existence:

They had us in a cage
To hold back our rage. Our eyes
smiled
anyway.[64]

Baraka's fascination with and romanticization of Black street life is
typical of the middle-class intellectual. To him ghetto life possesses a
drama that is missing in Black petit bourgeois life, provides the excitement of negotiating what Haki Madhubuti in "We Walk the Way of
the New World" calls the "dangercourse," and serves as the scene for
a middle-class boy's initiation or reintroduction back into the fold. Baraka recalls the time of his youth when he was "the only middle class
chump running with the Hillside Place bads,"[65] with these lines in In
Our Terribleness:

Hot souls
such as ones the
unimagined ecstasy of my childhood sometimes
what the thrust to completion is was in me
and thrilled me so
much. It shook me out of earth
I winged thru space man fine and clean.

There is to Baraka a vivid, almost sexual, exhilaration in the free world
of the niggers.

The art of In Our Terribleness is a definite success. The logic and political ideas put forth are something else again. The obvious contradictions of Black people remaining as Baraka imagines them to be and
then becoming rulers of the earth by dint of their past civilization, present intuitiveness, and future spirituality are an incredible proposition.
One begins to question whether Baraka, like most preachers, in his
rhapsodies on the superiority of Black intuition and the glories of the
street, is merely using a bit of persuasive rhetoric to win over a few

converts. For in one of his more calculating moods, he told David Llorens, a Chicago writer very much involved in the nationalist movement: "Most people are not rational, or they are just rational. . . .
They function on a less than conscious level. The reason you have to
teach people values, values, values is so they will do things that are in
their best interest without trying to reason about it. By the time the
average person reasons, especially the Negro in America, by the time
he reasons through anything . . . the thing has gone. . . . We're trying
to give people a value system so they can move, instinctively, to do
what is best."[66] His statement that people are "just rational" supports
his belief in the need for some added insight, some intuitive nature
that sees and feels beneath the surface. However, the same statement
seems to imply that Black people have neither the ability to reason nor
this special perception. According to Baraka and other advocates of the
Black Aesthetic, only the writer is privy to the secret of the universe,
or at least the political future of Black America, and must always "teach"
the people, "direct" the people, "give the people some values."

It was not long before the term "the people" began to mean the
small group of faithful who joined the church of cultural nationalism,
who gathered together at religious ceremonies they called political rallies or Black Theater, and who, with the pageantry of any Baptist Sunday, complete with the wearing of one's Sunday-go-to-meeting African
attire and the eating of a church supper (vegetarian fare instead of fried
chicken), participated in rituals, led by the high priest of the movement, the Black poet. After he or she delivered his sermon/
speech/poem in a chanting voice that captured the rhythms of Black music and the Black sermon, and after the choir (usually a jazz group or,
better yet, African drummers) had rendered its selection, the faithful, who were supposed to be inspired to rush out and fight the revolution, ventured homeward, buoyed up by the communal warmth of
fellow believers and drained of all anger and need for action by the
cathartic ceremony that concretized their hatred and resentment of the
white man, their new found love and/or old shame of being Black in
America, and their need to feel that someone cared and knew the answer.

However, sermons are believable only to the devotee or near-con-
vert. As a political tool, a propaganda weapon, poetry was a failure. It
became merely a means of reinforcing the previously ingested ideas of
those who already believe; and if gatherings of nationalists contained
other than true believers, they participated in what for them was just
another spectacle, a happening in which entertainment was provided
by one's fellow participants, wearing costumes and projecting images
thoughtfully designed for a show—a show directed by the poet, the
star and master of ceremonies of the 1960s.

This ritualization of political issues, instead of discouraging the move to robotize the people into smoothly functioning and unquestioning units, contributed to further dehumanization. For instead of struggling to teach people to reason in a society where the word already serves to mystify and the image that one sees disguises rather than reveals, the poets and other political leaders took upon themselves the duty of being the brains for the people. Unfortunately, or maybe fortunately, poets, especially romantic poets like Baraka, make inept political theorists and naive political practitioners, as Baraka's relationship with Kenneth Gibson in Newark proved.

Despite a concerted effort to wield political power on a personal level, the majority of the political poets of the 1960s were not guilty of some Machiavellian scheme to lead the unwitting masses into a revolution or into political action for purely self-serving reasons. The best of preachers, although acutely aware of the most effective means of playing on the emotions of their followers, generally are transported by the rapture produced by their own visions, by the hypnotic rhythms of their own voices, by the poetic brilliance of their own words. It is their immersion in and apparent emotional commitment to these visions that move the church to vicarious or active participation.

The inability of Black writers to accomplish the social and ideological goals of the Black Aesthetic movement stems directly from the varied and contradictory beliefs held by the different writers. Although Baraka and Haki worked closely together before Baraka's conversion to Marxism and both in their writings excoriate whites and middle-class Blacks with equal intensity (Baraka with a scathing invective, Haki with a rather haughty sarcasm), the two had demonstrable philosophical differences from the beginning.

Haki's portrayal of ghetto life in poetry and essay is a total repudiation of the exoticism reflected in Baraka's works. Despite the fact that Addison Gayle contends that Black art has to divorce itself from the tendency to explain the Black community in terms of pathology, Haki sees little else in Afro-American life.[67] His view of Afro-American culture very closely approximates the basically anti-Black (if one uses the term "Black" to describe the masses of Black Americans) position of the then Black Muslims. Elijah Muhammad's desire to obliterate the shame of the slave past, even to the extent of banning cornbread, is an elemental ingredient in the Muslim doctrine.[68] There are constant descriptions in Muhammad's *Message to the Black Man* of the proverbial laziness of the Negro[69] and the portrayal of the Muslims as an elite, the chosen few.[70] The self-proclaimed superiority and their puritanical lifestyle served to isolate them from the rest of Black people, and although Blacks were continually exhorted to love each other and rid themselves of self-hatred, Elijah Muhammad contends that our kinky hair was the result of our having angered God.[71]

Haki Madhubuti, who was still calling Elijah Muhammad "honourable" in 1971 and who sees Malcolm X mainly as a product and conduit of the Black Muslim religion,[72] grew up in circumstances that made it impossible to be romantic about poverty,[73] and when he writes of urban life it is rendered in stark and unsympathetic terms. Haki, who sees the Black ghetto existence as being synonymous with Black American life, describes the Negro as "a reflection of another man's imagination, a reflection of another man's fantasy, a nonentity, a filthy invention."[74] Negroes, the majority of Black people, are mindless, sad, impotent copies of the white man.[75] Our style that Baraka savors as something beautiful and unique, Haki scorns. He sees our concern with clothing and appearance as an example of our superficiality:

> why u bes dressen so funny, anyhow, huhh?
> i mean, is that u clean?
> why u bes dressen like an airplane, can u fly
> i mean
> will yr/blue jim-shoes fly u,
> & what about yr/tailor made bell bottoms, clean?
> can they lift u above madness.[76]

Of that toothpick that Baraka makes into a wizard's stick, Haki says:

> change-up
> that toothpick you're
> sucking on was
> once a log.[77]

And while Baraka delights in our legendary ability to sing, dance, and play ball, Haki views these talents as worthless skills that merely benefit the white man.

> listen, no doubt you're very smart
> we can tell by the size of yr feet that you dance too
> doin the kneeknot best in the land
> no doubt you're the best athlete to confront
> the 20th century since beaver bill
> expert ping pong player for the state department.[78]

Unlike Baraka, Haki sees no intuitive superiority in Black people and questions their ability to conceptualize at all: "We have, whether we admit it or not, been molded into beings that are mentally—in terms of our existence—just above animals, and just as animals, we are ruled by instincts which govern us from day to day."[79] Haki eventually per-

ceived any calls for revolution among such undirected and unconscious
people as a pipe dream, and his perception proved much closer to reality than the judgments of the revolutionary nationalists who did not
really believe that the system would deal death if necessary.[80] Unlike
Baraka and Baldwin, Haki is not even sure of our ability to survive,[81]
and in "Spirit Flight into the Coming" he makes the cruelest cut of all:

> . . . step in somebody
> Shine brightness for a dead people . . .
> Show us that there is value in ourselves
> prove to us that we are worth saving . . . [82]

Since Negroes are "dead people" and of questionable value, Haki
addresses all of his works to the "real people," to Black people, adding
in parentheses occasionally "and Negroes too"; and though in 1969 he
counseled against "closed societies" which demand that people pledge
allegiances to organizations rather than Black people and which set up
numerous stipulations for membership that result in the creation of
class divisions and racial disunity, as time went by the circle of the
saved for Haki got smaller and smaller.[83] By 1973 the list of "enemies"
had enlarged to include "Negroes, militants, revolutionary integration-
ists, soul brother number 15, black capitalists, colored politicians, and
pig-eaters lying about their diets."[84] Haki, a strict vegetarian, even proclaims in what seems to be a serious tone that it is impossible for a fat
person to be revolutionary (Poor Mao was suffering delusions all along).
Once the stipulation of having to know or, at least study, Swahili was
added, the possibility of being allowed into the promised land became
severely diminished.[85]

Despite his constant condemnation of the white man as enemy and
devil, a close examination of Haki's writings reveals that essentially the
white race or at least his conception of it is the standard by which
Blacks are to judge themselves. Again one can see in his concerns the
influence of the Black Muslim dogma, which, with its work ethic, authoritarianism, and emphasis on clean living, comes very close to rep-
licating good old American puritanism. One sees Booker T. Washington, Elijah Muhammad, and ultimately the Puritan fathers in lines like
this:

> times is hard rufus and they gointa be harder
> come on champ chop chop
> hit hard hit harda *catch up* chop chop [*my emphasis*]
> sleep less eat right rise earlier
> whup dust into the eyes of excuse makers.[86]

Haki talks of the need to groom leadership, as he believes whites do,
by selective educational processes and puts forth as a model the unfor-

tunate example of the career of Henry Kissinger, as if the world needed Henry Kissinger in blackface or whiteface for that matter.[87] Zionism is constantly cited as an ideal to emulate. "Afrika must exist for us like Israel exists for the Jews; every Jew realizes that his future . . . is dependent upon the continuation and growth of Israel."[88]

Haki paints Africa, which is somehow to be the salvation of Black people, in fantastic terms. Traditional Africa conjures up "memories of the once / to memories of the used to be / lost days of glory, the forgotten-forgiven history of the race: / when sun mattered and the night was for sleeping / and not for planning the / death of enemies.[89] Present-day Africa in *We Walk the Way of the New World* is portrayed as uncorrupted by the West, a picture totally contradictory to Africa's sociopolitical reality.[90] Yet whenever the exploitative nature of big business is examined, it is always in terms of imperialism in Africa, rather than domestic economic exploitation in America. Haki's discussions of substantive political issues and possible resistance are limited to an African context. It is never concretely stated, but perhaps he believes that through a reclaiming of natural resources and through political pressure Africa is going to force a reordering of America's system.

While Blacks wait for the time when they will "become the owners of the New World,"[91] they should, like the Jews, build their own institutions, buy Black, become a nation within a nation,[92] in other words, follow the Nation of Islam plan in African dress instead of black suit. The institutions, schools, presses, etc., are to be supported by using the methods of Black churches, by setting up retail outlets for a product that can be marketed locally and nationally, and by developing service-oriented businesses.[93] Haki seems oblivious to the fact that such a plan gives one a tremendous stake in the present economic system. He denies that this strategy has anything to do with capitalism since Blacks are only aspiring capitalists. His justification for nonresistance and actual cooperation with the system is a rationalization from Karenga which states that Blacks can be "rational and modern enough in their orientation to allow the exchange of goods and services within the society yet never become a reflection of it on the level of values and lifestyle."[94] Such statements belie any pretensions of the revolutionary or even rebellious character of cultural nationalism.

Of all the cultural nationalists Haki seems the most concerned about the development and education of the young, who must be prepared for the "21st century" which will demand from them "unknown effort, unknown discipline, unknown dedication . . . [and] will instill in [them] the necessary skills and values that will motivate them to serve Afrika and Afrikan people."[95] To prepare them for this awesome task, Black educational institutions must recreate in them an "Afrikan mind."[96] Haki prefers not the Senghorian model with its instinct and rhythmic abandon but rather the "African genius" defined by Nkrumah: "By African genius I mean something positive, our socialist conception of society, the efficiency and validity of our traditional statecraft, our highly developed code of morals, our hospitality and our purposeful energy."[97] Madhubuti proved later not to be serious about Nkrumah's socialism, but he was/is not alone in this tendency to read works selectively, to emphasize that which is reassuring, to redefine at will, and to ignore the rest.

To recreate this "Afrikan mind," alternative schools have been provided for young children. Although the schools, which are located in numerous cities, define their own pedagogical methods, they are probably greatly influenced by Haki and *Black Books Bulletin*, with its emphasis on children's literature and on the importance of redefining educational procedures. One hopes the methods described in a *Black Books Bulletin* article by Tayari Kwa Salaam of the Ahidiana Work/Study Center in New Orleans do not become typical of the Pan-African alternative schools. There is an air of militarism. "We begin activities together such as beginning meals with a leader who says, 'ready! Seats!' and then once we are seated, 'Ready! Sifa!' (*Sifa* is Swahili for *praise*)."[98] There are educational procedures that are pure B. F. Skinner:

> We develop discipline and concentration on an individual basis in Kazi (the work room) and on a group basis in Darasa (the classroom). In Kazi we develop these by first finding the child's attention span level, then requiring the child to remain working with an activity to his/her limit, reinforcing that accomplishment with praise and/or reward. The child is required to do this again later in the day or again the next day. Each time we increase the time limit in which the child must work on the activity (Skinner's Law on Temporal Summation). In Darasa we require the wato to be disciplined or they are not allowed to participate in the class at all.[99]

In this American society, which very skillfully provides baits and bribes, coopts that which is usable, and kills that which is not, we need children who know how to reason in adverse and ever-changing conditions, not little well-trained pigeons in some Skinner box.

The ultimate result of the type of cultural nationalism espoused by Haki Madhubuti is an isolationism which separates cultural nationalists from a world that grows continually smaller and more interconnected and a seclusion and exclusivity which will make them the New Amish of America. Haki himself became increasingly provincial with time. His early poems, which make reference to the similiarities between Blacks and the Vietcong, are later eliminated from the collected poems, *Directionscore*, and any Black involved in Third World allegiances is accused of merely being engaged in the romantic pursuit of Oriental women.[100]

However, this insular disregard of the world is not the crucial problem. The very cult nature of the organization described, the basically elitist and middle-class stipulations for membership, ignore completely the problems and reality of the "Negroes" who constitute the majority of Black people. Haki's defense of this separation from the rest of the world and the majority of Black people is that "corruption breeds corruption / the non-corrupt cannot live among / the corrupt and not become corrupt also, / one either leaves and exposes / or one become corrupt / there is no compromise ,/ there is no in between."[101] One can not question a man's desire to shape a warm and nurturing environment for his children, but to project this type of cultural nationalism as a viable solution to the problems of the masses of Black people or as some sort of present or future attack on the larger American system is to live an illusion. The children trained in watotos across the nation, who are supposedly being raised as cadres to lead Black people to freedom, will be as alien to and alienated from their own people as any little Black middle-class children reared in all-white environments. If they are not allowed to touch the real world and be touched by it, they will be ill-equipped not only for leadership but for survival.

The cultural nationalism of the late 1960s, early 1970s was essentially a movement of middle-class artists/intellectuals who assumed rather patronizingly that they knew what was best for Black people. Inherent in that patronization was an element of self-righteous contempt, the kind of contempt that prompted Baraka to say that "people who can't dig Trane are w/o [without] essential experience."[102] One had to dig Trane, Archie Schepp, Pharaoh Sanders, Ornette Coleman, Max Roach, Nina Simone, and Sun Ra. One had to be able to appreciate African art and give up at least pork. Carolyn Rodgers, in a rather poignant confession written in 1971, admits to the elitism, the isolationism. She recounts the rebellions of Black people in the cities of America and condemns "the Black, Blackest poets and scholars and students and historians, and artists and academicians who sat at home with their books and canvasses and theses and typewriters and AR-TIC-U-LATED, said, it's REVOLUTION, IT'S REVOLUTION!" In Rodgers's mind, the intellectuals reaped the profits, financial and otherwise, and the people stayed hungry. The next time, Rodgers predicts, the object of the people's rage might not be whites but the Black middle-class artist/intellectual who misled them in the 1960s.[103]

One of the positive attempts of the cultural nationalism of the 1960s was the move to make Black people aware of the crippling psychological effects of Black self-hatred so that they might rid themselves of a feeling of racial inferiority. The success or failure of that attempt is impossible to measure. According to John Runcie, psychological studies done on both lower- and middle-class Black children in 1972 show a correlation between the rising nationalism and a higher self-esteem

on the part of the children.[104] Fanon, however, implies in *Black Skin,
White Masks* that, since the inferiority complex of Blacks is based on
economic deprivation, the psychological effects of that oppression can
be eliminated only with the elimination of the actual cause.[105] However, if Fanon sincerely believed that recognition of a problem and an
attempt to cope with it on a psychoanalytical level were useless, then
there was no reason to write books like *Black Skin, White Masks*, whose
express purpose was to expose to Blacks the self-defeating effects of
racial shame. Carolyn Rodgers eventually decided that a great deal of
the Black-Is-Beautiful syndrome was pure self-delusion and wish fulfillment. She writes of her own transformation "from Super Ugly Black
to Super Black Beauty. I tried to believe. . . . I 'acted' like I was told.
Super Black Beauty, Fine Black Queen and my old and new (Black)
friends re-inforced me. We recorded each other's messages. We played
ourselves back to each other."[106] Since most cultural nationalists spent
the majority of their time recording messages for one another and had
no way of judging the effectiveness of their propaganda, *Superfly* and
its instant and massive effect on Black people came as a rather devastating and totally unexpected blow.[107]

Of all the movements of the 1960s, cultural nationalism was the most
easily coopted, mainly because it produced a plethora of artifacts for
commercialization (somebody in Taiwan probably got rich off all those
red, black, and green flags). Cultural nationalism paved the way for a
slew of Black politicians whose major contribution to the Black community seems to be the provision of patronage to friends and relatives,
paved the way for all those wretched Black exploitation films, paved
the way for Black capitalist pimps like George Johnson who ran an ad
in *Jet* evoking the names of Crispus Attucks, Nat Turner, Billie Holiday, Martin, Malcolm, Medgar, and hosts of other Black heroes and
heroines in order to market Afro-Sheen. Without African cultural nationalism, ABC probably would not have been able to sell us our slavery in the form of *Roots*, and the poor inhabitants of Gambia could
have avoided being stampeded by wild herds of Ugly Black Americans.
Without African cultural nationalism, however, we would have missed
the edifying sight of some Link from Chicago posing with her African
relatives in an issue of *Ebony*, and TWA would never have been able
to urge the Africans of America to fly home. Flo Kennedy would probably have never called that butcher Idi Amin a "precious nigger" on
"Sixty Minutes," and Andy Young would have missed all those trips
to Africa, in search of new clients for American goods and services.

There were, however, successes in the cultural nationalist movement. It was high time Black people shouted their collective hatred for
whites and centuries of slavery, oppression, and abuse, even if the end
result was merely catharsis. For silent and forgiving victims are never

respected, and hatred unreleased has a way of corroding the insides of those who hate. Furthermore, the 1960s revealed the white devils (a rather unfortunate choice of symbols since Black folks have always been more fascinated with and awed by the devil than God) to consist mainly of a bunch of ill-informed, powerless creatures, who, on the individual level, do not have to be feared or admired but who, on the group level, are prone to dangerous relapses of overt and violent racism that must be resisted. Cultural nationalism has kept Blacks cognizant of and sensitive to this recurring racism which surfaces from barely concealed hiding places in those times of crisis when America needs a scapegoat. More importantly, the nationalist movement of the 1960s has resulted in a more realistic world history by filling in the gaps and challenging the white nationalism that reduces human accomplishment to the legend of European hegemony, has served as a stimulus and a rejuvenating fount for the Black mythos that is the basis of the best of Afro-American art, has provided a beginning, if shallow, critique of the American system for a substantial number of Black people, and has created a place where a small group of Black people can recognize and avoid the all-pervasive materialism, the routinization of life, and the massification of culture that increasingly characterize America.

NOTES

1. James Turner, "Black Nationalism: The Inevitable Response," *Negro Digest* 15 (January, 1971), p. 6. See Adolph Reed, Jr., "Marxism and Nationalism in Afro-America," *Social Theory and Practice* 1 (Fall, 1971), pp. 1–39, for a comparison of the different nationalist movements.

2. James Baldwin, *The Fire Next Time* (New York, 1963), p. 49.

3. Ibid., p. 132.

4. Ralph Ellison, "That Same Pain, That Same Pleasure," *Shadow and Act* (New York, 1966), p. 27.

5. Larry Neal, "Any Day Now: Black Art and Black Liberation," *Ebony* (August, 1969), p. 55.

6. Ellison, pp. 39–40.

7. Neal, p. 56.

8. Frantz Fanon, *The Wretched of the Earth* (New York, 1967), p. 243. See the chapter "On National Culture" for Fanon's position on cultural nationalism.

9. Ibid., pp. 209–210.

10. LeRoi Jones (Imamu Amiri Baraka), *Tales* (New York, 1967), p. 89. For an indepth examination of Baraka's alienation and reentry into Black life, see Kimberly Benston's *The Renegade and the Mask* (New Haven, 1976).

11. Richard Wright, *Black Boy* (New York, 1966), p. 45. Wright, does, however, speak highly of Black folklore. See "Blueprint for Negro Writing," in *The Black Aesthetic*, ed. Addison Gayle (New York, 1971), pp. 315–26, and "The

Literature of the Negro in the United States," in *Black Expression*, ed. Addison Gayle (New York, 1969), pp. 198–229.

12. Adolph Reed, Jr., "Marxism and Nationalism," p. 16.

13. *Quotable Karenga* (Los Angeles, Calif., 1967), p. iii.

14. Ibid., p. 20.

15. Ibid., p. 26.

16. Ibid., p. 25.

17. Imamu Amiri Baraka (LeRoi Jones), *Kawaida Studies: The New Nationalism* (Chicago, 1972), pp. 9–10.

18. Stephen E. Henderson, "Survival Motion: A Study of the Black Writer and the Black Revolution in America," *The Militant Black Writer in Africa and the United States*, by Mercer Cook and Henderson (Madison, Milwaukee, 1969), p. 67. Harold Cruse felt that a democratization of America in which all ethnic cultures could be equal in a true cultural pluralism would be a revolutionary advancement. *The Crisis of the Negro Intellectual* (New York, 1967), pp. 188–189.

19. Fanon, *The Wretched*, pp. 221–222.

20. *Quotable Karenga*, p. 9.

21. Ibid., p. 2.

22. Ibid., p. 16.

23. Ibid., p. 6.

24. David Llorens, "Ameer (LeRoi Jones) Baraka," *Ebony*, August, 1969, p. 80.

25. LeRoi Jones (Imamu Amiri Baraka), *Home* (New York, 1966), p. 248, and Imamu Amiri Baraka (LeRoi Jones), *Raise, Race, Rays, Raze* (New York, 1971), p. 47.

26. Janheinz Jahn, *Muntu: the New African Culture* (New York, 1961), p. 124.

27. Sekou Touré, "A Dialectical Approach to Culture," in *Black Poets and Prophets: The Theory, Practice, and Esthetics of the Pan-Africanist Revolution*, eds. Woodie King and Earl Anthony (New York, 1972), p. 62. See also Fanon, *The Wretched*, pp. 233–248, and Amilcar Cabral, "National Liberation and Culture," in *Return to the Source: Selected Speeches* (New York, 1973).

28. Fanon, *The Wretched*, pp. 112–113.

29. Llorens, p. 80.

30. Baldwin, *The Fire*, p. 127.

31. LeRoi Jones (Amiri Baraka), "The Last Days of the American Empire," *Home*, p. 205. The phrase "Tonto syndrome" is probably based on a popular song by Oscar Brown, Jr., which has Tonto deserting the Lone Ranger in the middle of an Indian attack.

32. Ibid., p. 198.

33. LeRoi Jones (Imamu Amiri Baraka), "The Myth of a Negro Literature," *Home*, p. 114.

34. LeRoi Jones (Imamu Amiri Baraka), "Philistinism and the Negro Writer," *Anger and Beyond: The Negro Writer in the United States* (New York, 1966), pp. 54–55.

35. Antonin J. Liehm, "Foreword: On Culture, Politics, Recent History, the Generations—and also on Conversations," *The Politics of Culture* (New York, 1973).

36. See Eugene B. Redmond's chapter on the 1960s, "Festivals and Funerals," in *Drum Voices* (New York, 1976), pp. 294–417.

37. Stephen Henderson, "Introduction: The Forms of Things Unknown," *Understanding the New Black Poetry—Black Speech and Black Music as Poetic References* (New York, 1973).

38. See Larry Neal's "Some Reflection on the Black Aesthetic" and Julian Mayfield's "You Touch My Black Aesthetic and I'll Touch Yours," in *The Black Aesthetic*, ed. Addison Gayle (New York, 1971).

39. Don L. Lee (Haki Madhubuti), *Dynamite Voices* (Detròit, 1971), p. 24. See also LeRoi Jones's poem, "Black Art," in *Black Magic Poetry* (Indianapolis and New York, 1969), p. 117, and *The Quotable Karenga*, p. 22.

40. See LeRoi Jones's "Revolutionary Theatre," and "The Legacy of Malcolm X," in *Home*; Larry Neal's "Any Day Now: Black Art and Black Liberation," in Henderson and Cook, *Militant Black Writer*; Don L. Lee, "Black Poetry: Which Direction," *Negro Digest* 17 (September/October, 1968), pp. 27–32; Mari Evans, "Contemporary Black Literature," *Black World* 19 (June, 1970), pp. 4, 93, 94; Carolyn Rodgers, "Black Poetry—Where It's At," *Negro Digest* 18 (September, 1969), pp. 7–16; and Addison Gayle, *The Black Aesthetic*.

41. Don L. Lee (Haki Madhubuti), "The Black Writer and the Black Community," *From Plan to Planet* (Detroit, 1973), p. 96. Harold Cruse in *The Crisis*, p. 216, also feels that the only way a broad audience could be reached would be through the use of Black popular idiom and images but makes a seemingly paradoxical statement that the most important task of the artist is to mold "the lives and consciousness of the black intelligentsia, not the masses," p. 182.

42. Carolyn Rodgers, "The Literature of Black," *Black World* 19 (June, 1970), p. 10.

43. Carolyn Rodgers, "Breakforth. In Deed," *Black World* 19 (September, 1970), pp. 15–16, 20.

44. Pearl Cleage Lomax, *We Don't Need No Music* (Detroit, 1972), p. 9. Those poems written in a language more real to Mrs. Lomax show considerable promise. See "untitled," "vigil," "poem for neighbors," and "neighbor 1."

45. Don L. Lee (Haki Madhubuti), *Dynamite Voices*, p. 58.

46. Ibid., pp. 13–14. For further discussion of the communication problem, see Baraka, "Worknotes–66," pp. 12–13, and "Black Art, Nationalism, Organization, Black Institutions," p. 100, both in *Raise, Race, Rays, Raze*; also Haki Madhubuti, "The Black Writer and the Black Community," *From Plan to Planet*, p. 96. Harold Cruse addresses the problem of the dissemination of Black culture in *The Crisis*, pp. 84, 87.

47. Hollie West reports a figure of 250,000 books of Haki's poetry in "The Black Bard of Revolution," *Washington Post*, December 26, 1971, p. F1.

48. Baraka, "Black Art, Nationalism," *Raise, Race*, p. 98.

49. Madhubuti, *Dynamite Voices*, p. 73.

50. Richard Wright, "Blueprint for Negro Writing" in *The Black Aesthetic*, p. 321.

51. Liehm, p. 77.

52. Henderson, *The Militant Black Writer*, p. 106.

53. Marvin X and Faruk, "Islam and Black Art: An Interview with LeRoi Jones," *Negro Digest* 18 (January, 1969), p. 5. See Lee Jacobus, "Imamu Amiri Baraka: The Quest for Moral Order," in *Modern Poets*, edited by Donald Gibson (Englewood Cliffs, N.J., 1973), pp. 112–126, for an examination of Baraka's in-

terest in religion and its influence on his poetry from the beginning to the early 1970s.

54. Benston, *Renegade and the Mask*, p. 15, and Lee Jacobus, p. 126.

55. Imamu Amiri Baraka (LeRoi Jones) and Fundi (Billy Abernathy), "All in the Street," *In Our Terribleness* (Indianapolis and New York, 1970), n.p.

56. Marvin X, p. 8.

57. Baraka, "7 Principles of US Maulana Karenga," *Raise, Race*, p. 143.

58. Baraka, *Raise, Race*, p. 23.

59. Ibid., pp. 49–51.

60. Leopold Senghor, "What Is Negritude," *Negro Digest* 11 (April, 1962), p. 4. Abiola Irele, in "Negritude—Literature and Ideology," *Journal of Modern African Studies* 3 (1965), p. 518, and "Negritude or Black Cultural Nationalism," *Journal of Modern African Studies* 3 (1965), p. 339, contends that Senghor was greatly influenced by Lucien's and Levy-Bruhl's ideas on the so-called "primitive mentality" and Henri Bergson's theory on the superior nature of intuition.

61. See "Black Dada Nihilismus," in *The Dead Lecturer* (New York, 1964), p. 64, and "A Poem for Willie Best," *The Dead Lecturer*, p. 19.

62. "Word for the Right Wing," in *Black Magic Poetry*, p. 93.

63. This and the following quotes are from *In Our Terribleness* which has no pagination.

64. Cf. to Sterling Brown's "Strong Men":
They dragged you from hovel and
They chained you in coffles
They huddled you spoon-fashion
in filthy hatches . . .
You sang.

65. Theodore R. Hudson, *From LeRoi Jones to Amiri Baraka: The Literary Works* (Durham, North Carolina, 1973), p. 7.

66. Llorens, p. 65.

67. Addison Gayle, "Blueprint for Black Criticism," *First World* 1 (January/February, 1977), p. 43.

68. See statements on the "so-called Negro" in Elijah Muhammad, *Message to the Black Man in America* (Chicago, n.d.), p. 7.

69. Ibid., p. 26.

70. Ibid., p. 23.

71. Ibid., p. 31.

72. "Interview: The World of Don L. Lee," *The Black Collegian* 1 (February/March, 1971), p. 34.

73. Ibid., pp. 24–29. Interview contains biographical information on Haki's youth and early manhood. See also interview by E. Ethelbert Miller in *The Washington Review* 3 (Spring, 1977), pp. 12–13. A more extensive version of the Miller interview is on tape at the Afro-American Studies Resource Library, Founders Library, Howard University.

74. Don L. Lee (Haki Madhubuti), "Introduction: Louder but Softer," *We Walk the Way of the New World* (Detroit, 1970), p. 11.

75. There are numerous examples of this position in all of Haki's poetry. For specific examples see "For Black People," pp. 55–56; "Blackman/an unfin-

ished history," pp. 20–23; and "We Walk the Way of the New World," pp. 64–66; all in *We Walk the Way of the New World* (Detroit, 1970).

76. Madhubuti, "Move Un-noticed to be Noticed: A Nationhood Poem," in *We Walk the Way*, pp. 68–69.

77. Ibid., p. 71.

78. Madhubuti, "positive movement will be difficult but necessary," *Book of Life* (Detroit, 1973), p. 16. "Beaver Bill" was the only Black amateur Ping-Pong player touring with a state department team in exhibition games against the Chinese table tennis team during the initial diplomatic contacts with Red China. Haki sees him as a dupe of the white world.

79. Madhubuti, *From Plan to Planet*, p. 143.

80. See "Big Momma," p. 32, and "mixed sketches," p. 33, in *We Walk the Way*. In *Enemies: The Clash of Races*, Madhubuti predicts that capitalism will self-destruct and counsels Blacks to concentrate not on the revolutionary but a survivalist creed until the chaos subsides. (Chicago; 1978), pp. 173, 215, 219–220.

81. "u feel that way sometimes
    wondering:
    wondering, how did we survive?"
Madhubuti, "mixed sketches," *We Walk the Way*, p. 33.

82. Madhubuti, *Book of Life*, p. 30.

83. Don L. Lee (Haki Madhubuti), "Symposium: Measure and Meaning of the Sixties—What Lies Ahead for Black Americans," *Negro Digest* 19 (November, 1969), p. 12.

84. Madhubuti, *Book of Life*, p. 15.

85. Madhubuti, *From Plan to Planet*, pp. 49–53. In *Enemies* Haki urges co-operation with any Blacks who are interested in working for the race, pp. 125, 195–96.

86. Madhubuti, *Book of Life*, p. 14.

87. Madhubuti, *From Plan to Planet*, p. 23.

88. Ibid., pp. 23, 27. See also introduction to *We Walk the Way*, p. 15.

89. Madhubuti, *Book of Life*, p. 14.

90. Madhubuti, *We Walk the Way*, pp. 43–44. The Sixth Pan-African Congress of 1974, which was controlled by an African socialist contingency, disillusioned Haki, who returned with a more realistic view of the social and political realities of Africa and with a renewed dedication to Black cultural nationalism. See "Sixth Pan-Afrikan Congress," *Enemies*, pp. 62–73.

91. Ibid., p. 66.

92. Ibid., pp. 15–16. Haki reiterates this goal in *Enemies* and suggests the purchase of land in Africa as a second choice, pp. 214–223.

93. Madhubuti, *From Plan to Planet*, pp. 84–85.

94. Ibid., pp. 75, 79. In *Enemies* Haki rejects both communism and capitalism but advises Blacks to acquire both "money and power" if they are to survive in a capitalist world, pp. 219–220.

95. Ibid., p. 31.

96. Ibid., pp. 29, 45.

97. Nkrumah quote used as epigram in Madhubuti, *We Walk the Way*, p. 42.

98. Tayari Kwa Salaam, "Practices the Value and Love Revolution," *Black*

Books Bulletin (Winter, 1974), p. 49. A bit of Swahili is incorporated in the language used in most Pan-African schools.

99. Ibid., p. 42. See Benjamin B. Wolman, *Contemporary Theories and Systems in Psychology* (New York, 1960), p. 130, for discussion of behaviorism and Skinner's laws of behavior.

100. See pro-Vietcong poems, "Message to a Black Soldier," *Black Pride* (Detroit, 1968), p. 27, and "The Long Reality," *think black* (Detroit, 1967), p. 22. See poem denouncing Third World allegiances, "The Third World Bond," *Don't Cry, Scream* (Detroit, 1969), p. 56. Madhubuti in *Enemies* calls for knowledge of international politics and economics but reaffirms commitment to family, community, and race, in that order. He often refers to the survival tactics of the Amish and Mormons. See pp. 120–122, 175–176.

101. Madhubuti, *Book of Life*, p. 61.

102. Baraka, *Raise, Race*, p. 105.

103. Carolyn Rodgers, "Uh Nat'chal Thang—THE WHOLE TRUTH-Us," *Black World* 20 (September, 1971), p. 14.

104. John Runcie, "The Black Culture Movement and the Black Community," *Journal of American Studies* 9 (August, 1976), p. 213, quoting the *New York Times*, July 9, 1972, p. 21.

105. Fanon, *Black Skin, White Masks* (New York, 1967), p. 11.

106. Rodgers, "Uh Nat'chal Thang," p. 10.

107. Almost overnight the movie *Superfly*—whose hero is a cocaine dealer with shoulder-length hair, a keen interest in material goods, and a decidedly bourgeois mistress—made obsolete the nationalist notion of natural Black beauty and the nationalist rejection of wealth and luxury.

3

The "Black Revolution" and the Reconstitution of Domination

More than forty years ago Benjamin pointed out that "mass reproduction is aided especially by the reproduction of masses."[1] This statement captures the central cultural dynamic of "late" capitalism. The triumph of the commodity form over every sphere of social existence has been made possible by a profound homogenization of work, play, aspirations, and self-definition among subject populations—a condition Marcuse has characterized as one-dimensionality.[2] Ironically, while U.S. radicals in the late 1960s fantasized about a "new man" in the abstract, capital was in the process of concretely putting the finishing touches on *its new individual*. Beneath the current black-female-student-chicano-homosexual-old-young-handicapped, ad nauseam, "struggles" lies a simple truth: there is no coherent opposition to the present administrative apparatus, at least not from the left.

Certainly, repression contributed significantly to the extermination of opposition, and there is a long record of systematic corporate and state terror, from the Palmer Raids to the FBI campaign against the Black Panthers. Likewise, cooptation of individuals and programs has blunted opposition to bourgeois hegemony throughout this century, and cooptative mechanisms have become inextricable parts of strategies of containment. However, repression and cooptation can never fully explain the failure of opposition, and an exclusive focus on such external factors diverts attention from possible sources of failure within the opposition, thus paving the way for reproduction of the pattern of failure.

An earlier version of this article appeared in *Telos* (Spring, 1979), pp. 71–93, under the title "Black Particularity Reconsidered." Reprinted by permission.

The opposition must investigate its own complicity if it is to become a credible alternative.

During the 1960s theoretical reflexiveness was difficult because of the intensity of activism. When sharply drawn political issues demanded unambiguous responses, reflection on unintended consequences seemed treasonous. Years later, coming to terms with what happened during that period is blocked by nostalgic glorification of fallen heroes and by a surrender which Gross describes as the "ironic frame-of-mind."[3] Irony and nostalgia are two sides of the coin of resignation, the product of a cynical inwardness that makes retrospective critique seem tiresome or uncomfortable.[4]

At any rate, things have not moved in an emancipatory direction despite all claims that the protest of the 1960s has extended equalitarian democracy. In general, opportunities to determine one's destiny are no greater for most people now than before, and, more importantly, the critique of life-as-it-is has disappeared as a practical activity; i.e., an ethical and political commitment to emancipation seems no longer legitimate, reasonable, or valid. The amnestic principle which imprisons the social past also subverts any hope, which ends up seeking refuge in the predominant forms of alienation.

This is also true in the black community. Black opposition has dissolved into celebration and wish fulfillment. Today's political criticism within the black community—both Marxist-Leninist and nationalist—lacks a base and is unlikely to attract substantial constituencies. This complete collapse of political opposition among blacks, however, is anomalous. From the 1955 Montgomery bus boycott to the 1972 African Liberation Day demonstration, there was almost constant political motion among blacks. Since the early 1970s there has been a thorough pacification; or these antagonisms have been so depoliticized that they surface only in alienated forms. Moreover, few attempts have been made to explain the atrophy of opposition within the black community.[5] Theoretical reflexiveness is as rare behind Du Bois's veil as on the other side!

This critical failing is especially regrettable because black radical protests and the system's adjustments to them have served as catalysts in universalizing one-dimensionality and in moving into a new era of monopoly capitalism. In this new era, which Piccone has called the age of "artificial negativity," traditional forms of opposition have been undermined by a new pattern of social management.[6] Now, the social order legitimates itself by integrating potentially antagonistic forces into a logic of centralized administration. Once integrated, these forces regulate domination and prevent disruptive excess. Furthermore, when these internal regulatory mechanisms do not exist, the system must create them. To the extent that the black community has been pivotal in this new mode of administered domination, reconstruction of the trajectory of 1960s black activism can throw light on the current situation and the paradoxes it generates.

A common interpretation of the demise of black militance suggests that the waning of radical political activity is a result of the satisfaction of black aspirations. This satisfaction allegedly consists in: 1) extension of the social welfare apparatus; 2) elimination of legally sanctioned racial barriers to social mobility, which in turn has allowed for 3) expansion of possibilities open to blacks within the existing social system; all of which have precipitated 4) a redefinition of "appropriate" black political strategy in line with these achievements.[7] This new strategy is grounded in a pluralist orientation that construes political issues solely in terms of competition over distribution of goods and services within the bounds of fixed system priorities. These four items constitute the "gains of the 1960s."[8] Intrinsic to this interpretation is the thesis that black political activity during the 1960s became radical because blacks had been excluded from society and politics and were therefore unable effectively to solve group problems through the "normal" political process. Extraordinary actions were thus required to pave the way for regular participation.

This interpretation is not entirely untenable. With passage of the 1964 and 1965 legislation the program of the Civil Rights movement appeared to have been fulfilled. Soon, however, it became clear that the ideals of freedom and dignity had not been realized, and within a year, those ideals reasserted themselves in the demand for Black Power. A social program was elaborated, but again its underpinning ideals were not realized. The dilemma lay in translating abstract deals into concrete political goals, and it is here also that the "gains of the sixties" interpretation founders. It equates the ideals with the objectives of the programs in question.

To be sure, racial segregation has been eliminated in the South, thus removing a tremendous oppression from black life. Yet, dismantlement of the system of racial segregation only removed a fetter blocking the possibility of emancipation. In this context, computation of the "gains of the sixties" can begin only at the point where that extraordinary subjugation was eliminated. What, then, are those "gains" which followed the passage of civil rights legislation and how have they affected black life?

In 1964, the last year before the Vietnam boom (which in addition to other ways reduced black unemployment through military service) black unemployment averaged 9.6 percent; the 1971 average was 9.9 percent.[9] Moreover, among the most vulnerable groups—women and youth—unemployment rates in business cycle periods not only were not reduced in the 1960s but by 1975 were nearly twice higher than in 1957.[10] Black median income did not improve significantly in relation to white family income in the decade after passage of civil rights legislation,[11] and between 1970 and 1974 black purchasing power actually declined.[12] Moreover, blacks were still far more likely to live in inadequate housing than whites, and black male life expectancy declined, both absolutely and relative to whites between 1959 and 1961 and 1974.[13] Therefore, if the disappearance of black opposition is linked directly with the satisfaction of aspirations, the criteria of fulfillment cannot be drawn from the general level of material existence in the black community. The same can be said for categories such as "access to political decision-making." Although the number of blacks elected or appointed to public office has risen by leaps and bounds since the middle 1960s, that increase has not demonstrably improved life in the black community.

The problem is one of focus. The "gains of the sixties" thesis seems to hold only as long as the status of the "black community" is equated with that of certain specific strata. Although black life *as a whole* has not improved considerably beyond the elimination of racial segregation, in the 1970s certain strata within the black community actually have benefited. This development is a direct outcome of the 1960s activism: of the interplay of the "movement" and the integrative logic of administrative capitalism; and the "gains of the sixties" interpretation cannot spell out what "satisfaction" is because it is itself the ideology of precisely those strata which have benefited from the events of the 1960s within the black community. These "leadership" strata tend to generalize their own interests since their legitimacy and integrity are tied to a monolithic conceptualization of black life. Indeed, this conceptualization appeared in the unitarian mythology of late 1960s black nationalism. The representation of the black community as a collective subject neatly concealed the system of hierarchy which mediated the relation of the "leaders" and the "led."[14]

To analyze the genesis of the new elite is to analyze simultaneously the development of the new styles of domination in American society in general. Consequently, the following will focus on sources of the pacification of the 1970s and will expose the limitations of any oppositionist activity which proceeds uncritically from models of mass-organization politics which tend to capitulate to the predominant logic of domination.

Black resistance to oppression hardly began in Montgomery, Alabama, in 1955. Yet, it was only then that opposition to racial subjugation assumed the form of a mass movement. Why was this so? Despite many allusions to the impact of decolonization in Africa, international experiences of blacks in World War II, and so on, the reasons that black activism exploded in the late 1950s have seldom been addressed systematically.[15] Although resistance before 1955 was undoubtedly reinforced by the anticolonial movements abroad, what was significant for post-1955 growth of civil rights activity were those forces reshaping the entire American social order. An historically thorough perspective on the development of black opposition requires an understanding of the Cold War era in which it took shape.

Although popularity symbolized by "brinksmanship," "domino theory," fallout shelters, and the atmosphere of terror characterized by McCarthy, HUAC, and legions of meticulously anticommunist liberals, the Cold War was a much broader cultural phenomenon. Ultimately, it was a period of consolidation of the new mode of domination which had been developing for more than two decades. Piccone has noted that the Cold War era was the culmination of a dynamic of political and cultural adjustment to a dynamic of concentration that had attained hegemony over the American economy by the 1920s.[16] On the political front, the New Deal redefined the role of the state apparatus in terms of an aggressive, countercyclical intervention in the economy and everyday reality. At the same time, mass production required intensification of consumption. This requirement was met by the development and expansion of a manipulative culture industry and by the proliferation of an ideology of consumerism through mass communications and entertainment media.[17] Consumerism and the New Deal led to an intensification of the Taylorization of labor, which increasingly homogenized American life according to the dictates of bureaucratic-instrumental rationality. By the 1950s, Americanization had been institutionalized. Rigid political, intellectual, and cultural conformism (Riesman's "other directedness") evidenced a social integration achieved through introjection and reproduction of the imperatives of the system of domination at the level of everyday life.[18]

Pressures toward homogenization exerted for decades at work, in schools, and through the culture industry had seriously reformulated cultural particularity among ethnic groups. What remained were residues of the lost cultures—empty mannerisms and ambivalent ethnic identities mobilizable for Democratic electoral politics.[19] Moreover, the pluralist model was available for integrating the already depoliticized labor movement. In this context, the ruthless elimination of whatever opposition remained through the witch-hunts was only the coup de grace in a battle already won.

For various reasons, throughout this period, one region was bypassed in the monopolistic reorganization of American life and remained unintegrated into the new social order. At the end of World War II, the South remained the only internal frontier available for large-scale capital penetration. However, even though the South could entice industry with a docile work force accustomed to low wages, full domestication of this region required certain basic adjustments.

For one thing, the castelike organization of southern society seriously inhibited development of a rational labor supply. While much has been made of the utility of the segregated work force as a depressant of general wage levels, maintenance of dual labor markets creates a barrier to labor recruitment.[20] As a pariah caste, blacks could not adequately become an industrial reserve army since they were kept out of certain jobs. Consequently, in periods of rapid expansion the suppressed black labor pool could not be fully used, nor could blacks be mobilized as a potential strike-breaking force as readily as in other regions since employment of blacks in traditionally "white" jobs could trigger widespread disruptions.

The dual labor system was irreconcilable with the principle of reducing *all* labor to "abstract labor."[21] Scientific management has sought to reduce work processes to homogeneous and interchangeable hand and eye motions, hoping eventually to eliminate specialized labor.[22] A work force stratified on the basis of an economically irrational criterion such as race constitutes a serious impediment to realization of the ideal of a labor pool comprised of equivalent units. (Consider further the wastefulness of having to provide two sets of toilets in the plants!) In addition, the existing system of black subjugation, grounded in brutality, was intrinsically unstable. The racial order which demanded for its maintenance constant terror raised at every instant the possibility of rebellion and to that extent endangered "rational" administration. Given this state of affairs, the corporate elite's support for an antisegregationist initiative makes sense.

The relation of the corporate liberal social agenda to civil rights protest, though, is not a causal one. True, the Supreme Court had been chipping away at legal segregation for nearly twenty years, and the 1954 Brown decision finally provided the spark for intensified black protest. Yet the eruption of resistance from southern blacks had its own roots. Hence, to claim that the Civil Rights movement was a bourgeois conspiracy would be to succumb to the order's myth of its own omnipotence. Thus, the important question is not whether sectors of the corporate elite orchestrated the Civil Rights movement, but instead what elements within the Civil Rights movement were sufficiently compatible with the social agenda of corporate elites to prompt the latter to acquiesce to and encourage them. In order to answer this, it is necessary to identify both the social forces operative *within* the black community during segregation and those forces' engagement in civil rights activism. An analysis of the internal dynamic of the 1960s activism shows overlaps between the goals of the "New Deal Offensive" and the objectives of the "movement" (and, by extension, the black community).[23]

For the purposes of this analysis, the most salient aspects of the black community in the segregated South lie within a management dimension. Externally, the black population was managed by means of codified subordination, reinforced by customary dehumanization and the omnipresent spectre of terror. The abominable details of this system are well known.[24] Furthermore, blacks were excluded systematically from formal participation in public life. By extracting tax revenues without returning public services or allowing blacks to participate in public policy formation, the local political system intensified the normal exploitation in the work place. Public administration of the black community was carried out by whites. The daily indignity of the apartheidlike social organization was both a product of this political-administrative disenfranchisement as well as a motor of its reproduction. Thus, the abstract ideal of freedom spawned within the Civil Rights movement took concrete form primarily in opposition to this relation.

Despite the black population's alienation from public policymaking, an internal stratum existed which performed notable, but limited, social management functions. This elite stratum was comprised mainly of low-level state functionaries, merchants and "professionals" servicing black markets, and the clergy. While it failed to escape the general subordination, this indigenous elite succeeded, by virtue of its comparatively secure living standard and informal relations with significant whites, in avoiding the extremes of racial oppression. The importance of this stratum was that it stabilized and coordinated the adjustment of the black population to social policy imperatives formulated outside the black community.

Insofar as black public functionaries had assimilated bureaucratic rationality, the domination of fellow blacks was carried out in "doing one's job." For parts of the black elite such as the clergy, the ministerial practice of "easing community tensions" has always meant accommodation of black life to the existing forms of domination. Similarly, the independent merchants and professionals owed their relatively comfortable position within the black community to the special captive markets created by segregation. Moreover, in the role of "responsible Negro spokesmen," this sector was able to elicit considerable politesse, if not solicitousness, from "enlightened" members of the white elite. Interracial "cooperation" on policy matters was thus smoothly accomplished, and the "public interest" seemed to be met simply because opposition to white ruling group initiatives had been effectively neutralized.

The activating factor in this management relation was a notion of "Negro leadership" (later "black" or even "Black") that was generated outside the black community. A bitter observation made from time to time by the radical fringe of the movement was that the social category "leaders" seemed to apply only to the black community. No "white leaders" were assumed to represent a singular white population; but

certain blacks were declared opinion-makers and carriers of the interests of an anonymous black population. These "leaders" legitimated
their role through their ability to win occasional favors from powerful
whites and through the status positions they already occupied in the
black community.[25]

This mode of domination could not thoroughly pacify black life; only
the transformation of the segregated order could begin to do that. Furthermore, the internal management strategy generated centrifugal
pressures of its own. In addition to segregation, three other disruptive
elements stand out within the black population in the 1950s. First, the
United States' emergence from World War II as the major world power
projected American culture onto an international scene. Thus, the anticolonial movements that grew in Africa and Asia amid the crumbling
French and British colonial empires had a significant impact on black
resistance in this country.[26] Second, the logic of one-dimensionality itself became a disruptive element. The homogenizing egalitarianism of
the "New Deal" generated a sense of righteousness able to sustain a
lengthy battle with southern segregation. The challenge to racial domination was justified in terms of the "American Dream" and an ideal
of freedom expressed in a demand for full citizenship.[27] Thus, the same
forces that since the 1880s had sought to integrate the various immigrant populations also generated an American national consciousness
among blacks.

By the 1950s a sense of participation in a national society had taken
root even in the South, fertilized by the mass culture industry (including black publications), schools, and a defensive Cold War ideology. In
the face of this growing national consciousness "separate but equal"
existence was utterly intolerable to blacks. This is not to say that a
perception rooted in the nation-state was universal among southern
blacks in the 1950s, especially since the chief mechanisms of cultural
adjustment such as television, popular films, compulsory schooling,
etc., had not fully invaded the black community. Yet, mass culture
and its corollary ideologies had extensively penetrated the private
sphere of the black elite: the stratum from which systematic opposition
arose.[28]

Third, given the racial barrier, social mobility for the black elite was
limited, relative to its white counterpart. Because of de facto proscrip-
tion of black tenure in most professions, few possibilities existed for
advancement. At the ame time, the number of people seeking to become members of the elite had increased beyond what a segregated
society could accommodate as a result of population growth and rising
college attendance.[29] In addition, upward mobility was being defined
by the larger national culture in a way that further weakened the ca-
pability of the black elite to integrate its youth. Where ideology demanded nuclear physics and corporate management, black upward

mobility rested with mortuary service and the Elks Lodge! This disjunction between ideals and possibilities delegitimized the elite's claim to brokerage and spokesmanship. With its role in question, the entrenched black elite was no longer able effectively to perform its internal management function and lost authority with its "recruits" and the black community in general. As a result, a social space was cleared within which dissatisfaction with segregation could thrive as systematic opposition.

From this social management perspective, sources of the "Freedom Movement" are identifiable within and on the periphery of its indigenous elite stratum. As soon as black opposition spilled beyond the boundaries of the black community, however, the internal management perspective became inadequate to understand further developments in the Civil Rights movement. When opposition to segregation became political rebellion, black protest required a response from white ruling elites. That response reflected congruence of the interests of blacks and corporate elites in reconstructing southern society and helped define the logic of subsequent black political activity. Both sets of interests might be met by rationalizing race relations in the South. The Civil Rights movement brought the two sets together.[30]

The alliance of corporate liberalism and black protest was evident in the aggressive endorsement of civil rights activity that was mobilized by the New Deal coalition. Major labor organizations and "enlightened" corporate elements immediately climbed aboard the freedom train through the "progressive" wing of the Democratic party and private foundations. Moreover, it was through its coverage of black resistance in the South that television developed and refined its remarkable capabilities for creating public opinion by means of "objective" news reportage (a talent that reached its acme years later with the expulsion of Richard Nixon from the presidency). However, television was not alone on the cultural front of the ideological struggle. *Life, Look,* the *Saturday Evening Post,* major nonsouthern newspapers, and other national publications featured an abundance of photo-essays that emphasized the degradation and brutalization of black life under Jim Crow.

Even popular cinema sought to thematize black life in line with civil rights consciousness in films such as *The Defiant Ones* (1958), *All the Young Men* (1960), *Raisin in the Sun* (1961), *Band of Angels* (1957), and the instructively titled *Nothing but a Man* (1964). Those and other films were marked by an effort to portray blacks with a measure of human depth and complexity previously absent from Hollywood productions. By 1957 even the great taboo of miscegenation could be portrayed on the screen in *Island in the Sun,* and a decade later the cultural campaign had been so successful that this theme could be explored in the parlor rather than in back streets and resolved with a happy ending in *Guess*

Who's Coming to Dinner. It is interesting that Dorothy Dandridge became the first black in a leading role to be nominated for an academy award for her role in *Carmen Jones* in 1954—the year of the Brown decision—and that the most productive periods of civil rights activism and Sidney Poitier's film career coincided. Poitier's lead performance in the maudlin *Lilies of the Field* won an Oscar for him in 1963, on the eve of the passage of the Public Accommodations Act! Thus endorsed by the culture industry (which affronted White Supremacy in the late 1950s by broadcasting a Perry Como show in which comedienne Molly Goldberg kissed black ballplayer Ernie Banks), the Civil Rights movement was virtually assured success.

While the civil rights coalition was made possible by the compatibility of the allies' interests in reorganizing the South, its success was facilitated by the ideals and ideologies generated in the protest. Even though there had been ties between black southern elites and corporate-liberal elements for a long time, if the civil rights program had raised fundamental questions regarding social structure, the corporate-elite response may have been suppression rather than support—especially given the Cold War context. Instead, from the very beginning the American establishment outside of Dixie supported the abolition of segregation.[31] At any rate, it is clear that the civil rights ideology fit very well with the goals of monopoly capitalism. The Civil Rights movement appealed to egalitarianism and social rationality. On both counts segregation was found wanting while nonracial features of the social order were left unquestioned.

The egalitarian argument was moral as well as constitutional. The moral argument was in the bourgeois tradition from the Reformation to the French Revolution. It claimed equal rights for all human beings as well as entitlement to equal life chances. This abstract and ahistorical moral imperative did not address the structural or systematic character of social relations and therefore could only denounce racial exclusion as an evil anomaly. The predominant form of social organization was accepted uncritically, and the moral imperative was predictably construed in terms of American constitutional law. Extension to blacks of equality before the law and equality of opportunity to participate in all areas of citizenship were projected as adequate to fulfill the promise of democracy in the backward South.

Coexisting with this egalitarian ideology was the Civil Rights movement's appeal to a functionalist conception of social rationality. To the extent that it blocked individual aspirations, segregation was seen as restricting social growth and progress artificially. Similarly, by raising artificial barriers such as the constriction of blacks' consumer power through Jim Crow legislation and, indirectly, through low black wages, segregation impeded, so the argument went, the free functioning of the market. Consequently, segregation was seen not only as detrimental to blacks who suffered under it, but also to economic progress as such. Needless to say, the two lines of argument were met with approval by corporate liberals.[32]

It is apparent now that the egalitarian ideology coincided with corporate-liberalism's cultural program of homogenization. Civil rights' egalitarianism demanded that any one unit of labor be equivalent to any other, and that the Negro be thought of as "any other American." There is more than a little irony that the Civil Rights movement demanded for blacks the same "eradication of otherness" that had been forced upon immigrant populations. The demand hardly went unheard; through the blanket concept "integration" and the alliance with a corporate elite that was all too ready to help clarify issues and refine strategies and objectives, the abstract ideals of civil rights activism were concretized in a corporate elite plan for pacification and reorganization.

The elimination of segregation in the South altered the specificity of both the South as a region and blacks as a group, and the rationality in whose name the movement had appealed paved the way for reconstruction of new modes of domination of black life. The movement had begun as a result of frustrations within the black elite, and it ended with the achievement of autonomy and mobility among those elements. Public Accommodations and Voting Rights legislation officially defined new terms for the management of blacks and an expanded managerial role for the elite.

Although the Civil Rights movement did have a radical faction, that wing failed to develop a systematic critique of civil rights ideology or the alliance with corporate liberalism. Moreover, the radicals—mainly within the SNCC—never fully repudiated the leadership ideology which reinforced the movement's character as an elite brokerage relation with powerful whites outside the South. Thus, the radicals helped isolate their own position by acquiescing to a conception of the black community as a passive recipient of political symbols and directives. When the dust settled, the black "mainstream" elements and their corporate allies—who together monopolized the symbols of legitimacy—proclaimed that freedom had been achieved, and the handful of radicals could only feel uneasy that voting rights and "social equality" were somehow insufficient.[33]

Outside the South, rebellion arose from different conditions. Racial segregation was not rigidly codified, and the management subsystems in the black community were correspondingly more fluidly integrated within the local administrative apparatus. Yet, structural, generational, and ideological pressures, broadly similar to those in the South, existed within the black elite in the northern, western, and midwestern cities that had gained large black populations in the first half of the twentieth century. In nonsegregated urban contexts, formal political participation and democratized consumption had long since been achieved; there the salient political issue was the extension of the administrative purview of the elite within the black community. The centrality of the administrative nexus in the "revolt of the cities" is evident from the ideological programs it generated.[34]

Black Power came about as a call for indigenous control of economic and political institutions in the black community.[35] Because one of the early slogans of Black Power was a vague demand for "community control," the emancipatory character of the rebellion was open to considerably varied misinterpretation. Moreover, the diversity and "militance" of its rhetoric encouraged extravagance in assessing the movement's depth. It soon became clear, however, that "community control" called not for direction of pertinent institutions—schools, hospitals, police, retail businesses, etc.—by their black constituents, but for the administration of those institutions by alleged representatives in the name of a black community. Given an existing elite structure whose legitimacy had already been certified by federal social-welfare agencies, the selection of "appropriate" representatives was predictable. Indeed, as Robert Allen has shown, the empowerment of this elite was actively assisted by corporate-state elements.[36] Thus, "black liberation" quickly turned into black "equity"; "community control" became simply "black control"; and the Nixon "blackonomics" strategy was readily able to "coopt" the most rebellious tendency of 1960s black activism. Ironically, Black Power's suppression of the civil rights program led to further consolidation of the management elite's hegemony within the black community. The black elite broadened its administrative control by accepting without criticism and instrumentally deploying the inchoate elements of the Black Power agenda to gain leverage in regular political processes. Black control was by no means equivalent to popular democratization.[37]

This state of affairs remained unclear even to Black Power's radical fringe. Such a failure of political perception cannot be written off as crass opportunism or as underdeveloped consciousness. Though not altogether false, explantions of this kind only beg the question. Indeed, Black Power radicalism, which absorbed most of the floundering left wing of the Civil Rights movement and generated subsequent "nationalist" tendencies, actually blurred the roots of the new wave of rebellion. As civil rights activism exhausted itself and as spontaneous uprisings proliferated among urban blacks, the civil rights radicals sought to generate an ideology capable of unifying and politicizing these uprisings. This effort, however, was based on two mystifications that implicitly rationalized the elite's control of the movement.

First, Black Power presupposed a mass-organizational model built on the assumption of a homogeneity of black political interests embodied in community leadership. It is this notion of "black community" that had blocked development of a radical critique in the Civil Rights movement by contraposing an undifferentiated mass to a leadership stratum representing it. This understanding ruled out analysis of cleavages or particularities within the black population: "community control" and "black control" became synonymous. The implications of this ideology have already been discussed: having internalized the predominant elite-pluralist model of organization of black life, the radical wing could not develop any critical perspective. Internal critique could not go beyond banal symbols of "blackness" and thus ended up by stimulating demand for a new array of "revolutionary" consumer goods. Notwithstanding all its bombast, Black Power formulated racial politics within the ideological universe through which the containment of the black population was mediated.

Acceptance of this model not only prevented Black Power from transcending the social program of the indigenous administrative elite, but it also indicated the extent to which, as Cruse was aware at the time,[38] Black Power radicalism was itself a frantic statement of the elite's agenda—hence the radicals' chronic ambivalence over "black bourgeoisie," capitalism, socialism, and "black unity." Their mystification of the social structure of the black community was largely the result of a failure to come to terms with their own privileged relation to the corporate elite's program of social reconstruction. This state of affairs precipitated a still more profound mystification that illuminates the other side of Black Power rebellion: the reaction against massification.

The Civil Rights movement's demand for integration was superfluous outside the South, and Black Power was as much a reaction against integrationist ideology as against domination. Yet, while militant black nationalism developed as a reaction to the assimilationist approach of the Civil Rights movement, it envisioned an obsolete, folkish model of black life. This yearning was hypostatized to the level of a vague "black culture"—a romantic retrieval of a vanishing black particularity. This vision of black culture, of course, was grounded in residual features of black rural life prior to migrations to the North. They were primarily cultural patterns that had once been enmeshed in a life world knitted together by kinship, voluntary association, and production within a historical context of rural racial domination. As that life world disintegrated before urbanization and mass culture, black nationalism sought to reconstitute it.[39]

In that sense, the nationalist elaboration of Black Power was naive both in that it was not sufficiently self-conscious and that it mistook artifacts and idiosyncrasies of culture for its totality and froze them into an ahistorical rhetoric of authenticity. Two consequences followed. First,

abstracted from its concrete historical context, black culture lost its dynamism and took on the commodity form (e.g., red, black, and green
flags; dashikis; Afro-Sheen; "blaxploitation" films; collections of bad
poetry). Second, while ostensibly politicizing culture by defining it as
an arena for conflict, black nationalism actually depoliticized the movement inasmuch as the reified nationalist framework could relate to the
present only through a simplistic politics of unity.[40] Hence, it forfeited
hegemony over political programs to the best organized element in the
black community: the administrative elite. In this fashion, black culture
became a means of legitimation of the elite's political hegemony.

"Black culture" posited a functionalist, perfectly integrated black social order which was then projected backward through history as the
Truth of black existence. The "natural" condition of harmony was said
to have been disrupted only when divisiveness and conflict were introduced by alien forces. This myth delegitimated internal conflict and
hindered critical dialogue within the black community. Correspondingly, the intellectual climate which came to pervade the "movement"
was best summarized in the nationalists' exhortation to "think black,"
a latter-day version of "thinking with one's blood." Thus was the circle
completed: the original abstract rationalism that had ignored existing
social relations of domination for a mythical, unitarian, social ideal turned
into a militant and self-justifying irrationalism. Truth became a function of the speaker's "blackness," i.e., validity claims were to be resolved not through discourse but by the claimant's manipulation of
certain banal symbols of legitimacy. The resultant situation greatly favored the well-organized and highly visible elite.[41]

The nationalist program functioned also as a mobilization myth. In
defining a collective consciousness, the idealization of folkishness was
simultaneously an exhortation to collectivized practice. The folk, in its
Afro-American manifestation as well as elsewhere,[42] was an ideological
category of mass-organizational politics. The community was to be created and mobilized as a passively homogeneous mass, activated by a
leadership elite.

While the politicized notion of black culture was a negative response
to the estrangement and anomie experienced in the urban North, as a
"solution" it only affirmed the negation of genuine black particularity.[43] The prescription of cohesion in the form of a mass/leadership
relation revealed the movement's tacit acceptance of the black management stratum's agenda. The negativity immanent in the cultural myth
soon gave way to an opportunistic appeal to unity grounded on an
unspecifiable "blackness" and a commodified idea of "soul." Black unity,
elevated to an end in itself, became an ideology promoting consolidation of the management elite's expanded power over the black population. In practice, unity meant collective acceptance of a set of de-

mands to be lobbied by a leadership elite before the corporate-state apparatus. To that extent, "radical" Black Power reproduced on a more elaborate ideological basis the old pluralist brokerage politics. Similarly, this phony unity restricted possibilities for development of a black public sphere.

To be sure, the movement stimulated widespread and lively political debate in the black community. Although it hardly approached an "ideal speech situation," various individuals and constituencies were drawn into political discourse on a considerably more democratized basis than had previously been the case. Yet, the rise of unitarian ideology, coupled with a mystified notion of "expertise," effectively reintroduced hierarchy within the newly expanded political arena.[44] At any rate, "grass roots" politics in the black community can be summarized as follows: the internal management elite claimed primacy in political discourse on the basis of its ability to project and realize a social program and then mobilized the unitarian ideal to delegitimize any divergent positions. On the other hand, the "revolutionary" opposition offered no alternative; within its ranks the ideology of expertise was never repudiated. The radicals had merely replaced the elite's pragmatism with a mandarin version of expertise founded on mastery of the holy texts of Kawaida, Nkrumaism, or "scientific socialism." By the time of the 1972 National Black Political Convention in Gary, the mainstream elite strata were well on the way to becoming the sole effective voice in the black community. By the next convention in 1974 in Little Rock—after the election of a second wave of black officials—their hegemony was total.[45]

By now the reasons for the demise of black opposition in the United States should be clear. The opposition's sources were formulated in terms of the predominant ideology and thereby were readily integrated as an affirmation of the validity of the system as a whole. The movement "failed" because it "succeeded," and its success can be measured by its impact on the administration of the social system. The protest against racial discrimination in employment and education was answered by the middle 1970s by state-sponsored democratization of access to management and other "professional" occupations. Direct, quantifiable racial discrimination remained a pressing public issue mainly for those whose livelihood depended on finding continuous instances of racial discrimination.[46] Still, equalization of access should not be interpreted simply as a concession; it also rationalized recruitment of intermediate management personnel. In one sense the affirmative action effort can be viewed as a publicly subsidized state and corporate talent search.

Similarly, the protest against external administration of black life was met by an expansion in the scope of the black political-administrative

apparatus. Through federal funding requirements of community representation, reapportionment of electoral jurisdictions, support for voter
"education," and growth of the social welfare bureaucracy, the black
elite was provided with broadened occupational opportunities and with
official responsibility for administration of the black population. The
rise of black officialdom beginning in the 1970s signals the realization
of the reconstructed elite's social program and the consolidation of its
hegemony over black life. No longer do preachers, funeral directors,
and occasional politicos vie for the right to rationalize an externally
generated agenda to the black community. Now, black officials and
professional political activists represent, interact among, and legitimate
themselves before an attentive public of black functionaries in public
and private sectors of the social management apparatus.[47] Even the
ideological reproduction of the elite is assured: not only mass-market
journalists, but black academicians as well (through black "scholarly"
publications, research institutes, and professional organizations) almost invariably sing the praises of the newly empowered elite.[48]

It was in the ideological sphere as well that the third major protest,
that against massification of the black community, was resolved. Although authentic Afro-American particularity had been undermined by
the standardizing imperatives of mass capitalism, the black nationalist
reaction paved the way for the constitution of an artificial particularity.[49] Residual idiomatic and physical traits, bereft of distinctive content, were injected with racial stereotypes and the ordinary petit bourgeois *Weltanschauung* to create the pretext for an apparently unique black
existence. A thoroughly ideological construction of black uniqueness—
which was projected universally in the mass market as black culture—
fulfilled at least three major functions. First, as a marketing device it
facilitated the huckstering of innumerable commodities designed to enhance, embellish, simulate, or glorify "blackness."[50] Second, artificial
black particularity provided the basis for the myth of genuine black
community and consequently legitimated the organization of the black
population into an administrative unit—and, therefore, the black elite's
claims to primacy. Finally, the otherness-without-negativity provided
by the ideologized blackness can be seen as a potential antidote to the
new contradictions generated by monopoly capitalism's bureaucratic
rationality. By constituting an independently given sector of society responsive to administrative controls, the well-managed but recalcitrant
black community justifies the existence of the administrative apparatus
and legitimates existing forms of social integration.

In one sense, the decade and a half of black activism was a phenomenon vastly more significant than black activists appreciated, while in
another sense it was far less significant than has been claimed.[51] As an
emancipatory project for the Afro-American population, the "move-

ment"—especially after the abolishment of segregation—had little impact beyond strengthening the existing elite strata. Yet, as part of a program of advanced capitalist reconstruction, black activism contributed to thawing the Cold War and outlined a model to replace it.

By the latter 1960s the New Deal coalition was no longer able fully to integrate recalcitrant social strata such as the black population.[52] The New Deal coalition initiated the process of social homogenization and depoliticization Marcuse described as one dimensionality. As Piccone observes, however, by the 1960s the transition to monopoly capitalism had been fully carried out, and the whole strategy had become counterproductive.[53] The drive toward homogenization and the total domination of the commodity form had deprived the system of the "otherness" required both to restrain the irrational tendencies of bureaucratic rationality and to locate lingering and potentially disruptive elements. Notwithstanding their vast differences, the ethnic "liberation struggles" and counterculture activism on the one side and the "hard hat" reaction on the other were two sides of the same rejection of homogenization. Not only did these various positions challenge the one-dimensional order, but their very existence betrayed the limitations of the administrative state.

The development of black activism from spontaneous protest through mass mobilization to system support assisted the development of a new mode of domination based on domesticating negativity by organizing spaces in which it could be legitimately expressed. Rather than suppressing opposition, the social management system now cultivates its own. The proliferation of government-generated reference groups in addition to ethnic ones (the old; the young; battered wives; the handicapped; veterans; retarded, abused, and gifted children) and the apprearance of legions of "watchdog" agencies, reveal the extent to which the system manufactures and markets its own illusory opposition.[54]

This "artificial negativity" is in part a function of the overwhelming success of the process of massification undertaken since the depression and in part a response to it. Universal fragmentation of consciousness, with the corollary decline in the ability to think critically and the regimentation of an alienated everyday life set the stage for new forms of domination built in the very texture of organization.[55] In mass society, organized activity on a large scale requires hierarchization. Along with hierarchy, however, a new social management logic also comes into being to 1) protect existing privileges by delivering realizable, if inadequate, payoffs and 2) to legitimate administrative rationality as a valid and efficient model. To the extent that organization strives to ground itself on the mass it is already integrated into the system of domination. The shibboleths which comprise its specific platform make little difference. What is important is that the mass organization reproduces the manipulative hierarchy and values typical of contemporary capital-ism.[56]

Equally important for the existence of this social-managerial form is that the traditional modes of opposition to capitalism have not been able successfully to negotiate the transition from entrepreneurial to ad-ministrative capitalism. Thus, the left has not fully grasped the recent shifts in the structure of domination and continues to organize resis-tance along the very lines which reinforce the existing social order. As a consequence, the opposition finds itself perpetually outflanked. Un-able to deliver the goods—political or otherwise—the left collapses be-fore the cretinization of its own constituency. Once the mass model is accepted, cretinization soon follows and from that point the opposition loses any genuine negativity. The Civil Rights and Black Power move-ments prefigured the coming of this new age; the feminist photocopy of the black journey on a road to nowhere was its farcical rerun.

The mass culture industry in this context maintains and reproduces the new synthesis of domination. Here, again, the history of the "black revolution" is instructive. In its most radical stage Black Power lived and spread as a media event. Stokely Carmichael and H. Rap Brown entertained nightly on network news, and after ordinary black "mili-tancy" had lost its dramatic appeal, the Black Panther Party added props and uniforms to make radical politics entirely a show business propo-sition. Although late 1960s black radicalism offered perhaps the most flamboyant examples of the peculiar relation of the mass media to the would-be opposition, that was only an extreme expression of a pattern at work since the early days of the Civil Rights movement.[57] Since then, political opposition has sought to propagandize its efforts through the mass media. Given the prevailing cretinization and the role of the cul-ture industry in reproducing the fragmented, commodified conscious-ness, such a strategy, if pursued uncritically, could only reinforce the current modes of domination.[58]

That all forms of political opposition accepted the manipulative, mass-organization model gave the strategy a natural, uncomplicated appear-ance and prevented the development of a critical approach. The con-sequence was propagation of a model of politics which reinforced ov-ersimplification, the reduction of ideals to banalized objects of immediate consumption—i.e., the commodity-form—and to an alienated, dehu-manized hero cultishness with "revolutionary" replacing either hero or villain. In short, opposition increasingly becomes a spectacle in a soci-ety organized around reduction of all existence to a series of specta-cles.[59]

So monopoly capitalism has entered a new stage typified by the ex-tension of the administrative apparatus throughout everyday life. In this context, genuine opposition is checkmated a priori by the legitimation and projection of a partial, fragmented criticism which can be enlisted in further streamlining the predominant rationality. In cases where existing bureaucratic structures need control mechanisms to prevent excesses, diffuse uneasiness with predominant institutions ends up artificially channeled into forms of negativity able to fulfill the needed internal control function. Always a problem for opposition which seeks to sustain itself over time, under the new conditions of administered negativity, the one step backward required by organized opposition's need to broaden its constituency and conduct "positional warfare" becomes a one-way slide to affirmation of the social order. The logic of the transition to new forms of bourgeois hegemony requires adjustment of administrative rationality. The unrestrained drive to total integration now is mediated by peripheral, yet systematically controlled, loci of criticism; one-dimensionality itself has been "humanized" by the cultivation of commodified facsimiles of diversity.[60]

An important question remains: what of the possibilities for genuine opposition? The picture that has been painted seems exceedingly pessimistic. Yet, this should not be understood to mean that opposition is futile. It *is* necessary, though, to examine closely the customary modes of opposition. The theory of artificial negativity historicizes the critique of the post-Cold War left and suggests at the same time some broad outlines for a reconceptualization of emancipatory strategy.

This examination of black radicalism in the wake of its integration offers a microcosmic view of the plight of the left as a whole. Having accepted an organizational model based on massification, the radicals were forced to compete with the elite on the latter's terms—an impossible proposition since the elite had access to the cultural apparatus designed for mass mobilization. Moreover, even when opposition tried to reconstruct itself, it failed to generate systematic critique of its own strategy and was therefore unable to come to terms with shifts in the structure of capitalist social relations. Instead, it remained caught within a theoretical structure adequate for an earlier, preadministrative stage of capitalist development. Thus, the failure of mysticized black nationalism was reproduced in "ideological struggles" which reached their nadir in the 1978 dispute over whether Mao Tse-tung was really dead! Still, what of emancipatory possibilities? Certain general implications follow from the preceding analysis, but they become clear only through reflection on the forces currently driving the "really existing" American corporate liberalism.

Development into a sociopolitical order pacified through administration has been realized in the political sphere mainly through the integrative mechanism of a "progrowth" coalition that has cemented linkages institutionally between national and local elites, as well as between representative elites from the various member constituencies in the coalition at both levels.[61] From the vantage point of global system logic the drive to administrative pacification reached its limits in the 1960s, as the homogenizing imperatives of mass culture were challenged by black nationalists and white counterculturists from one direction and rightist populism and white ethnic resurgence from another. Typical to such popular reactions, these challenges began with only the conceptual language of the prevailing social order in which to phrase their revolt, and before genuine alternatives could develop they were integrated into the social management apparatus as supportive appendages. They were thus reconstituted as regulators of rationality deficits in the administrative system. In this essay I have traced the operation of that dynamic in the natural history of black activism.

At the level of practical political management, the growth politics model was undermined by its own contradictions. The strategy of maintaining social peace by ensuring payoffs through the elites of potentially disruptive constituencies works only so long as the number of critical constituent groups is restricted. In this sense corporate liberalism, despite its superficial appearances and the effusions of political scientists, is exclusionist and corporativistic rather than pluralistic.[62] Incorporation of activism in the 1960s forced open the circle of privileged constituencies to include first blacks and then a steady stream of other new claimants. The increasing volume of claims, in combination with other factors, pushed the costs of social control to a point that interfered with stable corporate profit-making, the basis of the growth coalition in the first place.[63] By the early 1970s a process of gradual retrenchment had begun, largely under the aegis of the Nixon administration.

The Reaganite phenomenon of the 1980s in this regard represents an attempt to reconstitute a new growth coalition that eliminates both the claimant groups mobilized as a consequence of 1960s activism and the traditional labor component. In addition to racism, crude self-interest, and fantasies of international vigilantism, Reaganism appeals also—albeit disingenuously—to popular discontent with bureaucratic regimentation and growing administration of social life.[64] A central justification for the program of retrenchment is that policies and programs aimed at new claimant groups have ensued primarily in creating unwarranted occupational opportunities for administrative elites.

Before such an argument, the post-Civil Rights era black elite—as principal beneficiaries of activism—is virtually helpless. As a growing segment of the black population is increasingly marginalized into a generally optionless condition, consigned to deteriorating urban areas and destined at best to low-wage, dead-end subemployment, the black managerial elite is hard-pressed to defend its claims to status and function. At the same time, this stratum—whose existence is an artifact of the old coalition—appears incapable of generating any substantive critique of the inadequacies of the Democratic model of growth politics and is left only with bankrupt demands that its own privileges be secured in the reorganization. Indeed, signs already are visible that the elite's interest-group organizations are retooling their focus away from "state interventionist" to direct "corporate interventionist" strategies that uncouple from the old coalition's social welfare focus and reformulate black interests openly and exclusively in terms of securing leverage for upper-income, professional strata.[65]

So, the wheels of corporate social reorganization turn, grinding beneath them the lives and hopes of the dispossessed and oiled by their misery. The legatees of activism, putative bearers of the principle of friction, simply cling to the wheels, hoping to go along for the ride—no matter what the outcome!

Yet, even if the current, draconian retrenchment is defeated, there will be little cause for celebration. Not only would a return to the old growth coalition be inadequate to meet the needs of large segments of American society, including a disproportionate element of the black population, but that coalition cannot be reinstated on its original basis. There is a sense, after all, in which Huntington's argument is sound. The partial success of 1960s activism in generating new status groups has intensified competition among noncorporate constituencies over the limited opportunities available for participation in the administrative distribution of privilege. Organized labor, feminists, and minority elites vie among one another in what they understand to be a zero-sum struggle for social and economic benefits. Added to these are the plethora of interest configurations arising from the maturing, upwardly mobile postwar baby boom—urban revitalization, localism, environmentalism, homosexual activism.

Not only are the agendas of these "Young Urban Professionals" often in objective conflict, if not overt antagonism, with those of minorities and organized labor, but that stratum's neo-Progressivist ideological orientation breeds fractiousness through its disposition toward the egoistic, single-issue activism of "citizen" initiative. Despite the hyperpluralism that this orientation promotes, it often masquerades—like its early twentieth-century predecessor—as defense of the public interest.[66] However, beneath the hollow "New Ideas" themes trumpeted by Anderson in 1980 and Hart in 1984 lies a "neoliberal" social agenda that at the national level would reinforce growth in the high-tech and information industries in which yuppies are concentrated and would accept decline of the old industrial base, as Hart's opposition to the Chrysler bail-out indicates. At the local level this agenda endorses a model of urban redevelopment that accelerates displacement of the poor under the guise of neighborhood renewal and advocates an expanding official role for neighborhood organization in local policymaking, which automatically advantages upper-income, better-endowed—and thus more easily mobilized—neighborhoods.[67] Moreover, the national neoliberal growth agenda promises to intensify local income stratification by exacerbating tendencies to labor market segmentation; that model for growth generates for those outside language and symbol manipulating areas only service sector or other poorly remunerative, optionless employment, and not much of that.[68] The prospect of recomposition of a growth agenda along these lines, therefore, does not portend a future for the general black population that is much different from that held out by Reaganism. Indeed, the neoliberal tendency identified with Gary Hart raises the spectre of a Democratic consensus that—like Reagan's—excludes blacks and other minorities, as well as the AFL-CIO.[69]

In this context one has to strain to find emancipatory possibilities. The dangers that the present situation poses for the black population cannot even be conceptualized within the myopic and narrowly opportunistic pattern of discourse defined by the black political elite. A first step, therefore, must entail breaking this elite hegemony over ideas in the black community. The spoken-for must come to master political speech and to articulate their own interests, free of the intermediation of brokerage politicians and the antirational, antidemocratic conformism preached by charismatic authority. This mastery can develop only through a combination of unrelenting critique of the elite's program and authoritarian legitimations and practical efforts to expand the discursive arena within the Afro-American population.[70]

The very success of the post-civil rights elite in imposing its agenda of administrative management has limited the terms of black political discourse to the options thrown up within the present arrangements of domination. Yet, inadequate though they may be, those options constitute at this point the only meaningful terrain for political engagement. Creation of a sphere of black public debate on issues arising from the current tendencies in capitalist social reorganization—ranging from the ramifications of public goods allocation decisions in a local political jurisdiction to national economic and social policy—is necessary to transcend the official black posture of quiet acceptance of any initiative that includes an affirmative action component. Stimulation of political controversy within the black community would lead to recognition of the diversity of interest configurations among blacks and is therefore a precondition to formulation of genuinely collective agendas, whose adherents may or may not be coterminous with the boundaries of racial identification. This ostensibly tepid call for the development of a political liberalism within the racial community offers, under the present circumstances, the only hope for combatting the sacrifice of a growing share of the black population to permanent marginality in the American social order. The principles of "bourgeois democracy," on which the black elite has grounded its demands for participatory rights in the distributive queue of growth politics, must be applied against the hegemony of elite interests within the Afro-American group.

At stake in the short term is the specific character of the governing synthesis that ultimately replaces the New Deal coalition. The concrete form of those new arrangements, including the position of racial minorities in them, will be determined through political contention, and the black political elite—for reasons that I have adumbrated—cannot be relied upon to press the interests of a population that exists for it primarily as private capital. Beyond the immediate situation, animation of a critical-democratic black political culture constitutes a necessary, though incremental, movement toward Afro-American participation in development of a more general critical dialogue which may produce the basis for a new oppositional politics—one capable of confronting squarely the irrational logic and mechanisms that constitute the mass capitalist order of domination.

The strategic proposal that I have sketched obviously provides no blueprint; it is modest and most contingent, and—even if implemented—it hardly guarantees social transformation. Its modesty only reflects the failure of oppositional forces to develop credible alternatives in the here-and-now. Acknowledgment of that failure, however, should not be misread as pessimistic assessment; admission of failure expresses the distance between actually existing conditions and a goal that lives beyond the shortfall. Although contingent responses offer no sure exits from a bleak situation, contingency itself is the source of real hope, that which lies in recognition of the openness of history. Such hope, grounded in an unyielding vision of human emancipation, seeks its possibilities even in the darkest moments of the present; it is despair that hides its head from history and refuses to see the undesirable.[71]

NOTES

1. Walter Benjamin, "The Work of Art in the Age of Mechanical Reproduction," in *Illuminations* (New York, 1968), p. 251.

2. Herbert Marcuse, *One-Dimensional Man: Studies in the Ideology of Advanced Industrial Society* (Boston, 1964).

3. David Gross, "Irony and the 'Disorders of the Soul,' " *Telos* (Winter, 1977–1978), p. 167.

4. Possible sources of the left's failure to interpret its past meaningfully are discussed also by Christopher Lasch, "The Narcissist Society," *New York Review of Books* 23 (September 30, 1976), p. 5ff; Russell Jacoby, "The Politics of Objectivity: Notes on the U.S. Left," *Telos* (Winter, 1977–1978), pp. 74–88, and *Social Amnesia: A Critique of Conformist Psychology from Adler to Laing* (Boston, 1975), pp. 101–118; and by Andrew Feenberg, "Paths to Failure: The Dialectics of

Organization and Ideology in the New Left," and David Gross, "Culture, Politics, and 'Lifestyle' in the 1960s," in this volume.

5. The work of Alex Willingham is the most consistent and noteworthy exception. In addition to his contribution to this volume see, for example, "California Dreaming: Eldridge Cleaver's Epithet to the Activism of the Sixties," *Endarch* 1 (Winter, 1976), pp. 1–23.

6. Paul Piccone, "Beyond Critical Theory," mimeo, and "The Crisis of One-Dimensionality," *Telos* (Spring 1978), pp. 43–54. See also Tim Luke, "Culture and Politics in the Age of Artificial Negativity," ibid., pp. 55–72.

7. See, for example: Thomas R. Brooks, *Walls Come Tumbling Down: A History of the Civil Rights Movement, 1940–1970* (Englewood Cliffs, N.J., 1974), pp. 290ff; Eddie N. Williams, *From Protest to Politics: The Legacy of Martin Luther King, Jr.* (Washington, D.C., n.d.), and Robert Smith, "Black Power and the Transformation from Protest to Politics," *Political Science Quarterly* 96 (Fall, 1981), pp. 431–443.

8. This slogan first rose to prominence on the back of the black elite's voluble reaction to the Bakke case, which is said to portend reversal of those alleged "gains." One interpretation of these gains is found in Richard Freeman, "Black Economic Progress Since 1964," *Public Interest* (Summer, 1978), pp. 52–68.

9. Dorothy K. Newman, Nancy Amidei, Barbara Carter, Dawn Day, William Kruvant, Jack Russell, *Protest, Politics and Prosperity: Black Americans and White Institutions, 1940–1975* (New York, 1978), p. 64. Since 1971, of course, unemployment among blacks has averaged more than 10 percent.

10. Ibid., p. 66.

11. U.S. Department of Commerce, Bureau of the Census, *The Social and Economic Status of the Black Population in the United States: 1974* (Washington, D.C., 1975), p. 25.

12. Barbara Jones, "Black Family Income: Patterns, Sources, and Trends," paper presented at the annual meetings of the National Economic Association, American Economic Association, Atlantic City, New Jersey, September, 1976, p. 2.

13. Bureau of the Census, *Social and Economic Status*, pp. 123, 137.

14. That the leadership elite projects its interests over the entire black population is neither unique nor necessarily suggestive of insidious motives; however, it is just in the extent to which the elite's hegemony develops unconsciously that it is most important as a problem for emancipatory action. Cf. Alvin W. Gouldner's critique of intellectuals and intelligentsia, "Prologue to a Theory of Revolutionary Intellectuals," *Telos* (Winter, 1975–1976), pp. 3–36, and *The Dialectic of Ideology and Technology: The Origins, Grammar and Future of Ideology* (New York, 1976), pp. 247–248 *passim*. More recently Gouldner attempted to elaborate a systematic theory of the place of intellectuals in the modern world that concludes that they function as a "flawed universal class"—a thesis that does not augur well for the emancipatory content of his theory—in *The Future of Intellectuals and the Rise of the New Class: A Frame of Reference, Theses, Conjectures, Arguments, and an Historical Perspective on the Role of Intellectuals and Intelligentsia in the International Class Context of the Modern Era* (New York, 1979). See also the critique of Gouldner's thesis in Michael Walzer's thoughtful review

essay "The New Masters," *New York Review of Books* 27 (March 30, 1980), pp. 37ff.

15. John Hope Franklin does not raise the question in his standard volume, *From Slavery to Freedom: A History of Negro Americans*, third edition (New York, 1969); nor suprisingly does Harold Cruse's *The Crisis of the Negro Intellectual: From Its Origins to the Present* (New York, 1967), which is a seminal contribution to a reflexive approach to black political activity. That Cruse and Franklin fail to raise the question is perhaps because both—reflecting an aspect of the conventional wisdom—see an unbroken, if not cumulating, legacy of black activism in the twentieth century. Franklin sees the Civil Rights movement simply as the culmination of a century or more of protest. Cruse, in establishing the continuities of the poles of integrationism and nationalism, projects them back and forth from Douglass and Delaney to Black Power, glossing over significant historical differences in the process. In *The Making of Black Revolutionaries* (New York, 1972), James Forman is so consumed by the movement's chronology and organizational unfoldings that he is unable to subordinate it to history. His account of the 1950s focuses entirely on his personal awakening. Louis Lomax, *The Negro Revolt*, revised edition (New York, 1971); Lewis Killian, *The Impossible Revolution? Black Power and the American Dream* (New York, 1968); and the two period volumes by Lerone Bennett, Jr., *The Negro Mood* (New York, 1964) and *Before the Mayflower: A History of the Negro in America, 1619–1964*, revised edition (Baltimore, 1969), all raise the question only to answer casually or to beg the question further. An all-to-common shortcoming exemplified by each of the writers cited and extending throughout the study of black political activity is a tendency to abstract black life from the currents of American history. The resulting scenarios of black existence suffer from superficiality. By the end of the 1970s some social scientists had begun to seek after the structural origins of black mass protest, but their accounts do not adequately consider political dynamics operating within the black community.

16. "Crisis on One-Dimensionality," pp. 45–46; "Beyond Critical Theory," p. 6.

17. John Alt observes that "The problem of legitimating industrial reorganization was solved through a new social practice and ideology structured around the pursuit of money, material comfort, and a higher standard of living through consumerism. Mass consumption, as the necessary otherness of Taylorized mass production, was itself offered as the ultimate justification for the rationalization of labor," "Beyond Class: The Decline of Industrial Labor and Leisure," *Telos* (Summer, 1976), p. 71. Stuart Ewen identifies the Cold War period as the apotheosis of consumerism, whose enshrinement during those years was aided by the continued spread of popular journalism and the "mass marketing of television . . . which carried the consumer imagery into the back corners of home life," *Captains of Consciousness: Advertising and the Social Roots of the Consumer Culture* (New York, 1976), pp. 206–215.

18. Cf. David Riesman (with Nathan Glazer and Reuel Denney), *The Lonely Crowd: A Study of the Changing American Character*, abridged edition (New Haven, 1961), pp. 19–22, and Jules Henry's perceptive and telling study of the period, *Culture Against Man* (New York, 1963). Marcuse went so far as to suggest that even the concept of introjection may not capture the extent to which the one-dimensional order is reproduced in the individual on the ground that: "Intro-

jection implies the existence of an inner dimension distinguished from and even antagonistic to the external exigencies—an individual consciousness and an individual unconscious apart from public opinion and behavior. . . . (However, mass) production and mass distribution claim the entire individual. . . . The manifold processes of introjection seem to be ossified in almost mechanical reactions. The result is not adjustment but mimesis: an immediate identification of the individual with *his* society and, through it, with the society as a whole," *One-Dimensional Man*, p. 10.

19. The point is not that ethnicity has lost its power as a basis for self-identification or associational activity. What has been obliterated, however, is the distinctiveness of the institutional forms which were the source of group consciousness in the first place. Warner and Srole pridefully acknowledge the centrality of the prevailing order in the determination of ethnic consciousness: "The forces which are most potent both in forming and changing the ethnic groups emanate from the institutions of the dominant American social system," W. Lloyd Warner and Leo Srole, *The Social Systems of American Ethnic Groups* (New Haven, 1945), pp. 283–284. Stuart and Elizabeth Ewen, "Americanization and Consumption," *Telos* 37 (Fall, 1978), observe that the dynamic of homogenization began with integration into the system of wage labor which "created great fissures and, ultimately, gaps in people's lives. Money . . . rendered much of the way in which non-industrial peoples understood themselves, and the reproduction of their daily lives, useless. The money system itself was a widely disseminated mass medium which ripped the structure of peoples' needs from their customary roots, and by necessity transplanted these needs in a soil nourished by the 'rationality' of corporate industry and the retail marketplace" (p. 47). Traditional ethnic ways of life hardly stood a chance under conditions in which the terms of survival were also those of massification! See also Maurice R. Stein, *The Eclipse of Community: An Interpretation of American Studies* (New York, 1960). Also see David Gross, "Culture, Politics and 'Lifestyle' in the 1960s."

20. See, for example: John V. Van Sickle, *Planning for the South: An Inquiry into the Economics of Regionalism* (Nashville, 1943), pp. 68–71; Gene Roberts, Jr., "The Waste of Negro Talent in a Southern State," in Alan F. Westin, ed., *Freedom Now: The Civil Rights Struggle in America* (New York, 1964), and Eli Ginzberg, "Segregation and Manpower Waste," *Phylon* 21 (December, 1960), pp. 311–316.

21. Harry Braverman, in *Labor and Monopoly Capital: The Degradation of Work in the 20th Century* (New York, 1974), notes the ironic circumstance that capital has appropriated as a conscious ideal Marx's "abstraction from the concrete forms of labor" (pp. 181–182). In the logic of monopoly capitalism—characterized in part by constant reduction of labor's share of the overall costs of production and increasing sensitivity for optimizing profits over time in a stable production environment, [cf. Andreas Papandreou, *Paternalistic Capitalism* (Minneapolis, 1972), especially pp. 80–89]—the short-term benefits likely to accrue from a dual industrial labor market situation need not be expected to hold any great attractiveness.

22. Braverman, *Labor and Monopoly Capital*, p. 319 *passim*. Also see David No-

ble, *America by Design: Science, Technology and the Rise of Corporate Capitalism* (New York, 1977), pp. 82, 257–320.

23. A clarification is needed concerning use of constructs "black community" and "black activism." Racial segregation and the movement against it were southern phenomena. Black Power "nationalism" was essentially a northern phenomenon for which legally sanctioned racial exclusion was not an immediate issue. Although the two historical currents of rebellion were closely related, they nevertheless were distinct. Consequently, they must be considered separately.

24. See, for example: Charles S. Johnson, *Patterns of Negro Segregation* (New York, 1943) and *Growing Up in the Black Belt* (Washington, D.C., 1941); C. Vann Woodward, *The Strange Career of Jim Crow* (New York, 1966); Wilbur J. Cash, *The Mind of the South* (New York, 1941); Robert Penn Warren, *Segregation: The Inner Conflict in the South* (New York, 1956); John Dollard, *Caste and Class in a Southern Town* (New York, 1957); James W. Vander Zanden, *Race Relations in Transition* (New York, 1965); George B. Tindall, *The Emergence of the New South: 1913–1945* (Baton Rouge, 1967); Arthur Raper, *Preface to Peasantry: A Tale of Two Black Belt Counties* (Chapel Hill, 1936), and *The Tragedy of Lynching* (Chapel Hill, 1933); William L. Patterson, *We Charge Genocide* (New York, 1951); Martin Luther King, Jr., *Why We Can't Wait* (New York, 1964); Mayo Selz and C. Horace Hamilton, "The Rural Negro Population of the South in Transition," *Phylon* 24 (June, 1963), pp. 160–171; Thomas Patten, Jr., "Industrial Integration of the Negro," *Phylon* 24 (December, 1963), pp. 334ff; Donald Dewey, "Negro Employment in Southern Industry," *Journal of Political Economy* 60 (August, 1952), pp. 279–293; and Herbert R. Northrup et al., eds., *Negro Employment in Southern Industry: A Study of Racial Policies in Five Industries* (Philadelphia, 1970). (The discussion here of the South draws freely from these sources.)

25. Certainly, the bizarre notion of black leadership was not an invention of the postwar era. That strategy of pacification had been the primary nonterroristic means for subduing black opposition since Booker T. Washington's network of alliances with corporate progressives and New South Bourbon Democrats. Moreover, the notion of a leadership stratum which was supposed to speak for a monolithic black community became the ideological model and political ideal for 1960s radicalism—especially in its "nationalist" variants. Johnson (*Patterns*, pp. 65ff) discusses stratification among blacks under segregation and white responses to the different strata. Perspectives on the phenomenon of black leadership in this context can be gleaned from: Tillman C. Cothran and William Phillips, Jr., "Negro Leadership in a Crisis Situation," *Phylon* 22 (Winter, 1961), pp. 107–118; Everett Carll Ladd, Jr., *Negro Political Leadership in the South* (Ithaca, 1966); Jack Walker, "Protest and Negotiation: A Case Study of Negro Leadership in Atlanta, Georgia," *Midwest Journal of Politics* 7 (May, 1963), pp. 99–124; Daniel C. Thompson, *The Negro Leadership Class* (Englewood Cliffs, 1963); Floyd Hunter, *Community Power Structure* (Chapel Hill, 1953); and M. Elaine Burgess, *Negro Leadership in a Southern City* (Chapel Hill, 1953).

26. King's fascination with satyagraha suggests, although exaggeratedly, the influence which decolonization abroad had on the development of civil rights opposition. Cf. David L. Lewis, *King: A Critical Biography* (Baltimore, 1970),

pp. 100–103, and King, "Letter from Birmingham Jail," in *Why We Can't Wait*, pp. 76–95.

27. Lomax, *The Negro Revolt*, p. 21 *passim*; Martin Luther King, Jr., "I Have a Dream," in *Speeches by the Leaders: The March on Washington for Jobs and Freedom* (New York, n.d.); Whitney Young, *To Be Equal* (New York, 1964); and Samuel DuBois Cook, "The American Liberal Democratic Tradition, the Black Revolution and Martin Luther King, Jr.," in Hanes Walton, *The Political Philosophy of Martin Luther King, Jr.* (Westport, Conn., 1971), pp. xiii–xxxviii.

28. This does not mean that *Life* magazine and "Father Knows Best" taught blacks to "dream the dream of freedom." Rather, the integrative logic of massification exacerbated disruptive tendencies already present within the black elite.

29. Enrollment in black colleges increased nearly sixfold between 1928 and 1961 and doubled between 1941 and 1950 alone, on the threshold of the Civil Rights movement. Doug McAdam, *Political Process and the Development of Black Insurgency, 1930–1970* (Chicago, 1982), pp. 101–102.

30. Concepts such as duplicity and cooptation are inadequate to shed light on why corporate and liberal interests actively supported the Civil Rights movement. Interpretations so derived cannot fully explain programs and strategies which originated in the black community. They suggest that naive and trusting blacks, committed to an ideal of global emancipation, allowed themselves to be led away from this ideal by bourgeois wolves in sheep's clothing. This kind of "false consciousness" thesis is theoretically unacceptable. Consciousness is false not so much because it is a lie forced from outside but because it does not comprehend its historical one-sidedness.

31. Of course, suppression was the reaction of certain elements, most notably within the state apparatus, whose bureaucratized priorities urged suppression of any disruptive presence in the society. Howard Zinn, *SNCC: The New Abolitionists* (Boston, 1965), as well as Forman, shows that the federal apparatus, which developed a reputation at the "grass roots" as the patron saint of equality, was at best lukewarm in response to black demands for enforcement of constitutional rights and often set out to suppress tendencies and distinct personalities in the movement. Nevertheless, the movement was not suppressed, and not simply because it forced its will upon history. That bit of romantic back-slapping has as little credence as the one that contends that the antiwar movement ended the Vietnam war. The state hardly was mobilized against civil rights activism; the Supreme Court had authorized its legitimacy before it even began. See also Cleveland Sellers (with Robert Terrell), *The River of No Return: The Autobiography of a Black Militant and the Life and Death of SNCC* (New York, 1973). Clayborne Carson details, though without acknowledging the ironic outcomes of the dynamic, the systematic attempts by the Kennedy administration and private foundations to steer the Civil Rights movement toward enfolding itself in the national Democratic agenda. He carefully, yet glibly, reconstructs the portentous tension this attempt generated in the movement. See his study, *In Struggle: SNCC and the Black Awakening of the 1960s* (Cambridge, 1981), pp. 35–39 *passim*.

32. John F. Kennedy picked up the line and ran it as if it were his own; see

his "Message to Congress," *Congressional Record*, 88th Cong., 1st sess., Feb. 28, 1963.

33. It was out of this milieu of muddled uneasiness that the Rev. Willie Ricks gave the world the slogan, "Black Power!" on the Meredith march in 1966. A flavor of the frustration of the radicals at the time can be gotten from Julius Lester, *Look Out, Whitey! Black Power's Gon' Get Your Mama* (New York, 1968). In some respects Lester's account, though more dated, has greater value for understanding this period than either Forman's or Sellers's because *Look Out, Whitey!* is written from within Black Power, rather than retrospectively from the vantage point of new ideologies and old involvements that need to be protected. See also, Stokely Carmichael, "Who Is Qualified?" in *Stokely Speaks: Black Power Back to Pan-Africanism* (New York, 1971). Carson's account in *In Struggle* meticulously rehearses the internal ideological and programmatic tensions and debates within SNCC during this period. Unfortunately, his treatment is bereft of conscious theoretical framework.

34. This is not to suggest, however, that events in the South and outside were totally unrelated. As a practical matter, Democratic willingness to accommodate southern activism may have been influenced by increasing prominence of blacks within the urban constituencies of the party's electoral base in the Northeast and Midwest after 1930. In this context—especially after black defections from the national Democratic ticket in 1956 along with erosion of white electoral support in the South after 1948—the party was given pragmatic incentive to acknowledge a civil rights agenda. Arguments to this effect are developed in Frances Fox Piven and Richard A. Cloward, *Poor People's Movements: Why They Succeed, How They Fail* (New York, 1977), pp. 214ff, McAdam, *Political Process*, pp. 81–86, and C. Vann Woodward, *Jim Crow*, p. 129.

35. See, for example, Carmichael, "Power and Racism" in *Stokely Speaks*. This essay is perhaps the first attempt to articulate a systematic concept of the notion Black Power.

36. *Black Awakening in Capitalist America: An Analytic History* (Garden City, 1969), pp. 129–192. Allen's interpretation, however, cannot move beyond this descriptive point because he accepts a simplistic notion of cooptation to explain the black corporate/elite nexus. Julius Lester charged by 1968 that the "principal beneficiaries of Black Power have been the black middle class," *Revolutionary Notes* (New York, 1969), p. 106.

37. Piven and Cloward observe astutely that "black power" assisted in the pacification of activism by "providing a justification for the leadership stratum (and a growing black middle class more generally) to move aggressively to take advantage of . . . new opportunities" opened by the movement. *Poor People's Movements*, p. 253.

38. Harold Cruse, *Crisis*, pp. 544–565.

39. Jennifer Jordan notes this "nostalgic" character of 1960s culturalism and its grounding in the black elite in "Cultural Nationalism in the Sixties: Politics and Poetry," in this volume. In the most systematic and thorough critical reconstruction of black cultural nationalism to date, Jordan identifies two core nationalist tendencies: one Afro-American preservationist, the other African retrievalist. Presumably, Ron Karenga is to be seen as a bridge between those

tendencies with his commitment to "creation, recreation and circulation of Afro-American culture." "From the Quotable Karenga," in Floyd Barbour, ed., *The Black Power Revolt* (Boston, 1968), p. 162.

40. Cf. Imamu Amiri Baraka (LeRoi Jones), "Toward the Creation of Political Institutions for All African Peoples," *Black World* 21 (October, 1972), pp. 54–78. "Unity will be the only method, it is part of the black value system because it is only with unity that we will get political power," Baraka, *Raise, Race, Rays, Raze* (New York, 1971), p. 109.

41. The legacy of this ultimately depoliticizing pattern of discourse can be seen in the 1984 Jesse Jackson presidential campaign in which criticism of Jackson's effort was denounced as heresy or race treason.

42. George Mosse examines the theoretical components and historical significance of folkish ideology as a response to mass society in *The Crisis of German Ideology: Intellectual Origins of the Third Reich* (New York, 1964), pp. 13–30.

43. The fascination shared by most of the nationalists with the prospects of consciously creating a culture revealed both the loss of genuine cultural base and the extent of their acceptance of manipulation as a strategy (cf. Karenga's "seven criteria for culture," *Black Power Revolt*, p. 166). The farther away the nationalists chose to go to find their cultural referents, the more clearly they demonstrated the passage of a self-driving, spontaneous black existence from the arena of American history. The ultimate extension of escapism came with the growth of Pan-Africanism as an ideology; that turn—at least in its most aggressive manifestations—conceded as a first step the inauthenticity of all black American life. See Carmichael, *Stokely Speaks*, pp. 175–227, and Ideological Research Staff of Malcolm X Liberation University, *Understanding the African Struggle* (Greensboro, N.C., 1971).

44. In this regard expertise translates into superficial articulateness and ability to negotiate within the social management apparatus.

45. After Little Rock, Ronald Walters was able to boast that the black elected officials had become the vanguard political force in the black community. "The Black Politician: Fulfilling the Legacy of Black Power," *Current History* 67 (November, 1974), pp. 200ff. Baraka, its former chairman and a central organizer, was very nearly expelled from the National Black Assembly in 1975 by a force of elected officials put off by his newfound "Marxism." Note, however, that even he had to admit the activists' marginality and weakness compared to the mainstream elite as early as 1970 at the Congress of African Peoples. Baraka, ed., *African Congress: A Documentary of the First Modern Pan-African Congress* (New York, 1972), p. 99.

46. This is not to say that blacks no longer are oppressed, nor that the oppression no longer has racial characteristics. Nor still is it possible to agree with Wilson's claim that race is receding as a factor in the organization of American society; as Harold Barnette notes, the integration of affirmative action programs into the social management apparatus suggests race's continuing significance. See William Julius Wilson, *The Declining Significance of Race: Blacks and Changing American Institutions* (Chicago, 1978), and Barnette's review in *Southern Exposure* 7 (Spring, 1979), pp. 121–122. With legitimation and absorption of antiracism by the social management system, race has assumed a more substantial and pervasive function than ever before in American life.

Moreover, this function is often life-sustaining; controlling discrimination has become a career specialty—complete with "professional," "paraprofessional," and "subprofessional" gradations—in public and private bureaucracies. However, "racial discrimination" fails as a primary basis from which to interpret or address black oppression.

"Racism" is bound to an "equality of opportunity" ideology which can express only the interests of the elite strata among the black population; equality of access to the meaningless, fragmented and degrading jobs which comprise the bulk of work, for example, hardly is the stuff of "black liberation" and is ultimately a retrograde social demand. It is not an accident, therefore, that the only major battle produced by the struggle against racism in the 1970s was the anti-Bakke movement, whose sole objective was protection of upwardly mobile blacks' access to pursuit of professional employment status.

Racism makes its appearance in black political discourse as an opaque reification grafted onto otherwise acceptable institutions. Small wonder it is the only issue the black elite can find to contend! Not only does racism carry the elite's sole critique of U.S. society, but the claim that racism creates a bond of equivalent victimization among blacks is one of the sources of the elite's legitimation. It is interesting to recall in this context that "racism" became the orthodox explanation of black oppression when the Kerner Commission anointed it as the fundamental source of the 1964–1967 urban uprisings. *Report of the National Advisory Commission on Civil Disorders* (New York, 1968), p. 203. This document goes far toward articulating the outlines of what became the new strategy for management of the black population.

47. The most significant shift in the occupation structure of the black population in the decade after the 1964 Civil Rights Act was relative expansion of its elite component. Between 1964 and 1974 the percentage of minority males classified as "professional and technical" workers increased by half; the percentage classified as nonfarm, salaried "managers and administrators" quadrupled over that period. Similar increases were realized by minority females. See *Social and Economic Status of the Black Population*, pp. 73–74. Hefner and Kidder discuss these developments which they laud as constitutive of a new era of black opportunity, even though they express concern—appropriate to an upwardly mobile stratum—that the rate of progress could be increased. See James A. Hefner and Alice E. Kidder, "Racial Integration in Southern Management Positions," *Phylon* 33 (June, 1972), pp. 193–200.

Moreover, where in the 1960–1970 period the proportions of black low-income families decreased and high income families increased at roughly the same impressive rate, between 1970–1979 the shares of families in both categories increased. In 1970, 30.6 percent of black families earned in the low income range, and 35.2 percent were high income. In 1979, 32.5 percent were low income and 38.6 percent high income while the middle income component fell from 34.2 percent in 1970 to 28.9 percent in 1979. Between 1979–1982 the low income category rose steadily to 37.8 percent; the high income category dropped to just over 35 percent in 1981 and stabilized at that level, while middle income families continued to decline, reaching 26.9 percent in 1982. Distribution of wealth by asset category is equally instructive. While proportions of total black wealth represented by equity in homes (the largest single category) and vehicles and in financial assets declined slightly between 1967–1979, equity in rental or other property more than doubled, from 12 percent to 25 percent of the total. See William P. O'Hare, *Wealth and Economic Status: A Perspective on Racial Equality* (Washington, D.C., 1983), pp. 18, 25.

An indication of the social management apparatus' centrality for this expansion in the black elite can be gleaned from consideration of the growth of the public sector as an avenue for black middle class employment. While government consistently has been more significant for black employment than white, between 1960 and 1970 the proportion of black males in managerial or professional jobs who were employed in the government sector doubled from 18.2 percent to 37.1 percent. Black females, whose professional opportunities had been more severely restricted to the public sector, realized more modest gains, from 57.9 percent to 63.3 percent. Despite a stabilization and slight tailing off, by 1980 nearly a third of black professional males and more than half of black professional females were employed in government. See Martin Carnoy, Derek Shearer, and Russell Rumberger, *A New Social Contract: The Economy and Government After Reagan* (New York, 1983), 133–134.

This is the context in which the Reaganite assault on public spending is most directly racial in its thrust. Indeed, the mobilization of Thomas Sowell, Walter Williams, and other ideologues of "black neo-conservatism" by the Reaganite forces is instructive. Sowell and the others seek to justify Reagan's reversal of racial palliatives and "entitlement" programs largely by pointing to the disproportionate benefits bestowed by those programs on middle class black functionaries. For critical discussion of this phenomenon see Jerry G. Watts, "The Case of the Black Conservative," *Dissent* (Summer, 1982), pp. 301–313, and Alex Willingham, "The Place of the New Black Conservatives in Black Social Thought" (unpublished).

48. The celebration of the new elite is not, as once was the case, restricted to black media. Stephen Birmingham has testified to their presence and allowed them to expose their personal habits in his characteristically gossipy style of pop journalism in *Certain People: America's Black Elite* (Boston, 1977). The *New York Times Sunday Magazine* twice at least lionized the beautiful black stratum of the 1970s. See Peter Ross Range, "Making It in Atlanta: Capital of 'Black is Bountiful,' " *New York Times Sunday Magazine*, April 7, 1974, and William Brashler, "The Black Middle Class: Making It," in the December 3, 1978, magazine. Each of these brassy accounts tends, despite occassional injections of "balance," to accept and project the elite's mystical view of itself and exaggerates its breadth and force in society. However, that the *Times* even would care to make the statement made by these two articles suggests minimally that the elite has been integrated into the corporate marketing strategy on an equal basis.

49. This distinction of "authentic" and "artificial" particularity is similar to Habermas's distinction of "living" and "objectivistically prepared and strategically employed" cultural traditions. A cultural particularity is "authentic" insofar as it: 1) reproduces itself within the institutional environment that apparently delimits the group, i.e., outside the social administrative system; and 2) is not mobilized by the mass culture industry. Cf. Jurgen Habermas, *Legitimation Crisis* (Boston, 1975), pp. 70–72. Therefore, in this usage, "authentic" par-

ticularity relates not to any notion of ethnic genuineness but to the oppositional impetus posited in a group's existence. This oppositional quality derives
from the otherness that characterizes the autonomously reproductive, unintegrated group's relation to the mass capitalist social order and that necessarily:
1) demonstrates the possibility of a form of social life alternative to that decreed
by the logic of administration, and 2) poses a practical negation of the order's
claims to cultural hegemony. As the group is integrated into the material and
cognitive frameworks of the prevailing order, the sense of alternate possibility
is lost, and the negativity that had mediated the group's relation to mass capitalism is overcome in favor of a nontranscendent, system-legitimizing, and
systematically authorized pluralism—which becomes the basis for what I have
described as "artificial" particularity. Authenticity thus is a category of emancipatory interest rather than ethnographic integrity.

50. Jordan even contends that radical culturalism was most susceptible among
all the 1960s' oppositional forms to the logic of commodification because of its
tendency to reduce identity to the artifact. Cf. "Cultural Nationalism in the
Sixties."

51. Compare for example: S. E. Anderson, "Black Students: Racial Consciousness and the Class Struggle, 1960–1976," *Black Scholar* 8 (January–February, 1977), pp. 35–43; Muhammad Ahmad, "On the Black Student Movement—1960–1970," *Black Scholar* 9 (May–June, 1978), pp. 2–11; and James and
Grace Lee Boggs, *Revolution and Evolution in the Twentieth Century* (New York,
1974), pp. 174ff.

52. The coalition's bankruptcy was demonstrated by the defections from its
electoral constituency to Nixon's "silent majority" in 1968 and wholesale collapse in the face of McGovernite and Republican challenges in 1972. Unable to
end the Vietnam war and adjust to a new era of imperialism or to address the
concerns of such postscarcity era advocacy centers as the student and ecology
movements, the productivist liberal-labor forces who had controlled the Democratic party for a generation also found it impossible to establish a common
discursive arena with the ethnic and feminist consciousness movements of the
1960s.

53. "Future of Capitalism"in this volume; "The Changing Function of Critical Theory," *New German Critique* (Fall, 1977), pp. 35–36.

54. Habermas calls these "quasi-groups" and maintains that they perform
the additional function of absorbing the "secondary effects of the averted economic crisis," *Legitimation Crisis*, p. 39.

55. Russell Jacoby, "A Falling Rate of Intelligence?" *Telos* (Spring, 1976),
pp. 141–146; Stanley Aronowitz, "Mass Culture and the Eclipse of Reason: The
Implications for Pedagogy," *College English* 38 (April, 1977), pp. 768–774; and
False Promises: The Shaping of American Working Class Consciousness (New York,
1973).

56. This integrative bias in mass movements is clear from Piven and Cloward's accounts in *Poor People's Movements*. Their interpretation, however, em-
phasizes the structural determinants of protest movements to an extent that
seems not to allow the possibility of transcendence.

57. Todd Gitlin carefully reconstructs the dialectic of mutually reinforcing
interaction between the mass media and the New Left in general, including

Black Power radicals, in *The Whole World is Watching!: Mass Media in the Making and Unmaking of the New Left* (Berkeley, 1980). Also see Carson, *In Struggle*.

58. Julius Lester was one who saw the prominence of a media cult in the movement (*Revolutionary Notes*, pp. 176–180). On the peculiar media-inspired style of the Black Panthers see Earl Anthony, *Picking Up the Gun* (New York, 1970).

59. "The spectacle presents itself as an enormous unalterable and inaccessible actuality. It says nothing more than 'that which appears is good, that which is good appears.' The attitude which it demands in principle is this passive acceptance, which in fact it has already obtained by its manner of appearing without reply, by its monopoly of appearance," para. 12, Guy Debord, *Society of the Spectacle* (Detroit, 1970).

60. A shift in advertising style captures contemporary life: during the national telecast of the 1978 Miss Black America pageant, General Motors, a sponsor of the broadcast, featured a commercial in which a utilityman at a plant listed the attractions of his job. Among them were pay, fringe benefits, security, opportunity to perform various tasks (a function solely of his particular position), congenial supervision, and a *good union*! In the metaphor of a colleague who is one of a vanishing breed of baseball fans, the bourgeoisie has a shutout going with two away in the bottom of the ninth!

61. For examination of the genesis of this growth coalition and its constituents and practices see Alan Wolfe, *America's Impasse: The Rise and Fall of the Politics of Growth* (Boston, 1981), and John H. Mollenkopf, *The Contested City* (Princeton, 1983).

62. R. Jeffrey Lustig develops this point in *Corporate Liberalism: The Origins of Modern American Political Theory, 1890–1920* (Berkeley, 1982). Samuel Huntington speaks explicitly of this characteristic of the American order and bemoans the disruptive qualities of the "democratic distemper" in *American Politics: The Promise of Disharmony* (Cambridge, 1981), and in his essay on the United States in Michel J. Crozier, Samuel P. Huntington, and Joji Watanuki, *The Crisis of Democracy: Report on the Governability of Democracies to the Trilateral Commission* (New York, 1975).

Lustig notes that the model of social management in which growth politics is embedded actually antedates the New Deal.

63. The various elements that combined to erode the efficacy of what they refer to as the "postwar corporate system" are described in Samuel Bowles, David M. Gordon, and Thomas E. Weisskopf, *Beyond the Waste Land: A Democratic Alternative to Economic Decline* (Garden City, N.Y., 1983), pp. 79–97. Barry Bluestone and Bennett Harrison emphasize the role of shortsighted corporate management strategies and capital flight in undermining the growth coalition's usefulness. See *The Deindustrialization of America* (New York, 1982).

64. Kevin P. Phillips examines this aspect of Reagan's base in *Post-Conservative America: People, Politics and Ideology in a Time of Crisis* (New York, 1982), especially pp. 193–204.

65. Earl Picard, "The New Black Economic Development Strategy," *Telos* (Summer, 1984). Picard develops this argument through a study of the current programs of the NAACP and Jesse Jackson's PUSH.

66. For a careful examination of the narcissistic style of new middle class politics and a refutation of the inherited wisdom that increased education and

income produce a "public-regarding" ethos, see Clarence N. Stone, "Conflict in the Emerging Post-Industrial Community," paper given at the American Political Science Association annual meeting, Denver, Colorado, 1982.

Stone charts the coordinates of conflict through examination of the narrowly self-interested politics of the mobile middle class in Montgomery County, Maryland, a largely upper-income jurisdiction in the Washington, D.C., metropolitan area. With its skills for organization and manipulation of language and image, this "yuppie" element is naturally suited to formation of political agendas along interest group lines.

67. See for example, Mollenkopf, pp. 261–266. Organizational and ideological mechanisms through which these advantages are realized in the natural workings of the political system are discussed in Clarence N. Stone, "Systemic Power in Community Decision Making," *American Political Science Review* 74 (December, 1980), especially pp. 983–984, and David Harvey, *Social Justice and the City* (Baltimore, 1973), pp. 82–86. See also J. John Palen and Bruce London, eds., *Gentrification, Displacement and Neighborhood Revitalization* (Albany, 1984).

68. For critiques of neo-liberal, high-tech development strategies see Carnoy, Shearer, and Rumberger, pp. 150–159; and Bluestone and Harrison, pp. 210–230. Systematic statements of neo-liberal reindustrialization strategy are: Lester Thurow, *The Zero-Sum Society* (New York, 1980); Robert Reich, *The Next American Frontier* (New York, 1983); and Felix Rohatyn, *The Twenty Year Century* (New York, 1983).

69. It is instructive that the postwar baby boom voted more consistently for Reagan than did any other age cohort in 1980. One view of this group's distinctive political style is proposed in Carter A. Eskew, "Baby-Boom Voters," *New York Times* (July 15, 1984).

70. A major focus of this project must be secularization of discussion of the black political situation. Certain elements in the left buttress the foes of democratic discourse in the black community by propagating a view that blacks—unlike other groups in the American polity—are moved to action only through the intervention of charismatic spokesmen who emobdy collective aspirations personalistically, outside of any discursive processes. Black religiosity is adduced to validate this authoritarian politics of cathartic *volkishness*, and these leftists opportunistically endorse the confounding of church and state in the black community even as they fret over the proto-fascist characteristics of the "moral majority." See, for example, Andrew Kopkind, "Black Power in the Age of Jackson," *The Nation* (November 26, 1983), and Cornel West, *Prophesy Deliverance!: An Afro-American Revolutionary Christianity* (Philadelphia, 1982).

I have developed critiques of these views in a review of West's book in *Telos* (Summer, 1984) and in *The Jesse Jackson Phenomenon: The Crisis of Purpose in Afro-American Politics* (New Haven, 1986).

71. "The main thing is that utopian conscience and knowledge, through the pain it suffers in facts, grows wise, yet does not grow to full wisdom. It is *rectified*—but never *refuted*—by the mere power of that which, at any particular time, *is*. On the contrary it confutes and judges the existent if it is failing, and failing inhumanly; indeed, first and foremost it provides the *standard* to measure such facticity precisely as departure from the Right," Ernst Bloch, *A Philosophy of the Future* (New York, 1970), p. 91.

Part II

New Left Politics and Counterculture

4

Culture, Politics, and "Lifestyle" in the 1960s

If a "culture" can be defined as a commonly held set of beliefs, values, and norms which bind a group together and give it a sense of identity, then nineteenth-century America contained a remarkable variety of such cultures. There were not only a number of identifiable class cultures (ranging from an elitist Brahmin culture down to an artisan and, below that, an urban working-class culture), but there were also many regional, religious, and ethnic cultures spread across the American landscape. Often these cultures had political worldviews embedded in them, though usually the politics remained muted or only half-articulated. At times, one culture might sharply clash with another, as happened for example when an Irish-liberal-Catholic culture confronted an English-conservative-Methodist culture. Occasionally, if two cultures lay in close proximity, one might try to dominate or discredit the other. As a rule, however, the various cultures left one another alone; consequently, each managed to acquire for itself enough cultural space to develop its distinctive characteristics in relative freedom.

Significantly, the nineteenth-century business entrepreneur had not yet learned to view culture as a market to be tapped for profit. True, the purveyors of the finest cultural goods found it useful to play on associations between "high" culture on the one hand and the images of status and success on the other. The upper-middle class in particular was encouraged to think that by possessing the trappings of a highbrow culture it would be signaling that it had arrived: that it was cultivated enough to at least know what appearances to keep up. Even in this instance the point was to move *up to* genuine culture by purchasing and then conspicuously displaying the most prestigious goods or objets d'art. The numerous regional or ethnic cultures were hardly touched by this approach. They were regarded as beneath consideration; they had nothing to do with real culture as it was understood by those eager to develop refined tastes.

Prior to 1900, then, American capitalism showed no great interest in invading and commercializing the plurality of existing cultures. There were no systematic efforts to commodify, package, or mass produce cultural qualities and then sell them back to people as if they were popular authentic expressions. There had not yet emerged, in other words, a standardized mass culture in America. Of course, in this very different climate of the nineteenth century some cultures possessed more prestige than others, but none claimed hegemony. At that time no culture, not even the most pretentious, ever imagined that it had the capacity to demolish other "lower" cultures, or make them lean on it alone for their guiding concept of reality.

In the decade or so before the First World War, this cultural situation began to change. During the 1920s and 1930s the change became even more pronounced until—by the period 1945–1960—an entirely new cultural reality had been created in America. This new reality may be briefly characterized by the following points. First, American culture became by and large a consumer culture. Second, the remnants of earlier ethnic, religious, or class cultures (to the extent that they persisted at all) were now relegated to the status of "subcultures." Third, culture lost its ties to communal modes of practice and hence no longer expressed much in the way of organic solidarity. Fourth, a good portion of what began to pass for culture either served as a conduit for commercial values or provided a stimulus for escapist sentiments, or both. Fifth, American culture became overwhelmingly depoliticized, especially after 1945.

By the 1950s it seemed to many that the plenitude of cultures in America had for all practical purposes been reduced to one: that of marketing or mass culture. In numerous symposia, the intellectuals of that decade fretted over the meaning of this new situation and offered explanations as to how it had come about.[1] If there was in fact only one cultural field in the United States, it must have come (they reasoned) as a result of factors which had not existed before. The sheer amount of corporate money invested in cultural goods and images between 1945 and 1960 was certainly one new factor. Because of both a higher educational level and growing status anxieties on the part of many Americans, culture became a hot market, and this drew unprecedented amounts of capital into the cultural arena. It also drew new kinds of entrepreneurs who became highly skilled at scanning the remaining subcultures in order to discover what in them was worth exploiting. Following the entrepreneurs were others who became experts in sanitizing, reproducing, and distributing the "fresh ideas" on a mass scale. (The most egregious examples of this process of appropriation occurred in the realm of popular music. Dozens of songs and lyrics were lifted from black culture, cleaned up, and then recorded by white performers mainly for white audiences.[2]) The unparalleled power of the advertising industry and the mass media, especially TV, also helped define, shape, and standardize culture in a way that would have been unthinkable a hundred years earlier.

The net effect of all this was the emergence, by the 1950s, of a powerful cultural apparatus which was able to legislate a particular set of tastes and values for all strata of the American public. By means of this cultural apparatus, as C. Wright Mills pointed out, "art, science, learning, entertainment, malarkey, and information are produced, . . . distributed and consumed. Inside it, . . . the images, meanings, and slogans that define the worlds in which men live are organized and compared, maintained, and revised, lost and cherished, hidden, debunked, celebrated."[3] Of course, many of the residues of earlier cultures still persisted in the corners of American life, but they were often viewed as quaint if not deviant survivals from the past; and for the postwar generation which grew up in suburbia in the 1950s, these traces were all but invisible. There were few occasions for a firsthand encounter with the marginalized elements of, say, a black or a chicano culture, since these were usually tucked away in the larger cities. If many young people in the 1960s became cultural radicals even before they became political ones, it was partly because of the cultural malaise they felt in their daily lives. Those whom Eldridge Cleaver once labeled the "vanguard of white youth" regarded their suburban TV culture as impoverished and one-dimensional; they were therefore more than ready to experiment with something quite different when the occasion presented itself.[4]

However, the occasion did not present itself during the period 1945–1960. At that time there were, culturally speaking, only three options available. The first was the option chosen by the majority of Americans, which was literally to buy into the official media culture, thereby absorbing its normative standards and values. Naturally this was the option most encouraged by corporate capital. It was a choice which led to the songs of the Hit Parade, the Book-of-the-Month Club selections, the *Reader's Digest*, TV serials, popular "light" movies, and other kinds of artistic kitsch which became part and parcel of 1950s mass culture.

The second option was to try and live as much as possible in one of the subcultures at the fringes of American life—for instance, in a black or Hispanic subculture (even though these were seriously weakened by commercial values). Similarly, one could try to carve out for oneself a private sphere which was *in* but not *of* the dominant culture. This was the course taken by the Beat poets. Their attempt at disengagement did represent an act of rebellion. The Beats clearly stood for a rejection of the prevailing cultural norms. They wanted nothing to do with the rampant "Moneytheism" that propelled American society. They defined themselves against the vacuous "neon wilderness" around them. Nevertheless, the rebellion of the Beats did not amount to much more than a withdrawal from the world of the "squares." They never challenged mass culture on its own terms. They simply wanted to be left alone, to "drop out," to retreat to their enclaves where they hoped they would not be bothered. Unlike the hippies a decade later, they made no effort to be conspicuous, to flaunt their dress or behavior. Moreover the Beats did not try to politicize their dissent from the mainstream. In an age of McCarthy and Eisenhower, they chose inwardness (drugs, jazz, art) or resignation (zen). Most Beats were self-consciously apolitical if not downright antipolitical.[5]

The third option was perhaps the most interesting. It accepted, formally and superficially, the general contours of the culture, but it did not internalize the values encoded in them. Rather, it *played* with popular cultural forms by pantomiming, deriding, and disparaging them— or simply putting them on a different register of valuation. In this way, the very cultural qualities which appeared to be embraced were secretly undermined. That group of young people whom Kenneth Kenniston termed "the uncommitted" represented this option.[6] In contrast to the Beats, the uncommitted youth of the 1950s did not overtly revolt against the consumer culture. They lived within it but at the same time embarked upon an inner emigration which effectively distanced them from it. Without creating new forms as some Beats did, they subverted the existing ones by deserting them mentally or emotionally. The blacks provided another example of this approach. They, too, only apparently accepted many aspects of white culture, but privately they manipulated the predominant cultural images and symbols, played on their ambiguities, and turned them upside down when they got a chance. This has at all times been the strategy of the powerless. When they have not been strong enough to overturn a culture, they have at least learned the tactics of avoidance, noncooperation, maladaptation, or conscious reversal of meaning.[7] Historically, the blacks in America (and other ethnic minorities as well) had often practiced this approach with considerable skill up through the 1950s.

What was new about the 1960s was that a fourth option, or a fourth way of relating to the established culture, explosively presented itself. This was the option of openly and forcefully attacking the major assumptions of mass culture, of contesting its values *on mass culture's own terrain*, and of seizing the cultural initiative by loudly and flamboyantly offering a variety of imaginative alternatives to commodity culture. This had never been tried during the period 1945–1960, which is why the cultural upheaval of the 1960s at first seemed so novel and refreshing. The new cultural rebels were clearly no longer content with passive withdrawal or strategies of avoidance or reconversion. Instead of retreating to the hidden spaces of American life, they tried to open and significantly expand precisely those same spaces. One result was the development (from below) of unexpected cultural forms which caught the merchants of popular culture off guard, at least at the beginning.

There were two elements which led the way in cultural experimentation. One was a white youth culture centered in music, drugs, personal openness, and (for large numbers) civil rights and antiwar activities. The other was a type of cultural nationalism which took root in black and other nonwhite ethnic communities, and which stressed ethnic pride, music, language, new modes of communalism, and (for many again) left-wing politics. Because I know more in terms of personal experience about the first of these two elements, I am going to confine my remarks chiefly to that side of the 1960s "cultural revolution."

It is now obvious in retrospect that both of these cultures appeared on the scene so quickly and assertively that the people involved in them were swept away by their own enthusiasm. The leaders, especially, were convinced that what was underway in America was absolutely unique and original—a fact which partly explains why nearly every important cultural document of that time was filled with the most unrestrained optimism. Typical was a statement such as the following by Charles Reich: "There is a revolution coming. It will not be like revolutions in the past. It will originate with the individual *and with culture*, and it will change the political structure only as its final act."[8] Similar professions of faith in the power of youth culture to transform the world can be found in Theodore Roszak, Abbie Hoffman, Jerry Rubin, Michael Rossman, Mitchell Goodman, Peter Martin, and many other spokesmen from the 1960s. All believed that the emerging culture of the young would usher in a new and much-needed emphasis on spontaneity, sincerity, and authenticity; it would also bring people together, give them a sense of cohesion, and yet foster liberating modes of self-actualization. However, it was always stressed that for all this to happen it would not be enough just to *think* differently. Putting it that way was the mistake of some aspects of the old culture which made the mind the pivot of everything important. Rather, the point would now be to *embody* the new culture: to enact it, demonstrate it, practice it day in and day out in one's personal life. Anything less would be hypocrisy—in fact, the same kind of hypocrisy which, as far as the young were concerned, completely discredited the "official" culture to which they had set themselves in opposition in the first place.

There was a great deal of truth in the idea that a culture, if it was to be at all meaningful, had to be really lived and not merely thought about. There was such stridency in the emphasis on the need to act out one's cultural beliefs, however, that it seemed almost to represent the return of Marx's "Eleventh Thesis on Feuerbach" with a vengeance. Nevertheless, this very issue of authenticity—of the necessity of fusing thought with practice—raised a very important question which had to be addressed. Exactly how does one incarnate a cultural worldview? If merely thinking differently is not enough, how does one go about translating changes in consciousness into changes in behavior?

The answer that a good portion of both the white youth culture and the nonwhite ethnic cultures arrived at was by means of a new *lifestyle*. Lifestyle became perhaps *the* key word of the 1960s. Taking on an alternative lifestyle came to be the primary means by which one manifested who one was. A lifestyle located a person on the cultural map; it signaled to others the nature of one's cultural values, and it demonstrated that one was by all appearances living up to them. Thanks to the concept of lifestyle, the cultural radical could (or thought he could) make two points at once. By his very looks and comportment he could be a living critique of everything he wanted to negate in mass culture, and by the same looks and comportment he could prefigure a new world of looseness, spontaneity, freedom, and sexual openness (and sometimes androgeny) which, it was hoped, might become the norm in America should such a style be taken seriously as a herald of things to come.

As the concept of lifestyle moved into the center of the discussion of culture in the 1960s, two problems emerged which relatively few people noticed at the time. One was: does culture really liberate? The other was: is transforming one's lifestyle the best way to think about a cultural revolution?

Huey Newton, among others, tried to confront these problems with regard to black culture. In his view, a new black lifestyle was not only not radical enough in itself but could easily deflect energy away from the more important goal of political revolution. African dashikis, Afro hairdos, black music, language, and cultural style admittedly stimulated ethnic pride, but these in and of themselves could only produce a radical "identity," not real freedom.[9] For true liberation to come about, Newton declared, "we're going to need some stronger stuff." Harold Cruse made a similar observation. The cultural nationalists of the 1960s were, in his opinion, on the wrong track in simply celebrating black cultural achievements or the "African personality." What the black community needed was not a flashy counterculture, but effective counterinstitutions to confront the white power structure. Yet aside from the efforts of a few, this was not forthcoming. "Most of the leading young nationalist spokesmen," Cruse wrote, "are apolitical." Cultural regeneration was more important to them than political or economic organization, but from Cruse's perspective this was not the correct way to think about revolution.[10]

Both of the problems mentioned above were equally evident in the white youth culture. Particularly in the middle and late 1960s, it was widely believed that the lifestyle associated with drugs, rock music, and "antisocial" behavior would shake and perhaps even bring down the Establishment. "(Y)outh lifestyle, . . . as we all know, is going to revolutionize the world" was an idea one heard so frequently in the 1960s that for many it achieved the status of a truism.[11] Jerry Rubin spoke for many thousands of his contemporaries when he argued in *Do It!* that the young, by actively embodying their new cultural consciousness, could nonplus and ultimately overwhelm the "pig power structure." Youth culture, he assured his readers, would automatically propel "9 millions of young people . . . into the streets of every city, dancing, singing, smoking pot, fucking in the streets, tripping, burning draft cards, stopping traffic."[12] According to many in the counterculture—and not only the Yippies—a lifestyle freely acted out would be the agent and maybe even the essence of radical social change.

Once the term "lifestyle" became pivotal, an interesting logic began to unfold. If the new culture was synonymous with a radical new lifestyle, and if this lifestyle was associated with certain acts or appearances, then a way was opened up to attach these acts and appearances to particular things (like clothes or records) which were said to manifest the "spirit" of the counterculture. Since much of youth culture was focused on images anyway, it was not hard to link an appropriate image to a plethora of objects which had to be owned or displayed if one was to be regarded as a bona fide member of the alternative culture. This linkage provided exactly the opportunity that marketeers of the dominant culture were looking for. It enabled them to package and sell "lifestyle" as a commodity. Admen and marketing experts cleverly played on the widespread yearning for symbols which accurately captured the mood and tone of the counterculture, as if possessing the emblems, badges, and symbols of a culture could be equated with possessing the culture itself (which no doubt it could be if the culture were a shallow one). Under these circumstances, it should not be surpising that a slogan such as "The revolution is the way you live your life" was used, and perhaps even devised, by promoters bent on selling a specific line of commodities to the emerging youth market. Similarly, Columbia Records ran an advertisement which proclaimed, in youth culture's own language, that "the Man can't bust *our* music. . . . Know who your friends are. And look and see and touch and be together. Then listen. We do."[13] Even Marshall McLuhan, who was supposed to be a guru of the counterculture, became instead one of the most prominent drum majors of commodification. The first task of a revolutionary, he insisted, was to *create new images*. This attitude played directly into the hands of the cultural entrepreneurs, who were only too glad to help revolutionaries develop—and more importantly, consume—their own images.

Another spokesman for the counterculture, Charles Reich, drew still more closely the connection between exhibiting a certain lifestyle and owning certain symbolic goods. In *The Greening of America* he indulged himself in a virtual paean to "jeans," which, he argued, were the perfect emblem and embodiment of the new cultural style. According to Reich, jeans represent a deliberate rejection of the "artificial look of the affluent society"; they are "earthy and sensual"; they "express an affinity with nature," since "browns, greens, and blues are nature's colors"; and they signal qualities of personal liberation because they "give the wearer freedom to do anything he wants." "Jeans make one conscious of the body" and are therefore a declaration of "sensuality as part of the natural in man . . . (beyond the) masculinity or feminity hang-up." Bell-bottoms are even better, since "they say much more." They are "happy, comic, and rollicking," and they "give the ankles a special freedom as if to invite dancing right in the street."[14] Reich carried this celebration of clothing to still greater lengths of absurdity which would be useless to follow. The point is that by pursuing a line of thought such as this, he and others like him helped reduce youth culture to specific things and images which the culture industry had no trouble exploiting for its own purposes.

Thanks to the benefit of hindsight, there is a great deal that can now be learned about the successes, and even more the failures, of the cultural explosion of the 1960s. For one thing, it is more evident now than it was then that capitalism has an unerring capacity to coopt practically everything that is original or expressive. The "new" is always raw material for commercialization, but most cultural rebels in the 1960s did not notice this, or if they did they were not on their guard against it. Second, it is more obvious today that a cultural revolution is not the same as a real revolution. Many in the 1960s simply failed to take account of the enormous difference between the two. A change in lifestyle means nothing unless culture is informed by politics. However, a good part of the cultural style of the decade was nonpolitical, and where there was a political tone, it was largely diffused by the cultural marketeers who were adept at sifting out what was salable from what was politically critical and retaining only the former. (The phenomenon of the Woodstock Nation in 1969 is a good example of this phenomenon.) Finally, it is now more apparent that any countercultural movement, if it is to maintain its identity, must carefully delineate its relationship to the dominant culture if it is to preserve its integrity. In the 1960s, however, the lines between the two spheres were often blurred. White youth culture never fully understood what position it wanted to take toward the cultural apparatus of the Establishment (which is one reason it constantly fell victim to the impresarios of rock concerts and "youth festivals," and why it bought into a musical star system which in theory it should have opposed). Then, too, not even the most avid of devotees of a counterculture, white or nonwhite ethnic, is able to get all his sustenance there. Everyone has to lean on the official culture to some extent, to make a living if nothing else. If a person does not sharply demarcate these two realms, it is all too easy for the values of the dominant culture to invade the alternative culture, thereby weakening its oppositional force. To a considerable degree this happened in the 1960s, which is why most aspects of youth culture were ultimately absorbed, with surprisingly little resistance, into mainstream commercial culture.

A minority within or at the edges of the counterculture (generally those with stronger political convictions) saw much of this, but, unfortunately, they were not able to do much with their insights, since they soon moved off into a number of confusing and often opposite directions. One faction—including Progressive Labor (PL), Young Socialist Alliance (YSA), and others—argued that cultural concerns as such were counterrevolutionary. Consequently, they labeled the whole cultural side of the 1960s as "petit bourgeois" and turned their attention instead to exclusively political or economic matters. Another faction, larger and undoubtedly more open-minded, acknowledged that cultural transformation was an essential part of the whole process of radical change, but *only* if it were politicized, i.e., if either the form or the content of cultural expressions carried critical or even revolutionary messages. However, those who took this position fell, in turn, into two different camps. One contended that the 1960s lifestyle *did* in fact contain a political content, broadly defined, and had therefore to be considered a radical development worth supporting.[15] The other camp disagreed. While accepting the idea that some cultural movements could indeed be radical, it was sure that a stress on cultural lifestyle alone, which is what the 1960s counterculture seemed to represent, was not.[16] A debate then ensued within this latter group as to whether youth culture could eventually be *made* radical by injecting politics into it, or whether it had to be written off as ultimately unredeemable.

This debate was never resolved, partly because the arrival of the 1970s made much of it obsolete. Still, it appears in retrospect that those who believed the issue of culture to be extremely important were on the right track. It may not be cultural activity itself, but only the narrow way it was thought about in the 1960s, that needs to be reconsidered. Generally speaking, no cultural opposition is likely to unsettle a given structure of power unless it is very focused politically, or unless it is intimately bound up with parallel movements of political or economic opposition. Usually culture, including present-day mass culture, serves as social cement for a status quo. For this reason, the cultural realm may be a good place to begin to challenge or destabilize prevailing myths or assumptions, but it is not necessarily the best place to mount a "revolution." Particularly if the revolution happens to be defined too exclusively in cultural or lifestyle terms, it may prove rather easy for the culture industry to dismiss, coopt, or nullify its overall force and effectiveness. Conceivably, people (as consumers) would then be allowed to make all the sweeping cultural changes they wanted, so long as such changes were confined to the individual sphere, and so long as major political and economic decisions were left to supervising elites.[17]

Though the sketch given so far of the 1960s counterculture is not inaccurate, neither is it the whole story. In truth, the cultural upheaval of that decade was a kaleidoscopic affair and hence more complicated than I have indicated. With approximately 10 million people involved to one degree or another (according to a *Fortune* article on the marketing possibilities of the new culture), it is obvious that there were many different constituencies and constellations of elements existing simultaneously. Staying focused as I have been on white youth culture, two groupings became especially prominent in the 1960s—the "politicos" and the "hippies."

The politicos were those who viewed the world, including the world of culture, through political lenses. In many instances their outlooks were forged prior to the countercultural surge of the mid-1960s. It was not initially music and drugs but the Civil Rights movement and the early New Left which shaped their basic orientations. Though politicos on the whole shared many if not most of the values of the youth culture, their *Weltanschauung* took on a quite different cast because it was forged through activism and informed by a specific range of readings. The bookshelves of politicos were likely to be stocked with works by the young Marx, Albert Camus, C. Wright Mills, Paul Goodman, Herbert Marcuse, Frantz Fanon, and Regis Debray. The journals they would have been disposed to keep up with would include *Ramparts*, *Liberation*, *Monthly Review*, and later probably *Radical America*, *Leviathan*, or *Telos*.

The hippies, on the other hand, came to the youth culture by a different route. From the beginning, what counted for them was a new consciousness, heightened perceptions, and enlarged personal vision. Not having passed through the crucible of political involvement, the hippies were generally more passive, less intellectual, and less socially aware. If anything, they represented an extension of the Beat movement of the 1950s in that drugs, Eastern religions, and music (rock rather than jazz) played as important a role for them as they did for the Beats. There were of course differences: the hippies were seemingly more frank than articulate, more honest than knowledgeable, and certainly more exhibitionistic than reclusive.[18] Also, for the hippies reading was not as important as simply experiencing life, but when they did read they worked through an entirely different canon than that of the politicos. It was not Mills or Marcuse who were formative influences, but primarily Alan Watts, Fritz Perls, Hermann Hesse, J. R. R. Tolkien, Timothy Leary, Georges Gurdjieff, and Carlos Castaneda.

Many politicos were suspicious of the hippies. They were afraid that the hippies were offering only a lifestyle protest, one that called for a transformation of consciousness or of taste and appearance but not of social reality. Though the politicos themselves also stressed the importance of the personal and the subjective—a glance at the Port Huron Statement (1962), to mention only one example, makes this clear—they also emphasized the indispensability of thought, criticism, and radical practice. However, these were precisely the qualities which appeared to be missing in the hippies. To them it seemed more desirable to bypass the mind as much as possible, since, from their point of view, everything purely intellectual only served to narrow perception and experience. As for political activity, this too was regarded as either fruitless or irrelevant. Just *living differently* would be enough to change the world. In fact, for some living differently was the be-all and the end-all of the revolution itself. As one hippie spokesman put it, "you don't change the world, you change yourself. The world is a projection of yourself, so you change yourself and you change the world around you, and this is like s-o-o-o true, man, it's incredible."[19]

Of these two orientations within the counterculture of the 1960s, the hippies gradually came to exert the greater influence, and this turned out to be decisive for the fate of youth culture.

At first it appeared that the opposite might happen, i.e., that youth culture might become politicized. It was certainly a strategy of many politicians to attempt to achieve just this. One theory had it that youth could be turned into a "radical class," another that it could become an "embryonic cultural basis for New Left politics."[20] Excited by the idea of "liberated zones" borrowed from Vietnam, many politicos imagined that the youth enclaves of Berkeley, Haight-Ashbury, Madison, Ila Vista, or the East Village could become the seedbeds of revolution, if not model revolutionary communities in their own right. By the late 1960s, however, these dreams were shattered. The hippie influence came to prevail and with it an emphasis on lifestyle over politics. In the end, the politicos were not successful in checking the drift toward primarily cultural modes of opposition to the Establishment. Consequently, youth culture lost whatever potential it may have had to become politicized. Instead, it became rapidly depoliticized, and not only because of the corroding effects of commercialization. Even without the pressure of the culture industry, there were forces at work within youth culture which favored depoliticization. The underground press, for instance, contained at the outset (in the mid-1960s) a more or less equal mixture of cultural expressiveness and political analysis; and as a matter of policy it sought to reach all elements of the counterculture without differentiation. By the end of the decade, however, most underground newspapers had become predominantly cultural in orientation. Their pages were opened to the advertisers of "hip capitalism," and they became generally uncritical of those aspects of youth culture which deserved censure.[21] Similar changes helped transform the free universities from essentially political counterinstitutions, which they were at the beginning, to promoters of lifestyle values, which is what they eventually became. By the early 1970s, one would have been hardpressed to find a free university course on, say, Marx or "power structure research" in the midst of a panoply of other courses on meditation, massage, Jungian psychology, tarot, Greek mythology, Eastern religions, the occult, psychic exploration, and health food preparation.

Actually, what I am calling the depoliticization of youth culture took two different forms by the late 1960s and early 1970s. On the one hand, depoliticization meant exactly what it says: politics was literally squeezed out of the counterculture. This was the path followed by someone like Charles Reich who, in the earlier-mentioned *Greening of America*, eschewed as "obsolete" virtually everything having to do with politics or power. It was also the path taken by even more extremist individuals within the counterculture who insisted that the whole world of politics was nothing but an illusion. "I don't believe," one member of the youth culture wrote in 1969, "that there is anything like rights and justice, and to the degree I would see myself as hung up with concepts like that, I would be in a circular bag, because there never have been rights and justice."[22]

On the other hand, depoliticization could be taken to mean something a little different, somthing closer to a "poeticization" of politics rather than the elimination of politics altogether. Whenever the will to change social reality was not eradicated, there was still present within youth culture a vaguely political urge to be effective, to make a difference, to improve the quality of life and not simply withdraw into a chrysalis; and no one can deny that sentiments such as these remained very strong within a segment of youth culture. When it came to figuring out *how* to be effective, however, what the counterculture (excepting the New Left politicos) mainly came up with were tactical methods that were mostly symbolic or poetic. Inherent political impulses, in other words, were given what earlier generations would have called nonpolitical forms. The very image of what political activity was supposed to look like was reconceptualized, and this happened to such an extent that in the end the counterculture had a far greater impact on politics, traditionally conceived, than politics had on the counterculture. The whole idea of "flower power," for instance, was a radical reformulation of previous modes of protest. So was the notion that demonstrations should be dramaturgical festivals, and so too was the view that authority is best challenged not by force but mainly by playfulness or unconventional behavior.

It was in this context that the Yippies—the Youth International Party— made their appearance in 1968. Though few in number, the Yippies were symbolically important because of their attempt to fuse politics and culture before each became permanently estranged from the other. Though their efforts at reconciliation were highly imaginative and provocative, the Yippies ultimately failed. They failed not only because they came too late but, more importantly, because their attempt at reconciliation really came down on the side of poetics more than politics. Their forte was the dramatic gesture or an absurdist rhetoric which had little to do with effective, long-term political activity. Despite good intentions, the Yippies turned New Left political protest into symbolic theater, so that once again meaningful politics got lost in the shuffle. Jerry Rubin might be taken as an example. Though statements such as the following reflect a typical Yippie bravado, they also reflect more of a cultural posturing than a credible political position:

I support everything which puts people in motion, which creates disruption and controversy, which creates chaos and rebirth.

What's needed is a new generation of nuisances. A new generation of people who are freaky, crazy, irrational, sexy, angry, irreligious, childish and mad. People who burn draft cards and dollar bills . . . who burn MA and doctoral degrees . . . who lure the youth with music, pot, and LSD . . . who redefine reality . . . who wear funny costumes.

(W)e are the guerillas attacking the shrines of authority, from the priest, to the holy dollar, to the two-party system, zapping people's minds and putting them through changes in actions in which everyone is emotionally involved. The street is the stage.

The longhaired beast smoking pot, evading the draft and stopping traffic during demonstrations is a hell of a bigger threat to the system than to so-called "politicos" with their leaflets of support for the Viet Cong and the coming working-class revolution. *Politics is how you live your life*, not whom you vote for.[23]

The net effect of all this by the end of the 1960s was the envelopment of politics by culture. Much of what remained of the New Left either migrated toward a variety of political sects or got absorbed into the countercultural lifestyle. Rubin was no exception. After passing through his Yippie phase, he experimented with practically every facet of the counterculture, from Transcendental Meditation, to vegetarianism, to est, and after consuming everything on this smorgasbord, he ended up as a Wall Street consultant.[24] An odyssey like this is not surprising once one realizes how much, for Rubin and others, politics had been swallowed up by lifestyle. In a sense, Rubin's later career was already predictable even during his most radical period when he wrote, with a confidence that turned out to be wholly unwarranted, that "Our politics is our music, our skin, our hair, our warm naked bodies, our drugs, our energy, our underground newspapers, our vision . . . *We cannot be co-opted because we want everything.*"[25]

I have made two overlapping points about the 1960s: first that youth culture gradually enveloped the original New Left, and second that cultural lifestyle similarly enveloped, and in the process displaced, a concern with focused political criticism. There is a third and related point to be made, namely that the concept of "personal development" also replaced the idea of "social commitment" as part of the same general cultural shift which was completed by the late 1960s.

At first sight, this last point may not be easy to notice. If, for instance, one looks at what was called the "movement" rather than at youth culture as a whole, the situation appears different. In the movement there were people who were motivated by genuinely selfless impulses—people who acted and often risked themselves because the circumstances seemed to call for commitment, not because they wanted to experience something enriching on a personal level. In these cases it would be wrong to speak of egoism or self-centeredness. However, it is now apparent that the movement was a minority tendency in the 1960s in perhaps the same way that the abolitionists were a minority tendency in the nineteenth century. At least in recent times, a stress on high-minded moral gestures or transcendental ethical values as a model for individual behavior has never been all that common in this country. The mainstream of American culture has instead emphasized the values of individualism and self-fulfillment, and the 1960s were no exception. Even collective experiences like be-ins were looked upon as another way to enrich the inner self or to add to the store of impressions which increased self-knowledge.

During much of our history, but especially during this century, one salient goal for Americans has been the development of what Robert J. Lifton has called the "protean man"—that is, the ever-changing, continually evolving individual whose main task is completeness and self-integraton.[26] For such an individual, ideas and idea systems, political concerns and political commitments, can be dropped as quickly as they are taken up because they are real and important only to the extent that they have a bearing on the self. It was not so different for a majority in the youth culture. As far as they were concerned, it was primarily the self and its processes which were essential; everything else, even the imperative to change the world, was treated as secondary.

If there was a single, unifying thread that ran through the counterculture as a whole, it was probably the drive for self-actualization. Once again, the diehard politicos would have to be regarded as an exception to this rule. For others, however, there was generally a personal motive, a search for "identity," that lay behind the style of youth culture. Of course, this is precisely what the culture industry played up to and helped encourage for its own purposes. If (or so the reasoning went) self-actualization could be defined as immediate gratification, and if gratification could be reduced to consumption, then the cultural rebels could be drawn into the very system they claimed to oppose. Much of youth culture fell into this trap, but *not* because something wholly foreign was imposed upon them from without. The potential for cooptation was there from the start, since the counterculture, despite all its apparent contentiousness, was also very much a part of American culture and therefore shared many of its basic assumptions.[27] Behind both the dissident youth culture and the dominant culture there was the same quest for therapeutic well-being, the same concern with self-discovery, and the same "ethic of self-fulfillment."[28] To a great extent, the rebellious anger of youth culture in the 1960s was directed against those institutional and value constraints *which made self-realization difficult*. Frequently political consciousness went no further than that. There was, for example, an attack on social "roles" but mainly because they promoted rigidity and hindered the unfolding of one's potential.[29] There was also a counterculture assault on sexual mores (which, incidentally, paralleled a similar assault going on in Establishment culture), but usually this call for sexual freedom was not informed by the political dimension which a Marcuse or a Wilhelm Reich believed had to be there if sexual liberation were to be at all threatening to the status quo.

Given all this at the heart of youth culture, it is conceivable that things could have gone differently—that some sort of new culture could have been created—but it is not entirely surprising that the counterculture got drawn into the mainstream of American life. There were some gains that came with this focus on personal development, not the least of which was an expanded notion (before commercialization set in) of what a many-sided self might look like. However, there were also many losses. The one that stands out most prominently, as I have been arguing, is a diminished commitment to radical social change. In order to engage in any social or political struggle, what is required is discipline, perseverance, determination, perhaps even a "fixed identity."

The history of revolutionary movements is filled with people who had these traits; but exactly the qualities of discipline, rigor, and the ability, as Kierkegaard put it, to "will for a long time in one direction" were rejected by much of the 1960s youth culture. Such qualities were invariably identified with the Protestant work ethic which it was the whole point to free oneself from, since this ethic allegedly prevented wholeness, versatility, and the well-rounded personality. In the distant past, a person went through, at most, one profound change in a lifetime, and that with great anguish and soul-searching. In the 1960s, however, it was not unusual to find people going through two or three changes a year, shucking off one personality or set of beliefs and taking on another, all more or less painlessly. However satisfying this may have been personally, it made sustained activity directed toward "larger loyalties outside the self" virtually impossible.

It was in just this setting that an old dilemma resurfaced in the youth culture of the 1960s. It was a dilemma which acknowledged that in order to arrive at a truly good society (one which advocates "individual autonomy, self-expression, and self-enjoyment") it would be necessary to use means which appear to negate exactly these qualities ("self-renunciation, devotion to a common goal, commitment to supra-personal values").[30] The tension between these two poles was never resolved in the 1960s, maybe because it is inherently unresolvable. However, for many the tension was too facilely overcome by simply opting for the first pole over the second, even within a "bad reality." This choice required that one forget about the higher demands of the Great Refusal and instead develop one's self and one's tastes in the here and now. "Don't do it if it doesn't groove ya" is the way one youth culturalist aptly summarized this ethos in 1967.[31] Such advice, which was followed to a significant degree, represented the end of any serious commitment to political or social change.

The easy choice of the Pleasure Principle over long-term opposition to the Reality Principle wrecked much of what was best in the 1960s counterculture. Now we have little more than the ruins of that decade to work with. Yet this is not to say that nothing is salvageable. For those who know how to pick their way through the debris, there is much to be retrieved. Even considering all that went wrong, the 1960s opened up vistas which have hardly been glimpsed in this century. These vistas are still there to be rescued or viewed again. They may have become blurred, but they have not vanished. Among those things that should not be permitted to disappear as *ideals* or *visions* are concepts like participatory democracy; projects such as the attempt to create nonhierarchical social forms; instances of exemplary behavior such as those provided by the Berrigans; and examples of original explorations in music, the arts, theater, and literature which, if grasped at the point *before* they became commodified, can still serve as inspirations for new beginnings. There were also inklings in the 1960s of what, with continued work, could develop into a thoroughgoing critique of everyday life, including a critique of the cultural apparatus itself.[32] Though the more "political" facets of that important period have by now been distorted, defeated, or simply not carried forward, they were once a vital if minority part of the counterculture and should not be allowed to slip away. There is still much there that can be returned to and rethought in a contemporary context.

NOTES

1. The two best collections which capture the mood of the intellectuals in the 1950s are *Mass Culture: The Popular Arts in America*, ed. Bernard Rosenberg and David Manning White (Glencoe, 1959), and *Culture for the Millions*, ed. Norman Jacobs (Boston, 1961), originally an issue of *Daedalus*, 1959.

2. Typically a song like "Sincerely" was taken from the Moonglows and then done differently by the McGuire Sisters. "Shake Rattle and Roll" was originally recorded in obscurity by Joe Turner but subsequently made famous by Bill Haley and the Comets. "Hound Dog" was initially sung by Big Mama Thornton in the mid-1950s but later popularized by Elvis Presley, who sold more than two million copies of the record. For more on this see Joe Ferrandino, "Rock Culture and the Development of Social Consciousness," *Radical America* 3, no. 6 (November, 1969), 27.

3. C. Wright Mills, "The Cultural Apparatus," *Power, Politics and People: The Collected Essays of C. Wright Mills*, ed. Irving Louis Horowitz (New York, 1963), p. 406.

4. Eldridge Cleaver, *Soul on Ice* (New York, 1968), p. 195. Cleaver was basically correct: "Bing Crosbyism, Perry Comoism, and Dinah Shoreism had led to cancer, and the vanguard of white youth knew it."

5. See Lawrence Lipton, *The Holy Barbarians* (New York, 1959), pp. 79, 306–309, and Ned Polsby, *Hustlers, Beats, and Others* (New York, 1969), pp. 144–182.

6. See Kenneth Kenniston, *The Uncommitted: Alienated Youth in American Society* (New York, 1965), especially pp. 68–73.

7. A brilliant analysis of how these tactics have been utilized in an earlier culture can be found in Robert Darnton's "Worker's Revolt: The Great Cat Massacre of the Rue Saint-Severin," *The Great Cat Massacre and Other Episodes in French Cultural History* (New York, 1984), pp. 75–101. See also Robert de Certeau, "On the Oppositional Practices of Everyday Life," *Social Text* 3 (Fall, 1980), 3–43.

8. Charles A. Reich, *The Greening of America* (New York, 1971), p. 4, my italics.

9. Huey Newton, interview in *The Movement*, August, 1968: reprinted in *Movement Toward a New America*, ed. Mitchell Goodman (Philadelphia and New York, 1970), p. 212.

10. Harold Cruse, *The Crisis of the Negro Intellectual* (New York, 1967), p. 441.

11. See Robert Christgau, *Any Old Way You Choose It: Rock and Other Pop Music, 1967–1973* (Baltimore, 1973), p. 95.

12. Jerry Rubin, *Do It!* (New York, 1970), p. 253.

13. This 1967 advertisement is cited in David Buxton, "Rock Music, the Star-System and the Rise of Consumerism," *Telos* 57 (Fall, 1983), 94, my italics.

14. Charles A. Reich, *The Greening of America*, pp. 234–237.

15. A typical defender of this position was Theodore Roszak. See his *The Making of a Counter Culture* (New York, 1968).

16. An example of this position can be found in John Heckman, "On the Role of Youth Culture," *Radical America* 4, no. 6 (September–October, 1970), 75–81; and Paul Piccone, "From Youth Culture to Political Praxis," *Radical America* 3, no. 6 (November, 1969), 15–21.

17. See Christopher Lasch, "Happy Endings," *New York Review of Books* 28, no. 19 (December 3, 1981), 23.

18. On this see Michael Brown, *The Politics and Anti-Politics of the Young* (Beverly Hills, 1967), p. 86, and Stuart Hall, "The Hippies: An American Movement," *Student Power*, ed. Julian Nagel (London, 1969), 191–192.

19. Gridley Wright, "Strawberry Fields," *Southern California Oracle*, August, 1967: reprinted in *The Politics and Anti-Politics of the Young*, p. 92. This is not to say that the hippies were *never* political. The boundaries were usually more fluid than that, especially in the mid-1960s. Sometimes the hippies joined the politicos in both local and national demonstrations. In the 1967 March on Washington they not only joined the protesters but attempted, in one inspired moment, to levitate the Pentagon.

20. See Theodore Roszak, "Youth and the Great Refusal," *Nation* 206 (March 25, 1968), 406.

21. See, for instance, Thomas Pepper, "Growing Rich on the Hippie," *Nation* 206 (April 29, 1968), 569–572.

22. Gridley Wright, "Strawberry Fields," p. 93. Carl Ogelsby, "The Hippies: Suburbanites with Beads," *The Activist* 20 (Fall, 1967), 10.

23. Rubin, *Do It!*, pp. 247–250, my italics.

24. See Jerry Rubin, *Growing (Up) at Thirty-Seven* (New York, 1976).

25. Rubin, *Do It!*, p. 240.

26. Robert J. Lifton, "Protean Man," *History and Human Survival* (New York, 1970), pp. 316–331.

27. "Whatever turns me on is a sacrament" was a statement by one member of the youth culture in 1967. The same attitude informed and still informs most of the established culture. See Hans Toch, "Last Word on the Hippies," *Nation* 205 (December 4, 1967), 582–588.

28. This is made very clear in a recent work by Yankelovich which explores all the various dimensions this "ethic of self-fulfillment" is now taking in the 1980s. Daniel Yankelovich, *New Rules: Searching for Self-Fulfillment in a World Turned Upside Down* (New York, 1981). Peter Clecak has also developed this theme in his *America's Quest for the Ideal Self* (New York, 1983).

29. One reason Richard Sennett's *The Fall of Public Man* (New York, 1977) was attacked by some critics was that he rejected this notion and therefore set himself against one of the prevailing assumptions of the 1960s. Sennett argued that roles are fulfilling and that a person discovers (or becomes) what he is by

taking on, not throwing off, a multiplicity of roles. This view was considered heretical by many of Sennett's contemporaries whose political outlooks, like his, were formed in the 1960s. For an excellent, but very different, discussion of the revolt against "roles" from the 1950s through the 1970s, see Barbara Ehrenreich, *The Hearts of Men: American Dreams and the Flight from Commitment* (New York, 1983).

30. John Edward Toews, *Hegelianism: The Path Toward Dialectical Humanism, 1805–1841* (New York, 1980), p. 369.

31. Hans Toch, "Last Word," p. 586.

32. The first steps toward such a critique have been taken by many whose perspectives were initially shaped by the New Left. See, for example, the works of (among others) Russell Berman, Stuart Ewen, Todd Gitlin, Lewis Hyde, Russell Jacoby, Douglas Kellner, David Noble, and Richard Sennett.

5

Paths to Failure: The Dialectics of Organization and Ideology in the New Left

ANDREW FEENBERG

CULTURE AND POLITICS

Introduction

The new left and the civil rights movement had at first an undeniably heroic character. In the name of the unrealized democratic ideals of American society, tiny groups of white students and blacks confronted bureaucratic intransigence and police brutality North and South. These struggles had a quality of righteousness and courage that captured the imagination of the world.

However, this phase of the history of the left could only last so long as radicals were naive enough to confound testimony to a universal moral law with an effective, instrumental strategy for implementing that law in the society around them. At first miracles happened, and their confidence was justified by the broad, sympathetic reaction of the American people; but miracles ceased as the 1960s faded and the 1970s began. Gradually the apparent failure of moral protest to bring about racial progress in the North and to end the war in Vietnam demoralized the movement.

For a time it was possible to believe that a "cultural revolution" in lifestyles would prove an inexhaustible source of renewal. However, it too was swept up in the debacle and became increasingly apolitical, irrationalist, and, finally, strictly commercial. To avoid this depoliticization, it would have been necessary to return to the roots of the social

This contribution, a revised version of a paper given at the 1977 Howard University conference, is reprinted by permission from *Humanities in Society*.

crisis of American society in this period, of which the existing movements were merely particular expressions, in order to devise a politics
capable of vehiculating the spread of opposition to new groups in forms
appropriate to their needs.

Inspired by China and Vietnam, new communist movements attempted to play precisely this role for a time, arguing with a certain
plausibility that they could break out of the growing cultural sectarianism of the new left. This attempted relay, however, failed as the
revolutionaries were systematically marginalized in the much weakened social movements of the 1970s. The Marxist ideology of those
activists served less to overcome the limits of the new left subculture
than to create a still narrower subculture of Marxists.

For a few years in the early 1970s, the left faced a crisis from which
it could only have emerged through radical changes in its assumptions
and methods. It had either to become a relatively structured political
movement, capable of maintaining itself for a long dry spell without
many spontaneous mass struggles to sustain it, or to sink into obscurity as these struggles faltered. In fact, it is the second of these alternatives which prevailed.

As this became discouragingly apparent, the heroic qualities of the
early years turned into their opposites: spontaneity became disorgani-
zation, courage became provocation, moral opposition sectarianism,
solidarity factionalism, and nonconformity a mere conformity to the
latest fad. This transformation proceeded with startling rapidity during
the early 1970s, repelling millions of individuals drawn to the movement at one time or another. Eventually, no demonstration of intelligence, sensitivity, or sincerity by those activists still seriously pursuing
the original aims of the movement could overcome the handicap of
association with these decomposition products of defeated radicalism.

Why did the movement fail to create durable organizations in this
period? I believe the answer lies in large part in the very strengths of
the new left, which was a profoundly innovative movement blocked
by its own early discoveries and successes from solving the problems
history posed for it as it grew and changed the world around it.

The new left was unique as a political movement in its emphasis on
cultural action and cultural change. Where earlier left movements focused primarily on the distribution of political power or wealth, the
new left was truly "new" in struggling first and foremost to alter the
culture of the society it challenged.

The cultural focus of the new left was a direct response to the emergence of systematic cultural manipulation by government and business
in the mass-mediated world of the postwar period. The oppressive but
brittle political consensus and social conformity of the 1950s testified to
the power of the new techniques of persuasion. It was the "integra-

tion" of this "one dimensional" society that the new left chiefly resisted, and in that it was remarkably successful.[1]

Subjected to new forms of control from above, the American people, or at least a significant fraction of them, innovated new forms of resistance and subversion based on cultural action from below. These new forms of action had the paradoxical property of enhancing the influence and support of the new left for several years while disorganizing it internally to such an extent that it soon disappeared from the scene.

My purpose here is to explain this dialectic. Why was such an exciting and innovative movement so vulnerable to internal disruption, so chaotic, and so oppressive to those who participated in it that it failed to sustain and reproduce itself? I believe that through addressing this question we can learn a great deal about the specific weaknesses of movements based on cultural action from below. Perhaps if we can gain a better understanding of the problems of the new left, we will not be condemned to repeat its errors in the future.[2]

Cultural Action in the New Left

The new left took America by surprise, arising as it did in the midst of an era of prosperity and general societal consensus on everything from sexual morality to foreign policy. Naturally, there were dissenting voices, but even dissent validated the consensus by its elitist tone and its hopelessness. The critics often shared the assumption that America was a success by its own standards, even if they dissented from those standards in the name of a more humane or spiritually satisfying way of life.

Nevertheless, beneath the smooth surface of the society, many problems simmered, problems that could not be articulated politically as they might have been in an earlier period because of the liquidation of the left in the 1950s. Without traditional left organizations and ideologies to represent them, the discontented generated spontaneous movements and new ways of experiencing opposition to the dominant society, independent of the socialist and Marxist heritage of the past.

As the 1960s brought disillusionment after disillusionment, it finally became clear that American society was not at an apogee of peace and prosperity but in the midst of a vast social crisis affecting it in almost every sphere. (The major exception was the economy.) This crisis resulted in the emergence of opposition on a mass scale for the first time since the Second World War, especially among blacks and students.

However, the opposition took unexpected forms. The minorities of the 1960s not only demanded political reform, but also rejected many of the dominant norms that governed the conduct of daily life, proposing an alternative "counterculture" characterized by new sexual practices, drugs, styles of dress, attitudes toward authority and work, and so on.

These cultural innovations reflected levels of discontent that could not find a political outlet because the public sphere had been radically narrowed in scope in the formation of the great American consensus of the day. Thus sexual issues and the family were too "shameful" or too "sacred" to be subjected to rational analysis; the enforcement of stylistic conformity drew extraordinary rigor from the unpatriotic associations of beards, drugs, and other deviations from the norm. Political authority, property relations, bureaucratic expertise, and administrative practices were all placed beyond criticism and cloaked in self-evidence.

Here were precisely the strongest underpinnings of the so-called "consensus" on which the American system was said to rest. To challenge these underpinnings of the system was subversive without being political; it was "cultural."

It is in this context that one must explain the revival of interest in African culture among blacks, the emergence of radical feminism among women, and "lifestyle" politics among young whites. In each case, ideological disagreements with official policy opened the way to a cultural alternative that appeared to provide a framework for personal self-transformation, beyond the oppressive restrictions of the dominant society. As time went on, the role of culture grew relative to ideology in the broadest sectors of the movement.

The political goal of the movement was, to be sure, the creation of a new and more humane social order, but the means to this end was increasingly thought to be not so much political power as the creation of a new human type in the movement itself. Revolution, it was argued, would not create the "new man," but rather the contrary.

The new left also innovated culturally at those decisive pressure points where the social crisis of the 1960s provoked intense political opposition. It was not so much the new left's political demands that were new as its political style. Its practice was a spontaneous adaptation to political struggle in a society dominated by cultural manipulation from above. The new left's great achievement was to find a way to counter such manipulation by acting directly on widely held assumptions governing the framework of public discussion.

In each of the great debates in which it engaged—discrimination, sexual politics, Vietnam—the essence of the new left's political practice consisted in finding persuasive symbols and gestures for signaling its refusal of the accepted terms in which the issues had hitherto been discussed. New left politics shattered the official consensus from the very outset by redefining the issues according to very different assumptions and frames of reference.[3]

So, for example, the black movements sought first and foremost to redefine what it meant to be black in America, as a necessary precondition for accomplishing specific legal or social changes. In the civil rights movement blacks worked to demonstrate their equality by the dignity of their claim to it. Later in the Black Power period, they attempted to manifest themselves as a threat worthy of the respect implied in the recognition of equality, however grudging. In both phases of their movement, the immediate object of blacks' political action was not so much specific laws and institutions as the official social definition of blacks as kowtowing Jim Crows, undeserving of respectful treatment and legal rights by reason of self-imposed dependency.

The new left generalized such challenges to well-established assumptions built into American political culture, and it is this which marked its originality as a movement. It was, in fact, the first modern left movement to employ cultural action from below as its principal form of practice. In this respect the new left resembled many previous major social movements which not only imposed new political demands, but also innovated in the very definition of politics and the public sphere.[4]

There is yet another aspect to the cultural strategy of the new left, and this is the transformation of political identity at the individual level in the context of small "consciousness-raising" groups. This approach, largely but not exclusively identified with the women's movement, involved bringing unconscious cultural assumptions to awareness in order to free the individual from oppression in personal life. Social roles were particular targets of attack, on the assumption that the domination introjected along with the roles could only be fought when the roles themselves were consciously contested.

The strategy of consciousness-raising was based on intrinsic potentialities of modern forms of individuality, the political implications of which had never before been systematically explored. Modern individuals possess what has been called an "accidental" form of individuality, accidental because the individual chooses his or her role, under objective constraints to be sure, but nevertheless with a certain degree of consciousness and responsibility.[5] Precisely because individuals are involved in the choice of their own social destiny, they can distinguish themselves from their roles and sometimes change them. The goal of the consciousness-raising group is to enhance awareness of the gap between the aspirations and potentialities of its members and the possibilities offered them in the roles they have accepted. It provides a social space in which they can become aware of the accidental relation between their own individuality and their social existence.

Consciousness-raising shifted the boundaries between the private and public spheres in ways favorable to emancipatory action. By identifying the oppressive elements in supposedly "private" roles, the left was able to transpose modes of action and resistance customarily associated with the public political sphere into the private sphere, where the dominant practice of civility effectively reproduced subtle forms of oppression and made struggle against them impossible.

The three forms of cultural action described above have in common what I will call a "reflexive" focus on the subject of the action. In each case, the actors are primarily engaged in a self-transformation or self-definition by which they hope to alter their position in the world and their relation to other social groups. It is generally characteristic of cultural action from below that in it the actors begin by taking themselves as the object of their own action. This is, for example, essentially what is meant in Marxist theory by the formation of a "class for itself." Later writings on racial and sexual politics confirm the point that reflexivity is the basis of revolutionary consciousness.[6]

However, we will see that reflexive cultural action in the new left posed problems as well as opened possibilities. The most serious of these problems was exemplified in the total self-absorption of sectarian groups.

A SECTARIAN MOVEMENT

The Politics of Self-Definition

The new left had a contradictory impact on its potential audience. It did accomplish an incredible amount of political work with an enormous variety of people, weakening the hold of the dominant ideology if not overthrowing it. At the same time, the left itself became the chief obstacle to the consolidation of a new political force representing its views on a lasting basis. The objective obstacles to success were of course very great, but all too often the way the left went about overcoming its difficulties demoralized and disorganized its own potential base. In this it proved to be more effective than all the police repression and conservative propaganda arrayed against it. Its own sectarianism and ultra-leftism sustained its energies for several decisive years while dispersing its audience.

Sectarianism in the movement was based on a sense of moral superiority that was effective in motivating an in-group but incompatible with its expansion among those sympathetic to its program. Moral heroism mobilized the troops, but it was accompanied by a characteristic romantic elitism rooted in a sense of differentness, of sacrifice and oppression. A feeling of "alienation" from the supposedly passive and ignorant masses corresponded to this romantic sense of self. Contempt for these masses expressed itself in some movements by identifying them with the enemy; in others this same contempt was veiled in the philanthropic concept of "service to the people." On this basis groups with the most various programs isolated themselves while acquiring internal cohesion and the passion to act.

New left sectarianism was often conjoined to ultra-leftism, the systematic failure to employ strategies realistically adapted to the situation at hand. Instead, many new left groups preferred to substitute individual morality for politics and became obsessively concerned with establishing the revolutionary personal identity of their members at the expense of effective action on the real world. Ultra-leftists became adept at driving a wedge between principle and practice in every kind of situation, blocking the employment of even the most elementary instrumental intelligence in political work.

Both sectarian and ultra-left tendencies in the new left can best be understood as specific disorders of a movement based on cultural action. They are ways in which the reflexive actions of a culturally conscious movement can become disconnected from political and social struggle and transformed into means of personal self-definition.

For many in the movement, its ostensible goal of social change was never a primary preoccupation in any case: the movement was so weak, the prospect of real revolution so dim, the actual achievements of political activism so difficult to compass that the mere existence of the movement became more important to many of its members than any political objective. The scene of the revolution shifted from society at large to the movement itself, where individuals could have an immediate effect on their surroundings through grasping and manipulating the movement's own codes of behavior. These codes made the pursuit of revolutionary purity a respected role through which personal desires for accomplishment and status frustrated in the larger society could be fulfilled.

In the course of making endlessly involuted revolutions within revolutions, the movement's perceptions of the political as an autonomous sphere of social reality grew increasingly dim. Activists tended less and less to measure their actions by their real effects, and more and more sought to conform to symbolic archetypes drawn from the history of revolutions, which came to signify power magically through association with it in theory or in other times and places. Internal movement struggle over the choice of archetypes replaced politically oriented social struggle.

Finally, the most compelling contest in which the movement was engaged placed it not in conflict with the state or the ruling groups but with itself. It was in such an environment that cultural action turned inward and destroyed the movement. Through sectarianism and ultra-leftism the individuals could transform their own personal self-definition, if not the world around them.

The Loss of a Mass Audience

The gradual narrowing of the constituency of the new left was hidden for many by the fact that its numbers constantly increased in the late 1960s and early 1970s even as it lost its most important allies in the society at large. The hope of new allies replaced the real ones whose defection left the movement isolated and exposed to repression.

The new left acquired its significance and identity in the middle-1960s through a style of politics adapted to liberal middle-class allies. At first small groups of radicals, usually students, sought a common ground with oppositional liberal forces outside the movement. This was the case with the civil rights movement, insofar as it involved whites, and at a later date with a large segment of the women's liberation movement. The antiwar movement followed a similar strategy for several important years. The mechanism of these movements consisted in bringing injustices to the attention of the media and then riding the crest of the wave of liberal discontent fomented around the issues in the early phases of the process of cooptation.

This type of movement had a characteristic life history. At first the alliance between radicals and liberals generated a great deal of optimism and activity. It seemed, during this period, that important reforms were about to be made. Everyone concerned got the exhilarating feeling that something new was occurring in the history of politics.

Then everything would go sour, however, and the coalition of radicals and liberals would fall apart. Frustration, impatience, and repression would drive the radicals toward ultra-left strategies while interest, fear, conformism, and common sense would drive the liberals to the right in the face of the increasing militancy of the movement. The situation was "polarized," the middle class "alienated." Isolated and discouraged, the radicals would seek a new issue on which to base the "new politics."

The collapse of the movement on campus was usually an effect of sectarianism. The familiar division of the student leaders of the late 1960s into an "action faction" and a "praxis axis," the one dedicated to militant activity, the other to political propaganda, veiled the common sectarianism that united them. The split between the most ideologically sophisticated or committed students and the mass constantly widened because the former made little effort to meet the latter halfway.

As the generation gap on campus widened, the movement became an ever more artificial replay of earlier occasions, refracted for the mass of participants through the media image of the left. In the worst cases, the search for allies gave way to the striking of impressive poses before the omnipresent cameras that alone made real the objects at which they aimed. The reproduction of the movement was arrested, and the expected relay from one generation of students to the next was interrupted. The four-year cycle of the universities quickly purged them of leaders, and soon the left appeared to most students to be little more than a particularly unsavory form of campus posturing. Similar disasters later struck the movement in each of the other constituencies in which it briefly found a place.

These disappointments did not stimulate much self-criticism, but instead gave rise to a theory justifying sectarian ultra-leftism as a highroad to revolution. This theory was in fact merely the rationalization of an obsessive fear of cooptation. Cooptation meant the loss of independent identity as a movement, absorption into the orbit of liberal democratic reform, a process thought to be far easier than it actually proved to be. Cooptation also meant the integration of entire social strata, such as blacks, through reforms that, it was feared, would remove their motives for revolt; this too has proven more difficult than was assumed.

Cooptation was a threat to be resisted at all costs by asserting the independent identity of the movement through uncooptable demands and gestures and through the development of revolutionary lifestyles. Sometimes political victories were actually feared as contributing to integration and betrayal.

The point is not that the new left should have endorsed Hubert Humphrey as the lesser of two evils; the movement was right to resist assimilation into the official party system where it could only have accomplished institutional and legal reforms at the expense of its capacity to act on the dominant political culture that sustained the evils against which it fought. However, the obsessive fear of cooptation went well beyond the rejection of party politics and ultimately extended to any and all effective political action.

The fear of cooptation testified to a moral rather than a political sense of the struggle. The movement was in fact hostile to politics per se and felt safe only in an atmosphere of pure cultural struggle that posed no threat of compromise. Implicit in the ideology of uncooptability was the categorical imperative that difference must be maintained, that the left must preserve its ostracism and unpopularity as its claim to virtue in an evil world. The imaginative leap from virtue to victory was easier to make in that era than it is today.

The bad faith involved in this obsession is now obvious. In fact the movement thrived on cooptation, which legitimated its attack on the society by conceding the gravity of the problems and the need for reforms. Given its weakness and lack of a mass base, this was the only way it could have achieved an audience at all. The search for the un-cooptable movement as a quasi-magical route to power completely inverted the actual state of affairs. In reality the power of the movement depended directly on its cooptability or, rather, on its ability to spread radical consciousness among some of the enormous masses it artfully involved in movements so just and right that even the authorities had to concede reforms.

The idea that power was a mere function of the counterplay of strategies of demand and cooptation and not an independent reality rooted in institutions, organizations, and the strategic application of force reflected the endemic political weakness of the new left, its overriding concern with self-definition, and its inability to combine cultural action with more conventional instrumental strategies. Eventually, the increasing radicalization of the new left, which was supposed to bring it closer to real power by making its cooptation impossible, forced the entire movement back into narrow political subcultures where it grew in numbers for a time among those predisposed by their position in society to share the illusions of its organizers; simultaneously, it lost most of its support in the larger society.

The Sectarian Dynamic

It would not be fair to attribute the problems of the new left to the personal or political failings of its members. There was no "typical" new leftist whose aggregated defects were writ large in the movement as a whole, nor can the problems be explained as "mistakes" due to bad political decisions. The existence of self-destructive behavioral and ideological styles in the new left is obvious, but the real question is why and how they prevailed against all competing alternatives. The answer to this question lies in the organizational dynamics of the movement. Sectarianism and ultra-leftism were not representative phenomena, but rather triumphed through a specific dynamic that offered bad leaders means for capturing status for themselves and motivating commitment in their followers while discrediting more tolerant and sensible leaders and approaches.

The sectarian dynamic was often initiated by individuals claiming "vanguard" status in the movement by reason of the particularly advanced line of the group to which they belonged or the daring action they proposed, or for reasons of sex or race. Belief without accomplishment, courage, or inherited status now entitled one to power in the movement in place of such customary qualifications for leadership as deeds done, risks run, decisions wisely made. In this way whole social and political categories acquired status in the movement in a hierarchy that mirrored that of the dominant society.

In the student movement, such vanguardism often took the form of claiming that only workers were truly revolutionary. This position demoralized the student movement by telling it that politics was none of its business. Naturally, those who proposed this view were, like their fellows, rarely "proletarians" but most often ordinary "middle class" students who had merely chosen an ideology in which workers held a certain imaginary place.

Those who initiated sectarian struggle could always count on some support from others in the group who accepted what was called the "guilt-trip" "laid on" them by the perpetrators. These happy victims would borrow status in the movement from those who claimed it by reason of race, sex, class, daring, or ideology, and use this borrowed status to dominate others or to survive psychologically in the increasingly hostile environment of their political group. Frequently sectarian minorities would win out through sheer persistence, as the majority of the group they attacked fell away in frustration and self-doubt. A successful sectarian offensive would shatter whatever bonds of solidarity and sense of reality individuals had initially brought to their political work, irreversibly substituting entirely new orientations.

Organizations gripped by the sectarian dynamic often went through a typical cycle. Strong leaders attempted to "raise the level of ideological struggle" by harsh denunciation of political co-workers and potential allies. Within the organization, all those who stood for other policies were stigmatized as "petit bourgeois," "opportunist," "racist," or "sexist," and life was made so miserable for them that they quit. The remaining in-group then began to make fantastic demands on its members in terms of both personal style and labor. Members were encouraged to withdraw from all "bourgeois" institutions in which they worked or organized, and the group abandoned whatever institutional positions of strength it might have acquired before its sectarian mutation.

The developed sectarian group usually behaved in a systematically self-destructive way, making unsuccessful "mass" appeals over the heads of potential allies it had rejected and finding itself ever more isolated. Painful personal conflicts often exploded as everyone sought to shift the blame for difficulties onto others. Frustrations built up which might lead to splits, new attempts, and failures with diminishing numbers. Sometimes the individuals would respond to what they interpreted as the passivity of the masses with the useless sacrifice of terrorism. More often the organization would dissolve as its members "burnt out."

Sectarianism was thus unable to create anything lasting, and yet the unhappy experiment was begun again and again in one group after another all over the country throughout the late 1960s and early 1970s. The movement was so vulnerable to this kind of takeover because sectarian offensives applied typical new left forms of practice within the movement and against it. The legitimacy of these forms of practice was taken for granted, so when "authority" was challenged, "oppression" denounced, meetings "disrupted," or symbolic protests made against the movement itself and in the name of its goals, the movement was disarmed and unable to resist.

The new left was based on challenging the exclusions that formed the negative counterpart of the American consensus. Ideas and groups that did not agree with the consensus and had therefore been denied a voice spoke loud and clear in the movement's protest marches. The new left appealed to a very fundamental assumption about public communication in choosing symbolic protest rather than violence or practical politics as its primary means of action. This is the assumption of reciprocity according to which all participants in public dialogue share an equal right to speak and be heard. If this is true, however, then any participant who is excluded may interrupt the dialogue in order to challenge the fairness of the premises on which it is based.[7]

The new left devised specific rhetorics through which to make such reflexive challenges to the conditions of public communication in American society. The ad hominem regression to racial, sexual, or social status was one of the chief of these rhetorical devices. It was this device that typically was used within the movement to enforce a sectarian turning. The challenger would claim that he or she was subtly suppressed in group discussion by those with white male status or class advantages such as education and, on that basis, would demand a larger share of attention and power. The charge of "elitism" was a sort of generalized rhetorical figure available for use against anyone who seemed to have acquired influence.

The ability of sectarians to impose their views was further enhanced by the new left's challenge to the boundaries of public and private life. To grasp the connection between the "personal and the political" meant identifying and criticizing introjected domination present in the everyday social relations of the races, sexes, and classes of American society. However, in bringing the personal into the political domain, the new left exposed individuals to forms of personal abuse and manipulation they were poorly equipped to resist. The customary protection of the privacy of personal life fell away, and individuals had great difficulty discriminating between acceptable and unacceptable comment on personal behavior and attitudes.

These problems were particularly apparent wherever techniques of consciousness-raising or "criticism/self-criticism" were employed. From a method of emancipatory critique and role distancing, these techniques would be transformed into authoritarian exercises in "re-education" of the "less advanced" by the "more advanced" members of the group. Skill in manipulating the unfamiliar communication system of the consciousness-raising group and the sheer nerve to go for the jugular vein were often effective and rewarded.

In this way, the politics of personal life entered the movement as a means of establishing the ground rules for discussion and decision-making. The prestige of this means as a guarantee of justice often eclipsed conventional democratic appeals to the views of the majority, especially where leftist groups placed a high premium on consensus in decision-making.

Sometimes this procedure had the salutary effect of calling the group's attention to its own hypocrisy in perpetuating hierarchies and exclusions typical of the society at large. However, the left was not armored against the abuse of these rhetorical devices and possessed no well-understood code for countering them. All differences inside the movement, and especially those on the basis of which leadership emerged, were thus exposed to a form of attack against which there was no defense. In the absence of rhetorical equipment for dealing with these problems, and once given the rejection of the customary means of protecting personal privacy, participants in the movement had either to adapt to an environment of high-stakes psychic struggle or to withdraw altogether from the left. Most chose to withdraw.

THE ORGANIZATIONAL DILEMMA

Split!

In the late 1960s and early 1970s, ideology became the subject of endless, agonizing debate in the new left. A split was in the air; the will to unity that had held the new left together through its early years was broken. Thousands of local organizations fractioned along ideological lines between 1969, when the SDS exploded nationally, and the 1970 student strike against the invasion of Cambodia which marked the apogee of the movement. In this section I will consider some of the causes and consequences of the split in the movement.

The polarizing issue at this time was whether or not the left should attempt to build a base in the working class. Ideally, the movement could have encouraged the development of working-class organizing alongside other approaches. In practice, the organizational preconditions for getting in touch with workers were not compatible with those required to develop the movement in its already established constituencies. Not only did the organizational methods appropriate for approaching these two constituencies differ, they were experienced by all concerned as mutually exclusive. Ideology intervened in these splits less as a cause than as a rationalization and an exacerbation of conflicting organizational styles.

As the new left entered this critical period, the majority of radicals abandoned the failing liberal-radical alliances for a more militant politics modeled on the antiimperialist struggles of the late 1960s. These radicals sought above all else to continue this new style of politics, which they saw as alone truly revolutionary. Alliance strategy and organizational methods were therefore subordinated to this prior stylistic commitment.

Central to this new model was a spontaneism hostile to all durable organization and to the attempt to devise instrumental strategies. This spontaneism blocked efforts to build bridges to the small radical minorities emerging in new constituencies in this period. In fact, there was no way to adapt the tried-and-true methods of student organizing and antiimperialist struggle in the streets to the task of contacting radical workers, soldiers, the unemployed, and others scattered among the conservative or indifferent mass of the population, and awaiting the initiative of the left with curiosity and interest.

At this point two routes opened. One could argue that the difficulty of bridging the gap between radicals and these new groups demonstrated the need for organizations employing new methods to bring them together. Left ideas could only be spread among the population at large through abandoning the symbols of the hippie lifestyle and finding new ways of meeting and cultivating isolated radicals or potential radicals in the new constituencies. Partisans of this position generally argued that the habit of reliance on spontaneity formed in the past had to be unlearned if the movement was to deal with its new tasks.

However, it was also possible to argue the opposite position: that the impossibility of spontaneously bridging the gap between the established constituencies of the left and these new ones demonstrated that it was premature or inappropriate to attempt to do so at all. Workers, it was said, would only be radicalized in the wake of the gradual spread of the hippie lifestyle into the factory. Sometimes workers were even dismissed as the "Enemy" and all attempts to appeal to them rejected out of hand.

It is easier now to see the bad faith and self-deception involved in the splits which resulted from this organizational dilemma. On the side of youth revolt, what must frankly be acknowledged as subcultural chauvinism and class prejudice made it difficult even to discuss the need for new styles of organizing. The dismissal of working-class politics was made especially easy by the foolishness of its advocates. They did not confine themselves to pointing out the usefulness of reaching new constituencies, but, rather, they denounced youth politics as positively counterrevolutionary, raised utterly unrealistic expectations, and offered a whole program swathed in an unctuous rhetoric of service and a stilted old-left style.

Given the disastrous results of the splits of this period, it is tempting to blame them for the downfall of the movement, but it was not so much the splits that destroyed the movement as the mark they left on those who went through them. The dialectic of their enmity determined all their later positions. Locked in a bizarre reciprocal sectarianism, each succeeded in excluding the other only at the expense of excluding the entire society as well.

The majority of the movement, committed to the dying youth subculture, lost itself in wild schemes, terrorism, and hopeless "Third World" alliances against the American people, and eventually succumbed to mysticism and the banalization of lifestyle. Meanwhile, the minority that went out "to the people" tried to use the ideology that had justified its break with the mainstream of the movement as a basis for organizing the masses. In fact, the "working-class politics" that motivated the split bore no relation at all to the needs and expectations of the new constituencies to which these radicals appealed for support. Instead of building a base in the working class, they built many "vanguards" and disappeared from view in ideological hairsplitting.

The Mirage of Revolutionary Youth

The debate over organization within the movement was usually formulated in terms of the probable "agent of revolution." Organizational choices were felt by many to depend on the answer to the question, "Who will make the revolution?" However, this formulation was at least partially misleading and usually hid prior ideological and organizational choices.

In fact, the discussion of revolutionary agency was futile since most of the participants had chosen their respective "agents" more on the basis of the kind of political work in which they wished to engage and the kind of revolution they wished to support than on the basis of a serious understanding of the society. To argue that youth or workers were the true agent of revolution was usually to justify an exclusive concentration of tactical energies on the preferred social group and often implied that other groups should accept its leadership.

The predominant spontaneist option was formulated in terms of the concept of "youth" as a new revolutionary agent, displacing the working class in advanced capitalist society. This orientation resulted in the most important misadventure of the left in this critical period, the attempt to rebuild something exactly like the old student movement in the society at large on the basis of the still-spreading cultural revolution.

Radicals who argued that youth culture would be the basis of the revolution usually claimed to be "undogmatic" and offered as proof their rejection of the outdated concept of a working-class movement. They were, in fact, dogmatic in another way: they only recognized as revolutionary those actions which were spontaneous and even violent, actions which created a sense of "community" through struggle and which manifested the revolutionary self-definition of the actors.

The ideological background to this spontaneist orientation is to be found in the attempt of the early new left to found radical politics on opposition to authority rather than on the traditional socialist demand for a change in property relations. Strangely enough, much of the new left shared with the ideologues of the most powerful capitalist society in history the conviction that relations of status and authority could be understood in abstraction from property relations. This made sense in the ideological environment in which the new left arose, which was characterized by total disillusionment with official communist ideology and the absence of any competing form of socialist ideology.

The antiauthoritarian movement was deeply rooted in the crisis of bureaucratic domination in America, in the rebellion against technocratic manipulation in both political and social institutions. As such it was a progressive force and made a lasting contribution to the left by engendering mass awareness of authoritarianism and alienation in both capitalist and communist societies.

The exclusive focus on these themes, however, also helps to explain why the emergence of short-lived spontaneous communities of struggle at peak moments of conflict took on a special pathos and, indeed, for many in the movement, became its essence. Berkeley gave the signal. The 800 students in Sproul Hall seemed to be living an anarchist's dream, demonstrating in practice the possibility of nonauthoritarian forms of social organization freely created and accepted by all in terms of the needs of the moment.

This became so important a revelation to many radicals that they struggled less for the ostensible goals of the movement than for a renewal of the experience of revolutionary community. Around this experience a fetishism of spontaneity developed, counterposing instant and total release from societal repression to the dominant technocracy and the communist alternative as well. From this standpoint, only the spontaneous struggle prefigured the ideal of liberation; hence, only groups available for or engaged in this sort of struggle were truly revolutionary.

The eventual consequences of systematic spontaneism were catastrophic. The struggle against bureaucracy and elitism in the left quickly became a prime mechanism of the sectarian dynamic, disorganizing the groups it was supposed to save. Democratic decision-making was frequently rejected as coercive for the minority under the influence of this spontaneist ideology, but of course charismatic leaders quickly filled the vacuum with their own unacknowledged authority. Often all specialization of political skills was rejected, and any movement requiring technical knowledge or information, such as the environmental movement, was considered ipso facto "coopted" or elitist. Views like these confined the movement to established constituencies that already understood the significance of its codes and symbols.

The movement fared little better in the constituencies off campus. It did succeed in spreading hippie lifestyles and the social freedom they represented, and it created an "underground" press in every major city in the country. However, the youth subculture soon lost its critical thrust, and serious drug abuse and intense competition from religious fanaticism eventually isolated and demoralized the left within it.

The Failure of Socialist Organizing

In the late 1960s and early 1970s, a significant minority of leftists believed the situation in America resembled that which lay at the origin of the great socialist parties. The objective contradictions of the society had produced reform movements in the middle class, at the extreme left wing of which socialist minorities had emerged. Simultaneously, these same contradictions had provoked lower-class opposition, sparking movements of blacks, welfare recipients, soldiers, chicanos, Puerto Ricans, Indians, prisoners, and others. These new movements, however, still lacked socialist political leadership for the most part.

The organizational task was clear: to draw together middle-class socialists and workers' opposition, theory and practice, in the creation of a revolutionary socialist party. Lost allies in the reformist middle class would then be replaced by the traditional union of a left-wing intelligentsia and plebeian social movements.

Implausible as this scenario may sound today, many of its elements taken individually were correctly observed, and the rediscovery of the history of the Russian and Chinese communist movements provided a framework within which many phenomena of American society could be interpreted as steps on the way to the formation of a new revolutionary movement. Most importantly, those who offered this analysis had seen the real need for the movement to overcome its social isolation by reaching out to new constituencies, and they were right to conclude that socialists needed to achieve organizational autonomy within the larger radical movement in order to accomplish this.

Unfortunately, the Progressive Labor Party dominated discussion of the working class in the movement from very early on, and soon other "communist" organizations added their sectarian notes to the chorus. Progressive Labor figures prominently in many histories of the new left, usually as a nemesis. Kirkpatrick Sale, among others, sees it as a subversive force on the left, so totally external to the "real" movement that its victory is inexplicable.[8] This is an inaccurate image of the pro-working-class wing of the movement. While PL and the other "vanguard parties" had a decisive impact on the SDS, it is essential not to confuse these old-left political sects with the tendency of the movement they succeeded in capturing.

This tendency consisted in small local "collectives" or circles of activists formed around tasks associated with labor projects, underground newspapers, socialist bookstores, military organizing, union work, and other community struggles. These were the local groups in which the national "communist" parties fished for members, but the parties did not create the local circles; rather, the circles grew out of the movement and responded to populist beliefs that had always been present in it.

For a time these circles were fairly effective at enabling the socialist minority of the radical movement to unite around new tasks. Despite the bad press this wing of the movement received later, it did serve for a while to support the political development of workers, soldiers, and others attracted to the left, and to spread socialist ideas to constituencies not informed of the activities of the movement by the sympathetic "radical chic" journalism read by better-educated groups. As a result, the left gained a brief presence in the broadening crisis of the army, the ghettoes, and, to a lesser extent, the world of work.

However, these socialist circles were abundantly contradictory phenomena, stretched between their hatred of the larger movement they had left behind and mythic representations of the new one they were attempting to create. These contradictions haunted them from the start, permanently wracked them, and frequently destroyed them. They were like whirlpools on the surface of the society, drawing in large numbers of individuals on one side and thrusting them out on the other. In their passage through these circles, some few people solidified their convictions, gained experience and competences, and went on to seek new activities, but most gave up in discouragement and confusion.

The fatal flaw of these groups lay in their origin, in their harsh rejection of the movement of which they formed a contradictory pole. These groups emerged through the working of the sectarian dynamic, usually on the basis of a poorly digested Maoism. To succeed, the circles would have had to transcend these origins, to forget not only long hair and dope—as they often did—but also the confused ideologies that had originally rationalized their break with the mainstream of the movement. This they usually failed to do, and so they rarely found a new ideological basis for their activities better suited to the task of rooting themselves in the real contradictions and concerns of the constituencies they hoped to influence. Instead, they attempted to involve millions of ordinary people in the internal movement squabbles that had motivated their formation. They were in fact engaged in a typical sectarian maneuver, which consisted in redefining themselves through a reflexive action that they confused with and substituted for effective instrumental action.

The sectarian dynamic through which the circles split off as a minority reinforced their sense of forming an advanced "party," a role they seemed to be fulfilling in breaking with the mainstream of the movement on the basis of socialist principles. This made them extremely vulnerable to the overtures of the national "vanguard parties," which promised to validate this status from above. So long as the circles were involved with fairly significant social movements, the demands of their activities preserved them from the worst consequences of their illusions, but as these movements declined, the independent socialist groups declined with them, became ever more ideologically involuted and divided, and finally the "vanguard parties" recruited the debris.

What was inadvertence, incompetence, and occasionally ill will in the small circles became a matter of principle and a basis for organizing these parties. Thus, as the circles slowly gravitated into the orbit of the parties, whatever openness and effectiveness they had was quickly lost. The parties seemed to believe that their antagonistic relation to the real social movement was the proof of their doctrinal purity. This purity, in turn, confirmed in their own eyes their right to lead the movement they had spurned. The "correct" programs all these parties pushed, however, were unrelated to contemporary American conditions and reflected instead clumsy attempts to impose models drawn from the utterly different conditions of semifeudal societies like prerevolutionary China. Pointing out the discrepancy usually brought on a severe regression to "principle."[9]

The situation of these parties, in direct conflict and competition with the spontaneous movements generated by the social crisis, had disastrous consequences for their self-image and behavior. Relative isolation, pseudo-revolutionary rhetoric, political ineptness, compensatory attachment to foreign models, all combined to produce astonishingly sectarian attitudes and methods of work. It is now clear that the essence of this whole trend in the left was the negation not of the existing society but of the movement. Around this negation there grew up a specific political subculture, as obsessed with self-definition as the hippies, as isolated from the society as the campus, and equally impotent to change it.

THE SOCIAL MOVEMENTS

A Fragmented Movement

Much of what has been described above becomes clearer when viewed in the light of the experience of the most militant new leftists in the major social movement of the time. Their failure to work out reasonable relations with and between the mass movements of blacks and women was decisive. The youth movement was doubtless condemned by its cultural narrowness to remain aloof, and at best working-class organizing would have begun very slowly to alter the ideological environment in the factory. However, the movements of blacks and women were, on the contrary, really powerful and had almost infinite potential.

The new left was betrayed by all its instincts and prejudices in its work within these movements, in particular by its reluctance to admit the need for a "material" level of motivation in the struggle and its demand for ideological and stylistic purity (which was not incompatible with a certain pragmatism that allowed for frequent revision of the principles to which dogmatic adherence was required). These attitudes led the left ever further from the realities of the movements and their actual potentialities toward mythic projections of their vanguard role, unrealistic expectations of the tiny socialist minorities within them, or outright contempt for their "nonproletarian" character.

The traditional socialist movement was always structured around a distinction between "primary" and "secondary" areas of struggle. The party was based on the primary contradiction of labor and capital. The party also helped form and support mass movements based on the various secondary contradictions, such as age, race, sex, and national oppression. Traditional strategy attempted to link up the various arenas of conflict by showing the dependence of the secondary contradictions on the primary one.

The new left was "new" in substituting for this traditional class politics a "radical" politics which rejected the old Marxist emphasis on class struggle in favor of a nearly exclusive emphasis on the secondary contradictions. The new left based its assault on the system not on the struggle of labor and capital but on other contradictions that had always been judged less important in previous left movements. "Radical" social theory in the 1960s and 1970s was characterized by the belief that class struggle had been permanently superseded in advanced capitalist society by struggle around these other issues.

Organizationally, the new left rejected the traditional subordination of the movements around the secondary contradictions to a party rooted in the primary contradiction. Separate and specialized organizations were built on the basis of the various sources of conflict in the society, without a centralizing socialist party to link them together. Organizational separatism freed each radical movement to develop its own leadership and its own self-interpretation without having to depend on traditional socialist parties and codes; but separatism also posed difficult strategic problems. The new left was never able to construct a strategy by which the movements that made it up could be united to attack the sources of power in American society.

What was its strategy in these movements? This is not an easy question to answer: there were many, too many strategies. To the extent that one can identify some main emphases, the following seem to me to be the guiding threads: first, a constant orientation toward cultural action in view of effecting attitudinal change, or change in "consciousness" specific to the secondary contradiction on which each movement was based; second, the pursuit of "equality" through legal reforms and civil rights; and, third, the attempt to combine the strength of the various organizations struggling around the secondary contradictions through a political alliance capable of projecting the power of the left as a whole.

Laid out in this way, the strategy looks more coherent than it proved to be in practice. While organizational separatism did make it possible for each movement to give a high priority to its concerns, it also proved an insuperable obstacle to alliance. Often the separate movements claimed the right to provide leadership for the entire left, in competition with each other. Theories became popular less by explaining than by justifying and perpetuating the divisions in the movement. When the "generation gap" was in vogue, radicals were not supposed to trust anyone over thirty. Radical feminists sometimes argued for the permanent division of the movement by sex. Nationalist theories ratified the separation of the races within the movement.

These fragmenting tendencies were supercharged with emotional content by the overemphasis on personal morality characteristic of the new left. Each movement tended to demand that individual attitudes of potential allies toward race, sex, and authority be fully transformed before the revolution, as a condition for common action. As a result, contacts between groups often contributed to intensifying antagonisms between radicals who claimed to be oppressed in different ways, not only by the "system," but also by each other. Ultimately the new left relied so heavily on attitudinal change that it did not realize until very late that divided it lacked the power to make equally important institutional changes.

The Dialectics of Ideological Development

The fragmentation of the movement was a consequence of its profoundly social character, its rootedness in the problems of everyday life. Where new constituencies emerged, sensitive to new issues, they had to find their own way of understanding the social problems that concerned them, often in isolation from and even against the will of others in the movement. Questions of politics and power came later, more as a way of encoding and articulating social opposition than as a central preoccupation of the new movements.

The initial radicalization of the new constituencies involved a slow subversion of the dominant ideology from within and did not take the form of a clear and sharp ideological break with capitalism. In the absense of a powerful socialist movement, or even of a minor socialist strain in the prevailing political culture, the various movements had no common organization and code through which to unite and communicate. The organizational ideal of the old left, a class-based movement controlling fronts based on other secondary issues, was never a realistic possibility, although one of the political side effects of these new left movements was to provoke widespread interest in socialism as an alternative way of organizing social life.

The resulting "radicalism" was based on what I will call "transitional ideologies," because of their role in mediating between the dominant ideology and the development of a socialist standpoint. Transitional ideologies motivated and rationalized opposition to society by contrasting its most progressive ideological claims with its actual achievements. The participants in these new movements at first reacted against their oppression in terms of the internal contradictions in the dominant ideology they had discovered through their struggles, rather than by reference to a socialist critique of capitalism. Usually transitional ideologies also played a crucial role in articulating the cultural changes and changes in personal self-definition furthered by the movements.

At first transitional ideologies had an unquestionably progressive function because of their ability to rationalize oppositional activity and to articulate new cultural conceptions. At some point, however, these ideologies began to play an ambiguous role. On the one hand, individuals who were exposed to the idea of social criticism and struggle in the more accessible transitional forms soon began to be interested in socialism. On the other hand, whole movements were by this time based on transitional ideologies and demands, and these movements and their leaders were threatened by the rising influence of socialist ideas. At this point, some leadership groups, for example in certain black movements, became consciously and openly hostile to socialism in an effort to fixate the evolving consciousness of their followers at the transitional level. Socialism was no longer perceived as an alien and vaguely daring concept but as a competitor for hegemony.[10]

At one level, the level of practical politics, the moderate leaders were surely correct in identifying the actual limits of the movements they led. At another level, in terms of the growth of an independent movement of the poor and oppressed, these leaders were engaged in a kind of betrayal. Their political realism rationalized the existing relations of force in the society and, in fact, strengthened and conserved these very relations. For this they were legitimately criticized by socialists in ideological struggles that had as their goal making the leap from the transitional to the socialist stage of ideological development. It was in the course of such ideological confrontations that the socialist left was defeated in the social movements.

Unfavorable objective conditions undoubtedly set the stage for defeat, but these conditions probably did not condemn the left as badly as it condemned itself through its inability to adjust to them. A realistic view of the situation would have shown the socialists ways of achieving modest long-term gains. Unfortunately, they were incapable of realism in the exciting atmosphere of the period.

Their experience with the dialectics of ideological development had been lived out on campus and in small radical communities where the passage from pacifism to solidarity with world revolution had been made in a few years' time. This experience continued to shape their implicit expectations, fostering illusions about the effectiveness of ideological confrontationism and about the ideological flexibility of those in society at large. Socialists were quickly marginalized because they did not appreciate the enormous difference between linking the student movement to socialism and performing the corresponding task with social movements such as those of women and blacks.

Two approaches to this task were commonly taken, both of which led straight to defeat. The "proletarian revolutionary" approach was based on the immediate rejections of the transitional ideological basis of the reform movements, of their goals and leaders, and, most importantly, of the new cultural identity the participants had defined for themselves through these movements. For this identity, socialists attempted to substitute a proletarian label that would not stick. Marxism, which might have helped socialists to understand the poor, had been so clumsily assimilated that it merely provided the rhetoric of sectarian polemics, serving rather as an alibi than as a critique of class, sex, and race prejudice.

Simultaneously, other socialists adopted a contrary approach which had a different sort of sectarian outcome. These socialists accepted the cultural innovations of the reform movements and attempted to combine these immediately with certain aspects of socialist ideology. They insisted that the women's and black movements were in fact new revolutionary vanguards, substitutes for the missing revolutionary agency of the politically passive American proletariat. Expectations traditionally associated with the working class were transferred to the new groups, and their revolutionary candidacy for power was proposed. This position led to active involvement with the social movements, but usually on the basis of positions that were so extreme the socialists had to form their own separate groups in the shadow of, and often in polemic opposition to, the larger mass reform organizations they failed to seize and influence.

The most serious example of the first form of sectarianism occurred in relation to the movements of the racially oppressed. Newly Marxified students and ex-students sometimes found it inexplicable that blacks supported reformism and nationalism instead of revolutionary socialism. However, reformism and nationalism were precisely the transitional ideologies blacks needed to free themselves from the dominant racist cultural assumptions under which they labored. No doubt a time would have come when ideological confrontation with reformist and nationalist leaders could have inaugurated a new, socialist phase in the history of black protest in America; but the open and permanent warfare by certain white groups against most black ones in the name of a nonexistent revolutionary proletariat was profoundly offensive to those who daily experienced the reality of racism from all segments of the white population.

Meanwhile, other white radicals attempted to cast the Black Panther Party in the role of vanguard of a revolutionary movement of Third World peoples within the boundaries of the United States, as a replacement for the failed agency of the old proletariat. In fact, blacks could not assume the role of a revolutionary leadership by themselves, with support from insignificant white groups, but had to find some sort of acceptable modus vivendi with American capitalism to survive. Only a great progressive movement capable of altering the real relations of force in society could have freed blacks to pursue massively a more adventurous strategy. The Panthers proved the reality of these limits by the example of the repression they suffered.

The attempt to substitute a female agent of revolution for the old working class was popular among leftists in the women's movement for a time. The most committed discovered a revolutionary vocation as women and tried to organize an autonomous radical feminist movement that would be able to right not only the wrongs done to women, but all the injustices of American society.

In the period under consideration, the women's movement was growing rapidly in an atmosphere of surprising good will. Mass reform organizations arose to which these more radical women had access, and for a time their version of feminism escaped the blistering ideological counterattack of the media and the police to which the rest of the left was exposed. At a later stage, the sectarian dynamic caught hold in the women's groups too and led to the isolation of an important

fraction of the radical wing of this movement from the reformist mainstream of feminism and the rest of the left. The women's movement as
a whole survived these splits better than did the other social movements of the time but not without paying a high and quite unnecessary
price.

CONCLUSIONS

The wisdom of the weak is to advance wherever possible, not at the
strongest point of enemy resistance. The new left simply failed to appreciate its own weakness and the weakness of the social movements
with which it worked. At the turning point in its developent, the left
needed to elaborate the basis for its long-term participation in the social
movements. However, this would have meant abandoning the ambi-
tion to take them over in the short run and to convert them into mass
revolutionary movements.

What was possible, and this was after all quite a lot, was to contribute to growth of these movements, to unity of action between them,
and to the gradual spread of socialist ideas within them. For this, a
prolonged period of political subordination was necessary, but the search
for the revolutionary identity so characteristic of the new left precluded
this solution and tempted leftists to isolate themselves from the only
mass forces active in the society.

The new left contributed new methods of cultural action and dra-
matically changed our conception of sexual and racial politics. It revived concern with the problem of authority and freedom on the left,
which for too long had been indifferent to this whole dimension of its
heritage. As a result, it is now possible to reconceptualize progressive
struggle in advanced capitalist society. As the left gradually reemerges
in the Unites States, it will be able to draw on these achievements and
will find elements of continuity with the past so lacking in the 1960s.
Perhaps the left will someday succeed in playing an oppositional role
while resisting the sectarian temptation. A future movement may find
a way of combining cultural and instrumental action, responding to the
need for a politics of self-definition that became apparent in the new
left not through sectarianism but as a by-product of the growth of solidarity.

NOTES

1. Herbert Marcuse's *One-Dimensional Man* (Boston, 1964) is essential reading for anyone who wants to understand the atmosphere in which the new
left arose.

2. The analysis which follows is abstracted from many cases, some studied

in books, others personally experienced. The interested reader may wish to consult some of the immense secondary literature on the new left for examples. Some starting points: M. Teodori, ed., *The New Left: A Documentary History* (New York, 1969); M. Cohen and D. Hale, eds., *The New Student Left* (Boston, 1967); L. Hamalian and F. Karl, eds., *The Radical Vision* (New York, 1970); Hal Draper, *Berkeley: The New Student Revolt* (New York, 1965); R. Morgan, ed., *Sisterhood Is Powerful* (New York, 1970).

3. For an important study of the strategy and impact of the new left in relation to the media, see Todd Gitlin, *The Whole World is Watching* (Berkeley, 1980). For the background to my approach to consensus here, see Pierre Bourdieu, *Outline of a Theory of Practice*, R. Nice, trans. (New York, 1977). Bourdieu writes:

In class societies, in which the definition of the social world is at stake in overt or latent class struggle, the drawing of the line between the field of opinion, of that which is explicitly questioned and the field of doxa, of that which is beyond question and which each agent tacitly accords by the mere fact of acting in accord with social convention, is itself a fundamental objective at stake in that form of class struggle which is the struggle for the imposition of the dominant system of classification. . . . It is only when the dominated have the material and symbolic means of rejecting the definition of the real that is imposed on them through logical structures reproducing the social structures, . . . i.e., when social classifications become the object and instrument of class struggle, that the arbitrary principles of the prevailing classification can appear as such. (p. 84)

4. Important and very different analyses of the ways in which new social movements alter the definition of the public sphere are contained in Jürgen Habermas, *Strukturwandel des Offentlichkeit* (Neuwied und Berlin, 1962), and Francois Furet. *Penser la Revolution Francaise* (Paris, 1978).

5. The concept of "accidental" individuality is suggested by a passage in *The German Ideology*. See L. Easton and K. Guddat, eds., *Writing of the Young Marx on Philosophy and Society* (New York, 1967), pp. 458–459.

6. For further discussion of the Marxian concept of class consciousness, and the relation of that concept to the new left, see Andrew Feenberg, *Lukács, Marx and the Sources of Critical Theory* (Totowa, 1981), ch. 5, and Feenberg, "Culture and Practice in the Early Work of Lukács," *The Berkeley Journal of Sociology* (1981).

7. For more on these problems, see Jürgen Habermas, "Some Difficulties in the Attempt to Link Theory and Practice," *Theory and Practice* (Boston, 1973).

8. Kirkpatrick Sale, *SDS* (New York, 1974).

9. As Lenin himself is reported to have said: "Principles are invoked by many revolutionary-minded but confused people whenever there is a lack of understanding, i.e., whenever the mind refuses to grasp the obvious facts that ought to be heeded," R. Tucker, ed., *The Lenin Anthology* (New York, 1972), p. 696.

10. In the movements of blacks there were occasions on which this competition led to the assassination of members of the Black Panther Party by members of other organizations.

6

The Medical Committee for Human Rights: A Case Study in the Self-Liquidation of the New Left

RHONDA KOTELCHUK AND HOWARD LEVY

The Medical Committee for Human Rights (MCHR) was on the Selma Bridge at the Meredith march during the height of the 1960s civil rights movement. It attended to the injured during the Washington, D.C., urban riots and at the 1968 Democratic Convention. It served the Black Panthers, Young Lords, and other Third World organizations of the early 1970s. It was with women in support of legalized abortion, with welfare rightists fighting for supplemental food programs, with prisoners rebelling at Attica, with the National Liberation Front fighting to end the war in Vietnam, with hippies running free clinics, and with workers struggling for occupational health and safety.

In short, the MCHR was anywhere and everywhere there was movement in the decade from 1964 to 1974. There were, to be sure, other health organizations that for shorter periods during that decade also played important roles. It is conceivable that in the long run some of them may prove to have been of greater historical importance. As a reflection of the turmoil, conflict, and contradictions of political movements as it pertained to the health Left, however, only the MCHR provides an adequate canvas on which to depict that period in the richness, color, and tone required for accurate interpretation.

What follows represents an attempt at an analytic history of the MCHR. It is our hope that this account will catalyze serious reflection, discussion, and debate concerning the many issues confronted by the movement of the 1960s, issues that promise to recur, albeit perhaps in different forms, in the movement of the coming decades.

An earlier version of this contribution appeared in *Health PAC Bulletin* (March/April, 1975). Reprinted by permission.

The MCHR suffered from many of the same unresolved theoretical and practical limitations as did the rest of the American Left. Further, its wane was coincident with that of the larger movement. This fact, however, provides scant solace or excuse for those concerned with building a viable radical movement. It is our contention that unless the shortcomings of the past are presented, understood, meditated upon, and ultimately overcome, we can except nothing but a repetition under new guises of the same errors that plagued us in the past and that still plague us. We realize that this runs contrary to a strong tendency pervading the American Left and having its roots in the character of American pragmatism: to forget or ignore the past and to turn optimistically to the future, vowing to "try harder next time." Nonetheless, it is our hope that such resistance can be surmounted and that at least the beginnings of such a process will be stimulated by what follows.

One night in June, 1964, three civil rights workers were arrested for speeding in Neshoba County, Mississippi, while investigating the burning of a black church. The sheriff claimed to have released them shortly after their arrest. A month later their savagely beaten and mutilated bodies were found buried eighteen feet under a clay dam. The names James Chaney, Michael Schwerner, and Andrew Goodman flashed across television sets all over the country. Millions of Americans were shocked, angered, and more determined than ever to complete the crusade for which the young men had given their lives. Mississippi was to be liberated by exorcising racism and hatred from its bowels.

The year was that of the Mississippi Summer Project or, as it became known, Freedom Summer. Though supported by a coalition of civil rights organizations including the Congress of Racial Equality (CORE), its phosphorescent guiding light, moral impetus, and catalytic energy was provided by the Student Non-Violent Coordinating Committee (SNCC). The silent 1950s were over as thousands of Americans, mostly students, trudged off to the front lines of Mississippi to be greeted by bombings, beatings, arrests, state troopers, ferocious dogs, and sometimes death.

Up to this time the medical community had been mostly quiescent. There were, however, progressive medical organizations still functioning as holdovers from the Old Left of earlier eras. Despite their low energy levels, they represented latent forces for social commitment within the medical community and set the stage for the MCHR's emergence.

In New York City, the Physicians' Forum held educational meetings, issued pronouncements on current issues, and wrote legislative proposals that were almost invariably ignored by a Congress that with all deliberate speed was going nowhere. Not that members of the Physicians' Forum and similar organizations had never known struggle. Many had a history of political activity dating back to the Communist Party of the 1930s; some had been on the front lines of the founding of the CIO; a few had been on the even tougher front lines of the Spanish Civil War fighting on the side of the Loyalists. They may in practice have accepted the 1950s ideology of the end of ideology, but, unlike their medical colleagues, they had been bitten and sensitized by the political bug. Their concern was heightened now by the fact that many had children who had gone South to join the fight for freedom and justice. With the killings of Chaney, Schwerner,and Goodman, they, as well as similar groups in other cities, were galvanized into action.

Toward the mid-1960s organizations with a more explicit civil rights focus sprang up within the medical community. In 1963, for example, a group of doctors, mostly from New York City, organized the Medical Committee for Civil Rights (MCCR) in response to the growing militance of the civil rights movement. Its first officers included John Holloman and Walter Lear, both destined to play central roles in the MCHR. Other MCCR members later to join the MCHR included Tom Levin, Aaron Wells, Charles Goodrich, and Paul Cornely.

The MCCR saw its role as challenging segregated medical facilities in the South and segregated local medical societies. In early June, 1963, the MCCR wrote to the president of the American Medical Association (AMA) appealing for the " . . . termina[tion of] the racial exclusion policies of State and County Medical societies . . . direct membership in the AMA [for] Negro physicians who are denied membership in their State and County medical societies . . . oppos[ition to] the 'separate but equal' clause of the Hill-Burton Act." On June 20, following AMA inaction, twenty MCCR doctors, all wearing suits and ties, shocked the medical community by picketing the annual convention of the AMA in Atlantic City, New Jersey, in what the MCCR described as a "dignified public protest." Later that summer the MCCR published its first newsletter, announcing its support for the upcoming March on Washington for Jobs and Freedom, which had been promoted by all the leading civil rights organizations. The MCCR that year also testified before Congress in support of pending civil rights legislation.

Another group, albeit a nascent one, played a role in the genesis of the MCHR. In the early 1960s Tom Levin, a clinical psychologist in New York City, gathered together a mailing list of psychologists and social workers who had given money and support to the civil rights movement. The group, called the Committee of Conscience, became the first medically oriented group to make contact with the Southern-based civil rights movement when Levin went to Mississippi to obtain firsthand information about brutality against civil rights workers. The contacts Levin made, in particular with the SNCC and CORE, later proved to be the direct link to the MCHR.

In Los Angeles the Charles Drew Society had an ongoing concern with discrimination against black doctors. In Chicago the Committee to End Discrimination in Medical Institutions (CED) was the MCHR's direct predecessor. Indeed, two of its members, Quentin Young and Irene Turner, were to assume preeminent leadership positions (nationally and locally, respectively) in the MCHR.

The killings of Chaney, Schwerner, and Goodman resulted in a panicked telephone call to Tom Levin from James Forman, head of the Council of Federated Organizations (COFO). Although neither Forman nor Levin had a clear idea of what should be done, a series of hurried phone calls resulted in a meeting two days later of twenty-five to thirty largely older white and black professionals held in the office of Dr. John Holloman.

One of the doctors present was Edward Barsky, a surgeon who had served as the chief medical officer of the Lincoln Brigade during the Spanish Civil War. Perhaps out of his experience it was proposed that a "sort of Abraham Lincoln Brigade" be sent to Mississippi. By July 4, 1964, with vague sense of action and little sense of strategy, the first team of doctors flew to the Magnolia State on what was called a fact-finding mission. The team included Tom Levin; Elliott Hurwitz, chief of surgery at Montefiore Hospital; Les Falk, a deputy director of the United Mine Workers' health program, the national office of which was located in Pittsburgh; and Richard Hausknecht, a private-practicing New York City gynecologist.

Once on Mississippi soil the team scattered in different directions. Those more or less sharing a public health perspective, such as Falk, spent their time investigating segregation in local health facilities and exploring the local health establishment, particularly the black medical establishment, in search of people willing to meet the needs of civil rights workers. They concluded that what needed to be done was to directly fight segregation in southern health institutions. They suggested that the separate-but-equal clause of the Hill-Burton Act was a potential "action wedge" for such a program.

Tom Levin, on the other hand, spent most of his time "on the front lines" with Bob Moses, SNCC leader of the Summer Project. After touring the battlefield, Levin concluded that what was needed was "medical presence" to directly aid the beleaguered civil rights workers and to employ the prominence and wealth of northern doctors in support of the civil rights movement (the idea, in fact, behind Levin's Committee of Conscience).

When the team returned to New York City everyone agreed about one thing—that an organization was needed. At the suggestion of Falk, it was named the Medical Committee for Human Rights. As to exactly what, however, the organization was to be and do, there was disagreement—in a form that was to become prototypical of future debates within and about the MCHR. At stake was the question: What is the MCHR?

The seemingly more militant camp identified with CORE and the SNCC, the most militant civil rights organizations, and pushed the notion that the MCHR should be a support organization for the civil rights movement, providing medical care on the front lines, that is, medical presence. Those less enamored of civil rights militance argued for a direct assault upon Mississippi's two-class health-care system. Paradoxically this apparently less militant approach would have given the infant organization an independent and self-defined role. The seemingly more militant approach of medical presence won out, however, and defined the MCHR as an adjunct of the civil rights movement.

In this decision lay the kernel from which the MCHR's legacy would grow. Later the civil rights movement would be replaced at different times by the antiwar movement, the Black Panthers and the Young Lords, the American Indian movement, the prison reform movement, poor Appalachians and workers on the job. However, the MCHR would never escape the legacy (some might say the curse) of being a service-and-support organization attached to whatever movement was most current or fashionable at the time; and at every step of the way, those within the MCHR pushing for the closest association and identity with other movements would be regarded as the militants and radicals.

In the MCHR's earliest days the position of the less militant faction was not helped by their nagging, mostly behind-the-scenes opposition to Aaron Wells, a black New York City doctor, as the first chairman of the MCHR. Several black doctors who had been present alluded in retrospect to the opposition to Wells as the first sign of latent racism within the organization, a charge that was to be echoed before the MCHR completed the civil rights phase of its history.

Every two weeks like clockwork through the summer of 1964 the MCHR sent twenty to forty doctors, nurses, and students into Mississippi. The nerve center of the operation was the Congregational Church (United Church of Christ) in midtown Manhattan which, at the request of Dr. Connie Friese, a member of the church and of the MCHR, made space available free of charge. At first Tom Levin directed the project; later the job was assumed by Des Callan, a young New York City doctor working at the Columbia Neurological Institute. During this period John Parham, originally within the Urban League, had responsibility for the day-to-day operation of the national office. In the South the MCHR found a dependable ally in Bob Smith, a black doctor who had been providing most of the medical care to the civil rights workers. The MCHR decided to set up a full time office and hire staff. By 1965 Dr. Alvin Pouissant headed the Jackson office.

Early leaders of the MCHR stated their goals in amorphous terms, but most members shared at least some of the following purposes:

1. provision of direct medical aid to civil rights workers;
2. provision of a medical presence at demonstrations and marches, designed to forestall brutality against participants;
3. appeal to the conscience of health professionals and the general public to gain support for the movement; and
4. raising money for the civil rights movement.

With the exception of providing medical aid for civil rights workers, the remainder of the program was necessarily geared toward public relations and placed strong emphasis upon professionals, especially doctors. This posture was reflected by the operation of the national office of the MCHR in New York City. An early advertisement in the *New York Times*, for example, raised an astounding $80,000. There was something incongruous about the high-stepping fund-raising parties and dinners at some of New York's poshier hotels, the Columbia University Faculty Club, and the Caprice Restaurant ("entertainment by Bobby Short!"), all ostensibly for the benefit of black sharecroppers in the Deep South. In the bewitching spotlight of publicity in which MCHR doctors basked, the organization lost sight of the fact that much of the day-to-day nitty-gritty work down south was being done not by doctors but by nurses, who barely had access to the wings of the stage, let alone the footlights.

Nurses such as Phyllis Cunningham, who had formerly worked with the SNCC, along with a few doctors such as June Finer, worked full time, night and day, traveling sometimes dangerous backroads of Mississippi to provide first aid for civil rights workers and community people and to hold classes on childhood diseases and nutrition for black mothers. They also observed firsthand the effects of segregated hospitals, clinics, and doctors' offices and became less and less enamored of simple medical presence.

Members of the MCHR originally thought of Mississippi as a battlefield and romantically envisioned themselves going to give first aid in the trenches. According to Des Callan, however, once MCHR doctors got to Mississippi they discovered that despite isolated physical attacks on civil rights workers, their gory expectations had been greatly exaggerated. This fact, together with the growing demands of SNCC militants and the perceptions of the MCHR's nurses, threw the emphasis upon medical presence and its public relations foundations into serious question. As Cunningham later commented regarding the visiting-fireman approach, "Pompous liberal doctors could think highly of themselves by daring a two-week voyeuristic trip to the wilds of Mississippi but then go back home and without batting an eye continue their lucrative, and often racist, private practices." Most galling of all to the nurses was that while the MCHR was paying them "peanut butter and jelly" wages for unstinting service, it, at least during the first year, was usually paying its doctors their plane fare and expenses for their brief appearances. Nor did it help matters when the doctors, according to Cunningham, referred paternalistically to the "grand work being done by our little maids in Mississippi."

The tensions felt, particularly by non-doctors and women, were barely articulated in the 1960s but were to erupt with devastating fury by 1971. In the meantime, on the surface at least, the MCHR appeared the picture of health. Participation increased and financial stability seemed at hand. In September, 1964 the MCHR decided to form an ongoing national organization with locally based chapters. Chapters rapidly sprang up in New York City, Washington, Boston, Chicago, Detroit, Philadelphia, Los Angeles, and San Francisco. By April, 1965, at its first annual meeting in Washington, at-large membership was extended to people in cities where no local chapter existed.

Local chapters, as spelled out in the Executive minutes, were "to have maximum local autonomy consistent with a functioning national body." Ostensibly membership would not be limited to doctors or professionals, although those same minutes reveal the MCHR's ambivalence on the question: "Anybody interested and *who can function* [italics ours] is welcome." On the question of voting rights the MCHR's professionalism and paternalism were undisguised: "We should not restrict ourselves to medical personnel; the majority will always be physicians. Let us act in magnanimity and not limit ourselves."

Whatever the interpretation of the rhetoric, in the years 1964 to 1966 the MCHR's style was dominated by doctors, though by 1965 there was a large influx of nurses and medical students into the organization. An indication of the leaders' real resistance, however, to consumer involvement was their reaction when a group of Mississippi black people asked to address the 1966 annual convention in Chicago. After much haggling, each consumer was allowed one minute to address the dignified assembly. To compound the irony, the convention's keynote speaker was Dr. Martin Luther King.

As early as 1965 the MCHR began to lose ground and support, at least of its original base, through quiet attrition. Early leaders such as Tom Levin began to drift away, in part because of the doctor-dominated atmosphere of the MCHR. The black doctors who had provided so much of the early leadership were also early departers. Some merely wished to devote more time to the pursuit of their growing private practices. Others moved on to organizations more appropriate to their social concerns than the MCHR. Several turned toward the National Medical Association (NMA), and in 1966 John Holloman was elected to the NMA presidency.

At about the same time the MCHR lost many of the public-health-oriented doctors who had made up its early roster. For some, who surmised that a movement could not be created to confront the southern two-class, racist health system, the alternative was to push for foundation and federal money to establish community health centers to serve the black community in the Deep South. Eventually Jack Geiger, one of the members of this group, succeeded in opening the much-heralded Mound Bayou Health Center in Mississippi. However, the very decision to seek an alternative represented both the failure and the abandonment of the earlier struggle, and those sharing the alternative vision soon left the fold of the MCHR—and the movement.

Still through 1966 there was no sense of crisis. The MCHR tried to "keep on keepin' on" with the civil rights movement, providing medical presence as it marched that year through Mississippi on a mammoth voter registration drive. It was on this march that James Meredith, the first black student admitted to Ole Miss, was shot. It was also during this march that Stokely Carmichael, an SNCC militant, first shouted "Black Power!".

The contagion of these two words threw the civil rights movement into disarray, as the more militant leaders and soon the SNCC itself began to question whether white participation was more a hindrance than a help. Having been rejected by the very cause for which they felt they had sacrificed, whites abandoned the civil rights movement. White participation plummeted and with it white support and financial contributions from the North.

No less than other organizations, the MCHR was thrown into a tailspin. As one MCHR communique put it, "The financial situation has not improved during the summer and it seems that there is little interest by MCHR members since the Meredith March." Indeed, only 25 percent of MCHR members responded to urgent fund-raising appeals. For the first time there was discussion of whether the MCHR should continue and, if so, what its role should be.

By this time many of the prominent and busy doctors who had founded and shaped the early MCHR had left it. They had been happy to step into a heroic role when history called on them, but must had no ongoing radical commitment and certainly no ongoing commitment to the MCHR. It had become clear that the early MCHR had been dominated by too many generals and had too few soldiers. The generals had no patience to stick around at a time of great confusion to chart out a new course for the organization. To the extent that a few may have wondered about sticking it out, they were soon enough dissuaded from doing so by the shift to the left that the MCHR was about to take.

A harbinger of this shift had taken place at the 1965 annual MCHR convention when younger members, mostly doctors and medical students, proposed that the MCHR adopt a resolution denouncing the war in Vietnam. Although the resolution was defeated that year by a narrow margin, it was passed at the next convention.

The old guard within the MCHR was not ready to take a stand on the war and could see little relevance of the war to the MCHR's civil rights concerns. Their qualms were greatly magnified by the fact that those who pushed the antiwar position were also beginning to vocalize, largely in response to demands of Black Power militants, the need to do something about medical care back home in the North. This meant attacks upon the medical system in which many of the older members had vested interests. This was the last straw; nearly all of the remaining older members bid the MCHR adieu.

By 1967 the MCHR was a dead letter in New York City, but there was still vitality in Chicago, and it was logical to move the national office to the Midwest. From that time on no name stands out more clearly in connection with the MCHR than that of Quentin Young, who came to be regarded by many as "Mr. MCHR."

In 1967 Young was a youthful-looking forty-four-year-old internist with a private practice catering to the mixed university community of Hyde Park and assorted movement people. He had been active in the MCHR since its founding in 1964. Earlier, Young had been involved with the Committee to End Discrimination in Medical Institutions in Chicago and before that with various political activities of the Old Left. Even with this extensive political experience under his belt, Young clearly had his work cut out for him with the MCHR.

With the eclipse of the civil rights movement Young inherited in the MCHR an organization in danger of losing its raison d'être. Nor was there any new issue current on the Left that could provide the holistic, even if transitory, sense of direction that the civil rights movement had so readily furnished.

For a while it looked as if the MCHR might be successful in turning the corner. In June, 1967, it was applauded with front-page headlines when, in conjunction with the Poor People's Campaign, an MCHR member disrupted the AMA convention in San Francisco by seizing the microphone to denounce the MCHR's arch foe, while other activists picketed outside the auditorium. Aside from keeping the name of the MCHR alive and helping recruit new blood to the organization, the event also served as a model for similar demonstrations at subsequent AMA conventions in other cities.

In 1968 the MCHR again hit the front pages, this time for its role in ministering to the victims of the police riots at the Democratic National Convention in Chicago. Shortly afterward the MCHR again gained prominence when Quentin Young was subpoenaed to testify before the House Un-American Activities Committee (HUAC) concerning the MCHR's role at the Democratic convention. Again in 1969 the MCHR was in the public eye as it provided aid and medical care to the 2,400 poor residents of Resurrection City in Washington, D.C.

The MCHR's success in the newspapers, added to its earlier civil rights reputation, gave it an important asset. It acquired a national prominence and recognition among the medical community that would bring it new recruits for years to come. More than that, these spurts of activity offered the hope of carrying the organization through a period of confusion and dissipation. For at no time was the MCHR more in its prime than when it was responding to the dramatic medical needs of one or another movement group. A need which these spurts of activity did not fill and, in fact, may well have hidden, was the need for an ongoing political program that could guide the organization when the dramatic requests faded and that could engage old members as well as integrate new ones. When it came to articulating such a program the MCHR fell back on grandiloquent pronouncements, such as "we argue that health care is a human right . . . that our economy should . . . make available to all the people." Hard to disagree with, but hardly a prescription for a program.

That the MCHR could articulate no meaningful national program during this period should come as no surprise, for the years 1967 to 1971 were not in general good years for national organizations. Rather this was the era of suspicion of leadership, structure, and central direction, of extreme local autonomy, and of "doing your own thing." While the national organization shrank to a mere vestige, local chapters attained varying degrees of apparent vitality.

The year 1967 introduced an almost entirely new cast of characters into the MCHR. As the older doctors left, they were replaced by younger doctors, nurses, and, more importantly, by nursing and medical students. Many of the medical students, in particular, had been activists within the Student Health Organization (SHO), which had burst onto the radical health scene in 1966.[1]

This is not the place to discuss the politics of the SHO, except insofar as they impinge on the MCHR. Perhaps because its summer project orientation so successfully capitalized on student energy (even as Freedom Summer had) or perhaps because of its early success in gaining funds and support, the SHO during this period was viewed by all as the more vibrant and vital of the two organizations. Many identified with both, and the more committed SHO members graduated into the MCHR in the late 1960s as they graduated from their medical schools.

It is important to recall that many SHO members had been recruited into political activity as undergraduates and were influenced by the Students for a Democratic Society (SDS) and the model it presented for community organizing, the Economic Research and Action Project (ERAP). For SHO as well as many MCHR members, this influence, in addition to the influence of Black Power, was all important. Members of SHO tried to respond to the insistence of their former black civil rights compatriots: they went back to their communities in the North to fight against white racism. This often resulted in projects seeking better services for Third World and poor white communities. When applied to health, these projects occasionally confronted institutions such as local health departments that denied adequate care to the poor or medical schools that refused to admit significant numbers of Third World students. By and large, however, early SHO and later MCHR projects had a distinctly service-and-support-oriented flavor. This was the genesis of projects like lead screening, sickle cell testing, childhood immunization, and rat control.

Despite the new faces and the emphatic orientation toward local as opposed to national projects and organizations, however, much of what the MCHR was during 1967 to 1971 was a continuation of what MCHR had always been—a medical support group for movements outside the health-care system itself. All that had transpired between 1964 and 1967 was that the unitary civil rights movement had fragmented into half a dozen movements, with the MCHR now trying to serve them all. This is not to say that medical support work was bad. It was not, and often the MCHR's services were urgently needed. It is only to say that the MCHR never developed a conception of itself that went beyond support, a fact that was to prove severely debilitating, if not devastating, as the political movement of the 1960s moved into the disillusionment, fragmentation, and demise of the 1970s.

No movement shows the MCHR's orientation more clearly than that against the war in Vietnam. While the war may have been driven home to many participants by the threat of the draft, the tone of the antiwar movement was one of support and service to the Vietnamese people. It was for many the direct descendant of the civil rights movement transported by American militarism and imperialism some 10,000 miles away.

Like others in the antiwar movement, the MCHR members organized opposition to the war in their own institutions. Leaflet and literature tables blossomed at medical schools, and contingents carrying bold banners inscribing the names of local MCHR chapters, schools, and hospitals appeared at antiwar demonstrations. So overwhelming was this political thrust that for an entire year the New York City chapter of the MCHR was literally submerged into the Medical Committee to End the War, which in the spring of 1967 turned out over 2,000 health personnel for an antiwar rally in Central Park.

The MCHR went beyond general antiwar activities to play a more specific support role, serving as the medical arm of the antiwar movement. Hence almost all MCHR chapters set up a system of draft counseling and referrals for physical examinations to serve young men seeking medical exemption from the draft. One exceptional draft panel in Los Angeles proved an embarrassment to the MCHR when it turned out that participating doctors were pocketing thousands of dollars in private fees for performing draft physicals.

An even more direct transfer of earlier tactics was the medical presence MCHR members provided at antiwar demonstrations and marches. In San Francisco, for example, the local MCHR chapter was largely absorbed by the pressing need for medical presence in the Bay Area. Hardly a day went by without the police attacking a group of demonstrators, ofen antiwar, but also black students (as in the San Francisco State strike) and years later white community-control advocates (as in People's Park). Necessary and commendable as such support work was, still the episodic nature of this sort of activity forestalled coming to grips with consideration of the development of a more organic program for MCHR members.

Although a bit more complicated than the antiwar movement, the role played by the MCHR in the second great activity of the late 1960s—the counterculture movement—was fundamentally similar. The year 1967 marked the birth of the Haight-Ashbury Free Clinic, the flower child, and the long-haired hippie. The counterculture proved to have a magnetic attraction to young health workers and students.[2]

Indeed the counterculture suggested a way out to health science students, interns, residents, nurses, and technical personnel who felt oppressed by years of grueling study, regimentation, pleasure denial, and hierarchically ordered health institutions. These young professionals had come to understand that health-science education involved more than learning about disease diagnosis, treatment, and (least of all) prevention, but rather involved a total socializing process. Doctors and nurses were being taught to accept their class and professional roles, along with the attendant alienation.

If medical and nursing school and hospital medical practice seemed to embody the objectivization of young professionals, then the recovery of subjectivity that free clinics and the counterculture seemed to offer came as a godsend to many. They represented a strong antidote to the treatment of students as computer punch cards. (The "do not bend, fold, or mutilate" mentality of college deans pertained no less to health-science school officials and hospital administrators.) In free clinics young professionals saw the promise of rebellion, a new lifestyle, immediate fulfillment, and an overcoming of the personal alienation, ego disintegration, and humiliation that had been their daily bread for all of their lives. Free clinics seemed to offer not merely a vision of the future but a utopia in the here and now. Moreover, so it was claimed, by the sheer weight of their example they would undermine the values of the health system.

While few local MCHR chapters actually set up their own free clinics, almost all chapters had members whose major energies were expended working in them. Some were attracted to this work by the "good vibes" of the counterculture, but more politically sophisticated MCHR members rejected as fatuous the political claims made in support of free clinics. Indeed, for many MCHR members the attention paid to the middle-class, white hippie clientele of the earliest free clinics represented a self-indulgent waste and sellout of the needs of the most oppressed members of American society.

Free clinics, however, were not long to remain the preserve of the counterculture; free clinics fit perfectly into the community-organizing strategies of the Black Panthers, I Wor Kuen (a revolutionary group in New York City's Chinatown), and various revolutionary Chicano, Puerto Rican, and immigrant white Appalachian groups in the Midwest and on the West Coast.

The dilemma in which MCHR activists working at free clinics found themselves illustrates a bind inherent in the MCHR's service orientation; MCHR activists began by simply asking how their medical skills could be used to best advantage on behalf of movements for social change. They thereby unwittingly imported a medical model of social change. Given the free clinics' severely limited resources, their choice was to serve a minuscule number of people in a model of humanized care, in which case the clinic was medically irrelevant, or to accommodate a greater load of patients in traditional assembly-line fashion, in which case the clinic had abandoned its original ideal of providing an alternative to mystified, alienated, and hierarchical forms of medical practice. In many cases, clinics tried to do a little of both, which resulted in no one's being satisfied. The simple transfer of medical expertise to the service of the movement resulted paradoxically in a failure to politicize health care—an objective that should be the very quintessence of a health movement.

The attachment to the counterculture and to political free clinics were both misdirected approaches in that both obscured the socially determining role played by established health institutions in distorting health care toward dehumanized services for patients and an alienated work environment for health personnel.

During the civil rights era, MCHR militants were those who, through medical presence, allied themselves most closely with the most militant civil rights organizations. Likewise, during the late 1960s, a similar identification took place, except that now MCHR militants were those who worked for the most politically "radical" free clinics. The analogy can be carried further: in both instances MCHR militants sought their identities through transference to groups that purported to represent a class, and often a race and culture as well, that were different from their own.

This search for identity through identification with society's most oppressed groups was not limited to MCHR members but was endemic to large parts of the movement. It stemmed from an unresolved and unmediated sense of guilt deriving from the activists' own privileged class and professional status. However, without coming to terms with this dilemma, MCHR members could not accept themselves as legitimate agents of change, much less consider the legitimacy of their own needs. The alternative for health radicals was to submerge their own needs (and hope they would not reassert themselves in too distorted a way) and to look to ostensibly more revolutionary groups for leadership. This is not to say that there is an easy resolution to the conflicting needs of these two groups—the poor, driven by their deprivation to seek material gain and inclusion in society's benefits, versus the more privileged, driven from materialism by alienation and a sense of their own impotence. At the very least a viable radical movement in America will have to recognize and deal with the needs of both groups.

Unfortunately, the tendency of the more politically aware MCHR members to define their identities through the eyes of a class other than their own led to what can only be called a compulsive need to constantly raise the ante: if political commitment was defined as service to radical groups, then one's self-assurance as a radical required constantly seeking out and attaching oneself to what appeared to be the most radical group on the scene. Anything less was a copout.

This dynamic meant that the MCHR was at the beck and call of whatever group could most skillfully manipulate its guilt. In 1970, for example, a group of medical students at Northwestern University Medical School in Chicago, on behalf of a coalition of political free clinics, challenged the MCHR's doctors' commitment: " . . . why hasn't MCHR contacted these bullshit physicians and demanded their participation?" The students went on self-righteously to demand that if the doctors refused to donate their time, " . . . they are to be removed from the organization." Finally, if this was not done, the Northwestern Health

Collective threatened to "expose [MCHR] as a liberal front for health professionals." This psychological blackmail extended beyond MCHR doctors in Chicago. In December, 1969, for example, an MCHR statement extended the indictment to the rest of the nation: "To the people of America, we say that if the [Black] Panthers are destroyed, we are all guilty."

Aside from the personal debility engendered by the politics of guilt, there were other, no less serious, consequences. The point came when local MCHR chapter activity, like much activity of the New Left, degenerated largely into a set of political slogans and mindless rhetoric. It was apparent to many, for example, that the political free clinics could not meet the health needs of the poor and that—what was worse— their existence had taken people's attention far away from the institutions that were ultimately responsible for the denial and distortion of health services to the poor in the first place. Indeed, no amount of serve-the-people rhetoric could disguise the fact that the community people allegedly being served were, with few exceptions, disinterested in and aloof from the work being done at the most political free clinics.

The truth is that the orgy of guilt that permeated both the MCHR and the Left in general in the late 1960s had led to the divorce of political language from reality. Slogans—meant, after all, to crystallize people's comprehension of reality—instead made this reality more opaque than ever. Middle-class radicals suffering conflicts over their identity were more concerned with their own radicalism and militance than they were with the task of convincing others of the correctness of their position. An observation of Norman Fruchter on other parts of the movement applies with equal force to the MCHR: "Radicals . . . were rarely about to cut through their rhetoric to argue their position so that it connected with people outside the small, increasingly isolated circle of the radical left."[3]

Russell Jacoby's writings about the same years draw an even sharper conclusion, namely that the distortion of political thought and action that characterized the movement of the 1960s was not a mere accident or mistake but was the movement's rhyme and reason. According to this perspective, its rhetoric concealed the movement's driving force, which was an effort to recoup what advanced capitalistic society had taken away—the individual's very identity and personal experience, one's ability to act as the subject of one's historical destiny.[4]

According to this analysis, the creation of a mass of socially impotent men and women in American society ultimately stems from the expropriation by capital of the free labor of individuals, by which bourgeois society originally defined the free individual. The next stage in the historical process was the conversion by capital of these amputated individuals into a mass of supposedly free commodity buyers. However, whether seen as a source of labor or as a potential customer, the individual had been robbed of the totality of personhood that alone defined his or her humanity.

The economic antidote for this dissolution of the personality has been the systematic effort of capital, with no small assist from its advertising, product design, and packaging subsidiaries, to personalize the consumer products of advanced capitalist industrial society. As depicted by Marcuse, even the most intimate of human activities, such as sexuality, is grist for the mill of commodity production and sale.[5] Nor has medicine escaped this fate, as a glance at the ads in any medical journal will demonstrate.

This analysis accounts for much of the common dissatisfaction with a medical care system that the health movement, in particular the women's health movement, correctly perceives as being insensitive to need, bureaucratically administered and technologically determined. Such a system necessarily drives the human element out of the patient and at the same time necessarily deprives health workers of what should be the gratification of work based on serving people in need. Both health workers and patients become interchangeable parts of technologic machinery and as such mere tools for those who control and administer the health system for profit and aggrandizement.

In response to this loss of genuine subjectivity, the MCHR, like the health movement and the rest of the movement in general, engaged in what Jacoby calls the politics of subjectivity. If monopoly capital had deprived men and women of their very selves and egos, the corrective, so the logic went, was to create a movement solely concerned with feeling, friendship, brother/sisterhood, good vibes, communality, and the like. However, "if the intensification of subjectivity is a direct response to its actual decline it actually works to accelerate the decline." As the cult of subjectivity spread to every movement group, individuals became less and less able to combat the brutal objective imperative of American society to "eclipse the individual."

Paradoxically, the end result was that the two seemingly divergent movements—the counterculture and the revolutionary political—merged imperceptibly into one another. The counterculture drew its strength from its recognition, long denied by traditional Marxist/Leninists, that individuals and their alienation matter and are of political concern; it erred, however, in believing that alienation could be righted with larger doses of subjectivity or, put another way, "with just a little help from our friends." Or to follow Jacoby, "To the damaged loss of human relations it proposes more of the same."[6] The revolutionary political movement, on the other hand, insisted that "offing the pig" and "armed struggle" were the answer, refusing to understand that sloganeering unmediated by thought and analysis does "not serve to popularize thought but replace it."[7]

Both thrusts were reverse sides of the same coin, and both ultimately made the same mistakes—ahistoricism, contempt for theory and analysis, and the flight from reality into wishfulness. Both parts of the movement finally opted to counter American society's drift toward the obliteration of the individual by seeking to create the experience of the individual here and now. Invariably, however, since the individual cannot now exist in society, this approach must lead to psychologizing reality, when in fact what is needed is an objective appraisal of reality. The initial need is for the development of an objective theory of subjectivity. From here one would hope for a political movement aimed at realizing the objective development of the subject.

Of course no one, either in the movement generally or in the MCHR particularly, was equipped in the late 1960s to deal with these, and many other, underlying points of theoretical confusion. Still, unless they were dealt with, it was just a matter of time until its foundations of sand guaranteed the collapse of the entire movement. These weaknesses may have been invisible to the MCHR as long as its members could believe that they were in the thick of "where it was at," but as the movements of the 1960s began to wane, the MCHR was once again left high and dry. Further, the nature of the support role by which the organization defined its existence had obscured (and possibly even created) inherent structural weaknesses in many MCHR chapters. These chapters had always drawn members in ones, twos, and threes from widely diverse institutions, situations, and interests. The very nature of chapter membership thus constituted an obstacle to developing an independent role for the MCHR. Beyond service and support, the question of what the MCHR should be doing seldom had an answer because it was asked of the wrong people in the wrong situation.

The MCHR's service-and-support role illuminates one last curious feature of its activity. While everyone acknowledged the importance of the organization, it had a strangely peripheral relationship to many, if not most, of its activities. Most such activities would have gone on, and most MCHR members would have participated with or without the existence of the MCHR.

At long last in October, 1970, a group of health workers and MCHR members living together in Brooklyn who called themselves Hampton's Family, after Fred Hampton, the slain Chicago Black Panther leader, tackled many of the questions the MCHR had stubbornly refused to recognize or had been unable to come to grips with during its first six years.

After suggesting that the MCHR had failed both locally and nationally, the Hampton's Family Paper went on to say that "this failure at both levels can be traced to the fact that MCHR as a whole lacked a sense of its own proper role in these struggles, a clear understanding of who its constituency was, how to reach them, and in general, a strategy for challenging the health empires and their subsidiaries."

The paper went on to argue strongly for the development of a "progressive organization" that could organize "large numbers of middle level health workers" who would relate to community and worker (presumably lower-echelon) struggles. It suggested that the MCHR be that organization and that its priority be a "commitment on the local level to build political activity in local institutions and health science schools." Hampton's Family thought an MCHR national office should exist "to provide and support a full-time staff as well as regional coordinators," presumably to foster the local priority aims.

In summary, the Hampton's Family Paper called for a membership drive designed to attract upper-level and middle-level health workers, concrete struggles around institutional organizing, and a strengthened national office of the MCHR to assist these efforts. Although the clearest exposition up to that time of the MCHR's problems, the Hampton's Family Paper was not without its own ambiguities. To begin with, its suggested role for the national office was left only implicit, a fact that was soon to have dire consequences for the MCHR's development.

Further, when it came to concretizing its suggested theoretical program, the paper repeated many of the same errors that the MCHR had already made. For example, it called for more and better (meaning "more political") service projects, medical presence, draft exams, and support for sundry movement organizations, and, finally, opposition to chemical and biological warfare. However, it was precisely these diverse and multifaceted approaches that had up until then prevented the MCHR from doing what in the main the Hampton's Family Paper argued it must do—define its identity around organizing in health institutions, with a constituency of upper-level and middle-level health workers and health-science students.

To be sure, as the Hampton's Family Paper argued, "Our perspective must be broader than our local hospital or medical school. We are part of a national and international movement and must link up in our struggles to other issues." Unfortunately, the national leadership of the MCHR that was elected in the next year readily seized upon the "larger perspective" without ever bothering about the local building blocks that could have made such a perspective concrete.

Although the Hampton's Family Paper had grasped, albeit tenuously, the critical issues facing the MCHR and had generated discussion within the organization, by the time of the 1971 annual convention, held in April at the University of Pennsylvania it was an idea whose time had already passed. The paper was hardly mentioned at the convention and, insofar as it had any impact, it helped to push the MCHR in directions diametrically opposed to the intentions of Hampton's Family. Even more ironically, despite profound differences bubbling just beneath the surface, an atmosphere of unanimity and good feeling prevailed at the convention in which there was little if any disagreement or debate. These anomalies stemmed from at least two sources.

First, there was little political sophistication or leadership in the MCHR as of 1971. New recruits swelled the MCHR's ranks, but even old-timers lacked the theoretical and practical political knowledge and experience to recognize the essential issues, think through their organizational implications, take an unwavering stance, and engage the organization in meaningful debate. By shortly after the convention it became clear, in fact, that few enough of the members of Hampton's Family themselves really understood the implications of the position put forth in their paper, as several went over to articulating precisely the opposite perspective.

Second, the more politically experienced members, who might have been expected to take leadership, were intimidated from doing so by a sense of guilt for being largely white male doctors and professionals, although these had been among the MCHR's chief constituencies in the past. This pervading sense of guilt was exacerbated by the theme and attendance of the convention but had its roots in developments taking place in the larger movement.

Organized around the theme "The Consumer and Health Care," the convention for the first time drew substantial numbers of articulate and organized women, Third World people, nonprofessional health workers, and consumers. The growth of independent Third World groups, such as the Black Panthers, and the emergence of the women's liberation movement engendered in the MCHR, as in many other groups, a consciousness and concern about its internal racism, sexism, elitism, professionalism, and organizational style.

This consciousness and concern were at once the MCHR's critical strength and its critical weakness. They constituted the basis upon which the organization could broaden its membership. Yet at the same time, the guilt borne of the charges of racism, sexism, and elitism led the MCHR to throw out the baby with the bath water, repudiating a major part of its historical constituency (and those with whom it could work most effectively). Indeed, the MCHR carried over a disdain for organizing doctors or medical students who, it was reasoned, if organized could only act ultimately in their own already privileged self-interest, which would of course be counterrevolutionary. Instead, the MCHR tried to transform itself into precisely what it was not—an organization of women and Third World nonprofessionals and consumers.

In this atmosphere, the MCHR charted new organizational directions, involving decisions on constituency, program, and structure, and elected a leadership that foreclosed for the immediate future the possibility of the organization coming to terms with the critical issues facing it. In many ways the subsequent years are but a playing out of those decisions, and it could be argued that our story could stop here. Yet what happened during and after the 1971 convention is worth examining in some detail because the issues then faced by the MCHR continue to be serious and unresolved ones, admitting of no easy solution. Moreover, while the fallacies of the course adopted by the MCHR in 1971 are readily evident in retrospect, the approach, perhaps because it offers a simple formula, continues to have currency for many organizations and activists today.

The April, 1971, convention decided that it was paramount to open the MCHR's doors to women, Third World people, nonprofessionals, and consumers—a decision implemented in the context of a growing militant national women's movement, the influence of which was enhanced by the large number of militant women at the convention. To their strong voice was added that of the smaller but still significant number of Third World delegates.

While there was no disagreement on this decision, there were radically different interpretations of what it meant—differences that went undiscussed and unresolved. To some this decision meant addressing manifestations of racism, sexism, and elitism within the MCHR and opening up the organization to a broader though still limited constituency of middle-level health workers. To others, including what came to be the national leadership, it meant transforming the MCHR into a mass organization incorporating all strata of health workers and of consumers as well. The MCHR was to be the radical vehicle of both the doctor and the dishwasher, the medical student and the ward clerk, the administrator and the consumer, the privileged and the poor, the Third World and the white, the man and the woman.

In short, there was no one who was not part of the MCHR's newly defined constituency. It would no longer simply serve the vanguard— MCHR would be the vanguard by shedding its skin and wishing itself a new one. The impact of this shift was devastating. One minimal advantage of the previous serve-the-vanguard approach had been that at least it allowed MCHR professionals, especially doctors, to embrace their own identities. They could still be who they were and use their skills and positions, as privileged as they might be, toward the support of groups judged to be more revolutionary. With its new decision on constituency, the MCHR lost even this.

Now the MCHR was no longer simply at the beck and call of whatever outside group could lay the greatest claim to militance, oppression, or other hallmarks of legitimacy. At least in that circumstance the organization had the theoretical right to decide where to give its support. Internalizing this process, the MCHR now rendered itself superbly manipulable by whomever within its ranks was most adept at social-psychological blackmail. Also, because the MCHR had indeed been guilty of racism, sexism, and elitism, it now lost its right to question or judge the validity of their claims or how they fit into the MCHR's agenda. Those who tried could be discredited as racist, sexist, and elitist.

Two major proposals, both written and circulated before the convention, dominated the discussions of structure and spoke to the issue of broadening the MCHR's constituency. The first, written by the Chicago chapter, argued for a strong national office. It met with hearty response, since many MCHR activists had seen the loose-knit, locally based, almost anarchistic structure of the MCHR's middle years dissipate energy in frenetic activity. What was not agreed on, incredibly enough, was the key question: should a strong national structure exist to give central direction, create a national image, and build the MCHR from the top down, or should it rather exist to serve, support, and coordinate local activities, building the organization from the bottom up (the Hampton's Family position)? Debate eluded the issue, however, and once more everyone took home his or her own interpretation of the subsequent decision.

The second proposal, drawn up by the East Coast Women's Caucus, also endorsed a strengthened national structure but emphasized expanding the leadership to include women, Third World people, and nonprofessionals as a means of broadening the MCHR's membership. This broadening, they contended, could evolve only if the MCHR adopted a collective style of leadership, a concept clearer in its criticism of the past than its prescription for the future. The women's caucus at the convention demanded a guarantee that half of those comprising the MCHR's leadership structure be women, and the Third World Caucus followed suit, demanding one-quarter. The result was an elaborate structure that was to prove as unwieldy and dysfunctional as it was superficially democratic.

The convention agreed, virtually unanimously, to set up a strong national structure that would function in a collective manner. The National Executive Committee (NEC), the interim governing body, was to consist of four national officers and four representatives from each of four regions. Each set of four regional representatives was to include at least one Third World person and two women, assuring that the whole body would be at least 50 percent female and 25 percent Third

World. Travel funds were assured so that no NEC member would be excluded from participation because of financial need or geographical isolation. Permanent caucuses of women and Third World people were to be established, which would be given the opportunity to meet at every MCHR gathering and which would assure that women's and Third World representation and participation in the organization met with their satisfaction.

Thus in 1971 the MCHR painstakingly created the forms of democracy and egalitarianism in its national structure. In so doing it pioneered an approach to addressing issues by implementing changes in form rather than changes in substance—an approach that was to become the hallmark of the later organization. No one asked what the MCHR had to offer women or Third World people, or how it would have to change to meet their needs sufficiently to give them a reason to make the investment that leadership requires. Rather it was assumed that having established the quotas and caucuses and having elected the right number of people of the right race and sex to the leadership, these problems would somehow resolve themselves.

The result was predictable. People were frequently elected to leadership positions because they fit a quota, not because they had necessarily demonstrated interest, commitment, or leadership ability in the MCHR. These representatives in many cases fell away as soon as they were elected, often, one suspects, because they had not resolved the questions whether the MCHR was the most appropriate vehicle for their concerns and whether they were prepared to deal with its residual racism, sexism, and professionalism. The end result was that the newly elected representatives exercised little leadership and the old-timers, intimidated by their own sex, race, and status, withdrew from leadership—leaving a vacuum too inviting to go long unfilled.

Quentin Young was elected to head a strong, centralized national office, which was moved from Philadelphia back to Chicago. Felicia Hance and Barbara Maggani, both members of the Eastern Women's Caucus and both part of Hampton's Family, were elected vice-chairperson and secretary, respectively, and Ann Garland, a Philadelphia nurse and leader of the Third World Caucus, was reelected treasurer. The convention also resolved to hire three full-time staff members of the United Auto Workers, a friend of Hampton's Family was hired as national organizer, and Pat Murchie, a member of the MCHR's Chicago chapter, was hired as executive secretary. Later Tanganyika Hill, a black activist from Houston, was hired by the Third World Caucus to be the Third World organizer. (Her tenure was short and she was never replaced by the caucus.) The three staff members shared one striking trait—all were virtually brand new to the MCHR.

While the 1971 convention sported the usual panoply of workshops and passed the usual multitude of resolutions, it focused primary programmatic attention on national health insurance. In fact, an air of excitement pervaded the convention, for everyone felt that the country was on the threshold of this momentous change in health care. Just six months before, Sen. Edward Kennedy had introduced his sweeping bill (the Health Security Act) into Congress, and the political climate of that time was such that it appeared to be a viable if not leading candidate in that arena. Everyone felt that national health insurance would be *the* major campaign issue of the 1972 election if it had not been passed before then. Indeed, it seemed that issues of health policy were reaching a historic moment in which the MCHR might, just might, be asked to play a vital role.

Prior to the convention, Tom Bodenheimer of the San Francisco chapter drafted and circulated a national health-care proposal embodying the MCHR's principles, which might serve as its alternative to existing national health insurance bills. The 1971 convention, again with seeming unanimity, adopted the national health-care plan with minor alterations as the basis of a campaign of education and agitation; again there was little understanding of what this action would mean.

This campaign offered several immediate advantages to the MCHR. It addressed an issue seemingly capable of uniting many diverse constituencies; it capitalized on the national interest and momentum around the national health insurance issue; and it seemed tailor-made for the new national role that the MCHR had adopted. Indeed, it offered the hope of being to the later MCHR what the civil rights movement had been to the earlier organization, with one critical difference—there was no popular movement afoot for national health insurance.

Thus the 1971 convention did not come to grips with the critical issues facing the MCHR; it turned the organization in opposite directions. Whereas the Hampton's Family Paper called for a broader but still focused constituency, a more focused program, and a local orientation, the convention gave license for the national leadership to move ahead with a united-front approach to constituency and program and a centralist, as well as centralized, national structure.

At the urging primarily of Frank Goldsmith and Quentin Young, the MCHR's new program was dubbed the National Health Crusade and was designed to promote five principles or, perhaps more accurately, five slogans, boiled down from Bodenheimer's alternative health plan. These included an end to profit-making in health; financing by progressive taxation; provision of complete and preventive health care; local administration of health centers through patients and health workers; and nationalization of the drug and medical supply industries.

At the national level, the National Health Crusade (NHC) was to consist of a series of nationally coordinated local press conferences and the mass distribution of polls, petitions, and a series of leaflets and brochures on the MCHR's alternative national health plan. The first leaflet came out in May, headlined "If you needed it [health care] right now . . . Could you find it? Could you pay for it?" It provided a brief critique of present health care, set forth the five points of the MCHR's alternative plan, and invited those interested to join the MCHR. Local chapters were urged to distribute these leaflets at shopping centers and department stores, in addition to medical schools and hospitals, and to conduct press conferences, polls, and petition-signing campaigns.

Most chapters ignored or laughed off the NHC; some were incensed at its public-relations style. At least one chapter—the one in New York City—actually attempted to follow the NHC's directives but came to an impasse when it could not figure out what was newsworthy enough to warrant a press conference. Many agreed with the NHC's educational potential but, assuming success in educating and mobilizing people, no one could answer the question that followed: "What can I do?" The MCHR did not wish to thrust people into the legislative arena to support existing bills (although later there was to be disagreement on this); it could not pass off its proposal as legislatively viable; and it could not point convincingly to local programs that would make it viable.

As criticism of the programmatic poverty of the National Health Crusade grew over the summer of 1971, the national leadership became more and more defensive, until it eventually was arguing that implementation of the NHC could include virtually all forms of MCHR activity. Free clinics, occupational health initiatives, lead poisoning and sickle cell screening, institutional struggles, antiwar activity, military organizing, student organizing, prison health—any and all could be seen as implementing some aspect of the NHC. When by late summer some of the underlying questions about the viability of the NHC were raised at an NEC meeting, the doubters were resoundingly put down by the national leadership for being disruptive.

By the fall of 1971, the NHC had begun to quietly collapse under the weight of its own contradictions. Even as it fell apart, however, it highlighted important elements emerging in the style and politics of the national office. First the NHC had the form of a political program, but little consideration had been given to its content—the essence of political bureaucratism. More than this, its lack of programmatic content pointed to the disturbing signs of political opportunism. Sometime between spring and fall it became clear that the MCHR did not take the goals of the NHC seriously in their own right and perhaps never had. Instead of asking what the MCHR could do for a national health care plan, the MCHR instead asked what a national health-care plan could do for it. The answer was that it could project the MCHR's name and image to facilitate its mass organizing and membership recruitment strategy. Thus its genius was closely akin to its vacuousness: It could encompass all constituencies and mean all things to all people. Further, through the NHC it became evident that the idea of centralization of the MCHR also embodied the idea of centralism. Dissent from within the ranks was not welcome.

The NHC was the MCHR's last attempt to adopt a single programmatic focus and the last juncture at which that was possible. Shortly after its demise the MCHR adopted the model of task forces as the answer to its programmatic problems. Task forces were designed to coordinate similar activities going on around the country and were modeled after the strongest and most successful programmatic undertaking of the latter-day MCHR—the occupational health task force.

The occupational health task force was organized by a small group, including Phyllis Cullen from Denver, Don Whorton from Washington, and later Dan Berman. They began by organizing a training session that could draw together interested workers (both union leaders and rank-and-file) and health activists. The task force spent much of the winter traveling from place to place generating interest and activity in occupational health. The task force raised (and personally contributed) money to hire a full-time staff member in the person of Dan Berman, who had previously worked with the Teamsters in St. Louis. Soon it was publishing a newsletter, pouring forth literature, and holding conferences.

Other task forces were encouraged to follow the pattern of raising money, hiring national staff, producing newsletters and literature, and organizing conferences. Soon the MCHR's list of task forces burgeoned to include prison health, national health plans, institutional organizing, community/consumer organizing, women's health, community health programs (including lead poisoning and sickle cell programs and free clinics), antiwar activities, mental health, rural health, patients' rights, nutrition, nursing, house staff, health-science students, and health care for the aged.

However sensible it may have appeared, the task force approach had serious drawbacks for the MCHR. First, it codified in a sophisticated form the more primitive do-your-own-thingism that had plagued the MCHR's past. More disturbingly, it could be and was used to deflect or absorb those who argued that the MCHR needed a programmatic focus. Now such dissenters could simply be told to set up their own task force. For the only programmatic approach acceptable to the national leadership was one which, like the unsuccessful NHC, could embrace all constituencies, a formula in which ultimately everything equaled nothing. Moreover, the task force model could be and also was used to abet the MCHR's publicity and recruitment drive by magnifying embryonic and often virtually nonexistent projects. The vast majority of task forces represented nothing more than a handful of people scattered around the country who shared a particular interest and who saw one another at MCHR gatherings. Yet when asked what it was doing, the MCHR could point with pride to its vast array of task forces.

During the summer of 1971, the MCHR national office began to function as it never had before: membership and mailing lists were organized; literature began to be massively produced; two internal communications, "The Office News" and "The Organizational Newsletter," were initiated and sent to key contacts on a regular basis; liaison with other groups was systematically established; and *Health Rights News*, the MCHR's house organ, began to appear on a regular basis. During that summer the MCHR raised $60,000 in foundation grants and received $20,000 more in membership dues. There was widespread appreciation throughout the organization that there now existed an organized and responsible national office.

However, with the appreciation there coexisted a growing apprehension about the style of that national office. The upbeat tone of office communications, while possibly appropriate for potential recruits, struck MCHR old-timers as overblown and condescending. "You received a sample of the national petition [for the NHC] which should be reproduced locally. Please do this as soon as possible so your friends and neighbors can Sign Up for quality health care," read an early office communication. Another enthused: "Now is the time to fill your local committees with active new enthusiasts. The last three months has proven that people are ready to move if they are just informed of the opportunities awaiting them with MCHR."

The accomplishments of the MCHR as reported in MCHR media were often magnified beyond recognition. When four MCHR members attended a two-day occupational health meeting, another internal communique characterized that fact as "This excellent attendance, spurred by MCHR's new emphasis in this health area," and whenever an MCHR member participated in a project or a struggle, the MCHR rushed to add that project to its burgeoning list of accomplishments.

Numbers became the standard of the MCHR's success—numbers of chapters, numbers of members, numbers of names on mailing lists, numbers of leaflets and newsletters distributed, numbers of meetings, numbers of projects, numbers of letters and telephone calls made and received, numbers of resolutions, numbers of alliances. There was little concern for what the numbers meant, and there was hostility toward those who asked. While heralding the formation of the fifty-third MCHR chapter, for example, the national organizer, when pressed, admitted that it consisted of three people, none of whom had ever met one another. Their names had simply been lifted from letters of inquiry received by the national office and, ipso facto, another MCHR chapter had materialized. *Health Rights News* became, at times, little more than a cheerleading sheet, recounting victories and editing out problems. The national office began reprinting any and every article laudatory of the MCHR from the national media, some in spite of the fact that they contained serious misinformation about the organization including one, for example, in which it was claimed that the MCHR supported the Kennedy-Labor national health insurance bill. In addition to promotional reprints, brochures, and buttons, MCHR balloons ascended for the first time at the October, 1971, American Public Health Association Convention in Minneapolis.

The bureaucratic style and public-relations tone of the national office combined with its stance on programs make clear that, all protestations to the contrary, the only significant concern of the national office during this period was membership recruitment, publicity, and image-building, and that all its activities were in one way or another tailored to that end. It appears, in fact, that the national leadership espoused a critical mass theory of social change, in which what members did was essentially irrelevant, so long as they indicated allegiance to the "right side," which would presumably grow and grow until by sheer force of numbers it would assure power.

The chinks in the armor of the national leadership were not hard to find. New recruits might for a short time buy the MCHR's salesmanship, but for its older members—many of whom had been attracted to the New Left precisely because of their alienation from the Madison Avenue aspects of commodified American life and from the rigid bureaucracy, hierarchy, and hypocrisy of their institutions—the style and tone of the new MCHR national office were thoroughly repugnant. Finally, no amount of glib salesmanship, hyperbole, or Sears-Roebuck cataloguing of task forces and projects could disguise the MCHR's lack of a focused and actionable program.

Some within the organization perceived the limitations of the national office's top-down bureaucratism. These members, largely from the older big city chapters, including New York City, Boston, San Francisco, and Los Angeles, were unimpressed with the large numbers of new recruits flocking to the MCHR. They saw the numbers as reflections not of the success of present leadership and policy but rather of the ferment created by the civil rights and antiwar movements, as well as the past reputation and visibility that the MCHR had established for itself. What did impress them, however, was the fact that both nationally and locally the MCHR had become a gigantic revolving door. Interested people came to it, looked around for meaningful involvement, more often than not could not find it, and then left in droves almost as large as those in which they had come. For this syndrome the MCHR's array of task forces offered no remedy. This faction shared an acute sense of the MCHR's being in trouble—not for lack of projects, but for lack of a unifying program, a direction that would inform not only national organizing but local struggles as well.

Correct as their criticisms may have been, this group found itself in an untenable position. Its members were united by little more than opposition to the style and politics of the national office and, in answer it it, by a vague sense of the need to limit constituency and to focus on institutional organizing which itself went hardly beyond the level of slogans. What the group needed but lacked was both a theoretical and a practical sense of what it might do to actually act upon these vague parameters. Necessarily this shortcoming allowed the national office to charge, with partial plausibility, that the effect of the dissidents was merely destructive and obstructionist.

The true weakness of the dissidents can be seen in their inability to implement their own strategic orientation in a situation where they exercised complete control—at the level of their local chapters. Even in New York City and San Francisco, cities that had already experienced collectives doing institutional organizing, MCHR dissidents were both peripheral to these efforts and were unable to emulate or go beyond them.

The weakness of the dissidents' position stemmed from their inability to develop three elements critical to the launching of a successful strategy: a concrete, human, and unrhetorical explanation of how and why the existing health-care system devalues human experience; an analysis of the contradictions inherent in the system that could inform organizing pespectives by providing the bridge between theory and concrete reality; and, finally, the incorporation within an organizing strategy of a means of realizing intermediate stages of an ultimate vision of a health-care system in which the needs of patients were the central focus and in which control was vested in an egalitarian workforce. Nothing less than the forging of these three links could create the conditions that would make possible the desired result—enabling individuals to experientially understand that it is both their responsibility and potentially within their power to become the agents of the construction of their own future.

In some ways the existence of groups such as those at Lincoln Hospital and San Francisco General Hospital may even have obscured the possibilities of institutionally based organizing with middle-level and upper-level health workers. The embarrassing truth was that at a very early stage of the organizing of such institutions, it was clear that the organizers had themselves very little sense of strategy and direction.[8] Worse yet, the romanticization of these early institutional struggles, while intending to move health workers elsewhere to join the struggle, ultimately had the opposite effect—the blocking of a process of thought that might lend clarity, direction, vision, and strength to strategic options and implications of institutional organizing.

Some of the onus for this state of affairs must fall on Health/PAC, whose bulletin more than any other intellectual organ fostered the idealization of these struggles. This posture sprung from the felt need, conveyed in dozens of ways by movement groups during these uncritical years, of presenting a positive image of the possibilities of social change so as to encourage the growth of the movement. The end results of such unreflective and unwarranted positive thinking were epidemic disillusionment, divorce from reality, and fostering of false premises, all of which without doubt were self-defeating. Finally, this intellectual euphoria depleted groups such as Health/PAC of their ability to delve deeper into an analysis of the health-care system and its oppressiveness to workers and consumers, which analysis alone can ultimately form the foundation of a movement for social change.[9]

The national office faction consisted of Quentin Young, Frank Goldsmith, and Pat Murchie—the editors of *Health Rights News*—and the leaders of both the Third World caucus and the Occupational Health Task Force. Although later events would reveal the fragility of this coalition, to the dissidents this group at the time seemed monolithic, if not conspiratorial as well.

Fueling the dissidents' readiness to see a conspiracy were the facts that several people in the national office faction were open or reputed members of the Communist Party and that the national office faction could depend on support from groups and/or individuals in New York and the South that had long been associated with the party. Whether or not particular individuals were actual party members and whether or not the party made a conscious policy of putting forth its line in the organization, there is no question that many aspects of the national office leadership were reminiscent of the Old Left, including its united-front approach to constituency, its mass-line, least-common-denominator approach to the program, its bureaucratic style, its opportunistic use of issues, and its centralist orientation, with its intolerance of differences or criticisms from within the organization.

The national office felt that the success of its political leadership was confirmed by the large numbers of new people turning out to MCHR functions. Because it was better organized and shared more political unity than anyone else, it felt no need to discuss political directions or develop a program for the organization. Instead, it felt threatened when others wished to do so because this felt need in itself represented criticism and because such discussion could not but weaken its position. Indeed, before long the energy expended by the national office at thwarting criticism and fending off dissent almost came to define its entire operation.

It was in the end the unwillingness of either faction to back off and the repressive tactics stemming from the centralist stance of the national office that led the MCHR down the road to factionalism and demise. The national office honed a set of tools with which it attempted to discredit, silence, and eventually expel dissenters. Questions probing the content or meaning of the numbers, the claims, or the style of the national office were taken as hostile attacks. From a disturbingly early stage in the new regime, people were seen as either friends or enemies, and there was little in between. New activists were warmly embraced and solicited by officers and staff until the first time they expressed doubts or criticisms, whereupon they became pariahs. Old friends who dissented were at first ignored or dismissed out of hand and later branded as negative, destructive, localist, and ultra-Leftist.

The most subtle of these tools for repressing dissent was the structuring of MCHR gatherings so that it was difficult if not impossible for dissidents to meet or talk. This tactic involved rigidly tight scheduling and the use of constant fragmentation into small groups, all for the purpose of precluding any occasion for a broad discussion of overall politics. At the 1972 convention in Chicago, for example, the leadership scheduled some forty workshops and fifteen constituency caucuses. As a result, the four-day convention provided only a short Sunday morning plenary session as a forum for oganizational business. Older members were both frustrated by this maneuver and resentful of the fact that every MCHR gathering was geared to the recruitment and needs of new people, who were invariably neither interested in nor experienced with MCHR internal affairs, rather than to the needs of those for whom those internal affairs were of paramount concern.

When older members began to organize occasions compatible with their needs, they were slashingly criticized by the national office. One such occasion came when leaders of the Northeast Region, out of dissatisfaction with the organization of the Chicago convention, organized a largely unstructured retreat to soberly analyze the organization's directions and viability. The national organizer, when informed of the meeting, threw a virtual tantrum, branding the members involved as elitist, exclusionary, and racist, and castigating them for having "No Workshops! . . . No Caucuses! . . . No Women's Caucuses! . . . Task Force and Constituency Organizing Completely By-Passed!"

The national office wrapped itself in the cloak of a united-front constituency and bureaucratic structural solutions to the MCHR's problems of racism, sexism, and elitism, in an attempt to immunize itself from criticism. It then used these concerns as epithets to be hurled at its critics. Those who wanted a focused constituency were dubbed exclusionary and elitist, anticonsumer, and antiworker. Those who felt frustrated by the constant fragmentation into special-interest caucuses were dubbed sexist and racist.

By 1972 the MCHR national leadership under Frank Goldsmith's direction had decided upon its tactic—dissidents were to be smeared with the volatile charge of racism. In a written report the MCHR leadership pointed out that the big city chapters had few black members. Unmentioned was the fact that this was true of everywhere.

In New York City an MCHR trip to China provided the nidus for the manipulative use of the racism issue. Partisans of the national office—none of whom theretofore active in the New York City MCHR chapter—suddenly constituted themselves as a separate chapter at Columbia-Presbyterian Medical Center. The group's sole activity was to nominate a black physician, Calvin Sinnett—himself never involved in the MCHR—as New York City's delegate to the China sojourn. Protests from the New York City chapter were to no avail and were denounced by the MCHR's Third World Caucus as "racist."

Of course, as with any organization wracked with factionalism, specific tactics are often only the paint to cover the deeper cracks. At the 1972 MCHR national convention the underlying centralist thrust of the leadership and the latter's need to expel dissidents became clear. Proposed constitutional revisions would have had the effect of lengthening the chairperson's term of office, hiring of staff without the approval of the Executive Committee, and finally would have permitted the NEC to remove from its own ranks members whom the chapter membership had duly elected in the first place.

Although these antidemocratic proposals were soundly defeated, the national office was not to be easily deflected from its goal of eliminating its critics. It now alleged the right of the NEC to simply expel chapters after "investigation," the grounds of which were not explicit. (In special cases it was proposed that chapters could be "temporar[ily] disaffilia[ted]" prior to investigation.)

By now polarization within the MCHR had become so great that productive organization and political work, including fund-raising to support critical staff functions, had come to a standstill. Having been ultimately rebuffed at every turn by the MCHR's members, Frank Goldsmith and his staff finally threw in the towel and quit in the fall of 1972. With the demise of the national office and chapter activity at a low ebb, the MCHR fell prey to all the forces then undermining what little remained of organized left activity.

With the antiwar years over, the larger movement was in disarray. The SDS and the Black Panthers had split, been repressed, and faded from the national scene; many local community struggles had faded as well. With the fall of the larger movement rose the star of the Left sectarian groups, whose attraction to activists was their simple, complete, and prepackaged sets of answers to the thorny issues facing the American Left and—probably more importantly—their apparent sense of purpose and community, a welcome contrast to the confusion, fragmentation, and isolation that now characterized the independent Left. Political parlance came to be studded with talk of the Progressive Labor Party, the Communist Party, the October League, the Revolutionary Union, and the National Caucus of Labor Committees, to mention only the most prominent.

The MCHR had never anticipated the demise of the many groups that had lent it its raison d'être. More than that, its residual reputation and appeal to new recruits, its breadth of politics, and its lack of self-definition made it a perfect breeding ground for sectarian groups. Once entrenched, such groups added still another obstacle to the MCHR's addressing the critical issues, since it was then put in the reactive position of having constantly to respond to the initiatives of better organized outside forces. The New York and Boston chapters withstood the onslaughts of the Progressive Labor Party only to have the Revolutionary Union rise to take its place there and in other Eastern cities. At the national level, the Communist Party began to function more overtly, and in the following years MCHR members closely associated with the party were elected as officers and served as staff.

From 1972 on, the MCHR was reduced to the old-hat plight of sectarian Marxist/Leninist intrigue. The Communist Party vied with the Revolutionary Union (later rechristened Revolutionary Communist Party—RCP) for organization control. While a few "independents" remained and were occasionally allowed access to national office, they did little more than act as credible fronts to disguise the MCHR's overt turn to "democratic centralism."

The old, mostly Communist Party-based, MCHR leadership was accused by RCP upstarts as having presided over a sputtering organization. Greater militance was the RCP's rallying call, and indeed in several major cities the RCP initiated meetings and demonstrations mostly on the issue of budget cutbacks of public health services. By 1974, the RCP's organizing energy, coupled with the collapse of the nonsectarian left, had won the day and control of the MCHR. The old MCHR leadership stepped aside with Quentin Young left hurling verbal brickbats at his successors from the sidelines.

By 1978 the RCP itself was split asunder with its own internal sectarian dispute. The issue at stake was whether to support or denounce China's Gang of Four (dubbed "Gang of Five" by the RCP who claimed the ghost of Mao as the holy-spirited fifth member). That an issue so remote from American political experience should become a fulcrum for an ideological split might leave most Americans bewildered. For the

Communist Party-oriented former members of the MCHR it might ironically have recalled an earlier decade's bitter wrangling over the issue of Stalinism.

Nationally, the Gang of Four hardliners won out and retained control of the RCP. Within the MCHR, however, the RCP was expelled to be succeeded by a new offshoot calling itself Revolutionary Workers Headquarters.

All of this bitter infighting resulted in an emaciated and enervated MCHR. The 1979 national convention attracted a scant fifty or so participants. Still the organizational bureaucracy ground on, passing resolutions and proposing initiatives. For the most part organizing promised to proceed along traditional liberal left/trade unionist political lines on issues such as occupational health and fighting public hospital budget cutbacks. In addition, efforts were begun to organize nurses upon the issue of proposed legislation that would require by the mid-1980s nurses to hold four-year baccalaureate degrees. The effect of this is alleged to be severalfold: the numbers of working class and minority nursing students are minimized. Further, those who graduate such programs are destined to assume supervisory functions with less well-paid personnel assigned to more demanding on-line nursing and technical duties. As far as they go these may be legitimate concerns; however, they skirt the larger unresolved issue of the role of nursing in today's increasingly technologically oriented medical practice. Similarly, fundamental questions concerning other organizational tactics, including occupational health and budget cutback issues, are left unaddressed.

Observers within the MCHR point to the broad-based appeal of the forementioned organizing initiatives as evidence of a shift away from narrow sectarianism. However, this is merely the woof and warp of all Marxist/Leninist politics: sectarianism is employed to wrest organizational control to be followed by broad-based united-front politics to later recoup membership which is invariably lost on the way to power. There is nothing on the MCHR horizon to suggest that this seesaw will not be repeated ad nauseum.

CONCLUSION

For the decade between 1964 and 1974 the MCHR was the standard bearer for the health left. Though often standing in quicksand, it still has claims to success.

The MCHR was an important, frequently effective ally of the civil rights movement. More than any other organization it alerted the health community to the truth about the war in Southeast Asia. It acquitted itself well throughout by allying itself with the weakest, most oppressed and despised members of American society. More often than not its heart and muscle were on the right side at the right time.

Internally, for all its faults, the MCHR could boast of accomplishments that no other health organization could claim. Even in its days of greatest doctor domination, it opened itself to other health workers and to those outside the health-care system altogether. It issued an early challenge to a racist health-care system both in terms of its delivery of health care and in terms of the treatment afforded minorities within it. Almost alone of all health organizations, the MCHR saw the sexism within the health community and strove to banish it from within the organization.

Finally, the MCHR was hardly alone among organizations, either in the health movement or in the movement generally, in its inability to come to terms with the two critical questions: who was to be its constituency and what was to be its strategic thrust? The long MCHR experience, in both its positive and negative aspects, brought some MCHR activists to understand the importance of focusing their energies on a limited constituency of middle-level and upper-level health workers in the setting of those growing bastions of power and resources—America's health institutions.

The MCHR experience did not, however, point the way past this most elemental step in understanding toward a strategic path which might lead to the objective of a health-care system humane to both its workers and its patients. To do this, we believe, will require at least two tasks, both analytical and to some extent abstract in their nature and both, we fear, going against the grain of the impatient, action-oriented movement of the 1960s and 1970s.

The first task is that of concretely analyzing and understanding the health-care system, including both an overview of its political economy and an analysis of how it more immediately shapes the values, perceptions, and relationships of the workers and patients upon whom it impinges. At the level of an overview, it is hard for us to imagine a successful movement which has not addressed such questions as: By what forces or combinations of forces is the health-care system controlled? Is it by doctors? by administrators? by banks? by insurance companies? For what purposes is it controlled? profit? social control? empire building? What is the relationship of the health system to other controlling interests in American society, for example, to multinational corporations? to finance capital? to labor unions? What role does the government play? Is it simply a handmaiden of the controlling interests? a mediator of them? an independent force? Clearly these questions are only suggestive.

Likewise, at a more immediate level, it is hard for us to imagine a health movement serious about health workers and institutional change which does not have a firm understanding of such questions as: How has increased technology, specialization, and corporatization affected the role definitions, the self-perceptions, and the felt needs of health workers? Is their course, and with it the course of increased fragmentation and alienation of the workforce, unalterable? What forms of resistance and rebellion have different workers' groups taken, and what are the implications for the workforce as a whole and for patients? Can trade unions deal with such wide-ranging issues? Are they necessarily limited vehicles for worker defense? Or contrariwise, do they serve to regulate the workforce and integrate it into the designs of management? To what extent can worker concerns mesh with those of patients, and to what extent do they conflict with them?

Finally, the success of the health movement as well as of the left at large rests on one last and possibly more difficult analytical task. We believe that the Left must apply equal intellectual and analytical rigor to itself—its own forms, styles, and modes or organizing. For it is only in doing this that opposition can effectively focus and conserve its precious energies and resources, and not squander them in impulsive reaction, outmoded models, and acting out unconscious needs.

At least three serious obstacles stand in the way of accomplishing these tasks, particularly the latter. The first is that, needless to say, activists obviously have large personal stakes in the struggles and organizations of the 1960s and 1970s which, much rhetoric notwithstanding, inhibit candid criticism of political practice. Indeed, not unlike the establishment, movement organizations structure themselves to ward off criticism.

An even more serious obstacle, we think, is an anti-intellectualism woven into the very fabric of the movement, stemming from a paradoxical and often unconscious amalgam of American pragmatism and Marxist historical determinism. From American pragmatism comes an ethos of "nothing succeeds like success" and "what works, works." Moreover, this philosophy dictates that what "works" will be found in action, not words, although in practice the action more nearly resembles trial and error. From Marxist historical determinism comes the assumption that socialism will emerge inexorably from the contradictions of capitalism and that individuals can only hasten or hinder the course of history, not alter it. Thus they are also relieved of the responsibility of determining it. Together these two traditions undergird the tendency for the movement to mindlessly laud any and every activity, project, and organization as signifying success by their very existence and hence bringing the movement that much nearer to final victory. Likewise, they underlie the tendency of the movement to recoil from sober evaluation of its activities in the context of larger directions. Indeed, not to accept the very existence of these activities as signifying success, to even press the need for sober evaluation, is likely to cast the critic as a defeatist when, in fact, he is like the proverbial messenger who must suffer the consequences of the message he brings.

The final obstacle is the absence of an intellectual tradition in the American Left which, when activists finally recognize the need for theory and analysis, makes them susceptible to the formalistic and outdated answers lifted from the Marxist classics and mechanically applied out of time and context to twentieth century America.

Not to address and overcome the antiintellectual and unreflective undercurrents described above guarantees a future resembling the past, where the movement responds to rather than directs the course of history. Indeed, it is as if activists have stood attempting to discern the first swell of a wave, have leapt on and ridden it as long as possible, and then have been cast on the shore to have the process repeat itself; and at any point in time, success has been measured by the height, splash, and roar of the waves. Rather, we would suggest, it is the responsibility of activists to take account of the waves but to turn their attention to navigating the tide on the way to their chosen goal.

NOTES

1. Barbara and John Ehrenreich, eds., *The American Health Empire* (New York, 1970), pp. 242–252.

2. C. Bloomfield, H. Levy, R. Kotelchuck, and M. Handelman, "Free Clinics," *Health/PAC Bulletin* (May/June, 1971), and C. Bloomfield and H. Levy, "The Selling of the Free Clinics," *Health/PAC Bulletin* (January/February, 1972).

3. N. Fruchter, "Movement Propaganda and the Culture of the Spectacle," *Liberation* (May, 1971).

4. Russell Jacoby, *Social Amnesia: A Critique of Conformist Psychology from Adler to Laing* (Boston, 1975).

5. Herbert Marcuse, *One-Dimensional Man: Studies in the Ideology of Advanced Industrial Society* (Boston, 1964). See also idem, *Eros and Civilization* (Boston, 1955).

6. Jacoby, *Social Amnesia*, pp. 114–115.

7. Ibid., p. 106.

8. M. Kenny, "Taking Care of Their Own," *Health/PAC Bulletin* (April, 1969); M. Kenny, "Battle for Heads, Beds and Territory," *Health/PAC Bulletin* (May, 1969); and Health Policy Advisory Center Staff, "Empire Round Up: Caught in the Squeeze," *Health/PAC Bulletin* (October, 1970).

9. Ibid.; see also Kenny, "Battle for Heads, Beds and Territory."

Part III

Critical Theory and the Changing Social Context of Activism

The Modern Service State: Public Power in America from the New Deal to the New Beginning

TIMOTHY W. LUKE

A new irony pervades the leading academic, corporate, and government circles in the United States as the current debates over the malaise of advanced industrial society have unfolded during the present decade. It now appears, somewhat ironically, that the complex bureaucratic tools of corporate and state intervention—which initially were conceived during the Progressive Era, haphazardly constructed under the New Deal, and then eventually employed after 1945 to manage economic growth and social development—in the last analysis dangerously have eroded the most basic psychological and social foundations of industrial life. Ultimately, bureaucratic intervention has become a form of cultural subversion whose corrosive impact now manifests itself in profound social-psychological crises: the "cultural contradictions of capitalism" the "fall of public man," and the "culture of narcissism."[1] My purposes here, then, are to illustrate briefly how the emergence of managerial capitalism, the formation of the service state, and the development of consumer society have led to these unexpected outcomes in present-day political affairs, and, in turn, I hope to suggest tentatively how the ensuing cultural crises possibly might be mitigated.

MANAGERIAL CAPITALISM AND THE SERVICE STATE

Over the course of America's rapid industrialization from the 1860s through the 1890s, farsighted corporate and managerial leaders began

Excerpts from this essay initially appeared in *Telos* 35 (Spring, 1978), *New Political Science* 8 (1982), and *The Journal of Sociology and Social Welfare* (1984). Reprinted by permission.

to see the promising light of industrial cooperation and corporate regulation gleaming through the cracks of their competitive entrepreneurial practices. Throughout the Gilded Age, as production became more technology-intensive, as distribution increasingly demanded more elaborate managerial structures, and as mass consumption began to concentrate in new urban centers, traditional liberal philosophies espousing individual initiative, market competition, and free enterprise seemed to point only down dead-end roads. To find a new formula for economic growth beyond classic liberalism, corporate leaders, such as International Harvester's George W. Perkins, increasingly favored market regulation and corporate concentration "because the end of competition would lead to more efficient industrial practices and the production of cheaper and better goods."[2]

Entrepreneurial capitalism's gradual expansion, which began during the fourteenth and fifteenth centuries,[3] encountered its practical limits in the late 1880s and early 1890s. Until that time, entrepreneurial capital transformed global economic relations by *extending* its rationalization influence through trade and conquest into the comparatively prerational societies of the Eastern and Southern hemispheres. Yet, as the ink dried on the Treaty of Berlin in 1885—formalizing Europe's subdivision of the last unclaimed regions of the precapitalist world—and as Frederick Jackson Turner called attention to the closing of the great North American frontiers in the mid-1890s, the world economy was shaken severely by a massive depression in 1893 whose impact forced the shaky entrepreneurial-capitalist mode of production to change its operational rules.

To effect these operational innovations, the more progressive business, industrial, and intellectual elites of America and Europe recognized the necessity of transforming capital from its traditional mode of *extensive* expansion via entrepreneurial commerce to a more organized mode of production, namely, centralized corporate concentration based upon *intensive* technical rationalization guided by scientific research. Hence, the transitional strategy from entrepreneurial to monopoly capital demanded greater state intervention, produced in the form of regulatory services, in order to coordinate the rational concentration of capital, the technical reorganization of labor, and the central management of social interaction in labor unions, schools, and the family.

Many leaders of the American corporate community recognized that such a transformation could only be worked out in a partnership with the federal government, which was the only political institution with the powers to unite the diverse regions, classes, and industries of the pluralistic American polity into a cooperative whole. These individuals, in turn, organized groups like the National Civic Federation in 1900 to encourage "some form of government regulation which would allow for the continued existence of the new corporate structures" in addition to collaborating with organized labor.[4] During the Progressive Era, such figures as Herbert Croly in *The Promise of American Life*[5] and Woodrow Wilson in *The New Freedom*[6] both maintained that Yankee industry, modern science, and governmental authority should be used to place "our businessmen and producers under the stimulation of a constant necessity to be efficient, economic, and enterprising."[7] Croly maintained that "in becoming responsible for the subordination of the individual to the demand of a dominant and constructive national purpose, the American state will in effect be making itself responsible for a morally and socially desirable distribution of wealth."[8] Similarly, International Harvester's George W. Perkins nominated Washington as the arena to "which our great business problems could go for final adjustment when they could not be settled otherwise."[9] Obviously, for Perkins and many corporate leaders, the mechanism for coping successfully with the unprecedented demands of stabilizing corporate industrial capitalism "would seem to lie through the medium of co-operation, with federal supervision."[10]

At this juncture, corporate managers and the leadership of the central government laid the foundations of a service state by assuming "that a democratically elected government, *together* with a business system dominated by private enterprise, can and should work *in consonance* to achieve certain economic objectives."[11] These "objectives" turned out to be jointly defined, but corporate-provided and government-protected "minimum standards of income, nutrition, health, housing, and education, assured to every citizen as a political right."[12] Consequently, the historic task of the service state was to create the new collective forms of industrial labor, personal consumption, high technology, and social services that managerial capitalism required for its continued rational growth and productivity. Since the inception of the service state idea, then, as Alfred D. Chandler, Jr., observes, "the government's most significant role has been in shaping markets for the goods and services of modern business enterprise."[13]

Beginning slowly with Theodore Roosevelt's and Woodrow Wilson's administrations, and maturing fully under Franklin D. Roosevelt's New Deal, a new state formation gradually was pieced together from: 1) executive departments and federal judiciary of the national government; 2) the managerial cadres of the new corporate elite; and 3) the corporate design for a society based on the mass consumption of material goods. Roscoe Pound has identified this political formation as a "service state," or a "state which, instead of preserving peace and order and employing itself with maintaining the general security, takes the whole domain of human welfare for its province and would solve all economic and social ills through its administrative activities."[14] There arises with it "the idea that all public services must and can only be performed by the government—that politically organized society and that alone is to be looked to for everything, and that there is no limit to the services to humanity which it can perform."[15] The service state fully embodies "the idea of regimented cooperation for the general welfare"; and, as it develops, it becomes "*par Excellence* a bureau state. From the very nature of administration, the bureau state calls for a highly organized official hierarchy."[16] Hence, the ultima ratio of the service state regime flows out of its instrumentally rational administration, typically mediated through the large, centralized bureaucracy, whose dominant inclination is to foreclose alternative institutional and political options in order "to organize the entire society in its interest and image."[17]

In doing so, the service state openly supports the operations of the corporate economy and society *bureaucratically*: 1) by intervening in industrial production through manipulation of aggregate demand, the money supply, employment levels, the price structure of commodities, or trade conditions to manage the business cycle; 2) by stimulating increased technical innovation and scientific research developments to rationalize the technical means of production; 3) by providing on a uniform, mass basis new educational, health, welfare, regulatory, commercial, and legal services to improve productivity and expand consumption; 4) by generating new markets for new public and private goods ranging from suburban housing, interstate highways, or advanced weaponry to expanded leisure time, new consumer goods, or mass college education: and, 5) by encouraging new forms of social individuality based on clientage in providing "helping" social, personal, and family services.

Still, the service state could not assume this administrative mission in a vacuum. On the contrary, the impetus behind its administration of social relations came through its close collaboration with the managerial structures of corporate capital. In addition to encouraging state intervention and regulation, many corporate groups altered their internal control structures by expanding the organizational roles played by professional engineers and managers vis-à-vis the owner-entrepreneur within the firm. To assure the survival of corporate industrial production, these new corporate leaders gradually separated the functions of "managing" from "owning" and "planning" from "producing," which took control of corporate capital away from owners and control of productive skills away from the workers to entrust it to these new professional administrators and technicians.

Therefore, in 1900, General Electric opened the first corporate industrial laboratory in the United States to apply systematically rational scientific investigation to the business of production. By 1913–1914, Henry Ford installed the continuously moving assembly line in his Highland Park plant, which had been made possible, in part, by Taylor's, Fay-

ol's, Gantt's, and Gilbreth's contributions to "scientific management."[18] By separating "planning" from "doing," or theory from practice, skill from activity, and thought from action, Taylorization began
to strip the American working classes of their skills. Because of their
alleged command over "the art of bringing ends and means together—
the art of purposeful action"[19] in the daily management of the large
industrial firm, these organizational trends legitimized the growing administrative regime of state bureaucrats and corporate managers.

In turn, the classic entrepreneurial capitalist forms of social exchange, personal identity, individual needs, and ethical beliefs slowly
have been redefined in the United States to suit the demands of instrumental rationality, namely, corporate capital's economically efficient,
large-scale, high-volume exploitation of material and social resources.
Thus, many large, multidivisional industrial firms such as Westing-
house, DuPont, General Motors, Standard Oil, and General Electric began after World War I to link closely their *productive* capacity with their
newly formed *innovative* (intracompany and interfirm advertising, marketing, financial, and service divisions) capacities to not only produce
familiar products for existing markets but to actually create and then
administer completely new markets for new kinds of goods and services that would satisfy *newly created* and *corporate-defined-individual needs.*[20]
As Chandler suggests, "After World War I the most important developments in the history of modern business enterprises in the United
States did not come from enterprises involved in carrying out a single
basic activity such as transportation, communication, marketing, or finance. Nor did they come from firms that only manufactured. They
appeared rather in large industrials that integrated production with
distribution . . . by moving into new products for new markets."[21]

These corporate goals, however, necessarily assumed the creation of
a new kind of social individuality that no longer counterposed the respective interests of individuals and society, but rather integrated them
by subordinating the former to the latter. Theodore Roosevelt, as an
exponent of progressivism, called for the United States to develop "a
system under which each individual citizen shall be organized with his
fellows so that they can work efficiently together."[22] Only by fitting
exactly the specialized tasks to which corporate capital might fit him—
both as a producer and consumer—could this individual adequately
fulfill his new socialization which "consists primarily in the discipline
which he undergoes to fit him both for fruitful association with his
fellows and for his own special work."[23]

Yet, with intense specialization in one area, each individual becomes
incapable of dealing with an increasingly complex existence beyond the
scope of his own narrow expertise. This trend, in turn, requires the
further "stimulation of infantile cravings by advertising, the usurpation

of parental authority by the media and the false promise of personal fulfillment"[24] to accommodate individuals to the new needs being presented in the consumer-based society of managerial capitalism. Also, "having surrendered most of his technical skills to the corporation, he can no longer provide for his material needs"; thus, this corporate-designed form of social individuality slowly erodes "everyday competence, in one area after another, and has made the individual dependent on the state, the corporation, and the other bureaucracies."[25]

Despite the central government planning experience of World War I and the expansion of corporate diversification in the 1920s, all of these attempts at macroeconomic organization could not forestall, in turn, the economic and political crises of the Great Depression in the 1930s. Of course, the American service state initially resorted to socially repressive legislation, such as accepting the organization of corporate "sociology" departments, beginning prohibition, and pursuing the Palmer raids, as a means of disciplining the populace. However, these direct interventions proved inferior to the gradual construction of "consumption communities."[26] Instead of state bureaucracies overtly repressing the working classes, the workers *as* consumers were prompted to discipline *themselves* strictly in order to satisfy "their" new needs and gain access to Model Ts, the suburbs, Woolworth's, and the movies. Still, "the creation of these markets necessitated an abolition of the social memories which militated against consumption."[27] In the process, a great deal of the social self-reliance, ethnic uniqueness, and personal autonomy that were cultivated under entrepreneurial capitalism were eclipsed by the new needs imposed by mass consumption and government regulation. For the self-sufficient individuals who matured beyond the reach of managerial capitalism, the new service state promoted the consumption of their traditional relationship to nature, the destruction of skills by which that relationship was carried on, and the exhaustion of the social forms of customary life as the primary projects of American mass industrialism.[28]

During Wilson's administrations, a number of programs and policies launched the activities of the service state in America. The Federal Reserve Act (1913) and the Federal Trade Commission Act (1914) gave the federal executive and its bureaucracies the rudimentary tools to manipulate corporate activity and expansion through the national money supply and commercial codes. The Underwood Tariff Act (1913) and the Federal Farm Loans Act (1916) enabled the central government to open the hitherto restricted American market to crucial new centers of production and consumption around the world and to begin experiments in financing domestic agricultural production. By the same token, the spirited enforcement of the Sherman Anti-Trust Act (1890) and the passage of the Clayton Act (1914) "hastened the growth of big business in the United States" inasmuch as their interpretation by the court system "provided a powerful pressure that did not exist elsewhere to force family firms to consolidate their operations into a single, centrally-operated enterprise administered by salaried managers,"[29] and, each of these new policies slowly solidified the bonds between managerial capital and the national service state as they "fulfilled the same purpose of bringing private interests into the interior processes of government."[30]

Moreover, a whole new wave of new debates and legislation arose as part of the Progressives' visions of the "New Freedom." As part of the ongoing effort to discipline each individual to more closely integrate him into the administrative regime of large corporate and state bureaucracies, the Nineteenth Amendment (1920) granted women a greater stake in the system through the formal right to vote. Similarly, the Eighteenth Amendment (1919) empowered state bureaucracies with the task of policing the adult population's leisure time activities through prohibition to make them more "responsible" citizens and workers. Perhaps more importantly, to finance this new regime of bureaucratic administration, the Sixteenth Amendment (1913) was enacted to rationalize the tax system of the central government, but, in so doing, the service state began to severely limit individual choice in that it gradually took "from the people more and more of their personal property and has determined how it should be distributed."[31]

To illustrate, however, the tremendous expansion of state control over social relations that emerged with managerial capitalism, one need only consider the revolutionary fiscal, labor, and social welfare legislation of the New Deal. With the crisis of the 1930s, the political caution and corporate hesitation that had characterized many of the Progressives' modifications of the classical market formulae disappeared under the federal state's bureaucratically contrived plans for a national industrial recovery. As the national income fell by half from 1929 to 1932, corporate leaders became more willing to cooperate, especially as the large multidivisional firms—such as General Motors and General Electric—saw themselves operating at 25 percent capacity in 1932.[32] As Gardiner C. Means claims, the New Deal was a "complete turning away from the classical model" in a collective search for "policies consistent both with the changed market structure and with a democratic society."[33] Consequently, the service state redoubled its interventionalist efforts to control the *intraclass* (divisions among corporate groups, industrial sectors, and financial circles) and *interclass* (clashes between labor and management, agriculture and industry) conflicts that had abetted the coming of the 1930s depression.

Here, the service state mobilized a familiar solution, namely, the "delegation of state power to monopolistic private organizations"[34] largely based in the corporate sector. Its initial, and most important, moves came in overhauling the monetary system and credit structure. Banking reforms, monetary circulation changes, and international banking connections were altered mainly under the Banking Act of 1935 to transfer "power over open market policies from New York to Washington," making the credit supply and monetary management "a practical instrument of government."[35] At the same time, federal fiscal management turned to deficit spending as an instrument of stimulating production and market demand.

Simultaneously, a whole series of bureaucratic agencies charged with the task of encouraging administratively the corporate sector's productivity were organized by the state. The industrial codes of the National Recovery Administration (NRA), despite its brief term of operation, successfully launched a general economic recovery during Roosevelt's first administration and accustomed many corporate leaders, in spite of their grave reservations, to the state's activist role in the economy. Similarly, a whole series of diverse agencies were founded to stimulate production, provide jobs, give access to services, and regulate economic activity. Here the Agricultural Administration, the Reconstruction Finance Corporation, the Works Progress Administration, the Tennessee Valley Authority, the Rural Electrification Administration, and the Civil Works Administration all provided a variety of services by means of the federal state recruiting its personnel from and sharing its power with the corporate or private groups most directly affected by its administrative intervention.

The same principles held true for organized labor. Continuing the theme of corporate collaboration, Samuel Gompers maintained that "the trade union movement is labor's constructive contribution to democratic regulation of large scale production."[36] Although many of labor's leaders shared this perspective, most corporate groups continued to oppose organized labor even after it was granted its "Magna Carta" in the Clayton Act during 1914. Before 1933, most American workers basically remained craft-oriented in their skills, shop-floor society, and labor organization. Partly broken by the scientific management movement and the assembly-line system after 1910, the American working classes were still politically resistive and collectively unorganized up to the 1930s. Only one in ten American workers belonged to a union— mainly craft unions—and individual workers, as citizens and consumers, were subjected to the repressive policies of prohibition, political harassment of their ethnic society, and a rigid assimilation myth rooted in WASP conformity.[37]

Beginning with the NRA and its Section 7A, however, the American labor movement slowly was integrated into the service state regime to assure that labor militancy would not short-circuit the national industrial recovery. The principle of federally mediated collective bargaining was established as a firm precedent and gradually acknowledged by business circles. Passage of the Norris-LaGuardia Act, the National Industrial Recovery Act, the National Labor Relations (Wagner) Act, the Public Contracts (Healy) Act, and the Fair Labor Standards (Wage and Hour) Act all contributed to the halting efforts being made toward the rational administration of labor. In keeping with the logic of the service state, the determination of issues central to the individual's identity, independence, and dignity—such as minimum hours, wage scale, unionization, hiring, firing, disability compensation, personal welfare, and contract bargaining—all were reduced to regulated routine procedures by the bureaucratic administration of the federal labor bureaus, the large corporations, and the national labor unions. What is more, in being promised some limited say over these material concerns, the union membership sacrificed job control issues and subsequently "almost never asked to participate in decisions concerning output, pricing, scheduling and resource allocation"[38] in corporate decision-making.

All of these varied measures, in turn, were further strengthened during World War II as "the mobilization of the war economy brought corporation managers to Washington to carry out one of the most complex pieces of economic planning in history."[39] The bureaucratic rationality of the service state continued to unfold in the new wartime administrative offices—the National War Labor Board, the Office of Price Administration, the War Manpower Commission, etc. The relative success of these measures "lessened ideological anxieties about the government's role in stabilizing the economy. Then the fear of postwar recession and consequent return of mass unemployment brought support for legislation to commit the federal government to maintaining full employment and aggregate demand."[40] Passage of the Employment Act of 1946 and the Labor Management Relations (Taft-Hartley) Act of 1947, followed World War II, reaffirmed the partnership of the service state and managerial capital to direct bureaucratically the internal processes of mass consumer society by maintaining programmed levels of aggregate output, guaranteed employment, predictable consumer demand, and bureaucratically mediated labor conflict. By 1948, one in three workers belonged to a labor union in the United States, and, even in the 1970s one in four workers remained affiliated with these corporate-modeled and state-monitored unions.

Thus, by the late 1950s, the American service state and managerial capitalism effectively had dismantled many traditional forms of community, which had evolved under entrepreneurial capitalism. These interventionalist policies from the New Deal had been meant only to be temporary transitional expedients; indeed, they had been forced upon capital by the national emergency of the 1930s depression. The federal commitment to rational management and the electoral mandate for public spending to advance that end, however, entailed the extension of the New Deal—under Roosevelt, Truman, Eisenhower, and Kennedy—through the advent of the Great Society.[41]

The New Deal program utilized government spending, largely in the public sector, for "resource creation." To combat the massive unemployment and price deflation of the 1930s, federal authorities used public spending to boost private productivity, which, in turn, increased general consumption by providing new employment. This overarching policy of resource creation by the federal government, under bipartisan Republican and Democratic management, resulted in close to full employment that indirectly stimulated greater levels of consumption. Hence, public policies in this era took the form of the TVA, the interstate highway system, the WPA, or the national defense education legislation.

With the Great Society, however, the policies of "resource creation" that prevailed from 1932 to 1964 gave way to a new regime of "transfer payments," which aimed not so much at *full employment*, but rather at *income maintenance*. Instead of *indirectly* stimulating consumption through increased employment and greater private productivity, the Great Society *directly* subsidized consumption through transfer payments and public service deliveries to compensate those groups (that had lost out in the labor marketplace) with income maintenance. Consequently, public policies of the Great Society era, running from 1964 to 1980—despite Nixon's efforts to close down many social programs—took the form of the Job Corps, Headstart, CETA jobs, or food stamp programs.

The Great Society's policies of "income maintenance" moved away from the formulae of resource creation and full employment engineered during the New Deal. Instead, these policies entrusted federal, state, and local government with the responsibility of running the transfer payment and service delivery systems that paid a social wage to boost consumption directly. A respectable number of new jobs—nearly 2 million—was created in the process.[42] Still, these employment gains reflected the fifteenfold increase in federal grants-in-aid for social welfare over two decades—$4 billion in 1960 and $60 billion in 1980—to state and local governments.[43] Likewise, grants for social welfare increased twentyfold from $1.5 billion in 1960 to $30 billion in 1980.[44]

The New Deal order devoted a significant level of resources to welfare services. It is only with the Great Society, however, that the federal, state, and local governments committed themselves decisively to maintaining incomes in the underclass through transfer payments, government services, and public employment at levels fifteen times greater than 1960 in 1980 as expenditures reached $90 billion. These shifts developed because the New Deal state arguably had lost much of its purposiveness and effectiveness in pursuing full employment into the 1960s. By 1964, it was the *unemployable* underclass and outsider groups—such as inner–city blacks, Hispanics, women, poor rural whites, Indians, and students—that demanded direct income maintenance and transfer payments in order to maintain the social contract. Hence the Great Society simply adapted many of the New Deal's old instruments for rational planning, bureaucratic control, and central management to serve its new goals. Under the regime of resource creation, corporate and public instruments had created new economies of scale, solid returns on social overhead, and tangible efficiencies in many welfare programs. Yet, with the rapid increase in funding, mainly in the 1960s, a powerful social welfare economy emerged. Its operations soon involved tremendous diseconomies of scale, decreasing returns on social overhead, and displaced inefficiencies in the secondary or tertiary impacts of its primary welfare programs.[45]

Clearly, pockets of "outsiders" hung on in the South, the West, and in the decaying cores of many of the nation's largest cities. Yet, with the steadily expanding economy, the corporate sector and federal government stimulated the revolutionary rearrangement of American urban life. The private automobile, suburban housing, and urban "automobilization" were placed at the center of American consumer society in the 1950s and 1960s. Federal fiscal and tax policies purposely subsidized corporate groups to expand private housing construction in new suburbs, redesign urban transportation around automotive expressway systems, and provide relatively cheap automotive transportation and fuel in response to both producer and consumer demands. As a result, the traditional forms of community and social organization slowly disappeared into the new community structures of consumer society, while the inevitable contradictions between workers and owners, consumers and producers, labor and capital, citizens and the state became managerial problems to be dealt with by the experts of large administrative bureaucracies in both the "public" and "private" sectors.

THE STRATEGY BREAKS DOWN

Meanwhile, internal political or social opposition to the service state and managerial capitalism continually was discouraged and repressed. Groups and individuals preferring to define and satisfy their own needs were encouraged through advertising, public education, and social pressure to let their needs be defined by state or corporate bureaucracies, and then satisfied by government-provided social services and corporate-produced goods. The state-employed professional educator was presented as knowing more and better than the parents; government-certified health and medical workers were billed as more effective and rational than traditional household hygiene, and store-bought goods were packaged to appear better than homemade products. Also, subsequent waves of government-sponsored Red scares, witch hunts, counterintelligence activities, and McCarthyist purges, beginning in the 1900s and extending up to the present, stymied most political opposition movements. Consequently, the service state system, instead of recycling the new ideas and practices of its internal opposition as important innovations, oppressed its opponents in order to manage the popular political process.

However, in having so strictly created the administrative conditions for the advanced rationalization of corporate capital, the service state after 1945—as it continued to grow through the Fair Deal, the New Frontier, and the Great Society—systematically stifled traditional forms of communicative interaction and individual independence. The purposive-rationality of bureaucratic organization became both less purposive and less rational as it eliminated prerational forms of social interaction.

How was this possible? At one level, the corporate and state health delivery systems, for example, can train—in a very purposive-rational fashion—more doctors, build more hospitals, and encourage more office visits to improve national health care and individual life expectancy. Yet, this same system can function only by relieving individuals of their own health and medical care skills. So as the complex health-care system comes on line it continues to expand to the point that capital-intensive hospitals and expensively trained doctors are dealing mainly with ingrown toenails, common colds, and minor medical operations. Despite purposively and rationally building a sophisticated health delivery system, the robbing of health and medical skills from individuals by bureaucracies leaves life expectancy and other health indicators steady or declining.

Similarly, under service state administration, state-supported mass education made possible a tremendous expansion of the schooling system that purposively and rationally kept youth in school longer learning increasingly more sophisticated technical and social skills to better integrate their labor power and personality into the consumer society. However, the construction and operation of these educational administrations have led, at the same time, to rampant indiscipline and the failure to transfer skills. A major implication of taking away skills and responsibilities from most workers doing most jobs has been the falling rate of expectations and skills within education. Functional illiteracy begins in elementary school students, and thousands of college graduates are systematically overtrained and underemployed given the needs of the larger society. Again, the bureaucratic administration of education is neither purposive nor rational.

Eventually, many potential bases for social resistance, personal autonomy, or political opposition gradually were buried in the onslaught of mass-marketed commodities, mass public education, and collective benefits of social welfare programs. Tradition succumbed to technique; yet, technique could evince such superiority only against and over tradition. Once rationalized to suit bureaucratic administration, the communicative interactions of historically evolved communities lose *their* unique *purposes* and *rationality* under "purposive-rational" bureaucracies. Once the purposive-rational mode of action was left only to its own bureaucratic devices, as occurred increasingly during the 1960s, it proved neither purposive nor rational either within its own formal operations or in terms of its efficient delivery of services. Limited intervention, ironically, in the process of rationalizing social activity, turned into comprehensive domination. By doing so, it often destroys the very bases of personality, society, and community which it sought merely to regulate. Therefore, and equally ironic, one survival tactic of the service state and managerial capital during the present crises is a move toward revitalizing new forms of social, political, and cultural *reason* to serve as alternative countervailing powers against the instrumental *rationality* that guides bureaucratic administration.

The "Social Revolutions" of the 1960s

Seen in this light, the rise of the New Left, the New Right, and other "countercultural" forces might be seen as one outcome of limited decisions made within the corporate and state structures to encourage weak oppositional forces in academia, the arts, the press, and the electronic media, which might serve as countervailing goal-setting forces against the service state's administrative regime. In a parallel fashion, one might identify the emergence of professional public interest lobbies, such as Ralph Nader's task forces, Barry Commoner's environmental institute, John Gardner's Common Cause organization, Jerry Falwell's Moral Majority, or Howard J. Phillips's Conservative Caucus,[46] which strive to bureaucratically mobilize interests against the bureaucratic decision-making of large corporations or the federal bureaucracy, as the new form of political opposition of managerial capitalism. Instead of being repressed, these weak, oppositional forces are subsidized, lionized, and encouraged to prod the bureaucratic apparatus to perform more efficiently or humanely.[47] However, these counterbureaucratic forces do not become powerful enough to disrupt or dismantle the apparatus as it currently functions—as Nader's failure to get a meaningful consumer protection agency established, or Commoner's inability to gain support for an effective energy conservation bill, or

Gardner's frustrations at winning a meaningful electoral reform program, or Falwell's difficulties in resurrecting "traditional American values" all further illustrate.

In addition to these professional counterbureaucratic lobbies, new oppositional mechanisms are being built into the service state itself. Beginning with Nixon's slow sabotage of various Great Society programs and continuing under Reagan's supply-side revolution, a new form of federalism has been developing which seeks to halt the continuing subordination of state and local governments to central decision-makers. Instead of a single welfare state system operating from Washington, the instruments of revenue sharing, block grants, and community action programs are giving state and local decision-makers back some of the administrative discretion appropriated by the federal bureaucracy since the New Deal. Hence, the welfare state idea has been injected into cities, counties, and states as they too set up their own welfare divisions, community development agencies, and economic intervention bureaus. In doing so, these multiple centers of power and decision-making are checking, countering, and countervailing the organizational dictates of the federal administrative regime.

Similarly, Congress has counterattacked against the presidency in the early 1970s to contain its "imperial" authority. Most importantly, the Senate Watergate investigations and the House impeachment committees finally challenged the overwhelming power of the president and ended an executive regime that sought to undermine the very democratic structures which made its rule possible. The War Powers Act of 1973, the Budget Act of 1974, and the extensive expansion of the congressional staff after 1974 all are significant new constraints on the president's ability to make war, to dispose arbitrarily of legally appropriated monies, and to unjustly manipulate information. These important legal developments, in turn, are not simply fortuitous reactions to the Watergate affair. Rather, they amount to a systematic attempt to revitalize the constitutional contradictions and political conflicts between the executive and legislative branches to keep the federal government more manageable, responsive, and controlled.

A variety of internal reforms have developed to correct other excesses of the service state. A number of bureaucratic insurgency tactics ranging from whistle-blowing to public employee unionization to information leaks, as well as a series of new antibureaucratic legislation, such as sunshine laws, sunset provisions, and zero-based budgeting policies, have begun to make bureaucratic decision-making more accountable and responsible as the aura of total power and total knowledge are pulled away from bureaucratic practices. Similarly, the service state is encouraging increased citizen participation as part of its standard operation procedures. Under Carter, these practices were fostered as exercises in democratic participatory management, while Reagan has recast them as advances for personal initiative, states' rights, and Yankee self-reliance.

To rebuild older cities or to reform the welfare system, the service state is favoring municipal action over federal action, neighborhood action over municipal action, and individual decisions over state decisions. Thus, the revitalization of personal decision-making, as a source of opposition in the consumer society, gradually is being built into the bureaucracy in the form of professional community organizers, citizen committees, community liaison offices, and public hearings to improve the bureaucratic delivery systems. Yet, the common thread uniting all of these developments remains their attempt to derail the purposive-rational uniformity of the service state in favor of their self-defined choices and community. These efforts emanate, in large part, from within the bureaucratic administration of the service state but are directed against the increasing irrationalities of its administrative activity. As a result, these newly engendered negative forces have kept three presidents—Ford, Carter, and Reagan—well within the weakened scope of the postimperial presidency.[48]

The "Reagan Revolution" in the 1980s

In certain respects, however, the Reagan Revolution represents the most radical attack to date on the "rationalization" of the service state. Here, the Reagan administration, following up on Nixon's abortive efforts at reform during his first term,[49] has launched a program of corporate and state "rerationalization" by turning parts of the central state against itself to recapture its past levels of purposive efficiency at a lower equilibrium of control, expenditure, and management. If increasing expenditures on income maintenance programs like social security, food stamps, or workmen's disability, as the supply-side technocracy maintains, deliver decreasing general benefits with increasing specific costs, then the service state must rerationalize itself by discarding such key bureaucratic instruments, which were originally constructed to regulate the inefficiencies of job markets in corporate society. Like traditional American society prior to 1932, the Reagan formula seeks to leave responsibility for the young, the old, the hungry, and the disabled to the "private" sector or fifty states.

Since the interventionist service state apparatus itself now emerges—in the Reagan analysis—as the real fetter on the purposive rationality of the economy and society, Reaganism seeks to streamline or wholly dismantle those initially "rational" social welfare programs whose doubling and tripling in funding allegedly has promoted simultaneously the halving, quartering, or worse of corporate America's growth, productivity, and innovation.

Rather than being managed by federal bureaucratic "politics," corporate guidance will be mediated through the tightly regulated "markets" that transnational capital has constructed under the interventionist regime of welfare capitalism. The rerationalization of the old service state instead allows the cost-effective bureaucracy in Washington to be efficiently supplanted by the more cost-beneficial technocratic management of transnational capital in New York, Houston, Atlanta, Chicago, Denver, and Los Angeles as concentrated corporate power supersedes the Great Society's obsolescent concentrations of central state power.[50] Of course, the balancing role of the state will continue to surface throughout this process. However, the dictates of rerationalization require that it shift from Washington to the more accessible, pliable, and corruptible centers of power in city halls, county courthouses, and state capitols. Confronted by the immense resources and wealth of large national firms and transnational capital, but without the backup power of federal authority, these decentralized, disorganized, and downsized subnational state power centers will not be able to easily resist the strategic management of corporate capital.

The austerity of the new corporate state does not imply the total abolition of the welfare state as much as it means its partial *privatization* and *decentralization* to stimulate a supply-side economic recovery.[51] Therefore, as the Department of Energy is dismantled, Exxon planners will again draw up Washington's energy policies. As the Department of Education is reorganized, churches and businesses can again provide "suitable" educational materials to replace federal handouts. As the Social Security Administration is pruned back, trust funds, banks, and insurance firms will cook up more flexible or profitable retirement schemes. As the Department of Health and Human Services is pared away, indigents can become "productive" on "workfare," and the disabled can drag down to local churches, civic associations, or soup kitchens to savor born-again Christian charity. As the Department of Justice slacks off on trust-busting, young corporate lawyers can cut their teeth on union-busting or supercorporate mergers. As the Department of Interior economizes on environmental inspection and resource supervision, strip miners and power–planters can more efficiently gut the earth and foul an atmosphere already fouled, as President Reagan has observed, by the natural metabolism of trees.

Reaganism, then, as a social and political revolution of rerationalization, boils down to a comprehensive contraction of the costs, impact, benefits, and effectiveness of the service state. The New Deal state, on the one hand, enlarged its structures and functions to rationalize the concentration of macroeconomic resources. These policies facilitated the global expansion of national monopoly capital so that it could attain its present transnational corporate form. On the other hand, the Great Society system levied increasingly larger claims on corporate capital to fund the income-maintenance policies that it provided for the groups excluded from the New Deal's full employment formulae. The exponential expansion of these welfare capitalist schemes after 1964–1965, however, has provoked corporate capital to aid and abet the dismemberment of the Great Society apparatus by attacking many of the same public entitlement programs, service delivery agencies, and regulatory bureaus that materially assisted its post-World War II growth.

Reagan's program for a new corporate service state, then, works along several fronts. First, seeing no other immediately accessible surplus of capital, the Reagan Revolution aims to "soak the state" rather than the rich, reducing government spending from 35 percent of the GNP to 25 or 20 percent in the late 1980s. With such trimming, billions supposedly will be available to reignite "private" enterprise. Second, reducing the funding of the Great Society, it is hoped, will lessen the tendency in public welfare programs to contradict, confound, and cancel out one another with irrational implications. If the purposive rationality of federal employment programs becomes so costly as to decelerate economic growth through inflation, government waste, and creating a dependent underclass of federal "makeworkers," then, in the Reagan formula, such employment-producing policies must be junked as being no longer purposive or rational. Third, Reagan's rerationalization reconsiders the cost-benefit matrices of bureaucratic entitlements by asking *who decides* in these government programs and *who benefits* from them. Should those public decision-makers and larger blocs of welfare beneficiaries in question *not* be part of the New Beginning coalition then their funding is cut back or cut completely. Finally, the new corporate service state of the New Beginning grounds its rerationalization not in traditional liberal-statist *cost-benefit* judgments but in a new conservative-corporate *cost-effectiveness* analysis—except in defense spending—that asks not what benefits might accrue on the demand-side given increasing revenues but rather how costly these programs actually are on the supply-side given their questionable benefits.

As they were developed since the 1930s, the New Deal state and the Great Society state did "more" with *more*. Today, however, the New Beginning state will do "less" with *less* as the cost effectiveness calculi of Reaganism promote stringent cost-containment in government programs instead of serving the benefit-enlargement policies of the New Deal order. By turning the agency of rationalization—the central service state apparatus—against itself, Reaganism's rerationalization rolls back the Great Society. What is more, in revitalizing the resource creation role of the New Deal to restore the legitimacy of the corporate economy, the new corporate service state will allow the "rationality" of corporate capital to operate unfettered by the "irrationality" of income-maintaining welfare capitalism.

This design for the new corporate service state, then, undoubtedly will punish precisely those underclass and outsider groups that the old New Deal system proved incapable of absorbing in the middle-class, white, male, suburban "happy days" of the 1950s. Black unemployment, for example, increased from 15 to 27 percent in the private sector from 1960 to 1976. Fifty-five percent of 2.3 million black nonagricultural employment gain, as opposed to only 26 percent of the growth in white employment, from 1960 to 1976 came in the public sector—particularly in jobs within the social welfare system.[52] These trends, in turn, have parallels in Hispanic, Indian, female, and youth employment. The Great Society concept, despite its many flaws, did promote the formation of new "black," "Hispanic," and "female" middle-class employment, whose material basis crumbles away with each new round of Reagan tax and budget cuts.

In the last analysis, of course, there are no guarantees that the Reagan Revolution's solutions for the contemporary crises of advanced capitalism actually will succeed. The incredible Reagan budget deficits are both a cause and a sign of the difficulties involved in this rerationalization strategy. Furthermore, the supply-side technocrats' design for turning the Great Society inside out threatens to quicken the delegitimization of the federal state by abruptly cutting off or trimming back the material goods and services it has provided to the groups and individuals which were ignored under the New Deal. Rerationalization may serve the best interests of corporate capital by returning to a minimalist state; yet, the interventionist regulation of the New Deal state and the positive income transfers of the Great Society economy also mitigated the intrinsic irrational competition, short-sighted profit-seeking, and unresponsive planlessness that historically has characterized competing capitalist groups in the United States. Thus, the internal conflicts, economic self-seeking, and technical constraints inherent in corporate capital itself may aggravate further the present economic crisis once Reagan's rerationalization lessens the state's regulative roles. In addition, returning by the corporate road to a supply-side prosperity does nothing to lessen the depoliticized dependence of the populace on technocratic managers, which has prevailed in America since 1932. Instead of fulfilling Reagan's vision of sparking new entrepreneurial initiatives and voluntaristic participation, the new corporate service state merely will shift the operational location and professional loyalties of technocratic managers from federal office buildings to the even less accountable and accessible executive suites of corporate towers.

BEYOND THE SERVICE STATE

As the economic, political, and social crises from the late 1960s and early 1980s have illustrated, the state and the corporate social formations have confronted challenges that their purposive-rational logic no longer seems capable of successfully managing. That is, even under the Reagan Revolution, the current alliance of the service state and managerial capital still is gripped by a "rationality crisis" which, in turn, entails an equally threatening "legitimacy crisis." [53] Once the *prerational* communicative interaction of the larger society was submitted to the *rational* imperatives of purposive-rational management, the instruments of social administration began to lose their original purpose. Having gone beyond mere intervention in the ongoing historical processes of economic exchange and social relations, the bureaucratic administration of managerial capitalism and the service state became forms of complete domination. In doing so, however, the service state destroyed the very forms of organic community and individual autonomy that promoted such administrative intervention. In turn, the Reaganauts' efforts to revitalize such institutions thus far have proven to be failures and/or farces.

Communal communicative interaction and emancipatory development, which rational administration after the 1930s was to have assisted and advanced, became frozen unnaturally in the purposive-rational control of corporate and state bureaucracies. The service state's essential mechanism of legitimation lies in its administrative effectiveness at providing the collective social "goods" of political stability, economic growth, mass consumption of consumer goods, and social welfare services. However, the interruptions in its technical control over these goods has led to a legitimacy crisis. As the service state's rationality crisis disrupts its purposive-rational management of the economy, polity, and society, however, the administrative effectiveness at delivering the system's own self-defined social "goods" is weakened substantially, which severely shakes its legitimacy and rational purposes. [54]

Counteracting the ironies of intervention under these conditions, however, means more than simply reconstituting critical intellectual analysis and debate. The essential need for *individual participation* necessarily demands the *repoliticization* and renewed *education* of every individual to cultivate and use his personal choices, political skills, and individual discipline. Here, activists must do more than merely define and criticize the mass depoliticization of the service state. Instead, the theoretically informed politicization of free individuals in the organic communities of the family, neighborhood, or urban locality must help individuals escape from the naturalized social behaviors of personal commodity consumption, political apathy, and the passive acceptance of bureaucratic policies and mass culture to create new communities of competence.

Political activists and social theorists must elaborate new political forms of realizing a *social individuality*—rooted in the organic community of the neighborhood, the family, or the city—instead of a commodified consumerist personality; for *personal political autonomy*—based upon renewed popular interaction and displacement of bureaucratic rule by reviewing individual skills for popular participation—instead of passive political clientage; and for *individual social judgment*—grounded in the substantive rationality of organic community—instead of the technical policy sciences of the service state's administration. Such a psychosociological renaissance, clearly, will demand the rapid revitalization of these autonomous public and private spheres given their past fragmentation by the service state. Nevertheless, these fresh political spaces seem to be opening with new social movements: the voluntary simplicity movement, radical feminism, the black consciousness movement, alternative technology groups, the new ethnicity, and the ecology movement. These groups, in turn, could serve as the institutional foundations for renewing personally initiated and collectively conciliated communicative interaction.

By imparting skills and values for individual self-definition, self-construction, and self-determination as a free individual interacting in a collectively constituted public sphere, these new social movements might be guided toward redeveloping personal autonomy. By critically reassessing politics in this fashion, the frozen social relations of consumer society—the bureaucratic objectification of human behavior, the internalization of personal domination, and the justification of human dependence by reducing social relations to a technocratic elite's "authoritative allocation of values"—can be attacked to regenerate individual choice and automony. At the same time, the passive life of administered commodity consumption must be demonstrated decisively to be degrading, dehumanizing, and inferior to the active praxis of communal creation promised by these participatory communal alternatives to the service state.[55]

NOTES

1. See Daniel Bell, *The Cultural Contradictions of Capitalism* (New York, 1976); Richard Sennett, *The Fall of Public Man: On the Social Psychology of Capitalism* (New York, 1976); and Christopher Lasch, *The Culture of Narcissism* (New York, 1978).

2. Joel H. Spring, *Education and the Rise of the Corporate State* (Boston, 1972), p. 8.

3. See Immanuel Wallerstein, *The Modern World System* (New York, 1974).

4. Spring, *Education*, p. 10.

5. Herbert Croly, *The Promise of American Life* (New York, 1909).

6. Woodrow Wilson, *The New Freedom* (New York, 1913).

7. Ibid., p. 22.

8. Croly, *Promise*, p. 23.

9. Quoted in Spring, p. 9.

10. Ibid.

11. Melville J. Ulmer, *The Welfare State: USA* (Boston, 1969), p. 4.

12. Harold L. Wilensky, *The Welfare State and Equality* (Berkeley, 1975).

13. Alfred D. Chandler, Jr., *The Visible Hand: The Managerial Revolution in American Business* (Cambridge, Mass., 1977), p. 494.

14. Roscoe Pound, "The Rise of the Service State and Its Consequences," *The Welfare State and the National Welfare*, ed., Sheldon Glueck (Cambridge, Mass., 1952), p. 211.

15. Ibid., pp. 212–213.

16. Ibid., p. 213.

17. Herbert Marcuse, *Counter-Revolution and Revolt* (Boston, 1972), p. 11.

18. For a well-argued historical treatment of the scientific management of labor and production, see Harry Bravermann, *Labor and Monopoly Capital: The Degradation of Work in the Twentieth Century* (New York, 1974); Siegfried Giedion, *Mechanization Takes Command* (Fairlawn, N.J., 1948); and, David Noble, *American by Design: Science, Technology and the Rise of Corporate Capitalism* (New York, 1977).

19. American Institute of Management, "What Is Management," *Dimensions in Modern Management*, ed., Patrick E. Conner (Boston, 1974), p. 23.

20. See Stuart Ewen, *Captains of Consciousness: Advertising and the Social Roots of the Consumer Culture* (New York, 1976).

21. Chandler, *Visible Hand*, pp. 472–473.

22. Spring, *Education*, p. 13.

23. Ibid., p. 18.

24. Lasch, *Culture*, p. 43.

25. Ibid., pp. 10–11.

26. See Daniel J. Boorstin, *The Americans: The Democratic Experience* (New York, 1973), pp. 89–166.

27. Stuart and Elizabeth Ewen, "Americanization and Consumption," *Telos* 37 (Spring, 1978), p. 48.

28. Ibid., pp. 49–50.

29. Chandler, *Visible Hand*, p. 499.

30. Theodore J. Lowi, *The End of Liberalism* (New York, 1969).

31. Raymond Moley, "What Liberties Are We Losing?" *The Welfare State*, ed., Sheldon Glueck, p. 187.

32. Chandler, *Visible Hand*, p. 496.

33. Gardiner C. Means, *The Corporate Revolution in America* (New York, 1964), p. 42.

34. Alan Wolfe, *The Limits of Legitimacy: Political Contradictions of Contemporary Capitalism* (New York, 1977), p. 144.

35. Means, *Corporate Revolution*, p. 31.

204 Critical Theory and the Changing Social Context of Activism

36. Spring, *Education*, p. 7.

37. See Jules Blackman, "Emerging Trends," *Labor, Technology and Productivity in the Seventies*, ed., Jules Blackman (New York, 1974), pp. 19–25.

38. Chandler, *Visible Hand*, p. 494.

39. Ibid., p. 496.

40. Ibid.

41. Paul Blumberg, *Inequality in an Age of Decline* (New York, 1980), pp. 65–107; and Wolfe, *The Limits of Legitimacy*, pp. 108–175.

42. See Michael K. Brown, "Gutting the Great Society: Black Economic Progress and the Budget Cuts," mimeo, Virginia Polytechnic Institute and State University (April 1982), p. 8.

43. Ibid.

44. See Morris Janowitz, *The Last Half Century: Societal Change and Politics in America* (Chicago, 1978), pp. 469–490, 507–545.

45. See Tim Luke, "Culture and Politics in the Age of Artificial Negativity," *Telos* 35 (Spring, 1978), pp. 65–73. Thus, according to the U.S. Census Bureau, in 1975 the top 20 percent of the income-earning population received 41 percent of the national income, while the bottom 20 percent obtained only 5.4 percent. In spite of the Great Society income-maintenance schemes, these figures were the same as 1947 levels. Yet, average family income among the lowest 10 percent of all families increased significantly from 1960 to 1980, and the number of families considered to be living in poverty also declined from 20 percent to about 8 percent of all families from 1960 to 1980. See John Schwarz, *America's Hidden Success* (New York, 1983).

46. See John Guinther, *Moralists and Managers: Public Interest Movements in America* (New York, 1976), and William J. Lanouette, "New Right Seeks Conservative Consensus," *National Journal: The Weekly on Politics and Government* (January 21, 1978), pp. 88–92.

47. Indeed, these oppositional forces have begun to form entire alternative policy programs. In addition, such institutions as the Brookings Institution, the American Enterprise Institute, the Institute for Policy Studies, or World Watch provide systematic policy critiques in their research and publications. See William J. Lanouette, "The 'Shadow Cabinets'—Changing Themselves as They Try to Change Policy," *National Journal: The Weekly on Politics and Government* (February 25, 1978), pp. 296–303.

48. Carter's Federal Personnel Management Project continued this decentralizing tendency. By using a personal incentive system to increase the efficiency of the administrative apparatus and to improve the delivery of state services, Carter sought to abolish the hierarchical command relations of the New Deal bureaucracy, and Carter was more intent upon reconstituting the apparatus than any of his recent precursors—Johnson, Nixon, Ford—who also had many of the same ideas. Still, as Reagan also learned, it is difficult to administratively deprogram the administrative programmers.

49. See Otis L. Graham, Jr., *Toward a Planned Society: From Roosevelt to Nixon* (New York, 1976), pp. 188–263.

50. See Hyman P. Minsky, "The Breakdown of the 1960s Policy Synthesis," *Telos* 50 (Winter 1981–1982), pp. 49–58.

51. See Thomas Ferguson and Joel Rogers, *The Hidden Election: Politics and*

Economics in the 1980 Presidential Campaign (New York, 1981), for further discussion.

52. See Brown, "Gutting the Great Society: Black Economic Progress and the Budget Cuts," p. 10.

53. Jürgen Habermas, *Legitimation Crisis* (Boston, 1975), pp. 33–75.

54. See Alvin Gouldner, *The Dialectic of Ideology and Technology* (New York, 1976), pp. 195–273; James O'Connor, *The Fiscal Crisis of the State* (New York, 1973); and Claus Offe, "Political Authority and Class Structure—An Analysis of Late Capitalist Societies," *International Journal of Sociology* (Spring, 1972).

55. This critical debate already has begun; see Bruce Brown, *Marx, Freud and the Critique of Everyday Life* (New York, 1973); Russell Jacoby, *Social Amnesia: A Critique of Contemporary Psychology from Adler to Laing* (New York, 1971); William Leiss, *The Limits to Satisfaction: An Essay on the Problem of Needs and Commodities* (Toronto, 1976); Claus Mueller, *The Politics of Communication: A Study in the Political Sociology of Language, Socialization, and Legitimation* (London, 1973); David Noble, *America by Design: Science, Technology and the Rise of Corporate Capitalism* (New York, 1977); and Richard Sennett and Jonathan Cobb, *The Hidden Injuries of Class* (New York, 1972).

8

Rationalization and the Family

JOEL KOVEL

In Kafka's *Trial*, K succeeds in proving to the Priest that the Door-keeper who keeps the man from approaching the Law is no more than a simpleton. The Priest, nonetheless, objects. No one has the right to pass judgment on the Doorkeeper, for he serves the Law; to doubt his dignity is to doubt the Law itself. K fights back: "I don't agree with that point of view . . . for if one accepts it, one must accept as true everything the Doorkeeper says. But you yourself have sufficiently proved how impossible it is to do that." "No," said the Priest, "it is not necessary to accept everything as true, one must only accept it as necessary." "A melancholy conclusion," said K. "It turns lying into a universal principle."[1]

True enough . . . and melancholy enough. Kafka is describing the predicament of those trapped by rationalized, lucid madness—the world of modern administration. To the extent that his vision is true, i.e., to the degree that the administrative mode is totalized, people living in this mode are as insects caught in the web of a spider to whose power they cannot help but aspire. This is not an encouraging picture, nor is it the picture of man Marx had in mind. Yet, it contains a deep human truth, one which may tell us something about the failure of the left and of the radical consciousness in general in advanced capitalist societies.

The prevailing tendency of late capitalism is to obliterate its class structure by creating a relatively undifferentiated *mass* of individuals who lack the consciousness of a class-for-itself. There are many aspects of this phenomenon which we cannot explore here. Whatever the

An earlier version of this essay appeared in *Telos* (Fall, 1978), pp. 5–21. Reprinted by permission.

mechanisms, however, one overriding fact stands out: The inertia of the masses cannot be comprehended on a purely objective level. No matter how relentless may be the social structures that culminate in a net of economic domination, one is yet left with the question: why do some—perhaps most—people knuckle under, while others resist? In other words, there is no quantum of social coercion. Whatever is set up to exert such coercion—and this would include the entire output of the culture industry, the educational apparatus, etc.—has to act through an individual subjectivity that, multiplied without end, comprises the mass. It has to *mean* something to that subjectivity; and, depending on what it means and how the specific subject is constituted, coercion either produces compliance or resistance. Viewed from this end of the process, the "inertia of the masses" can be rephrased as the failure of a *historical* subject to develop from the *individual* subject. To study this failure, one must examine the historical emergence of that individual subject in all its weakness and reproducibility; and one must study it in light of the notion of administration, for it is by this mode that history is delivered to the individual, much as medicine is administered to a patient.

What unites all the elements of social coercion in a historical totality is their formal subjugation to the administrative mode, their gathering by the tentacles of a universal bureaucracy. Ultimately, this inhuman process is made by and for humans. If the revolutionary spirit is gone, its elements have been seized and held hostage by administration. Adorno's phrase "The totally administered society," arid and impersonal as it may appear, nevertheless strikes a chord of terror. There is something both desolate and diabolic about the idea. We know that this is the heart of the matter: a heart of heartlessness, an icy rationality that paralyzes the will and numbs the senses. What we are not able to comprehend is the point of historical mediation between a labyrinth with its endless chambers, their lurid green walls pasted over with yellowing memoranda, their flickering fluorescent lights, stacks of forms and pockmarked bakelite counters—and the humans who line up quiescently behind them and succumb to its will.

For present purposes I shall use a set of congeneric terms, e.g., administrative mode, bureaucratic rationality, etc., to describe a peculiar way public life is delivered to persons within the terms of contemporary capitalist society. The mode is no discrete form but a dialectical compound of an established reasonableness and fairness on the one hand, and a certain mysterious inexorability on the other. It is designed to be sensibly pleasant but never gratifying, to provide a rationalized type of stimulation and a notion of order. Finally, it seems perfectly transparent and banal, yet invariably gives the impression of unseen forces at work. This is partly the result of a high degree of technological elaboration and partly the function of the extreme degree of alienation and division of labor characteristic of bureaucratic rationalization. The notion is not confined to bureaucracies as such but pervades mass media, health care, and other facets of contemporary life. The mode, in short, is superficiality of style with a deep hidden content. Although the bureaucratic mode serves the economic requirements of capital—notably by exerting some predictable control over the productivity of the work force and by regulating the consumption of commodities—there can be no doubt that it exerts a systematic cultural influence that transcends mere economistic considerations. Indeed, administration infiltrates every pore of personal existence, and by personal existence we mean life with other people, beginning with the family.

As Walter Benjamin[2] pointed out, one is never left in doubt that Kafka's fathers are right and have reason on their side—no matter how monstrous, filthy, seedy, and stupid they also happen to be. The capture of desire completes the triumph of administration. For after K's melancholy conclusion, he wearies of disputation and paces alongside the Priest, fearful of becoming "utterly dependent" upon him. The priest tells him how to leave the cathedral—and now K panics. "I can't find my way about in this darkness . . . don't you want anything more from me? . . . you let me go as if you cared nothing about me." "I belong to the Court," replies the Priest. "So why should I want anything from you? The Court wants nothing from you. It receives you when you come and it dismisses you when you go."

In love, the weaker is the one who loves the more. Administration wants nothing from anybody; hence it remains the stronger so long as a glimmer of desire comes toward it from the human subject who is its object; and administration wants nothing because it is constituted by the negation of desire. Desire presupposes a subject. It is the vector between the subject and some lost portion of the object world—real or imagined. Bureaucracy, however, is created insofar as subjectivity is wrung out of social intercourse. It is what is left behind: "rationalization," if one takes an ahistorical view; administrative domination if one thinks dialectically.

As Heydebrand has argued, bureaucratic organizations, far from being the "abstract march of functional rationality," always embody the fundamental contradictions of capitalist society even as they raise those contradictions to new historical levels.[3] From this standpoint, bureaucratic rationalization always has one superordinate meaning, namely, to increase the productivity of labor. Consequently, it drags along with it all of the contradictory moments inherent in the notion of productivity and the labor process.

In order to turn labor into a commodity, the worker must be objectified so that his activity can be placed into a calculable set of relations out of which surplus value can be extracted. At the same time, some modicum of subjectivity must thrive in order for value to exist at all. In concrete terms, workers must retain enough of a mind so that they may sell labor-power on the market as well as exercise some degree of choice in the consumption of commodities. Without these two ends of the economic process, capital would cease to circulate. Consequently, the existence, not to mention the expansion, of capital depends upon the combined maintenance of a ruthless objectification and the cultivation of a certain degree of subjectivity, but such a combination is inherently explosive. For by permitting the coexistence of subjectivity and objectification, capital becomes vulnerable to the adventitious development of genuine rationality as well as transcendent desire. In other words, capital necessarily permits the germination of what, sufficiently developed, could destroy it. Nothing is more important for its survivial than the thwarting of such a development, but this cannot be done automatically. People will not spontaneously accept the cultural terms of capitalist expansion, nor can anything so irrational be taught directly. The terms must be mediated so that stunted forms of human development can be passed off as the apex of human nature. In this struggle, administration becomes capital's stoutest legion.

Bureaucratic rationalization may then be read as the more or less continuous attempt to manage the interrelationship between the subjectivity and the objectification required by capital. It does so by mediating its peculiar brand of rationality—one that strips desire from subjectivity as it "humanizes" objectification, i.e., tries to make it fair and equitable while retaining a semblance of rational objectivity. Since the instruments of bureaucracy are constituted by the elimination of desire while the human subjects to whom they relate remain passionate, the conditions for bureaucratic domination are therefore automatically established. The question remains as to how these conditions become invested with desire, terror, and necessity.

In the immediate experience of life, the notion of necessity is rooted in the family—to be more exact, in those primitive intrafamilial images of self and others that congeal into the matrix of subjectivity. Since, as Kafka held, everything must merely be accepted as necessary for bureaucratic domination to exist, the alignment of the matrix of family relations must be secured within the prevailing conception of necessity.

The notion of necessity described here is quite phenomenologically distinct from that allowed by ordinary consciousness and factored into political economy. The latter is experienced as an imperative stemming from the outside world; it is rooted in an appreciation of the self's relation to that outer world, and it is felt in a framework of linear, sequential time, no matter how brief the interval. The structure of such necessity is generally of an "if-then" nature. "If I wish to survive, then I had better step out of the way of that oncoming truck." Or, from the economic sphere: "If I wish to retain my unemployment benefits, then I had better see to it that I am paid under the table for that free-lance job." The logic of this form of necessity varies from reflex to calculation; it can be readily assimilated into the prevailing reality principle.

However, this notion of necessity is not what Kafka's Priest had in mind, nor is it sufficient in itself to lock people into the order of things. There is another, more primary experience of necessity that does not arise from the outer world, although, significantly enough, it may be projected onto the outer world and be experienced as arising there. It rather emerges from a stratum of "deep" subjectivity—"deep" in the sense of being "thing-like," beneath verbalization, without "if-then" qualities, outside ordinary time sequence, and essentially unconscious, although with a certain degree of determinable structure. The pressure of this stratum into consciousness—and hence its phenomenological surface—is experienced as a murky yet peremptory urging; and the structure of this urging is given by the archaic mental traces of original caretaking others as they had been experienced by the infant through his or her body. Since this quality of necessity is suffused with desire for an outer source of power, and since the model for such a power was once a parent, it may be said that the family supplies a trans-historical substructure for the possibilities of domination. One says trans-historical because the structure is an outcome of a universal human disposition: in this case, infantile helplessness and the need for attachment. To this extent, we are introducing "biological" considerations, although we are dealing with a piece of nature that confers no determinancy and, indeed, sees to it that the nucleus of the human psyche is imaginary.

The family, then, is no "base" for historical domination. History neither abolishes nor is based on the trans-historical but is a continual transformation of it. If it should turn out that transactions with the mother are responsible for the primary experience of necessity, this does not make mothers responsible for historical domination (although it might help account for the profound and decisive fear of women which enters into the history of patriarchal domination).[4] Similarly, though men in fact rule in patriarchal-dominative orders up to and including capitalism, this does not make fathers as such responsible for the woes of family life. A much more complex account is needed to comprehend the relations between the personal microsphere and the societal macrosphere than has yet been forthcoming from radical thought.[5] Certainly, Marxism continues to flounder for lack of such an articulation.

Marx recognized that the self is an "ensemble of social relations" and that we construct our beings out of the ways we are with others, but he did not appreciate—and this became a particularly weak point in his system—that the self does not spring up all at once like Athena, but passes from an undifferentiated primordium through a number of intermediary stages, all of which are dragged along and play vital roles in later developments.[6] The first apprehension of self is of the reflection made by the infant in the eyes and gestures of the primary caretaking parent—an object that, for historical as well as biological reasons, generally happens to coincide with the mother. Before there is a well-structured "I" who can position him or herself with respect to the outer world and so enter the realms of economic necessity, there is the proto-self composed of the initial products of differentiation from the primordium. We may regard these products as comprising an elementary contradiction between the nameless urging that stems from the activity of the infant's organism, and the named construction that stems from incorporating the other's recognition. The former is a matter of sensation, the latter of an internalized perception; the energy comes from within, the form from without; and though they do not go together in nature, it is the job of the nascent self to put them together in its own realm, that of the psyche. In this fashion the primary or narcissistic self arises, the self as other, the self in which the subject fuses itself from a thing-like element drawn from its own bodily urge and an elementary word, or name, that belongs to the other.[7] When this fundamental elaboration of the self begins, individuals are readied for historical participation; insofar as it is ever completed, they become full historical agents.[8]

We may study the primitive manifestations of this organization with the aid of psychoanalysis which, by withdrawing the object of intersubjective dialogue from view, succeeds in decomposing the screen of ordinary language and in revealing the fundamental structures of subjectivity. Based upon these findings we can generalize that, for each human subject, there is a level beneath which the person can reexperience the empty unstructuredness of an original craving fused with the assignment of agency or structure to an unspecified other. Now this is a frightening and risky position and in ordinary waking experience tends to become sealed off—i.e., repressed—rather quickly. The mode of repression is itself a historically specific act which reflects the individual's internalization of the prevailing mode of social relations.[9] From a somewhat different angle, this means that repression achieves a synthetic unity between the most elementary properties of the self and the externally established system of domination; in this case, bureaucratic administration. Between these faces of the unity lie the intermediary structures of everyday life and their subjective correlates—more specifically, the subjective registration of the family, which coincides, in the most general sense of that term, with the Oedipus complex. In other words, no individual can react to any social force without bringing in all the particulars of his or her individual history. No matter how ant-like the denizens of an administered society may essentially be, each ant moves according to a "physiology" which is given by personal history. Within any concrete historical situation, all these elements are involved, although the particular conjunction of historical forces may bring one or another feature to the fore.

A brief psychological digression may be in order here. One is accustomed in psychoanalysis to distinguishing between two broad phases of infantile mental development, the pre-Oedipal and Oedipal. The former generally coincides with the oral and anal stages of psychosexual development, and the latter with the phallic and genital phases. However, the essential nature of pre-Oedipal and Oedipal phases do not reside in the sexual sphere as such, but rather in the orientation between the self and others in the world. In brief, pre-Oedipal relations are dyadic in quality, while those of the Oedipal period are triangulated. In the former, the self is related to another (generally the mother) into whom it can be more or less fully absorbed. As a corollary to this, the subjective boundaries of the pre-Oedipal self are blurred vis-à-vis the world and its own body.[10] By contrast, the Oedipal child has achieved a reasonably clear distinction (subject to numerous lapses throughout life) in relation to the body. Further, the other becomes others: there is always a third (classically, father alongside mother)—and beyond this third an endless elaboration of others in increasingly intricate patterns. It is for this reason that the Oedipus complex can be said to be the subjective registration of the family as well as the mediation between infantile life and social existence. However real the distinction between pre-Oedipal and Oedipal phases, of equal importance is their interpretation: the more deeply one studies an individual, the more problematic becomes any discrete segregation of mental elements into one phase or the other. In particular, one becomes impressed with the tendency of what seems Oedipal to dissolve into its pre–Oedipal forerunners. It often seems as if real participation in the world of discrete individuals—i.e., civil society—is necessary to keep the individual from sliding backward into a narcissistic pool of merger with an undifferentiated other. In any case, people seem considerably more vulnerable to manipulation around this point than had previously been realized by psychoanalytic students of society, who had made the Oedipus complex the alpha and omega of psychosocial transactions. There is a sense in which they were right, since Oedipal relations remain the point of intersection between the individual and the many discrete figures of society. However, once entry into subjectivity has been attained, a dialectic between Oedipal and pre-Oedipal takes over in which it often seems as if the more primitive layers are the decisive ones.

In other words, the Oedipus complex does not itself account for the subjective mediation of domination but is joined with, and indeed rests upon, a more fundamental pre-Oedipal mental organization that has to do with the origins of the psyche itself out of object loss. It is this original function that supplies the universal—i.e., "biological" or trans-historical—quality to the situation, whereas the Oedipal configuration is the inward reflection of the given historical state of the family and of relations of production in general. The Oedipal structures are no less critical for being yoked to more primitive pre-Oedipal functions, but their importance is linked with that of history itself as well as with the previously outlined universal and trans-historical core of subjectivity. Viewed from the angle of history, the Oedipal structures are the shadow cast by the fathers who seized control of society at the dawn of historical time. Viewed from the angle of a trans-historical subjectivity, however, Oedipus, his forebears, and his descendants are all hedges against self-dissolution and merger. Combining the two views, we may say that historical domination has been supported and reinforced by what it negates, i.e., a return to certain anxieties attendant upon the primary condition of the self.

These considerations do not make the real position of mothers irrelevant, either as transmitters or victims of historical process. Aside from their position in the Oedipal configuration (which is where children generally learn the key lessons about the role of the sexes in society), the actual behavior of the mother in the pre-Oedipal phase plays an enormous role in the future development of the child. The seeds of resistance as well as acquiescence are sown in the first phase of life. Indeed it seems to me that the refusal of history, which is after all the fount of the revolutionary impulse, is instituted in the pre-Oedipal—and presymbolic—experience of fusion with the mother. Being presymbolic, this experience belongs to the trans-historical, i.e., is removed from the historical system of significations. However, the trans-historical is no more an absolute category than the historical. Beyond good and evil, it still only survives under specific historical circumstances, as babies only survive in a given family which shapes and is shaped by them.

It is not easy to pinpoint the central attitude of capitalist society, to say when it began, when it achieved hegemony, or whether it is still in a process of development. For present purposes let us agree to see it as a more or less ruthless universalization of an objectifying attitude. This, finally, is responsible for the mystique of productivity and economism since, by stripping the world of value, it leaves human activity nowhere to go than to work upon lifeless matter. What most critics of this development have overlooked, however, is its irrational core and mediations in everyday life. Despite appreciation of the irrationality of the attitude in its overall historical context, it is somehow assumed that objectification is itself a position rationally chosen and held. There is a confusion here between a trans-historical need to objectify, i.e., to realize needs and subjective wishes by transforming the external world, and the perversion of this function which occurs under capitalism and is specific to it.

In terms of the above discussion concerning the deeper structures of subjectivity, it may be possible to make some headway into the problem through a consideration of the history of the family under capitalism. Here one essential development stands out as characteristic of the entire era in its effects upon personal life: the relentless separation between so-called productive work and domestic life.

This is not the place, nor have I the qualifications, to develop the history of the bourgeois family in any detail. Let me state as a matter of definition that by the bourgeois family I mean a mode of familial existence specific to capitalist society as a whole and imposed upon all who contribute to that society. There are important differences between the families of the working and the ruling classes; but all of them are stained with the mark of the totality.

The only point I wish to pursue here is the family's location within the central contradictions of capitalist society. It is perhaps not too sweeping a generalization to claim that the split between productive work and domestic life has cast a longer shadow across personal life than any other historical factor of the entire era.[11] The split has been necessary from the economic side as a means of developing the economic sphere and the primacy of production as such. It was the only way to develop a work force that could be inserted into a calculable system of wages and commodity relations. So long as production had been organized locally and in contact with the rest of personal life, no class hegemony could be established along the lines of economic domination. Once work has been broken from the hearth, however, it could be universalized, along with all its other cultural accoutrements—for example, social mobility, a technical attitude—and once these factors existed at large, they could become the signifying elements for the rising bourgeoisie.

The bourgeoisie, however, did not preexist outside Western history like some nation of Goths hammering on the Roman gates. Rather, it created itself from within European society. Bourgeois self-generation drew on antecedent elements in Western culture, but its specific qualitative distinction did not arise until work had been split from the home. The character of the class—and of subsequent class struggles—became defined by the scission between work and domesticity. To put it slightly differently, it is not productivity as such, or objectification as such, that characterizes the bourgeoisie, except in a symptomatic way. The class has, rather, drawn its cultural dynamic from the dialectic of two aspects of social existence, work and domesticity, that became severed in order that the bourgeoisie might rise.

Focusing for the time being on the domestic side, we can observe several remarkable and contradicting features. First of all, the bourgeois family was from the beginning a *decomposition* of older extended kinship systems that belonged to a precapitalist unity of work and domestic life. This decomposition began in feudal times and is by no means complete. In fact, if one recognizes capitalism's more or less systematic demolition of sustaining features of family life (for example, local rootedness, religious justification, or economic necessity), an essential feature of bourgeois society has been to destroy the family as such. If one were to look only at the exigencies of the pure accumulation of capital, the family would be wiped out as an institution—except for those brute "biological" considerations having to do with the reproduction of the work force that Marx was able to describe in a mathematized way within the framework of *Capital*.[12] However, what Marx was able to dissect out for the purposes of critique, capital made into the leading edge of its strategy of domination: the animalistic reduction of *praxis*—sensuous activity—into abstract labor power. The human thereby became sacrificed on the altar of productivity. The reality of this destruction cannot be denied: look at any nursing home and see the outcome of family life for those who no longer have their role to play in the circulation of capital.

Yet the bourgeois age is the age of the family in a very real sense—not simply the family as a decayed fragment of metabolic breakdown, but the family as centerpiece of the personal world, the family as location of a desire and intimacy that were not conceptualizable in precapitalist formations, the family that has been called "nuclear" in the twofold sense of being the cellular module of social organization and the heart of human emotional life. This latter functional trend inherent in the bourgeois family is no sentimental trifle, nor is it reducible to economic terms—i.e., it cannot be explained simply as a manifestation of the need to stimulate commodity consumption or to develop a highly educated and differentiated work force. If these elements were economically reducible, the capitalist state would not have to worry about its legitimation function—i.e., it could collapse legitimation into accumulation. Instead, the state is beset with a never-ending political struggle based upon the irreconcilable contradiction between those functions, a contradiction in which legitimation is always the weaker, yet never an erasable, element so far as the state is concerned. Hence, the political nature of the struggle.

The legitimation functions are real; they are grounded in bourgeois family existence and represent the impression made by love on political economy. Splitting work from domestic life did far more than permit the development of a fantastic level of wealth, i.e., of objects of desire: it freed the family from the constraints of precapitalist domination and permitted it to undergo a structural development of its own. At the same time, it burdened this new institution—and, in particular, the women within it—with the unmet needs peculiar to the capitalist mode of work, with its systematic alienation. It should be noted that alienation, and not mere brutalization of work, is involved here, and that alienation does not involve a simple degradation of the work process but a more complex function that includes the promise of a higher level of development along with frustration and mystification. In other words, alienated individuals have been exposed to a certain degree of stimulation; they feel at some level the promise of entitlement to better things, and yet they are systematically cut off from any real agency in public or workplace existence. It is this individual who turns to home for the fulfillment of unmet—and historically expected—needs. Typically, this has consisted of the man attempting to reflect the domination experienced at the workplace onto the others at home, while at the same time seeking consolation from his wife. With both power and nurturance alienated away from the workplace, the family has to pick up the check at the cost of the woman's individuality. Eventually, the costs are passed all around, appearing at length as neurotic crippling and in character types suitably twisted to conform to capitalist society. There are several themes and innumerable variations, but the basic story remains the same: the conjunction of the historical and trans-historical under capitalism devolves through the family to produce a host of damaged individuals.

So, the bourgeois family is assailed with profound contradictions from the moment of its inception. Its prominence is a product more of these intense contradictory demands than of any supposed "nuclear" structure it is said to have. A close look at the experience of the bourgeois family would probably disclose that the solidity connoted by the term "nuclear" is at most a metastable resting point in the history of its development and, more likely, just another piece of propaganda. Whatever the duration of the family's stability, it is plain that the forces to which it is subjected would tear it apart if the state did not undertake substantial interventions to patch things up.

One of the casualties of this development deserves some attention: the role of the father, or of patriarchy in general. The classic bourgeois family is patriarchal and it was in such a context that Freud observed the configuration of the Oedipus complex. Yet, at least for the past two centuries, the patriarchal quality of the bourgeois family has been no more than an outer shell steadily hollowed out from within.[13] In this respect, bourgeois patriarchy is like a house nibbled away by termites: it looks fine for quite a while but then collapses all of a sudden. The hegemony of capital, with its fluid objectification, sounds the knell of patriarchy, even though those who retain power appear for some time to be in the lineage of kings. Capital's ethos of calculating rationality, epitomized in the notion of administration, is antithetical to the spirit of myth in general, and to the Oedipal myth in particular. The arbitrary and capricious will of patriarchy, descended from Abraham and Isaac, yields to fairness, the fact-finding board, and peer review. When Louis XIV boasted that he was the state, he was already protesting too much: the mere fact of having to remind his audience of the identity signified that a defensive posture was about to be taken toward impersonal administrative forces. Since capital began to win, the real figure of the father has steadily receded. Kafka represents the last gasp of its hold over the imagination, a cry of longing for one who has passed through the door; and with Kafka, the father disappears from Western literature.

What then is the role of the Oedipus complex, and why does patriarchy persist? Is the Oedipus complex, as Freud suspected, ultimately a biological residuum that makes its claim in the face of the historical whittling away of its objective base? Or is there a Lacanian nom du pere that persists in the structure of language and cognition itself?[14] From extended observation of neurotic and psychotic people, it is clear that Oedipal dynamics continue to play a compelling role in their inner mental life; and this role continues to determine a good measure of their active relation to the object world. However, as previously noted, Oedipal dynamics cannot be regarded as the exclusive organizing principle of the deeper state of subjectivity. Indeed, with respect to the psyche, they are in a relation homologous to that between patriarchy and administration on the social level: the Oedipus complex being the outer (i.e., closer to consciousness) aspect concealing a more basic and decisive pre-Oedipal organization.

Whether this represents a real historical shift from Freud's time has to remain somewhat speculative at present. Early psychoanalytic formulations, as we know, were almost exclusively Oedipal; and Freud himself seemed quite remarkably obtuse on the subject of mothers in general and the pre-Oedipal relations with mothers in particular.[15] Was this a reflection of that portion of psyche offered up to psychoanalytic investigation at that particular time? Also, was this a real historical variation or a superficial change? Or did it merely manifest the bias of the analysts, which is itself a historical phenomenon? The question is impossible to answer fully at present (since it begs as well the ever-present factor of the narrow class basis of psychoanalytic discourse).[16]

However, whatever the precise contours of the shift in psychoanalytic interest from Oedipal to pre-Oedipal dynamics, it seems that a historical force has been at work, and that this force, in its broadest outlines, has had to do with the weakening of actual parental influence in a social order that has remained structured by patriarchy.[17] The early "Oedipal" neurotics Freud studied were by and large people in rebellion against actual fathers who could no longer hold them in check, while today's "narcissistic" neurotics (who have added to and not replaced the former category) reflect a more general fragmentation of relations with both parents. As for the bias of the analyst, this has always been a historical factor. It should be recalled for example, that the intense interest in the mother-infant bond did not simply emerge from intrinsically scientific deliberations but followed the political fortunes of women. As Juliet Mitchell has observed, it was only after World War II allowed great numbers of women access to the public sphere that psychoanalysis began to turn its eyes toward primary human relations.[18]

Freud pointed out that instincts were urges to return to earlier states of things.[19] While this insight was meant in a strictly biological sense, it can only be fully appreciated with respect to the historical—trans-historical dialectic. What is "instinctual" is a manifestation of that which is trans-historical clinging to what is historically passing away. Given the persistence of patriarchial structures along with the waning of immediate paternal influence, children, from their trans-historical position (which includes somatic givens as well as nurturant familial bonds), conjure up the Oedipal parents and relate intrapsychically to them. The instinctual structure stands in an inverse relation to the objective one, and an object is instituted in the mind after it has been lost in reality. Once established intrapsychically, instinctual structures propel the individual to re–find the object in reality. The installation of the Oedipus complex provides therefore the subjective conditions for the persistence of patriarchy in the face of its historical obsolescence. Pre-Oedipal formations, by contrast, are less capable of objective restoration on a social scale, although they structure much of the psychology of love, including its subversiveness. This is because of their dyadic, self-dissolving, and protosymbolic qualities.

The loss of real parental influence is associated with an Oedipal configuration of fantasy that is intense but incapable of serving as a platform for more mature development. Indeed the individual becomes all too readily suffused with pre-Oedipal fantasy and subject to experiences of personal disintegration. The Oedipal fantasies which articulate with these strata of mind are not the classical "positive" ones of conquest but the "negative" Oedipus complex of passive yearning for authority.[20] A further propping up by reality is required; and this support

both replaces the missing parental influence and articulates symbolically with the negative Oedipal fantasies as well as deeper pre-Oedipal
ones. It is into this space that administration is inserted, ostensibly a
rationalization of the objective disorder of the world, but no less a cor-
relative of the most primitive and thing-like strata of the inner mental
world. It is the conjunction of extremes of rationalization and irrationality that lends administration its sense of mysterious inexorability. It
is as though the shadow of love were cast by a loathsome and heartless
suitor.

The essential mode of relation between individuals and the bureaucracy is that of the self toward an undifferentiated other—i.e., it is a
relation desired from early infancy, of the self with its primary caretaking object. The triangulation of the Oedipal situation yields to the dyad
of an original bond, and capital in becoming post-Oedipal does so by
marshaling that which, in the family, is pre-Oedipal.

Such a development does not take place in a state of happiness. Immediate observation confirms this truth in a compelling way. In its es-
sentials, family life in advanced capitalist society is psychotic. There
are obviously enormous variations on the theme, especially with relation to different classes and ethnic groups, and many throwbacks to
earlier historical modes of family organization. Despite the disjunction
between the individual and the general social type, there can be no
doubt that a particular variation of family madness is specific to late
capitalism. The combination of heightened needs of nurturance with
the loss of a material human presence for delivering these needs leads
to a situation where the basic tie between the generations is one of
psychotic fusion. The essential relation is lack of distinction between
the self and other. In an age when increasing individuality is the ruling
trend, the child is seen less and less as an individual within the family.
The parents are forced to expend huge amounts of emotional energy
toward children; yet, lacking social autonomy themselves, they cannot
let them go. Children, from their side, feel craving but no structure: in
order to preserve sanity, a premature and violent rupture with parents
has to be made. The older generation is disparaged and jettisoned,
ostensibly with contempt but actually out of fear; for when the parents
are approached, ordinary logical relations are suspended and a panicky
loss of self, accompanied by extreme hatred, is experienced. Rather
than experience this actual state of affairs, a falsified subjectivity arises:
the whole panoply of inauthentic personal attitudes that provide the
raw material for psychotherapeutic trades.

The distance between generations—combined with a perpetual craving—creates, so to speak, vacuoles within personal experience into which
the organelles of administration can ever so neatly be inserted. Here at
last is a certified source of rationality, not to be valued for itself but as

a hedge against madness. The fact that the logic of administration is shadowed by the domination of labor, and that it enters as the embodiment of objectification, might make it seem an unlikely candidate for meeting the intense human needs that arise from the crisis of the family, and indeed it is, if needs are taken in a progressive sense, i.e., as what people "really" need. However, in the actual state of disordered subjectivity evoked by contemporary family life, the logic of administration, and the intrusions of the capitalist order in general, play into the given psychological state of affairs.

If the dialectical logic of the unconscious is kept in mind, then someone in the situation outlined above is clearly anything but ready for a full human relation. Indeed, their yearnings, intense as they may be, are primarily a source of anxiety, for they lead back to hatred and to the edge of dissolution. The false subject which represents a lifeline away from this edge demands a false object for its realization; and the instruments of capital, from school curricula and TV shows to the bureaucratic logic of corporations and state agencies, are thoroughly tooled to meeting such a need.

The administrative mode provides the objective template upon which the psychoanalytic notion of the ego is constructed. This notion, which is a good example of reification in contemporary discourse, depicts the ego as a quasi-independent mechanism capable of mediating—with the ambivalent aid of conscience, or superego—between the "animal" id within the self and external reality. As recent psychoanalytic critics have pointed out,[21] this idea of the ego is an anthropomorphic fiction that does little justice to the subtleties of mental life. However, although the notion of the ego is extensively reified as a theoretical object, it must be granted that this reification has a certain factual correspondence with personal life within bourgeois society, insofar as the conditions of social existence force upon individuals a profound split between inner and outer life and hence require the development—as a matter of psychological survival—of more or less alienated internal mental agencies. The ego certainly has a mental reality, but it exists as the internalized adaptation to the existing mode of administration. Since it is the imprint of an external social reality that goes its own way, antithetical to human desire, the ego—insofar as it can be postulated as a "thing" within the perimeter of bourgeois relations—is perpetually stretched out to the breaking point between the realms whose mediation it attempts. In this state of crisis, the ego turns to external objects for succor and stabilization, and it is at this juncture that the external social order has seized control. Through the administration of culture, the state sees to it that objects of desire, muted by the pale certification of rationality, are dispensed, whether in the form of Muzak, sex education curricula, or professional football. The sign of all these phenomena is the presentation of some deep wish of desire conjugated with the mask of a perfect and ultimate control by an unseen other. A new order of necessity arises. This, then, becomes the fate of the striving for transcendence, which, in unofficial hands, could move toward the revolutionary transformation of society itself.

What we are describing amounts to a conjugation between emotional states and objective structures, between desire and instrumental rationality. Each is falsified according to the operation of distinct dynamisms—the dialectic of the family and the commodity, respectively—and each demands of the other respect for its own falsity. Therefore, the conjugation between them is doubled falsification, the making of "lying into a universal principle." The only immediately common feature between the two realms is a sense of power and urgency, Kafka's notion of necessity, not experienced as the apprehension of real relations in the world of space and time but as the inchoate urge toward a distant and receding center of power. To the extent that such an urge has trans-historical qualities it is reflected in the universal human pull toward transcendence. What characterizes the age of capital, however, is the historicization of the desire for transcendence, its seizure and universalization within a host of material circumstances, from the watching of television to the waiting on line at the neighborhood bank or supermarket. People are not particularly fascinated by these phenomena. Indeed, what strikes one is the rather low level of libidinal investment characteristic of the conjugation between desire and rationality, compared with more immediate subjective attitudes toward, say, one's body or family members. The point is not that people desire the administrative mode. It is rather that administration protects them against the desires they cannot stand, while it serves out, in the form of diluted rationalizations, a hint of the desire and power lost to them.

Administrative rationality is nothing that anybody except a small segment of the managerial class is happy about. Indeed, its purpose is not to provide happiness but to offer a dialectical fusion of realistic self-preservation combined with a defense against the deepest anxieties. Since these anxieties are generated by the perpetual crisis of the family, all administration has to do in order to secure a more or less permanently docile population is to keep this crisis going. This task it has undertaken with alacrity, having made the family a prime subject of state concern since the beginning of the century. By thus appearing to be helpful in the human sense, the state manages to destroy the roots of family life and personal autonomy while introducing an endless procession of ego supports in the form of the various helping professions and agencies.[22] The fact that certain individuals may benefit from this arrangement only serves to legitimate it on a large scale, and it is on this larger scale that the process of destruction and rehabilitation is carried out.

Although the process has been going on for a century or more,[23] the post-World War II era has been the setting for its emergence. The New Deal had culminated in the massive state apparatus of monopoly capitalism, and the end of the war found the United States in a position of global hegemony confronted only by the Soviet Union as a potential threat. The resultant cold war was conducted on a level of totalization and paranoia which, from a mass-psychological viewpoint, effectively externalized all social perturbations and correspondingly buttressed domestic loci of social reproduction such as the family. Through the 1950s personal life slept with the imagined howling of communist wolves outside the reinforced door of domesticity. In this era of intense integration, repression functioned well and bureaucracy was able to impose its rationality upon family life.

In the 1960s, however, internal contradictions surfaced in the black uprising at the same time as imperialism was reaching its limits in Vietnam. The two crises played back and forth upon each other and conjointly led to a cultural explosion that stopped short of becoming a revolutionary situation only because the working class remained subject to corporate interests. Despite the failure to achieve revolutionary proportions—and in some measure because of it—the crisis refluxed directly into personal and family life. At least four conflagration points were manifest: the divorce rate maintained its rise as the search for individual gratification found intolerable the family's necessary limitations (especially in view of the material realities entailed in providing for others in a heartless economy); the feminist revolution caught fire from the others and made problematic that sacrifice of female individuality which had been the linchpin of the whole system of personal life; the weakening of patriarchy (in good measure hastened by the debacle of Indochina) permitted a derepression of sexuality, which erupted at a number of hitherto "perverse" points; and youth began to not only rebel against their parents, which had been the rule of generational conflicts for centuries, but to ignore them as well, which was something quite new on the world cultural scene. It is at this point that the scission between generations became an open one and—more critically—one toward which administration could not help but take an ambivalent attitude. For while the widespread loss in parental authority posed a tremendous challenge to capitalist legitimacy, the cult of subjectivity and the self engendered by the same breakdown proved most useful to the state from two closely related angles: first as a fount of consumerism ("You've come a long way, baby"—i.e., the commodification of desire) and second as a mode of *privatizing*, and so of weakening, resistance. It was necessary of course to keep these developments under close control; and this, in the broadest sense, is the proximate cause of the great concentration of administrative control over subjectivity that has occurred in the past decade.

It is scarcely necessary to add that this development coincides with the general contraction of the left in the 1970s and is in some substantial measure responsible for it. However, nothing stands still in the history of capitalism and fresh contradictions ceaselessly and necessarily arise. In this case the new contradiction is provided by the concomitant contraction of the economy as a whole (ascribable, in my opinion, to the watershed effect of defeat in Vietnam). For the administration of personal life is predicated on the existence of a healthy economic surplus. In an age of scarcity and increased political-economic confrontation such as we are now surely facing in the 1980s, its terms have to be rewritten. Only one thing is sure: administrative rationality will seek to dominate the process—and once again fail to meet human needs.

Thus, administrative rationality has become the great mediating mode between subjective and objective existence. Without creativity, spontaneity, or the capacity to make anybody happy, it becomes the primary gluing force of contemporary culture. As long as it works, there is a rough equivalence between the amount of subjective autonomy it demolishes and the ego supports it provides—and this suffices to keep a reasonably intact population of producers and consumers in line with the prevailing order of things. It is obvious, however, that this state of affairs can never provide more than brief periods of stability for a small segment of the population, and the weakest point is the family. Insofar as the family is so structured as to be unable to match the desires it inculcates with the objects with which it is provided, and insofar as administrative intrusions cannot but in the long run continue the crisis of the family, the present arrangement can be no more than an unstable equilibrium. The system is open to perturbations from any number of angles—from attendant economic shortages to outbursts of unmediable mass-psychological desires and anxieties. In this respect, it should be recognized that the disorders we may expect—the workings on a mass-level of that part of us called id—are the wellsprings of resistance no less than acquiescence, for desire is the wellspring of revolution. The opportunity arises afresh with each child born into the family. For administration, which destroys the autonomy and intimacy that people have become acculturated to need, also continually creates conditions that its own spurious brand of rationalization cannot encompass. By eliminating or otherwise alienating the need for human labor, bureaucratic capitalism leads to an increase in unbound time. It attempts to administer this (mainly through education and the cultural industry), but the attempt never succeeds—ultimately because the center of psychological gravity has shifted to more primitive mental levels. The ground forever erodes under the tread of administration. Watching children watch TV, one knows they are being dulled, rendered passive, made to numbly accept an unseen administered order, but one also senses that the programming never really captures their minds. Some portion of fantasy always escapes, not at all necessarily for better things, but available for something unexpected.

What this will portend I leave to the soothsayers. There are only two considerations for the future I would like to mention in closing. One is the inadequacy of any purely personalistic or family therapy—at least as presently construed—as a way out of the crisis. Whatever individual reconciliation this may offer—and I am not disputing its merits on a personal level—it is plain from the above that no therapy as such can unlock the point of conjugation where the economic order and the state penetrate into personal life. The second consideration follows from the first. It is the necessity of developing a conscious left strategy, more fully articulated than heretofore, in which the unity of personal and work life can be reestablished. This may have to proceed on a concretely microsocial or cellular level for a considerable period of time— time during which an understanding of its generalization to the totality of society, that is to say, its reunion with class struggle, can be formulated. The functioning of this strategy is neither to bypass nor reconstruct the family. Neither can be done, for intimate family relations remain a trans-historical given that cannot be gotten around, while the notion of reconstruction implies that there once was an ideal family unit to which we must return: a fantasy, understandable in infantile terms but foreign to a real historical understanding of that perpetually battered foundation of civilization. The job then is not to reclaim but to newly define love, work, and the generation of culture free from the tentacles of the state.

NOTES

1. Franz Kafka, *The Trial*, trans. Willa and Edwin Muir (New York, 1968), pp. 220–222.

2. Walter Benjamin, "Franz Kafka," in *Illuminations*, ed. Hannah Arendt (New York, 1969), pp. 111–141.

3. Wolf Heydebrand, "Organizational Contradictions in Public Bureaucracies: Toward a Marxian Theory of Organization," *The Sociological Quarterly* 18 (Winter 1977), pp. 83–107.

4. Cf. Dorothy Dinnerstein, *The Mermaid and the Minotaur* (New York, 1976).

5. John Fekete, "Administered Society and Its Culture Industry: Politics and Rationality in Science Fiction," paper delivered at the St. Louis *Telos* Conference, February, 1978.

6. Karl Marx, "Theses on Feuerbach," in *Writings of the Young Marx on Philosophy and History*, ed. and trans. Lloyd D. Easton and Kurt H. Guddat (Garden City, 1967), p. 402.

7. Cf. Joel Kovel, "Things and Words: Metapsychology and the Historical Point of View," *Psychoanalysis and Contemporary Thought* 1:1 (1978), pp. 21–88.

8. Lucien Seve developed this concept under the name "excentration so-

ciale." Cf. "Psychanalyse et Materialisme Historique," in C. Clement, P. Bruno, and L. Seve, *Pour une Critique Marxiste de la Theorie Psychanalytique* (Paris, 1973).

9. Wilheim Reich was the first to pursue this idea systematically; cf. *Character Analysis* (New York, 1945).

10. For a good survey of early self-object differentiation, cf. Margaret S. Mahler, Fred Pine, and Anni Bergman, *The Psychological Birth of the Human Infant* (New York, 1975).

11. Cf. E. P. Thompson: "The crime of the factory system was to inherit the worst features of the domestic system in a context which had none of the domestic compensations," *The Making of the English Working Class* (New York, 1963), p. 335.

12. Cf. chapter X, "The Working Day," vol. I, *Capital* (New York, 1967), pp. 231–302.

13. Christopher Lasch, *Haven in a Heartless World: The Family Besieged* (New York, 1977).

14. Jacques Lacan, *Écrits*, trans. Glen Sheridan (New York, 1977), p. 67.

15. Philip Slater, *The Glory of Hera* (Boston, 1971).

16. Michael Schneider, *Neurosis and Civilization: A Marxist-Freudian Synthesis*, trans. M. Roloff (New York, 1975).

17. Alexander Mitscherlich, *Society without the Father*, trans. Eric Mosbacher (New York, 1973).

18. Juliet Mitchell, *Psychoanalysis and Feminism* (New York, 1974).

19. Sigmund Freud, *Beyond the Pleasure Principle* (1920), standard edition, vol. XVIII, pp. 1–65.

20. Sigmund Freud, "From the History of an Infantile Neurosis" (1918), standard edition, vol. XVII, p. 6.

21. Cf. Merton Gill and Philip Holzman, eds., *Psychology vs. Metapsychology: Psychoanalytic Essays in Memory of George S. Klein. Psychological Issues.* Monograph no. 36 (New York, 1976). Also, William Grossman and Bennett Simon, "Anthropomorphism—Motive, Meaning and Causality in Psychoanalytic Theory," *The Psychoanalytic Study of the Child* 24 (1969), pp. 78–111. The trust of these critiques is to eliminate biologistic and mechanistic features from psychoanalytic theory. Their hazard is an attenuation of the depth of psychoanalytic discourse; cf. my "Things and Words," op. cit. Ego Psychology has come to bear a heavy share of the reification which has crept into mainstream psychoanalysis. In a particularly effective critique of Heinz Hartmann, the main exponent of Ego Psychology since Freud, Roy Schafer pointed out that Hartmann's Ego, rather than the self-subsisting biological agency it was portrayed as being, was more like an endopsychic representation of the efficient Austrian bureaucracy in which Hartmann's father had been a high official. Cf. Roy Schafer, "An Overview of Heinz Hartmann's Contributions to Psychoanalysis," *International Journal of Psychoanalysis* 51 (1970), pp. 425–447.

22. For a good survey of this kind of penetration into everyday life, cf. Peter Schrag, *Mind Control* (New York, 1978).

23. Cf. Edward Shorter, *The Making of the Modern Family* (New York, 1975). This is an abominable work that nonetheless contains many useful data.

9

The Future of Capitalism

PAUL PICCONE

Although it has been ritually declared dead, obsolete, or at least in a perennial "crisis" for about a century and a half, capitalism not only thrives but has successfully managed to fend off all its challenges and alternatives. Because of its ability to draw sustenance from precisely those movements seeking its obliteration, it has managed to emerge stronger out of almost every crisis it has faced. Yet, its well-known flaws and the high human price it exacts remain. So does the need to comprehend its logic in order to mitigate, if not eliminate, the damage it wreaks. For this reason, it is imperative to examine critically both the failures in theoretical understanding and in political practice since the 1960s, when it was widely believed that an alternative to capitalism was not only possible but also imminent. The following will analyze the theoretical failures of the most sophisticated analysis of advanced industrial societies and the "critical theory" of the Frankfurt School, and it will question the mistaken interpretation of recent history generated by such a flawed theoretical approach. Finally, it will investigate the new and more serious sociopolitical crisis engendered by these failures for a capitalist system addicted to a steady flow of radical criticism to further regulate and rationalize itself.

BEYOND ONE-DIMENSIONALITY

When the one-dimensionality thesis was fully enunciated in the early 1960s, it was already historically obsolete, not because of the student

An earlier version of parts of this paper was originally published under the title "The Crisis of One-Dimensionality," *Telos* (Spring, 1978), pp. 43–54. Reprinted by permission.

activism and antiwar militancy that exploded in the following years, but because it described an already obsolescent phase of capitalist development. Furthermore, the critical theory that had formulated such a thesis after 1940 turned out to be structurally unable to anticipate and explain new social processes. This failure was the result of key theoretical commitments made in the 1930s to explain those social developments that orthodox Marxism seemed unable to grasp, while retaining unchanged most fundamental Marxist assumptions. Rather than critically dissecting Marxism itself, critical theorists initially chose to merely modify it by taking out a mortgage that finally came due in the mid-1960s.

Contrary to Left conventional wisdom, according to which the quandaries of critical theory are the result of having jettisoned too much Marxist theory, the problem is the exact opposite: the unwarranted retention of too much traditional Marxist baggage. By the late 1930s, the Stalinist outcome of the Bolshevik revolution should have led to drawing certain unpalatable conclusions.[1] Far from ushering in socialism, Marxism had become the ideology of a party bureaucracy.[2] Such an outcome affected the very core of Marxist theory and demanded a radical restructuring of the whole conceptual edifice.

Although fully aware of the Stalinist travesty before most of their contemporaries, critical theorists failed to provide a satisfactory explanation of Stalinism, and, consequently they failed also to account for fascism and the New Deal. Their initially cautious attitude toward Stalinism and their inability to come up with a *sociopolitical* theory of fascism was also related to their reluctance to give up the traditional Marxist model. Rather, they chose to keep that model by adding to it a psychoanalytic epicycle which sought to explain the failure of revolution and the rise of fascism in terms of *individual* dynamics, leaving the traditional Marxist socioeconomic framework largely unaffected. Instead of curing the objectivistic cancer of Marxist theory this psychoanalytic turn intensified it, thus forcing the theory into a pessimism and political impotence from which it was never to recover—even after the organizational phase of capitalist development that they sought to explain gave way to a new state of affairs.[3]

The first victim of the psychoanalytic turn was the dialectic itself, which, in order to survive, had to be ontologized as the trajectory of all Western civilization or forced into a biological straitjacket. While in Hegel it had been possible only as the self-unfolding of the Absolute and could be grasped only *after* the completion of the process, in Marx it conflicted with the rest of the theory—as becomes embarrassingly clear in the *Grundrisse*—with the presupposed linear theory of history shipwrecking on the Asiatic mode of production.[4] Only with *History and Class Consciousness* was the dialectic successfully integrated into

Marxism, to be blown sky-high by its own internal assumptions.[5] In fact, if Lukács's "objective theory of class consciousness" was "the theory of its objective possibility," its validity was conditional on that new classless society and collective subjectivity that would have retroactively guaranteed its scientificity.[6] The failure of that epistemological wager necessitated the junking of the entire framework—something that Lukács himself soon came to realize. However, in Adorno and Horkheimer, the dialectic became dehistoricized over the whole of Western civilization as the genesis of the domination of the concept.[7] It ultimately became the first defender of particularity, autonomy, and nonidentity in the totally administered society where internal opposition is successfully instrumentalized toward further strengthening that very society.[8] Yet, the dialectic remained throughout anchored in an objectivistic theory of being—precisely what had to be discarded in order to salvage it.[9]

This unwillingness to break with traditional thought is reflected in the retention of the primacy of unequal exchange, a lingering faith in the unavoidability of the economic collapse, and an overestimation of the pervasiveness and effectiveness of the bureaucratized institutions of the administered society.[10] Psychoanalysis related the theory of the crisis of capitalism to a psychological dimension, which sought to explain why the explosion did not occur.[11] The subject tended to disappear, society became all-powerful, and intellectuals could only escape into abstruseness to avoid homogenization, instrumentation, and in extreme cases, annihilation.[12] What this approach lost was precisely that nonidentity which it pretended to preserve. Instead, it embalmed it, reified it in an increasingly rigid and objectivistic conceptual reproduction of a reality that had already been frozen by the all-pervasiveness of the concept.[13]

Psychoanalytic theory came in to vindicate a biological dimension that presumably resisted efforts to blend human nature to a fundamentally irrational social system, thus generating new dysfunctions and becoming the repository of emancipatory hopes.[14] This was both questionable as well as unnecessary. When the various social systems exhausted their one-dimensional models (fascism, Stalinism, and the New Deal) and attempted to reconstitute the previously destroyed individuality, the resulting regulated desublimation ended up reproducing the predominant social relations that it was meant to modify. This, of course, was undertaken not in the interest of emancipation, but in order to provide the overadministered society with new and badly needed internal control mechanisms. What Habermas desribes as a rationality crisis is *the* one fundamental crisis of the overadministered society, and it can be successfully managed only by reversing the logic of one-dimensionality.[15] The process of homogenization and fragmentation has been too successful, with the result that it has destroyed that autonomous otherness the homogenization of which constituted a major advance in the rationalization of capitalism. When, in the late 1960s, in order to guarantee the smooth functioning of monopoly capital, it became necessary to reconstitute artificially that negativity without which the system proved itself unable to operate effectively, the instinctual psychoanalytic fortress to which critical theory had retreated turned into a conceptual prison preventing an understanding of those qualitative changes apprehensible only through that very same dialectic that had earlier become ontologized and, therefore, deactivated. In the same way that the counterculture of the late 1960s ended up reproducing existing social relations under different labels, critical theory could see nothing but a mere extension of the same homogenizing processes, thus missing crucial new developments.

From a post–one-dimensional vantage point, the logic of the age of one-dimensionality becomes much clearer than can be surmised from the critical theorists' aphoristic presentation, resulting in a more accurate periodization of capitalist development and, consequently, a fuller understanding of the nature of many otherwise puzzling recent events. The age of one-dimensionality can thus be seen primarily as a transition between entrepreneurial capitalism and the full domination of monopoly capital.

Already prefigured at the turn of the century, when entrepreneurial capitalism seemed to have entered into its final crisis, but fully institutionalized only after the 1929 crash, the age of one-dimensionality meant the domination of collective capital over every facet of everyday life—to the point of even reconstituting character structure and personality in accordance with the new requirements of capitalist rationalization. The rapid expansion of entrepreneurial capitalism within a precapitalist context met its historical limit with the disappearance of the obsolescent precapitalist framework whose systematic erosion had fueled an unprecedented restructuring of political and socioeconomic relations. The 1929 crisis of entrepreneurial capitalism was successfully resolved by massive government intervention to turn extensive into intensive development, colonialism into imperialism, and internal conflicts into regulatory social mechanisms. Unlike in Europe, where similar measures could be implemented only by authoritarian means because of strong internal political opposition—in the United States, where almost all internal resistance had been destroyed during the 1920s, a more peaceful transition was possible.[16] A variety of both peaceful and violent projects of social reconstruction had already been devised and tested during the Progressive era—under the assumption that entrepreneurial capitalism could be kept alive by piecemeal social reforms. Thus, when it became obvious that only a major reconstitution would do, the sociopolitical means were already available. Furthermore, given the lack of internal opposition, the transition in the United States could be readily achieved with a "human face." Whereas most pre-World War I progressive legislation, scientific management, and the integration of the earlier forms of opposition were finally institutionalized as the New Deal, Prohibition and other overtly repressive projects could be safely dropped as unnecessary.

One-dimensionality came about as a result of the annihilation of all specificity and otherness typical of the entrepreneurial phase, in order to create the conditions necessary to rationalize a system in crisis. Both work and leisure had to be homogenized by turning people into the abstract labor power needed in the newly Taylorized productive process, and into the alienated consumers needed to buy the well-packaged, standardized, and carefully marketed junk that such a system could profitably produce.

Taylorization, capital-intensive technology, the culture industry, and consumerism combined within a capital-intensive system based on the automobile and military expenditures to facilitate the penetration of capital relations into almost every domain of life. The homogenization and depersonalization associated with this period—i.e., the domination of the concept and of the abstract instrumental reason of capital— constitute the historical limit of this transitory rationalizing phase. The triumph of one-dimensionality, however, also corresponded to its exhaustion.

Marcuse's and Adorno's accounts could not grasp the implication of this new crisis of rationality and overadministration. Respectively, they postulated either "a great refusal" that already presupposed an even better acceptance of the given world, or a retreat to an aesthetic dimension safeguarding the vision of an emancipated humanity yet unable to excogitate any possibility for its genesis. This explains Habermas's "linguistic turn" as an attempt to escape the problems of the older version of critical theory. His reintegration of the dubious achievements of "bourgeois" social science and philosophy within a critical theory, now critical in name only, eliminated the pessimistic deadend, but at the price of reintroducing a naive rationalism more appropriate and fashionable in the earlier entrepreneurial phase of capitalism. The second major leg of a critical theory of society in addition to the dialectical one (already truncated by the psychoanalytic turn), the theory of alienation, was cut off by reintroducing the frills and formalisms of communication theory. In a world increasingly populated by alienated individuals unable and/or unwilling to participate in undistorted political discourse and where, in any event, their alienated participation generally injects further irrational and particularistic dimensions to otherwise formally "rational" but actually particularistic decision-making processes—witness the phenomenon of fascism, most populism, and the recent religious revival—Habermas's account tends to degenerate into a new liberal apology or an intellectual's pipe dream where, presumably, talk rationally translates into changes in this, the best of all possible worlds. Far from increasing democratization or rationalization in the way postulated by Habermas's optimistic version of "critical" theory, recent developments have been characterized by the reintegration of the irrational and a decrease in democratic participation. Regulated chaos rather than rational organization is increasingly becoming the order of the day; and in this regulated chaos the new "critical" theory either regresses by seeking to recycle earlier and long-since transcended bourgeois ideals, or becomes politically impotent in grasping the complexities of the new social reality.

THE CATALYTIC FUNCTION OF THE VIETNAM WAR

Contrary to the widespread Weberian vision of a constantly rationalizing and bureaucratizing process of capitalist development, bureaucratization becomes counterproductive when it successfully penetrates what it seeks to rationalize. What makes its fragmenting formal mechanisms successful is the lingering resistance of that yet-unrationalized specificity which it constantly tends to destroy. The bureaucrat's linear logic remains effective only as long as it confronts a recalcitrant nonlinear reality. As Adorno, Horkheimer, and Marcuse vividly showed, Auschwitz, Hiroshima, and the Gulag are the logical outcomes of this process. Yet, they are not its fulfillment. Long before the attainment of total annihilation, this process threatens the very capitalist growth which it was meant to facilitate, thus necessitating radical changes. Marcuse himself already discussed how the system ends up creating and supporting its own opposition. However, at the beginning of the 1960s, the crisis of one-dimensionality was yet to explode fully, and, at any rate, Marcuse had already reduced his own theory to unidimensionality by grounding it on a psychoanalytic foundation, thus ruling out any possible qualitative reconstruction. In order to see how the age of what may be called "artificial negativity" increasingly displaces that of one-dimensionality, one need only analyze the structural changes that have taken place in various social systems. In the same way that the shift from entrepreneurial capitalism to the New Deal meant that in order to guarantee existing relations of domination a great deal had to be changed, the shift from the New Deal and its aftermath to the new state of affairs also necessitated a major institutional overhaul and a parallel conceptual retooling to fully understand it.

Consider the Vietnam War. The U.S. "defeat" is still celebrated in conventional New Left nostalgia as the greatest achievement of the stu-

dent movement and of the successful mass mobilization that it provoked. However, what was the Vietnam war other than the result of
the extension of the logic of one-dimensionality *after* that logic had been
counterproductive? It resulted from the uncritical continuation of the
Dulles imperialist policy at a time when that policy was patently obsolete, against the best interests of a large segment of capitalist interests,
and in the process of being replaced by a new one. Whereas during
the phase of entrepreneurial capitalism the appropriate form of foreign
expansion was colonialism, and during the one-dimensional phase it
was aggressive imperialism based on indirect political domination and
economic control, in the new phase all former overt coercive features
become unnecessary. In the age of the culture industry, the marines
give way to Coca-Cola and Xerox machines; cultural hegemony displaces political domination in a cybernated imperialism where the victims themselves yearn for their own oppression. Within such a context,
all that is necessary to guarantee imperialist relations of unequal exchange is merely unimpeded commerce between advanced and backward societies. As Emmanuel has shown, the very existence of different organic compositions of capital in the two worlds guarantees the
institutionalization of a new imperialist form of exploitation.[17] All that
is necessary today to safeguard international domination is trade and
cultural imperialism. The struggle is no longer fought in the battlefields
but in the disproportionate confrontation between the "American way
of life" and traditional cultures.

Thus, Vietnam was a kind of watershed between the old and the
new imperialism. In many respects, the liberal argument that it was all
a mistake and the conservative rebuttal that the war was lost at home
are both true. From the viewpoint of the new imperialism based on
multinational corporations and cultural hegemony, it was a mistake to
try to prevent the communist reunification, since in the long run relations of domination would not have changed anyway; only their management would have been different. Instead of the United States directly dominating Vietnamese society, this domination would have been
indirectly mediated by the USSR, itself indirectly tied to the United
States in a relation of subimperialism. From the right-wing viewpoint
of an *unopposed* one-dimensional imperialism, however, old traditional
relations could have been retained by using a few atomic bombs and
by seriously confronting the North. In terms of the most lasting consequences, the Vietnam war was decided in terms of a confrontation
between a progressive and a backward sector of capitalism. After all,
only the backward competitive sector of capitalism was interested in
retaining unchanged neocolonial relations of dependence in order to
externally generate a privileged position that would otherwise be internally eliminated. The monopoly sector fears no challenges from a

nonexisting potential competition and can allow new imperialist relations to develop "naturally" as a result of an already successfully established cultural hegemony. As it turned out, the progressive sector won.

The Nixon removal could also be seen as part of the same scenario, where righteous indignation against traditional corruption was opportunistically manipulated by the media to dispose of one major remnant of the old bankrupt policy. Similarly, the authoritarian Greek or Chilean solutions—all extensions of 1950 *Realpolitik*—gave way in the late 1970s to the human rights offensive, which is not only much more effective, but, in a context of restored U.S. world hegemony, is considerably more appropriate. Having already won the confrontation with traditional culture, human rights became useful for monopoly capital as a self-justification and at the same time as an indictment of the repression necessary to fill the gap in most of the Second, Third, and Fourth worlds between rising expectations and increasing underdevelopment as a result of what Carlo calls "the iron law of underdevelopment."[18]

Given a situation where either the opposition successfully overthrows the system or ends up strengthening and rationalizing it, it is now clear that the New Left performed the latter rationalizing function. Unable to translate its moralism into a qualitatively different form of social organization, it merely accelerated the shift to the new rationalized phase, where the United States can present itself as the champion of freedom, the bureaucratic collectivist regimes of the Second World can only solve their internal contradictions through increased economic dependence and/or political opposition to the United States, and the Third World ends up with the unpleasant predicament of having to choose between two equally disastrous modes of domination, ultimately under the same universal management.

PHASING OUT SURPLUS REPRESSION

A roughly similar state of affairs exists with respect to the repressive apparatus which is becoming increasingly more unnecessary and therefore in need of dismantling or otherwise rationalizing—which explains the scaling-down and closer scrutiny of previously untouchable police agencies such as the FBI and CIA. While during the phase of one-dimensionality, any type of opposition—real or imagined—had to be eliminated in the process of homogenization, overbureaucratization requires the opposite. In order for the system to function, it needs control mechanisms in the form of internal opposition, whether critics or social movements, to guarantee its viability. Far from being persecuted, the lingering opposition now needs to be supported to keep functional a bureaucracy in a state of serious involution. Counterbureaucratic bureaucracies become one of the paradoxical expressions of the frantic efforts to generate artificially constituted opposition and challenges. The problem with this system-generated opposition is that, to the extent that it is itself bureaucratically sanctioned, it becomes an extension of the very bureaucracy in need of control. Consequently, caught in the paperwork of funding, reporting, justifying, and such, it simply extends the bureaucratic logic it was meant to challenge and thus becomes counterproductive. The organic opposition needed to successfully sustain this challenge must develop *outside* and *independently* of the bureaucratic administrative framework. Yet, since both the organic community as well as the bourgeois individual have largely been destroyed during the period of one-dimensionality in the rush to homogenization, the conditions no longer exist which, in a context of decentralization and debureaucratization, would readily lead to the resurgence of a manageable internal opposition and, therefore, the much needed control mechanisms. One need only examine what has recently happened to the black movement, women's organizations, and criminality in general to realize the pervasiveness of this change.

While in Europe homogenization meant, among other things, a brutal policy of anti-Semitism, in the United States its paradoxical counterpart was the civil rights movement. Both aimed at eliminating specificity and otherness—one through extermination camps and the other through social integration. One-dimensionality cannot tolerate racial or ethnic differences: blacks had to become abstract and manipulable labor power just as the whites within the predominant administered rationality. However, with the shift to the stage of full domination of capital, the opposite is the case. It is no accident that black nationalism exploded on the American scene in the late 1960s, and in spite of the simultaneous implementation by the agencies of the old one-dimensional logic of a policy of extermination vis-à-vis the Black Panthers, the winds rapidly changed direction. The search for self-identity (also followed by all other ethnic groups) sought to artificially reconstitute an otherness that had long since been effectively destroyed. Thus, the pathetic efforts of American blacks to become re-Africanized were matched only by the increasing disintegration of the traditional black community centered around the church. Again, contrary to Left conventional wisdom, the civil rights movement was not the result of a sudden rise in militancy on the part of blacks; racist oppression and rebellion against it had been a constant feature of American life throughout this century. Rather, it was triggered by the Warren decision of 1954 and sustained subsequently by federal legislation and liberal funding agencies. Attempts to reconstitute a nonexistent black community are similarly structured from above, this time in accordance with new requirements.[19]

NEW AGENCIES OF DERATIONALIZATION

Although somewhat different because of its longer history of struggle, the women's movement met substantially the same fate. While its recent rise did not take place until the mid-1960s, it immediately fell into the logic of the one-dimensional phase: homogenization and formal equality. Only with the development of a feminist movement was the strategy updated. Thus, while attempts to obtain even symbolic formal recognition, such as the ERA, initially steamrolled through one state legislature after another, that piece of legislation was stopped cold in its tracks. Identified with the forced bureaucratization of the last vestiges of individuality and specificity, the ERA was progressive neither from the viewpoint of the new requirements of the system nor from the depersonalized perspective of the private woman who sees in her femininity the last protection against anonymity and vulnerability.

Radical feminism outflanked the women's liberation movement at the beginning of the 1970s by vindicating the particularity and specificity of women. Its aim was to reverse the logic of formal homogenization and de facto subordination to males, but it was immediately caught in a fatal self-contradiction that prevented it from moving beyond some initial successes. Unable to elaborate a biological foundation that would effectively preclude any possibility of universalization,[20] feminism had to seek a social one. It thus sought to theorize the generalization of feminine traits such as nurturing, against the predominant logic of (presumably patriarchal) instrumental rationality. However, in basing its project of social reconstruction on particular traits resulting from female socialization within patriarchal societies, it ruled out the possibility of qualitatively altering them by seeking the elimination of the existing sexist division of labor originally entailing its particular form of female socialization. Its success would thus destroy its very foundation by homogenizing male and female forms of socialization, thus eliminating that specificity which is hypostasized as the foundation of the movement. Thus precluded from universalizing itself, feminism lingers as the vocal wing of the women's lib movement, institutionalized as the formal expression of one more set of corporativist interests within the flagging pluralism of monopoly capitalism. Unable to radically alter existing social relations, feminism indirectly contributes to this erosion without being able to provide any meaningful alternative. It thus increasingly degenerates to the level of an ideology of upwardly mobile career women using affirmative action and its equivalents as means of social advancement while the lot of most women not only is not substantially improved but actually deteriorates because of the further disintegration of traditional institutions.

Similar patterns appear in other domains as well. Thus, the explosion of criminality since the middle 1960s is also connected with the process of reexternalization of repressive mechanisms whose earlier internalization—during the one-dimensional phase—destroyed spontaneity and creativity to the point of becoming counterproductive within the overhomogenized and overpacified system of social relations. However, the loosening up of repressive mechanisms could not restore the long-since destroyed personality molded by organic community life. Consequently, in the age of artificially created opposition, anomie and criminality become the rule rather than the exception—which also explains the need to reintroduce those external control mechanisms rendered obsolete during the phase of transition when internalization had successfully taken its toll. The reintroduction of the death penalty, the spreading drives against pornography, and the increase in prostitution are all signs of this phenomenon. The brutalized and depersonalized individual that breaks free of the shackles of internalized control mechanisms has to be externally kept in check with objective threats and prohibitions.

THE NEW INTERNATIONAL CONTEXT

Internationally, the situation takes on a bizarre configuration with the reversal of the U.S. international role. First Budapest in 1956, then Prague in 1968, and Poland in 1981 violently ruled out the possibility of reforming the "socialist" system either from below or from above, with the result that the Russian bureaucratic statist model could only intensify its internal contradictions without ever hoping to resolve them or to integrate them creatively in a dynamic framework. Consequently, the repressive apparatus can neither be dismantled nor significantly reduced, since it is an important social glue holding the system together. Thus, the conflict generated by this state of affairs increasingly pushes the intelligentsia toward mysticism and an uncritical pro-Western stance, the working class to drink more and produce less in an increasingly depoliticized existence whose long-range result can only be the resurgence of traditional religion, the peasants toward an intensification of a cynical individualism resulting in a chronic agricultural crisis, and the bureaucracy toward an unprincipled opportunism whose main goal is merely the retention of existing privileges. Confronted with an internal crisis manageable only be remedying the floundering consumer goods sector and agriculture, and unable to implement the reforms necessary to bring about improvements in these two areas since they entail unacceptable political costs (the dismantling of both the bureaucrats as well as the repressive apparatus), the only viable alternative is to seek external solutions carrying *acceptable* political costs, e.g., increasing dependence on the United States. To the extent that the retention and growth of U.S. hegemony requires primarily a continuous international trade, Russian needs feed directly into the logic of the new American imperialism. No matter what solution is provided, the result is the gradual deterioration of Russia to the level of a subimperialist power—notwithstanding its growing military might and occasional scientific breakthroughs.

Reagan's militaristic rhetoric and policies are meant more as means to generate support for increased military budgets to safeguard U.S. competitiveness vis-à-vis Western Europe and Japan by rebuilding the U.S. defense industries and thus reestablishing a declining technological hegemony than as responses to any genuine Soviet threats.[21] Notwithstanding occasional setbacks, East-West trade is constantly increasing, and the huge debts that they have generated only reinforce the new relations of indirect domination. Unable to undertake radical internal reforms,[22] the USSR needs the United States both as a military threat to artificially fan nationalist feelings and as a willing trade partner to meet otherwise unsatisfiable internal consumer demands. In such a system of fine-tuned international terror, both superpowers have stakes neither in significantly increasing nor in significantly decreasing the present precarious balance. A peace offensive would undermine U.S. economic hegemony by weakening defense industries and subsequently all other related sectors, while also taking away the ground from under Russian nationalism. Similarly, an escalation of hostility would eventually affect U.S. trade and subsequently create more consumer goods shortages in the USSR. The present precarious situation, while not a real long-term threat to world peace, is not likely to take too much of a turn either for the better or for the worse—unless unforeseen extraneous factors upset the present balance. United States world hegemony is alive and well managed, not by the Pentagon, but by Wall Street and Madison Avenue.

The Chinese model did not fare much better. Even if one ignores the fact that it was intended for and applicable only to a backward and precapitalist society, Chinese communism is also beset by hard-to-manage internal contradictions that not only make it irrelevant in the West but also raise serious doubts about its future. At any rate, China is only beginning to come to terms with its Stalinist mortgage, which increasingly poses the party, the bureaucracy, and the army as the crucial agencies running the system. Even at the peak of the cultural revolution, the army defined the sociopolitical space within which challenges could be made, and, throughout, the "primacy of politics" had an economistic justification: ultimately it was meant to provide a more efficient and legitimate path to economic development. A genuine process of politicization aiming at the creation of social individuality not only cannot be instrumentalized to immediate productivist requirements, but cannot exhaust the private into the public or dissolve the particular into the universal. Without an irreducible particularity to express and articulate it, the universal loses its concreteness and rapidly deteriorates to the level of a false totality enforceable only by a bureaucracy and a repressive apparatus. Thus, the inherent tendency of the Chinese model is not only increasingly toward bureaucratic collectivism but also toward increasing dependence on the United States.

Both Russia's growing dependence on the United States for agricultural goods and sophisticated technologies to manage crises in two vital areas, and China's internal struggle with backwardness and bureaucratic centralism play into the logic of American imperialism, which—buttressed by and in competition with Western Europe and Japan—far from being in a weak position after the Vietnam disaster, has emerged as the unchallenged world power. This overwhelming hegemony, however, is not based on sheer military superiority—in fact, if this were the criterion to measure hegemony, it would have to be admitted that there has been a relative decrease as a result of the growth of other military powers—but on its overwhelming productive superiority, the instrumentalization of internal contradictions as control mechanisms and propellants to growth, and the lack of a significant alternative to the predominant consumer ideology that automatically legitimates the system by retaining a framework of perpetual scarcity and glorifying the efficiency of the capitalist economy able to feed this consumerism. Given the tendency of the system to overproduce and underconsume, the thrust toward economic crisis can be averted only by successfully disposing of the surplus and exporting problems generated by intensified production. What is crucial at this point for the United States is the guarantee that international trade will continue and grow. The logic of unequal exchange, whereby any trade between a more advanced country and a less developed one will result in the former having the upper hand, not only places the United States in a favorable economic situation but also allows for the exportation of the ecological problems resulting from the continued effort to sustain economic growth. Increasingly, less developed countries will be able to offer in trade to the United States precisely those items whose continued flow raises ecological questions. Thus, the system's Achilles' heel is no longer economic or social or political, but cultural—and at this level there are no challenges anywhere.

As long as consumerism is not seriously challenged by simultaneously demystifying technocratic management, scientific ideologies, hierarchical relations in everyday life, and generally raising questions of the quality of life and *meaning*, capitalism will be able to thrive and grow. Communism, as the last step in the secularization of the Judeo-Christian tradition and understood as the maturation of humankind

through the elimination of exploitation and domination, has historically challenged capitalism on economic grounds while relegating questions of meaning and value to a cultural dimension degraded to epiphenomenal status. Yet, unless these questions are brought to the
political forefront, capitalism will remain unchallenged. In the present
sociohistorical context, however, the cultural challenge has no practical
meaning, since there are no meaningful alternatives to the status quo.
The last promising challenge, Eurocommunism, has by now been all
but forgotten, and its memory continues to have only a negative political and theoretical impact.

THE HERITAGE OF ONE-DIMENSIONALITY AND THE
POLITICS OF ENERGY

The weakness of the American Left in the long run becomes a liabil-
ity for the reconstitution that monopoly capital is in the process of carrying out. This phenomenon is nowhere more clear than in the inability of the American executive to come up with a workable energy policy.
Clearly, the question of energy will remin the central issue around which
most other socioeconomic decisions will revolve in the immediate future. Economic growth is closely tied to the costs of energy, and the
success of Reagan's policies is mostly a function of a number of factors
that, in the last few years, have successfully kept these costs down.
Consequently, even though "the energy crisis" as a political issue has
gradually faded in the background, it remains *the* key to the future of
capitalist development. After all, it was the massive shift from labor-
intensive to capital-intensive technologies that ultimately made the New
Deal age of one-dimensionality work.

The redesigning of the production process associated with Taylorism
discouraged any type of challenge to capitalist control by fragmenting
functions, sharply separating thinking from doing, and generally preventing workers from ever understanding the totality of the labor process. Combined with the higher wages made possible by a rapidly expanding economy (as a result of the shift from labor-intensive to capital-
intensive technologies), this created a pacified populace while also lay-
ing the basis of the recent energy crisis. The year 1968 meant the exhaustion of this two-pronged strategy of capitalist reconstruction and
the beginning of the energy crisis. Greater reliance on nonrenewable
fuels necessary for rapidly expanding capital- and energy-intensive industries laid the groundwork for a critical shortage of energy, and the
fragmentation and rationalization of the work process resulted in a
frustrated population unable to fully grasp the roots of its problem.

All this combined to bring about a new kind of antibureaucratic
populism, couched occasionally in traditional right-wing rhetoric seeking

a return to a long-gone entrepreneurial capitalism. This is the foundation of both Carter's and Reagan's political appeal. It is the unexpected coincidence of this new populism with the objective interests of monopoly capital that explains the political developments of the late 1970s and early 1980s.

Far from being a monolithic whole, American capitalism had developed a myriad of sectors with one major division being most important: that between the competitive and the monopoly sectors. While the competitive sector (steel, automobile, garments) was running into increasingly fierce international challenges, the monopoly sector (computers, aircraft, and high technology in general) was thriving. Furthermore, while the competitive sector was still besieged by all the problems that the strategy of capitalist reconstruction from the New Deal onward had sought to solve, the monopoly sector (largely composed of newer industries) had no such problems. Thus, given its privileged state, it had few if any labor problems, it produced little pollution, and it was in no way challenged by traditional efficiency, profit-sharing to greater legitimation. To people employed in the monopoly sector, socialism had ceased to be an alternative since in their particular context socialism would amount at best to the rhetorical displacement of "owners" by "party officials." It is this sector also that holds the key to political developments in the United States for the rest of this century. From its viewpoint, the competitive sector at home might as well be phased out and relocated abroad in a new international division of labor. The exporting of the whole competitive sector, of course, coincides with the change in strategy of capitalist reconstruction.

That an energy crisis was coming—unless drastic measures were taken—was a commonplace among ecologists well before the 1973 crisis. Oil eventually would simply run out. The answer to that, of course, was that nuclear energy would replace it and all would be well in this, the best of all possible worlds. Only when the problems with nuclear energy became widely known were hard questions raised about the fact that increasingly larger amounts of energy would be needed to sustain "progress." At that point it became clear that this "progress" meant essentially the indefinite extension of that American way of life that has a generally overweight American eating large amounts of nutritionally dubious junk food, using an incredible assortment of labor-saving devices, and then spending a good part of the day jogging in the latest sport fashions. This indefinite extension would also apply to the present technocratic system within which capital grows indefinitely and all of the world comes to resemble the United States.

In addition to the fact that only some sectors of American capitalism have an objective stake in this scenario—the most backward, older, competitive sectors—it should be recalled that the present system, where the American way of life is a deeply felt need not only in the United States but in the whole Western world (and an even larger sector of the Eastern world as well), is *historically constituted* and came about as a response to some very specific problems: the prevention of qualitative social change as the result of the 1929 capitalist crisis. Today it does not have to be ideologically inculcated, but it naturally flows from the way technology, the media, and even American cities have developed. Its main objective is the consumerization and the deactivation of the masses at the price of greater amounts of energy, whose extraction and use tend to cause irreparable environmental damage. *Even from the viewpoint of large sectors of capital, this is no longer necessary or desirable.* Its retention is a function of the political struggle between the two main sectors of American capitalism—the competitive and the monopoly sectors.

Despite ecologists' long-term forecasts, however, today's general awareness of the energy crisis can be attributed to contingent events, such as the Iranian revolution and the political need to mobilize broad support for a deeply troubled nuclear program. Even before the Three Mile Island accident, the American nuclear program was besieged by various environmental and public interest groups—many of them supported by interests in the monopoly sectors—and was likely to grind to a halt in the not-so-distant future. The energy crisis in its spectacular form of long gas lines at considerable inconvenience to the everyday consumer was meant as a harbinger of worse things to come unless nuclear power was fully developed. With nuclear energy, the American way of life could easily survive, and even the automobile could remain by using electricity instead of the internal combustion engine.

The task ahead in the United States would be to provide concrete alternatives to the American way of life, to expose its irrational and historically constituted character, and to work out specific proposals to restructure everyday life in such a way that the reduction of energy consumption will not be a matter of personal sacrifice (which will never work) or of bureaucratically enforced rationing (which will work only at too high a social and political price), but a matter of normal, everyday behavior. With a Left powerless to formulate cogently any alternative to the American way of life by seeking the cultural hegemony necessary to popularize new lifestyles not inextricably tied to capitalist growth, the shift from the transition phase to that of full domination of monopoly capital is thus temporarily stalled. The most tragic feature of the age of Reagan may well turn out to be the failure to develop an effective, alternative American way of life during the breathing spell provided during his first term by stable energy costs. This failure has a lot to do with the fact that there no longer is a Left making noise and energizing the system. This means that, far from being solved, the energy crisis will return with a vengeance and reintroduce all the problems that were unwisely forgotten in the early 1980s.

CONCLUSIONS

In retrospect, Marxism and traditional critical theory turn out to be, at best, theoretical expressions of earlier phases of capitalist development—entrepreneurial capitalism and the transition phase—which cannot adequately grasp the new coming phase of full monopoly capital. The new conflicts cannot be understood by means of their obsolete categories, and their rehistoricization yields paradoxical results. Far from being exhausted, capitalism is at the beginning of a new historical epoch during which monopoly capital ends up as the potential agency of emancipatory possibilities. In order to further develop, monopoly capital must recreate a previously destroyed public sphere. Whether this public sphere can, in fact, be recreated or whether it will only provide regulatory mechanisms rather than developing qualitatively new alternatives remains to be seen. One thing is clear: socialism is no longer a viable alternative in any of its various historical versions, and Leftist theory is in shambles. The annihilation of the emancipatory other has, however, reproduced those very contradictions externally eliminated within the very heart of capitalism with disconcerting consequences. In fact, the very success of monopoly capitalism today seems to be tied to its ability to carry out new emancipatory tasks.

NOTES

1. Most of these conclusions, however, could have been drawn much earlier—at least as early as the turn of the century, at the time of the Bernstein Debate. For a fuller discussion of this problem, see my "Labriola and the Roots of Eurocommunism," *Berkeley Journal of Sociology* 22 (1977–1978), pp. 3–44.

2. Cf. Cornelius Castoriadis, *L'Institution Imaginaire de la Societe* (Paris, 1975).

3. A full discussion of this problem is in my "The Changing Function of Critical Theory," *New German Critique* (Fall 1977), pp. 29–38.

4. For a fuller discussion of this point, see my "Reading the Grundrisse," *Theory and Society* 2 (Summer, 1975), pp. 235–256.

5. This point is developed in my "Dialectics and Materialism in Lukacs," *Telos* (Spring, 1972), pp. 105–134.

6. Georg Lukacs, *History and Class Consciousness*, trans. R. Livingstone (London, 1971), p. 81.

7. Max Horkheimer and Theodor W. Adorno, *Dialectic of the Enlightenment* (New York, 1972).

8. The defense of particularity, of course, became a main issue with Adorno, especially after his extended debate with Benjamin. Cf. Susan Buck-Morss, *The Origins of Negative Dialectics* (New York, 1977). The classical statement on the

integration of the opposition is Herbert Marcuse, *One-Dimensional Man* (Boston, 1964).

9.   Cf. Herbert Marcuse's various unsuccessful attempts to reformulate the dialectic in his "A Note on Dialectics (1960)," in *Reason and Revolution* (Boston, 1960), pp. vii–xiv, and "The Concept of Negation in the Dialectic," *Telos* (Summer, 1971), pp. 130–132.

10.   Good examples of this are Adorno's essays in his *The Positivist Dispute in German Sociology*, trans. G. Aday and D. Frisby (New York, 1976).

11.   Cf. Herbert Marcuse, *Eros and Civilization* (New York, 1962).

12.   See Adorno's analyses in *Minima Moralia* (Frankfurt, 1951).

13.   This becomes all too obvious in Adorno's *Negative Dialectic*, trans. A. B. Ashton (New York, 1973).

14.   It is not surprising that Marcuse wrote "A Biological Foundation for Socialism?" as the first chapter of *An Essay on Liberation* (Boston, 1969), pp. 7–22.

15.   Jürgen Habermas, *Legitimation Crisis*, trans. Thomas McCarthy (Boston, 1975).

16.   This thesis is best developed in Mihaly Vajda's work on fascism. See his "Crisis and the Way Out: The Rise of Fascism in Italy and Germany," *Telos* (Summer, 1972), pp. 3–26.

17.   Arghiri Emmanuel, *Unequal Exchange*, trans. Brian Pearce (New York, 1972).

18.   Cf. Antonio Carlo, *Crisi Economica e Dialettica Storica* (Rome, 1975).

19.   Cf. Adolph L. Reed, Jr., "The 'Black Revolution' and the Reconstitution of Domination" in this volume.

20.   Of course, some splinter groups reclaim a biological foundation, but that automatically defuses their revolutionary potential by downgrading the required universalistic claims to mere particularistic ones.

21.   For a fuller examination of this predicament, see Paul Piccone and Victor Zaslavsky, "The Socio-Economic Roots of Re-Armament," *Telos* (Winter, 1981–1982), pp. 5–18.

22.   Cf. Cornelius Castoriadis, *Devant la Guerre* (Paris, 1981). For a discussion of the remote possibility of economic reform, see Cornelius Castoriadis, " 'Facing the War' and 'The Socio-Economic Roots of Re-Armament': A Rejoinder," and the two replies that follow, in *Telos* (Fall, 1982), pp. 192–210.

Part IV

What's Left?: An Exchange

REED:

The opening paragraph of *The Eighteenth Brumaire* might be applied to radical activism in the 1960s. When the counterculturists and black nationalists proclaimed a revolutionary break with bourgeois culture, they did so in a language that affirmed the mass-marketing culture's principle of self-definition through commodity consumption. When the New Left sought wholesale theoretical clarity, the principal turns taken—Marxism–Leninism and Pan-Africanism—entailed departure from lived history and initiation of a search for authenticity in the past. In each case the goal of authenticity—ultimately a variety of the quest for self-fulfillment—overrode engaged political critique.

Each of the radical political and cultural movements of the 1960s endorsed a view that connected politics and personal revitalization. To that extent—notwithstanding their other considerable accomplishments—those movements hastened their own demise by overloading personal relationships (thus feeding the logic of "burnout") and banalizing political action by making it an instrument of self-realization. This tendency was exacerbated as actual political movement slowed, and, combined with the commoditized "alternative" vision of counterculturism—black and white—it left us in the last decade's apolitical and commercially orchestrated hedonism. A central aspect of the tragedy of 1960s radicalism, therefore, is its inability, even in its apparently most radical manifestations, to transcend the irony of mass culture—i.e., the fragmentation and reification of the atomized identity and the constraint of all types of purposive activity by the requirements of the (self-defeating) desire to overcome atomization.

Although this is hardly the only area that should be searched for clues about the natural history of the New Left, examination of the normative vision invoked by radicalism—tacitly or otherwise—may illuminate elements within New Left praxis that undermined the movement. Given that it at best addresses only one aspect even of the Left's normative vision, how do you react to the view proposed here? Is it accurate, even in a limited context? Does it help us comprehend the dynamics of dissolution in the New Left? Does it help us make sense of the present situation? Is it mean-spirited, misanthropic, "Marxist neoconservatism"?

LUKE:

These questions are difficult to answer. The contemporary social spectacle integrates anything and everything into its logic of commodification, including historical time itself. In the bright, familiar packaging of "the Sixties," a decade serves as the fungible containerization of uniquely diverse social upheavals, cultural innovations, and political struggles. Significance is marked in differences; the disjunctures from decades similarly packaged as the "Fifties," "Thirties," or "Seventies." To answer these questions and judge the New Left, one must pick through the incomplete pieces, last signs, and remaining fragments of an era jumbled into "the Sixties" container. But, in answering, one also feels like a *Vekhi* critic, writing off unhappily the sad realities of the 1905 revolution not knowing 1917 will come.

Still, like it or not, the opening passages of Marx's *Eighteenth Brumaire* accurately capture much of the radical spirit and substance of 1960s radicalism. Maturing in the wake of McCarthy's antileftist pogroms in the 1950s, New Left activists and black nationalist cadres clearly had to borrow from others the names, battle cries, and costumes of their revolutions. To grapple with the pressing crises of the "Other America" (as Harrington defined it) that the "Amerika" (as SDS epithet framed it) of mainstream suburban society ignored, 1960s radicals turned to Gandhi, Nkrumah, Mao, Che, and Ho for their critiques of advanced industrial society.

Images, illusions, and icons of revolution, packaged in film, voice, and videotape in Moscow, Peking, Algiers, Havana, Cairo, New Delhi, Accra, Hanoi, Leopoldville, Djakarta, Nairobi, Belgrade, and Conakry, incessantly were broadcast and rebroadcast in the American mass media as a spectacle of global revolution. From these prepackaged metatexts of transformation, 1960s radicals—black, white, brown, male, female, young, and old—borrowed the names, battle cries, and costumes of their revolutions. As a result, Marxism–Leninism and Pan-Africanism, which had virtually no groundedness in the lived history of advanced industrial America, were adopted as schemas of "wholesale theoretical clarity" into the countercultures of the 1960s. Yet, in presenting these time-honored disguises and borrowed languages as their own, America's Black Power, New Left, and counterculture movements fell far short of revolutionizing themselves anew or creating something new that had never yet existed. The New Left intended to create a revolution, but, in the process, it unintentionally revolutionized the workings of corporate America.

Clearly, the central tragedy of 1960s radicalism was its inability to transcend these ironies of mass culture. As members of a society of bureaucratically controlled consumption, telegenic spectacles of opposition, resistance, critique, or negativity projected from abroad in the mass media provided most of the revolutionary forms and goals of the New Left. With the eclipse of blue-collar industrial work by white-collar service work in the 1950s, and the effective domestication of proletarian union power in the 1940s, the strategy and tactics of America's Old left were defined as obsolete by 1960s radicals. Instead the spectacles of media culture projected new models of action: Gandhi's humiliation of British rule, Ho's defeat of French and American military force, Nasser's appeals for Pan-Arab/Pan-African unity, Che's call for Third World uprisings, Nkrumah's model of African revolution, and the new Islamic awakening across the Eastern Hemisphere. To transform America, many among the New Left mindlessly mimicked these anticolonial models of struggle, debating endlessly whether or not committed radicals should fight in the mountains, out in the countryside, or from within the ghetto. One need only remember those endless debates during the 1960s, late at night, in one, two, many dorm rooms, over the relative strengths and weaknesses of Gandhi's satyagraha, Maoist peasant war, or Che's *focoismo* in mobilizing "the people" of Oregon, Illinois, Alabama, or Vermont. In these spectacular images of rebellion, 1960s radicals found the illusions needed to conceal from themselves the corporate limitations on the content of their struggles, while keeping their enthusiasm on the high plane of great historical tragedy. Thus, America's counterculture, which had produced rebels without a cause in the 1950s, generated revolutionaries without a base in the 1960s and 1970s.

Likewise, 1960s radicals, armed with the names of peasant revolutionaries, shouting the battle cries of national liberation wars from colonies in European empires and clad in the costumes of Ho, Castro, or Gandhi, projected their quest for personal realization, communal authenticity, and self-development into the transformation of advanced industrial society. In turn, the revolutions of 1968—marking a single moment that summarizes an entire period—were failed revolutions, just as the uprisings of 1848 were failed revolutions. By the manifest criteria of their borrowed revolutionary theories, the revolutions of 1968 were a "failure" in America—as well as France, Czechoslovakia, and else-where in Europe—to the extent that both black and white radicals in the 1960s failed to substitute a new political order for the old regime through either force or nonviolence.

As revolutionaries, then, what exactly did the New Leftists and black nationalists change? Even after Johnson's resignation and the massive street demonstrations of 1968–1970, the Vietnam war did not end. Great Society legislation from 1964 to 1966 did more for the outsiders of the "other Americas" than did the SDS, Black Panthers, or La Raza Unida. The oil crisis of 1973 had more impact on changing the wasteful ways of the affluent society than did all the New Left's criticism during the Age of Aquarius. Yet, the New Left and black nationalist and counter-culture movements, both in the 1960s and continually ever since, have been identified in political debates, academic writing, and the mass media as powerful agents of social transformation. Why has the nar-row reality of revolutionary change not matched these expansive spec-tacles of revolutionary transformation?

A hardline analysis of the 1960s may miss the real thrust of these events. The "revolutionary break" of the New Left with "bourgeois" culture, society, and politics actually was defined almost entirely in the codes of mass marketing. The Woodstock nation plainly formed at a complex intersection of automobile, rock music, drug, and outdoor life-style consumption. The counterculture's ultimate principle was simple: individuals find their self-actualization through commodity consump-tion, material goods and wish-fulfilling images. Thus, the revolt of the repressed in the 1960s was denominated in the "product revolutioni-zation" of corporate capitalist product demography. Such revolutions, it now would appear, turn out as episodes of corrective, weak, nega-tive feedback than as events of destructive, system-transforming vio-lent change. "America," like everything in a society of the spectacle, was and is an evolving "product" for mass consumption.

In the 1960s, the American dream machine was not "performing" as its civics book operating manuals and formal constitutional warranties had guaranteed to the buyers. Urban squalor, black inequality, rural backwardness, spreading pollution, denials of civil rights, suburban anomie, mass poverty, and conscription for an undeclared war all were obvious signs of a poorly performing product or an increasingly falter-ing service. Hence, a complete change in methods, conditions, or models of operation—a product revolutionization—was launched in the 1960s, which the black and white countercultures strongly aided and abetted. Old, rundown, unimproved America was "broken with" in this "revolutionization" of 1960s radicals; but, as with most products of cor-porate change, this revolutionary breakthrough only led down the aisles of collective choice to a redesigned model: new, improved America.

Ironically, the revolution of the New Left, Black Power, and other counterculture movements in the 1960s assisted the previous projects of corporate growth and economic liberalism, accelerating the collapse of arbitrary limits imposed upon the *individual* pursuit of life, liberty and happiness. American had *not* delivered the individual goods of industrial democracy before the 1960s to entire categories of "individuals"—blacks, the young, women, ethnics, latinos, gays, old people, ghetto dwellers, the rural poor. Many social taboos, political rules, and cultural attitudes in traditional American society constituted a restrictive culture of petty apartheid, preventing goods and services from circulating far beyond the secure sphere of middle-class, middle-aged, male, straight, WASP communities.

Newsclips of the Watts, Detroit, or Washington, D.C. riots encapsulate the revolutionary situation of the 1960s. Within a society of spectacle—which defines identity, purpose, and meaning in terms of commodities—marginalized, underemployed consumers leap out of shattered store windows, carrying away the best icons of identity—TV sets, vacuum cleaners, air conditioners, reclining chairs, stereo systems. Denied the leisure time, wages, or legal equality to acquire these totems of consumption more conventionally, the outsiders rioted; and, in the revolt of the repressed, these riots became "the shopping spree" denied to them by the petty apartheid of the traditional marketplace. In the name of revolution, women's liberation, Black Power, gay rights, or flower power, the New Leftists—in their theories—fought for authenticity, personal fulfillment, and self-actualization, which meant—in practice—increasing access for these outsiders to corporate capitalist goods and services.

Despite its best radical intentions, the New Left unexpectedly served as the shock troops of mass culture and its corporate producers, tearing down the last constraints on circulating all commodities to anyone, anytime, anywhere. Except for the most radical fringe, the New Left engaged in guerrilla theater not guerrilla terror. Its agitprop was performed by the Doors, Jimi Hendrix, and the Jefferson Airplane rather than underground professional revolutionaries. The exemplary community of New Left activities was the rock concert and televised sit-in, both spectacles of consumption and personal self-definition in consumption. The diverse countercultures of the 1960s quickly were colonized and instrumentalized by corporate culture as a "look," a "style," or a "mindset" to be sold nationwide as corporate products. Hip capitalism, by the same token, emerged in sandal shops, waterbed stores, record shops, Leftist bookstores, health food outlets, and head shops to sell satisfactions for these newly mobilized needs. Revolution was a product. It could be bought into. With the correct investment of time and effort in new costume, language, and attitude, anyone could become a revolutionist. Yet, as New Left activists donned their berets, dark glasses, jungle fatigues, and leather jackets, their attempts to apply Maoism, *Fidelismo*, and Gandhism to America revolutionized not society but the corporate marketplace.

Not surprisingly, then, the New Left has not produced any texts of critical reappraisal, like *Class Struggles in France 1848–1850*, *Marxism and Philosophy*, *1905*, *The Prison Notebooks*. Instead, its self-understanding is memorialized in "Bye-Bye, American Pie," *The Doonesbury Chronicles*, and *The Big Chill*. Real revolutionaries in the 1960s would be either in power, dead at the hands of the state, still struggling underground, or plotting the final offensive from abroad (perhaps in Switzerland?). As *The Big Chill* reveals, however, the revolutionizations of the 1960s were only a valorous phase of youth, marked by a special mode of language, solidarity, dress, and attitude. The counterculture revolutionaries survived those days of fear and loathing; but, today, instead of instructing their cellmates in revolution along the Lena River or furtively sketching out new radical theories in jail, they sell running shoes, deal dope, practice law, raise kids, or work in the media. Yet, to its credit, this revolution *does* have a powerful soundtrack. Those rock and roll classics of the 1960s, which can be turned up all the way on the Walkman, will ease the sufferings of the long march through the institutions; and these tunes always take one back to the days of "revolution," recreating the illusion of rebellious upheavals, without forcing the renunciation of personal self-actualization in consumer goods.

With its street demonstrations, sit-ins, and revolutionary communiques, the counterculture broke with and broke down traditional America. In winning victories for the "other Americas," however, the Playboy philosophy, a Jordache look, Cosmo girls, a sense of Miller Time, the Dodge Rebellion, a New Pepsi generation, a Virginia Slims "progress," and L'Oreal values all were mobilized as the mop-up units, following behind the sweeps of the countercultures' shock troops against Nixon's–GM's–Wallace's–Dow Chemical's "Amerika." In the last analysis, the New Left cannot transcend the irony of mass culture because it is mass culture's ultimate irony.

Indeed, the spectacle system has not only survived the commodification of New Left revolution; it actually has been made stronger through occasional doses of this self-administered "artificial negativity." The videos, soundtracks, and texts of the revolutionary 1960s now are the spectacular models of social movements in the 1980s. The peace movement, the antinuclear movement, the Central American solidarity movements—now organizing thousands who were infants or not yet born in the 1960s—all have borrowed, in turn, the disguises and languages of "the Sixties" in their political campaigns. Here, the answers to hard political questions, rising from debates such as this one, might serve an important purpose. In recognizing the real roots of revolutionary activity in the 1960s, these new activists might not repeat the tragedies of the 1960s radicalism as the farces of a new "revolution" in the 1960s.

WILLINGHAM:

1) I don't think the search for authenticity was just in the "past" but in what I would call "extrinsic" directions of diverse kinds including the past. Thus those radical blacks who resisted Marxism, for example, because it was somehow *outside* the black experience did not realize that in their turn to Pan-Africanism they did the same thing, Pan-Africanism, of course, being just itself another specific ideological school(?). This may exclude Du Bois, of course, but they also excluded him! If this appears to equate Pan-Africanism with Marxism as a system it is not intended. This point merely extends and reinforces the point about how "engaged political critique" was avoided. I only want to assert that it was not just a turn to the past.

2) Political action was banalized by some kind of personal level needs, but I tend to see that (perhaps in retrospect) as certainly an effort to find in political movements, or better, to approach political movements with unresolved personalism(?) which skewed our view of politics. Some of this did come from the atomization caused by mass society/culture, but some of the rest of it came exactly as Marx saw in *The Eighteenth Brumaire*, i.e, from well-embedded values and identities settled in socializing agencies which formed so much of what we were. Thus from the perspective of the grandmothers and mothers of "the Sixties," radicalism was just one more temptation like loose women, gambling, or strong drink. That was one reason why I was always so sensitive to the association of radical ideas with "youth." The commonsense notion that "new ideas" will appeal to the young was one thing, but the very notion that a call for broadly transformative behavior (revolution?) should be restricted to those who have no experience not only flies in the face of the dynamism of the link between exploitation and remedy, but it raises the large question of what would be the basis of the humanism of the new society? Michael Jackson? My sixteen-year-old?

a. On the problem of burnout: there may be something respectable about this fortyish phenomenon, but I doubt it. It is difficult for me to treat as "burned out" one who made it by shouting the most radical (read unrealistic) slogans unless, like Baraka (who is *not* burned out), the end is in the assertion. I'll think more about this.

3) Is the view Reed proposes accurate? Generally speaking, yes. However, Karenga would argue that external forces caused the dissolution. He is wrong. Yet there is a need to make sure that we situate Left activity within a dynamic context composed of diverse "players," "allies," and such.

GROSS:

It's true: "the Sixties" explosion got caught up in and banalized by a mass-marketing culture; political action was too often (but not always) simply a facet of the quest for self-realization, and the Left destroyed itself partly because it became infatuated with foreign models at the expense of a regard for lived history.

An awareness of these failures is easier to come by now, thanks to the clarity of hindsight. Many of us didn't always notice them as they were happening—or, if we did, we expected that everything would somehow work out all right in the end, that even failures would dia-lectically turn into successes. In rereading much literature from the 1960s recently, I was struck by how much optimism there was then, only fifteen or twenty years ago. The world, it was assumed, was about to be radically transformed, and it would be youth (and youth culture) that would help do it. Jerry Rubin, for example, imagined that it would not be long before "every high school and college in the country will close with riots and sabotage. . . . Millions of young people will surge into the streets. . . . High government officials will defect. . . . Revolutionaries will break into jails and free all the prisoners. . . . and Workers will seize their factories and begin running them communally, without profit." This was only partly tongue in cheek. It's hard to re-member now, but hundreds of thousands of young people believed that this scenario, or something close to it, could actually happen—and soon. Not only the optimism, then, but also the naivete of that decade appears startling today. The Left and the counterculture as a whole could have stood some heavy doses of pessimism and been better off for it; or, if the optimism was to be kept, it ought to have been draped as Ernst Bloch once put it—"with funeral crepe flying." If this had happened, the letdown of the 1970s might have been endurable, sim-ply because people would have been prepared for it. Also, it might have been easier to continue some of the more important cultural and political projects begun in the 1960s instead of abandoning them alto-gether as many did.

All this, however, has to do with the 1960s and 1970s. We're now in the 1980s. One of the most pressing questions we have to face, there-fore, is how to deal with what happened. We are in a period of setback and defeat, there is no doubt about that. This means we live in the shadow of something that went wrong. We can't escape this depress-ing fact; we can't pretend to be able to start afresh with "new ideas" as if the past had never occurred. *That* road is a perilous one, though not a few are now in the process of taking it. On the other hand, we can't go back and try mindlessly to repeat what happened. That would do no good either: it would only lead, as Marx put it, to the repetition of tragedy which is farce. What, then, can we do?

I would suggest several things. First, we need to understand exactly what went wrong in the 1960s and why. I mean this not superficially; we need to grasp in detail the logic of failure, the mechanism of defeat and cooptation, or else all of it will likely happen again. Those of us who experienced the 1960s firsthand have to make ourselves wiser for the next time, if there is a next time. The counterculture has been criticized for its inability to "transcend the irony of mass culture." Actually it was a longshot that it would be able to do so, for the counterculture was little prepared to ward off the blandishments of the market and media. After all, virtually everyone in the counterculture had grown up within the artificial paradise of mass culture; even when the young rebelled against it, they still accepted many of its presuppositions. What is required, then, to break away from something apparently so all-consuming? How does one free oneself from a condition which seems able to buy or coopt everything, even dissent? These are questions which have to be addressed, and the 1960s provide an excellent setting for studying them.

Second, we need to go back to that tumultuous decade and try to recover its unrealized possibilities. There were a lot of things that happened during that period, both in the political and cultural realms, which were highly original. A great many imaginative forms of all types were created which briefly saw the light of day and then were quickly commodified. It might be well to return to these original moments and see what can be learned from them. They could serve as takeoff points for new developments in the future.

Third, those of us who were affected by the 1960s need to be careful not to turn on that decade like frustrated lovers. We expected much and it was not forthcoming. Under the circumstances, the inclination exists to reject what happened then as a mistake or a seductive illusion. This may be a natural reaction, but it is not the best way to handle disappointment. Actually we have almost exactly the opposite obligation. We need to do what we can, publicly and privately, to preserve the memory of what was highest and best in the 1960s before these traces disappear altogether. This is not an easy task because of the ambiguity many of us feel about that period and the problematic relationship we still have toward it. However, it can't have escaped anyone that we're now in the midst of a wholesale assault not only on the values of the 1960s but on the *factual truths* of that time, on what actually happened and why. Part of the assault is politically motivated; it's the usual kind of reinterpretation that the victors impose upon the vanquished. However, part of it also has to do with the way the culture industry chews up and reprocesses "facts" and "values" until they become cliches. In either case, the effect is the same. What was once meaningful soon gets reduced to trivia. Already the generation just now coming of age has no idea what the 1960s were about. How could they? They know nothing but distortions. This situation imposes a responsibility on those who believe that there are things worth salvaging from that decade. First of all, however, these things have to be seen before they can be salvaged. Simply making them visible is a task that cannot be shunned; if it is, then the best of the 1960s could be lost forever.

Finally, we need to learn better than we have so far how to live in periods of retrenchment. Perhaps a closer study of history would be useful here. It may be satisfying to read about the heady successes of earlier movements—the 1776s, 1789s, and 1917s—but what about the aftermath of defeats? How did people hold themselves together in bad times? What attitude did they take toward a past which they had once heavily invested themselves in, only to find it later effaced or denied by the new political and cultural realities? It might not be edifying, but it would be helpful to understand how the radicals of the French Revolution coped with Thermidor, or later with the Restoration; how the German revolutionaries of 1848 dealt with the bleak years of the 1850s; how the French working class preserved remnants of solidarity and hope after the devastating suppression of the Paris Commune; how German radicals tried to keep alive the "council idea" after the defeat of the Revolution of 1918–1919; or how disappointed Russian revolutionaries confronted the "betrayal" of their ideals in the 1920s and 1930s (a careful study of Victor Serge, to mention only one example, would be especially rewarding).

The list could go on; it is unfortunately a long one. The point I want to make, though, is that there is a lot more to be gained by looking back at this regressive side of history than one might think. To keep us going forward, the historical experience of the past is about all we have. We certainly can't fall back any longer on the kind of revolutionary optimism which led Rosa Luxemburg to declare that we may lose all the battles—but we would win the last one. We know now that there is no guarantee we won't lose the last one as well. Still, I think we could go at least a little way toward insuring against this by following some of the suggestions I have made here. The 1960s, it's true, have ended in shambles. Nevertheless, it's possible to try and pick up the pieces and put them together again but this time in different combinations.

PICCONE:

I can almost fully endorse Reed's statement. My possible reservations have to do with elaboration of details and different emphases. Let me begin with what I find most interesting in Reed's account.

Unlike most Left analyses of the New Left as either a consciously

mediated product of the more enlightened sectors of the Old Left (Den-
itch) or a spontaneous outburst of creativity and frustration (Breines)—
both accounts certainly true *in part*—Reed's statement relates the phenomenon to the dynamics of American mass culture: the extension of
commodification to intellectual production and political movements.
Seeing the New Left in this light allows us to focus on the logic of
system shifts from the New Deal to the post-New Deal model and relate the rise and demise of that New Left to broader social processes.
That the predominant visions tended to be derived from the past and
that their realization was sought by politicizing the personal dimension
testifies to the cretinizing effects of mass culture in blocking the formation of genuinely new visions and the instrumentalization of the
various movements as shock troops of the commodity form's penetration of the last bastion of resistance to further capitalist rationalization:
the self and the personal. This also explains why, with the effective
reconstitution of a new mediational black elite and the phasing out of
the Vietnam war the most lasting result was generalized narcissism.

However, the system shift for which the New Left may have been a
social catalyst did not quite take place as smoothly as it should have,
and the pathological recycling of a pre-New Deal model within a New
Deal administrative context that could not be effectively dismantled in
spite of immense efforts to do so only means that the conditions which
generated the New Left are still with us—only in temporary remission.
If anything, the original problems have been intensified: the more effective adminstration of black marginality, the intensified disintegration of the traditional family in the absence of an alternative working
model, the impossibility of the system to rationalize itself or function
independently of a growing and counterproductive central bureaucracy, the ineradicability of inflation and unemployment—these and
other anomic conditions make the introduction of a not-yet-existing alternative model of further capitalist rationalization all the more urgent.
When an alternative model will be eventually excogitated, and it becomes necessary to politically implement it in order to overcome the
forces of stasis and reaction, it will become expeditious (as usual in
American history) to precipitate a crisis and vent latent discontents. It
is then that a functionally equivalent version of the New Left will be
once again allowed its day. If the lessons of the history of the New Left
will have been learned, maybe the outcome will not be once again only
instrumentalization and integration into computerized misery, but also
emancipation and the beginning of qualitative change.

FEENBERG:
I think the view expressed in the opening statement of this section
is sadly accurate, but there was a real dilemma behind the problems.

Old Left styles of activism, what in French is called "le militantisme," could not be revived effectively in the 1960s. The mainstream of the movement rejected the impersonality and "puritanism" of traditional activism. The movement arose from a protest against a technocratic system in which, to paraphrase Fanon, "objectivity is always against the rebel." The struggle for personal self-realization on the Left contained an implicit protest against "reality," or what, in any case, American society used for reality in this period. There was no question of basing a long-term "disciplined" activity on an "objective" analysis of the situation in the traditional style.

The sectarian groups were engaged in what we might have called at the time a "nostalgia trip," doomed to failure from the start. The longing for an ordered world in which objectivity and discipline guaranteed success was necessarily frustrated by the absence of a traditional intelligentsia or working-class support for the movement. Thus the personality structures and motivations presupposed by traditional organizational forms were never available as a basis for old-fashioned activism. The caricature of the Old Left these sectarian groups managed to produce was a destructive dead end.

So what could the movement fall back on? The apparently radical refusal of normal daily life and the heavy burden of repression carried over from the 1950s led to ultimately cooptable changes in the sexual compensations for alienated labor. The moral fervor and hopes born in the struggles faltered or lost their immediate relevance. All attempts to find a middle term between counterculturism and sectarianism proved unable to resist attack from those currents, which were far more influential with the mass of participants in the movement.

I suspect that we are not so much clearer today than we were in the 1960s on how to organize and struggle effectively in a society that no longer produces the human types and problems out of which grew traditional forms, and in which traditional "bourgeois culture" has all but collapsed. If there should be another upsurge of mass struggle in the 1980s, for example, around war in Central America, I believe we would quickly confront similar problems once again. Perhaps the existence of a well-known historical precedent offers hope.

JORDAN:
I don't feel that Pan-Africanism ever "sought" or found "wholesale theoretical clarity." I do agree, however, that in its devitalized state during the 1970s its focus was personal actualization through a combination of ritual, nostalgia for a nonexistent, romantic Africa, and mysticism.

Pan-Africanism, or even black nationalism, was primarily a cultural, rather than political, position, but in its most radical period, probably around 1969 or 1970, Pan-Africanism (at least as it was expressed in art) talked of violent revolution and attacked the bastions of political power (both the predominantly white power structure and its black middle-class allies). Perhaps the hostility and rebellion expressed through rhetoric and art were no more than middle-class youth's equivalent of the riots of the poor. In many ways the antiwhite rage of black nationalists and their refusal to participate in the system were cathartic and, thus, primarily therapeutic.

The theoretical impulses underlying the Pan-Africanism of "the Sixties" were not initially egocentric (although one could argue that the rage and sense of injustice that create a radical is extremely personal). Pan-Africanism, or more generally black nationalism, was born out of a belief that to become a part of the American system was to integrate into a "burning house" and out of a sometimes sentimental and patronizing identification with the problems of the black poor. I feel that the reduction of Pan-Africanism to a cultish and mystical orientation (Islam, the Yoruba religion, an interest in authentic African culture that required considerable, individual study, plus accompanying interests like vegetarianism and astrology) resulted because political activity was stymied by repression and police violence. In other words, radical theory was not at first interested in "personal revitalization" that led radicals away from political action. Rather, the emphasis on "getting oneself together" came about because people had reached a state of alienation that made reform inconceivable to them but was not sufficient to fuel a revolutionary response. The failure to move the sincerely felt rejection of the system to another level and to redirect the political rhetoric to an analysis of ways to confront the system resulted from fear of harassment, imprisonment, and perhaps death, and from the Pan-Africanist's contentment with his essentially comfortable middle-class and/or bohemian existence.

KOVEL:

I think there is a problem if you start out by assuming that the New Left failed en bloc as if it were a total disaster and utterly failed in all of its emancipatory goals. Because the more grandiose expectations of the movement weren't fulfilled tells us nothing about the actual advances that may have been won during the period; more, it leads us in the direction of a nihilistic totalization instead of a critical analysis.

I am impressed, rather, with the fact that a considerable degree of transformation did take place as a result of the counterculture and the black nationalist movement, despite the overall failure to lead the faithful into the promised land or to overturn the main relations of domination. Some of this has been substantive in the sense of providing a matrix for ways of living that are absolutely more liberated now than they were in 1959, for example, those of the women's or gay movements, neither of which could have happened were it not for the opening provided by the counterculture. Some has been prefigurative, in the sense that the movements of the 1960s provided the theoretical break which permitted today's most promising movements, for example, the social-ecological, to take root. Another example, not widely appreciated: the Sandinista revolution in Nicaragua is profoundly affected by countercultural ideology, much of the leadership having grown up in that decade and having considerable exposure as students to the main emancipatory tendencies of the time.

In general, there is much more of a healthy distrust of authority now than in 1959, thanks in good measure to the movements of the 1960s. I am not trying to be Pollyannaish; the country as a whole is in disastrous shape, with most progressive social movements in disarray. Insofar as the Right has triumphed, some degree of the responsibility must be borne by the Left; and to a degree, the mechanism Reed outlines of the failure of the Left would apply: mass culture is that strategy chosen by capital to absorb, blunt, and fragment mass spontaneity, whatever form it takes. However, I don't think the process is seamless; it may shift the terms of the struggle but cannot abolish them. Also, I don't feel that the mechanism outlined is the only one by which the hegemony of the Right has been reasserted in recent times. Others have been more straightforwardly external, for example, the fact that Nixon abolished the draft and pulled U.S. forces out of Indochina, thus undercutting the material impetus behind the youth rebellion. Another mediation is more directly mass-psychological. I believe that the Oedipal implications of the youth and black rebellions provoked massive anxieties among the petit bourgeoisie and workers, and this, in turn, fueled much of the reaction that followed. Lacking material alliances with these classes—indeed, such alliances were inherently impossible given the basic alignment of forces in America—it was inevitable that the counterculture would be sacrificed. Once the culture industries figured out how to use the impulses behind it for the purposes of consumerism, its days as a major political force in America were finished. Under these altered objective circumstances, it scarcely mattered what choices the New Left made: it was bound to be squashed, to survive only as a prefigurative remnant of the revolution that is yet to come.

REED:
Your various responses raise several critical issues concerning the significance of the radicalism of the 1960s in relation to the developmental logic of the American social order. Taken as a whole, moreover, those responses suggest certain tensions which might be explored usefully.

1) I am struck that white and black radicalisms converged around a common orientation from very different directions. Not only were both camps disposed to commingle the personal and political, but also tended to search for "extrinsic" models, in Willingham's phrase. Both aggressively and self-righteously contraposed themselves to what they cast as the values and attitudes of their parents and fetishized their own youth and novelty. Both looked to the underdeveloping countries for spiritual revitalization (perhaps rejuvenation?) and were equally captivated by sloganeering that elevated peasant simplicity over technological prowess. The last was no doubt largely a rationalization of our powerlessness inside the United States, but it was a rationalization already connected with a model of opposition stylized from the mythology of the Noble Peasant either in revolutionary war or in assertion of pastoral authenticity. Is this convergence purely coincidental? Might it suggest a general condition of stratum or culture of which both types of radical expression were artifacts? In this light it may be interesting that in maturity the postwar baby boom cohort took as its political symbols John Anderson in 1980 (when not Reagan, who ran stronger in this cohort than in any other) and Gary Hart and Jesse Jackson in 1984—all of whom demand attention exclusively on the basis of theatrical images of novelty, simplicity, and self-improvement ideology. This may be off the wall, but the strong parallels between these aspects of New Left style and the antimodernist quests among an element of American intellectuals since the Gilded Age might suggest the mediation of a subterranean cultural tendency.

2) There is, of course, a tension around how we should see the New Left (generically, black and white) in relation to capitalist sytem management imperatives. This tension appears most sharply—not surprisingly—between the comments by Kovel and Piccone, although Feenberg's portrait of liberatory existential rebellion and Luke's depiction of that rebellion's embeddedness in the ontological principles of mass culture may best capture 1960s ambivalence.

A key issue is the extent to which radicalism fomented, precipitated, or was epiphenomenal to the crisis of the model of social management that had prevailed since the New Deal. The potential for political crisis certainly is intrinsic to the proto-corporatist logic through which the "service state" has cemented loyalties. The "squeaking-wheel" pluralism that has served as an integrative mechanism stimulates a proliferation of demands for privileged status that outstrips the normal capacities of the system to pay off. The "urban crisis" is a laboratory case. Now, activism pretty clearly exacerbated this crisis tendency by substantially increasing the level of demand and, as Bowles et al. demonstrate, increasing the costs of social management. In this sense radicalism helped to unravel the governing synthesis by propagating decentralist, participatory ideologies that stimulated the formation of new claimant groups.

At the same time, Piccone and others have argued that the forms that radicalism took in the 1960s drew attention to the irrational core of the social management configuration and provided mechanisms—through the same decentralized and participatory ideologies—for reformulation along more rational lines. From this vantage point, arguably, activism: a) ensured social peace by renegotiating the governing consensus to include black (as well as other racial minority and female) elites among privileged status groups, b) aligned with what we might now call the trilateral wing of the corporate growth coalition to refine the styles of American imperialism, and c) laid the foundation for a new, narcissistic politics that reconstitutes the growth coalition on a conceptual basis that—under the guise of localism and neighborhood on the one hand and national moral revitalization on the other—potentially excludes the labor movement from the matrix of privileged status groups and in the process deauthorizes a discourse of class politics in general and the role of the state as a guarantor of equality in particular. In this regard the Anderson/Jackson/Hart/Reagan phenomenon loses its ironic dimension; the popularity of that peculiar, mass-mediated populism—which began actually in a halting, inept fashion with Jimmy Carter in 1976—is a culmination of tendencies present in the New Left all along. This is a politics appropriate to the cultural radicalism that Gross, Jordan, Luke, and other have identified.

What sense can be made of all this? Was the New Left both a precipitant of crisis and agent of reactionary recomposition? Was Gus Hall right all along? Can we simply write these developments off to the tragic ironies of history, citing the flight of Minerva's owl through Hegel and Marx? How much was structurally determined? Is there any lesson here at all?

JORDAN:

I would venture an unsupported guess that the majority of 1960s radicals, black or white, had only a superficial interest in any organized and ideological transformation of the political structure of America or Amerika. In retrospect much of the rebellion and the critique seem anarchist in nature. One indulged in a kind of ritualistic chest-thumping and denounced the "pigs" or "whitey." The rejection of bourgeois values and lifestyle, the focus on the pastoral, and the emphasis on cultural transformation are reminiscent of the anarchist tradition of William Godwin, Shelley, and other romantics. The rebellion of the 1960s was primarily expressed through violent language; the so-called revolution was a battle of words. Radicals spent the majority of their time proselytizing the previously converted, engaging in verbal struggle *within* radical ranks, and intellectualizing about the struggle in what Ed Spriggs, formerly of the *Journal of Black Poetry* and the Studio Museum of Harlem, called "the tea rooms of our revolution" ("For the Truth").

The preference for talk over action in the insular environment of the college campus was accompanied by an extreme xenophobia. Luke is quite on the mark with his contention that we were revolutionaries "without a base." The radicals of the 1960s hated and envied the rich and scorned the middle class. However, the greatest contempt, despite all the talk of "the people," was reserved for the lower classes of America. Perhaps this refusal to transcend class lines was one of the reasons why it was so easy to denounce the Vietnam war without addressing oneself to the psychology, welfare, and revolutionary potential of the American troops. It was a rare breed of 1960s radical who gave any thought to the possibility that the American soldier was anything other than a baby-killer. We of the Black Nationalist persuasion sympathized with the Vietcong and excoriated the dumb niggers who couldn't avoid the draft or volunteered to be the murderous dupes of the white man.

The insularity of our radicalism grew not only out of class prejudices but also out of racialism. Most black radicals directed their rage against all whites and, except for the Panthers, were hostile to and fearful of the notion of coalition. White radicals seemed enchanted by the ghetto gangsterism of the Panthers and Cinque and were eager to form masochistic and fantastic relationships with the cowboys of black radicalism. Interestingly enough these same white radicals seemed unwilling to interact with their intellectual counterparts in the black world.

Black and white radicals were separated by a cultural and social gulf. Most blacks, whatever their political orientation, were indifferent to the Beatles and even Jimi Hendrix. Segregation was a reality in radical worlds. It is revealing that in *The Big Chill* the only blacks in that all-white, yuppie world existed for entertainment purposes. The blacks sang; the solitary Jew provided comic relief.

The revolution failed because nobody was really organizing the troops. How could there have been success when the only person you could convert to your vision of America was your roommate? Black and white radicals, despite similar analyses, were unable to communicate with each other, and neither group was able to convince even a substantial minority of Americans that something was amiss in their society. The subsequent cosmetic integration of a few black people and women into the system was never recognized by the majority of the people as a response to radical attack but rather was perceived as proof that radicals were wrong all along in their distrust and rejection of the American Dream.

GROSS:

I'm struck by the overall pessimism of the responses to this dialogue, but I don't feel uncomfortable with it. It doesn't seem to me that any other position is permissible just now. A note of strident optimism would not only be inappropriate, it would be false for the times we live in. For the present and the foreseeable future, pessimism is realism.

Of course, all of us have been reflecting on a decade which, objectively speaking, was a failure. At least it must be labeled such as far as we are concerned, for the things we imagined or hoped for in the 1960s have certainly not materialized in the 1980s. Already histories of postwar America are being written which treat the New Left, the Civil Rights movement, the black rebellion, and the various forms of cultural upheaval during the 1960s as little more than a footnote to the age. Though these developments are given some attention, it seems to be mainly for reasons of embellishment, since all good narratives need a dash of color or a touch of the flamboyant. In many of these histories it's clear that those events which continue to have an impact today originated not with the white or black revolutionaries; they stemmed instead from those other longer-lived "revolutions" of the 1960s—the revolutions which took place in technology and telecommunications, in global business investment and corporate mergers, in demographic shifts and the collapse of political party structures.

These texts make a valid point, though they exaggerate the irrelevance of the cultural and political explosions of the 1960s. Even if, as some have argued in this volume, these explosions were shallow or counterfeit; and even if, as others in this book claim, they were engineered by the system, and ultimately served the needs of the system, it is evident nonetheless that they also left residues and directions into the future which haven't been fully measured or charted—and can't be yet, since the full effects are still unfolding, still in process. This is not a statement of just that kind of optimism I've already said we need to avoid. Rather, it is an expression of the only philosophy I am able to defend today, a philosophy of open-ended pessimism (open-ended in the sense that I'm always ready and willing to reevaluate those things which, at the moment, seem to justify only the worst conclusions).

It appears to me that all but one or two of the participants in this discussion share this outlook. It's a strange legacy to have been passed down from the 1960s, especially given the generally upbeat tone of that decade, but that's the way things have turned out, and we have no choice but to face that fact. In light of this, and as a hesitant first step, what better can we do in these "dark times" than analyze the internal reasons for the failures of 1960s movements, or uncover and make known the external, managerial needs of the economy and polity which also helped undermine (or coopt) those same movements?

KOVEL:

I may be a little soft on the New Left, since I was not enough a part of it to feel betrayed. For me, the 1960s were a chance to escape from the 1950s. The epoch did not provide an identity so much as allow a previously imposed identity to be modified, and for this I remain grateful. For many others, though, the 1960s offered a great deal more. For all the eschewal of hierarchy, there was an expectation that those anointed in the New Left would somehow end up in command of a higher type of being if not of actual institutions. The hope was there, whether one called it revolution or social transformation; and as this hope became crushed, a sense of bitterness set in.

That the hope has been crushed is a certainty, but does this mean that the New Left was a fiasco? Frankly, I find much of the critique leveled at the movements of the 1960s to be rationalization of one personal setback or another. To have begun political life so spectacularly and to end up in the ignominy of a tenure battle is galling in the extreme. For the victim of such a humiliating turn of events to turn to grandiose theories of the integrative powers of the capitalist apparatus is understandable, no doubt, but nonetheless totalizing and undialectical.

The New Left failed, beyond question. In case no one has noticed, there has not been a social transformation, much less revolution, in late capitalist society; and, yes, Eldridge Cleaver, Jerry Rubin, and Rennie Davis have become figures of fun. More to the point (since leadership is never to be trusted), the great mass of once youthful rebels have made peace, however uneasy, with the corporate state (there is no real peace to be made with the corporate state). Ultimately, the failure of the movements of the 1960s is measured by the shape of the movements of the 1970s and 1980s. The lack of any coherent Left opposition today is a responsibility of the Left opposition of a generation ago. That the New Left never matured continues to haunt us now. As Reed points out in his introduction to this volume, invoking the cooptive power of capitalist society may be a valid description but is no excuse.

Still, the New Left was no fiasco, and to regard it as such is a wretched substitute for critical thought. Of course, the New Left did not bring the Vietnam war to a close on its own. Since when is a historical process on the scale of a war decided by any one movement? Is there a rational person, however, who can argue that the antiwar movements of the 1960s made no constructive difference? Only remember that Richard Nixon himself alleged that he would have used the Bomb on Hanoi were it not for his fear of the ensuing outrage on campuses. If this is indeed true—and there is no reason to doubt it—then all the failings of the New Left can be forgiven.

It makes as little sense to claim that the Civil Rights struggles got nowhere because racism persists in America, or the main activity of black politics has shifted to within the consensus of bourgeois democracy. Notwithstanding these unpalatable facts, real victories were achieved in the 1960s, and the changes in black consciousness resulting from them have been irreversible. The same could be said for a number of other struggles. After all, to say that the masses of participants have given up on radical change says only what everyone can see anyhow—that society was not transformed; but the masses are not everybody. What of the sizable minority of participants in the New Left who have kept their faith? It is not for nothing that the core of activists in the movements of greatest immediate potential—antinuclear, antiintervention in Central America, ecology—are the over-thirty generation shaped in the 1960s. The New Left failed, ludicrously at times, pathetically at others, but it did not sink without a trace.

Where does this leave us? Posed between apologetics and self-flagellation, and searching for the ever-elusive dialectic. There has never been—nor will there ever be—a revolutionizing process which turned out very much as its protagonists intended. This is true whether the revolution succeeds or fails by its own terms and no doubt has to do with the illusions immanent in all praxis. However, the only thing that matters is whether we can learn from experience and do better the next time. What, then, is to be learned from the 1960s?

Huddling against the savagery of Reaganism, it is easy to forget how much was signified by the Indochina War: for the first time, a decisive defeat suffered by Western imperialism in direct combat. It seems to me that what the movements of the 1960s were—and what they had to suffer as a consequence—was primarily shaped by this reality. Both of the main components of the New Left—the antiwar and the Civil Rights movements—were fundamentally anti-imperialist in nature. The antiwar movement was directly so; and the Civil Rights movements were antiimperialist because racism is ultimately an imperialism that has become internalized. Of course, these movements did not become anti-imperialist accidentally, but only because imperialism had been weakening, so that various nationally oppressed groups were able to launch coherent assaults upon the system of metropolitan control. The specifics of the 1960s were comprised by linkages between masses of youth in the metropolitan regions and these rising oppressed groups. This linkage was itself made possible because of the weakening of patriarchal authority under the conditions of the youth-centered consumerist culture of late capitalism.

It is, therefore, quite stupid to berate the movements of the 1960s for their concern with Third World models of liberation, when that concern was the expression of the raison d'être for the very historical emergence of the New Left. Obviously one has to remain critical of any romanticization that leaves behind the reality of Third World revolution while neglecting what is happening on the home front. A good deal of this happened. However, much of the criticism of the New Left goes further to suggest that it was a mistake in the first place to get involved with emancipation in the Third World. Setting aside the crypto-racism and anticommunism, it can be said that such positions deny the source of what was transcendent in the New Left. They take the very heart out of the 1960s, its universalizing motion.

The failure of the 1960s was, in my opinion, two failures rolled into one: no way was found to get across the generations; and no sustained grip was taken on any force of production. I am enough of an unreconstructed Marxist to believe in the latter as a sine qua non for any revolutionary process; and in the absence of the former conditions, namely, a bridging of the generations which would have permitted linkages with socially productive adults (i.e., workers), the movements of the 1960s were bound to remain ineffective and ultimately puerile. Thus as soon as Nixon removed the principal material incentive for rebellion, namely, the draft, youth had nowhere to turn save the established order, always ready to integrate their desire into its consumerism. It seems to me, then, that the incorporation by mass culture was more the effect than the cause of the collapse of the New Left. I don't mean to suggest by this that cultural engagement was not close to the heart of the politics of the New Left. It was the creation of a "counterculture" that kept the movement going, just as every truly radical force has to live by its own culture. However, the culture of the New Left, like every culture, could not feed on itself. Once it was established that the movement was not going to really take over, then it was only a matter of time before the counterculture would become negated by the very consumerist forces it had hoped to transcend. One can say that this tendency toward cooptation was present from the start; but that is no more than saying that the inability to develop a full-scale social transformation was present from the start. Ultimately, the New Left was brought down by the same egoism and failure of a genuine communalism as have plagued American radical movements from the beginning. In this sense, that is, in the sedimentation of history into subjectivity, consumerist society may be said to have won out in the end against the radicalizing forces of the New Left.

Can we do better the second time around, now that the crises in Central America, Southern Africa, and around the spectre of nuclear cataclysm provide fresh sources of antiimperialist energy? It's hard to be sanguine and impossible to offer blueprints, especially given the cretinization of today's youth. However, there is something in me—I hope you will call it nonrational rather than irrational—that refuses to accept the given as final. Revolutions are unpredicable not only in their outcome but also in the way they begin.

WILLINGHAM:

As with the volume itself, anyone reading these responses would be struck by the terminology of the discussion—there is the free and sometimes interchangeable use of such terms as "movement," "Sixties," or "New Left" to describe the object of analysis. In time, perhaps, scholars may stipulate which of these is to be the definitive term, but for present purposes the mixture remains—as if a special commentary on the complexity of the subject matter. Reed, in setting the call for the responses, speaks of "counterculturalists," and "black nationalists" operating within a "New Left Movement" whose search for theoretical clarity led to "Marxism–Leninism," and "Pan-Africanism," respectively. That equation is not entirely satisfatory, but it charts the terrain over which we can discuss the "radical activism of the Sixties."

Sometimes the terms do seem to beg for more systematic analysis, as when assertions about the fate of the movement turn on how we set the categories of the activity. Indeed, Feenberg asserts that the central dynamic of the movement's decline was the failure of "all attempts to find a middle term between counterculturalism and sectarianism." Ultimately, how we answer the question—what happened to the movement of the Sixties?—may be conditioned substantially by how we set the "terms" of discussion.

In his initial provocation Reed notes what all of these writers assume; namely, that a peculiar, important radical activism of the 1960s disappeared from the American political scene. To be sure there remain dynamic bands of activists seeking change in foreign policy, in the use of nuclear weapons, in opposition of the death penalty, or in support for voting rights among racial and ethnic minorities. Despite such efforts a sense of the decline in radicalism is hardly controversial—it is to say what everybody knows. However, to say "why" the movement disappeared raises challenging questions of interpretation which could reach to the very authenticity of the activism itself.

The decline of the New Left is to be found in the way it came into being, i.e., as an insurgent movement separating from its biological and ideological foreparents. Feenberg says a rejection of the "Old Left" was a precondition for New Leftism. Radicals of the SNCC rejected the ideas their elders had used to accommodate racial segregation; SDS founders annoyed by anticommunism repudiated ideology as such. The nonideology had the virtue of protecting the new movement from past squabbles among Left groups. It also eliminated one pretext the government had used to attack radicals (as in the Cold War). Early on, the New Left assumed a quality that set it apart in the evolution of American progressivism.

In avoiding the old anchors the New Left turned to its readiest resource—youth and the energy intrinsic thereto. This was a productive move. Simple, innocent idealism inspired massive, selfless political action that pointed the nation to important social relations in need of change. However, that idealism obscured the difficulty that children of middle-class America could have in forging serious structural change. In retrospect, these authors say, that difficulty came in no small part from the way in which the New Left developed on top of a certain sense of place wherein the activists retained an affirmative stance toward middle-class society and its terms for political change. Political/ideological inquiry was unnecessary as the activism became apolitical, seeking mere "social" change. Jordan: "I would venture [a guess] that the majority of 1960s radicals, black or white, had only a superficial interest in any organized and ideological transformation of the political structure." Indeed, both Jordan and Gross say that the real gains of the era resulted from the normal operation of American democratic institutions rather than a political program of the movement. The New Left was like a midwife to reform.

Kovel takes pains to credit this idealism with what it did, i.e., it brought some "real victories." He fears that those victories may be ignored even by the now older idealists looking back at themselves, but he acknowledges that the movement failed. First, it was unable to ever find a way to "get across the generations," and, second, it was unable to get a sustained grip on any means of production.

Gross makes a similar argument saying that the New Left was characterized by properties of youth—optimism and naivete. Such a perspective could not confront realistically the problems of the activism (failures, miscues) typically leaving the activists unable to counter the response from the state.

How did the state respond? There is pointed reference (especially by Jordan) to the repressive police actions, but there continues to be special emphasis on noncoercive action: factors internal to the movement itself, and the historical shift in late twentieth-century bourgeois society.

New Left radicalism occurred in the context of a society changing under its own expansionist impetus. This parallelism between change and Left demands meant that legitimations would be borrowed and confused between the two. Piccone and the others assert that the New Left was insufficiently aware of the parallel activity and of the possibility that the "system shift" would alter real relationships of injustice. They insist on an explanation that, in Piccone's words,

. . . relates the phenomenon to the dynamics of American mass culture: the extension of commodification to intellectual production and political movements. Seeing the New Left in this light allows us to focus on the logic of system shifts from the New Deal to the post-New Deal model and relate the rise and demise of that New Left to broader social processes.

Such a critique traces the "special quality" of the New Left to the atomization of the individual resulting from the rise of mass society, in which the search for personal identity becomes a central burden of everyday life. Our activists are unable to escape the burden as well. The individual searches for self-realization in movement activity. Such personalism avoided engaged political critique. Involvement became "meaningful" insofar as it was satisfying. The tension over whether activism should be judged by its "political" as opposed to its "cultural" impact caused excited debate that cut across racial and ethnic lines during the radical 1960s.

The New Left was reinforced by the satisfaction of expanding interpersonal contacts and experimentations—a hallmark of the movement. It was fueled by a commonsense view of justice which contradicted the restrictive (racial, ethnic) view of the middle class and its prudery. There was a ready and increasingly holistic repudiation of one's society, but it was more rebelliousness than rebellion. (Jordan notes how the white intellectual radicals were disinclined to engage in dialogue with their black intellectual radical counterparts due to an "enchantment" with "ghetto gangsterism.") There was "a preference for talk over action" (Jordan); getting oneself together, resulting in a conversion atmosphere which saw movement leaders swing between ideological positions widely different in content.

In those times such changes were seen as moves, indeed growth, to higher and higher levels of clarity; but the present critics now regard this change as functional at the personal level, if at all. As modes of radical thought, such changes seemed neither fastened on the developing American state (the readjusting New Deal structures) nor sufficiently aware of the seductive pull of political action as an antidote to personal uncertainty and insignificance. It is in this sense that, for all its confrontational aspects, our authors see in New Left radical critique rather more the quality of avoidance than engagement.

There was an inability to keep a critical perspective on the developing state and the changing mix of social repression. This is no easy task in any case. If we grant Marx's suggestive comments in *The Eighteenth Brumaire* that youth-driven efforts to break with ascendant institutions are constrained by dependency on the very terms of their upbringing, then the 1960s had even greater temptations. These entailed a variety of "extrinsic" phenomena including, we can now admit, a view that modern complexities are too frustrating given the unchallenged accomplishments of ancient African kingdoms, calming Eastern meditation, or simple life in pastoral Mississippi. There was the growing fascination with various Third World symbols and works (as well as that romanticism by white radicals of the black American "lumpen"). This seemed to substitute for the tight-fisted working-class focus that would have been provided by the Old Left. Our critics now argue that reliance on extrinsic ideology put the burden of accounting for the most advanced society on theories from less developed places. That presents no problem in matters of simple justice, but as one moved to interact with an elaborate market mechanism, things were more difficult. (Kovel warns correctly that this point can be overdrawn.)

The critics believe that, as a movement, the New Left never understood the market or the media. The Manichaeanism crucial to foreign colonialism would obscure the dynamics of pluralist society.

The demand for racial equality masked a state-inspired drive for "more effective administration of black marginality." The fight against poverty became more meliorative federal welfare programs. The struggle against the Vietnam war can claim more direct impact but mostly in redirecting temporarily dysfunctional imperialist strategy. On the whole the changes made were just enough to rationalize racial and other irrational categories into a system of consumption—to expand the domestic market society while cooling out any split-offs (consumers) that would require specialized appeals or sustain alternative competitive producers.

Thus those who may feel discomfort in subordination to the market are charmed when critics show up in the media. Affirmative feelings replace skepticism when characteristics of derision—being black, poor, gay, southern?—become a media preoccupation. Nasty questions about the shape of the economic pie or the conditions of work or the basis of allegiance lose momentum as the formerly despised find themselves projected in a welcomed format.

The spread, among the populace, of news about revolutionary personalities or activity is viewed as a saga of autonomous acts supportive of structural change. Free breakfast programs, communal living, neighborhood self-help, draft counseling, etc., seemed to be evidence of the surging appeal of the radical program. In reality the popularity of revolutionaries assumed the form of, and thus legitimated, the ordinary marketeering intrinsic to the capitalist enterprise. The artifacts of counterculture themselves become commodities. In celebrating the growing recognition of their works, the radicals were celebrating the redirection of their thrust. In his response Luke is blunt: "The New Left unexpectedly served as the shock troops of mass culture and its corporate producers, tearing down the last constraints on circulating all commodities to anyone, anytime, anywhere."

The movement, which enjoyed widespread popular attention, was nonetheless unable to establish reflective discourse to complement mass activity and to focus anticipatory attention to the defensive tactics of the state. The lack of a reflective attitude was due in part to the movement's open-endedness that had, since its very birth, set the New Left apart from both Old, especially Communist, Left and from the parent generation. However, the very open-endedness of this "belief system" would soon lead to a collective desire for a coherent "world view." The impatience of youth served the process. Its own superstars would come to ask, "But what is the correct ideology?"

Ironically in the mid-1970s when the New Left was in the throes of decline, an important ingredient was the serial conversion to one form or another of ideological lines promoted by the traditional radicalism. In one sense this was not surprising. The Old Left was anchored in one or another of the Leftist parties, in the labor movement, in academic or other intellectual professions. Of course, for the New Left these institutions were attacked as irrelevant.

It was this turn to ideology that made it difficult to "continue some of the more important cultural and political projects begun in the 1960s instead of abandoning them altogether as many did" (Gross). Ideological "debate" resulted in the introduction into the movement of formal thought systems with world views.

The Old Left, held at bay by the preclusive assumptions of the New Left, now became a sort of ultimate source for ideological clarity. The prefabricated mode of its thought, however, fitted, rather than challenged, the commercial dynamics and vitiated the emancipatory appeal it could have had. The emancipatory aspect of American progressivism, having at first been rejected by the youth, was now banalized in the way it was peddled by the party bearers. Energetic recruitment schemes into the Party, or the New party, utilized a form that could just as well have served recruitment into the Pepsi Generation.

Shopping among mutually exclusive ideologies and the reduction of movement conferences to arenas for competition among them became a perverse way of subjecting activists to the "market of ideas." Pretty soon it was not exactly clear what was meant when somebody called for "revolution." On one coast it was recommended that rape be used as an instrument for politics; on another hallucinogens were recommended. Any given idea deserved attention, a point of view at one with the commodification of thought.

Jordan and Kovel are careful to argue that the decline of the New Left is not fully grasped by mere analysis of ideas. There was an intransigent political system. " . . . people had reached a state of alienation that made reform inconceivable to them but was not sufficient to fuel a revolutionary response. The failure to move the sincerely felt rejection of the system to another level and to redirect the political rhetoric to an analysis of ways to confront the system resulted from fear of harassment, imprisonment, and perhaps death" (Jordan). Even under affluent conditions, not all revolutionaries are bought off. Those who aren't face real consequences. Militants found the administration of justice to be arbitrary, especially in rural, white-supremacy counties of the South, and conditions in the state jail systems were oppressive everywhere. On several occasions police got out of hand trying to manage mass demonstrations. Key losses in militant black leadership resulted from unofficial violent attacks by renegades with no formal link to public agencies. A strict ideological focus will obscure the way militancy provoked and suffered from oppressive acts during the 1960s.

Did the failure of the activism of the 1960s mean anything? Were there consequences for actual people? Was there some injustice that lived on? Well, if Malcolm X were to somehow return and pronounce the chickens home to roost, some fingers would have to point not to the physical death of a popular president, but to the deathly social conditions (survival!) of people caught in the self-reinforcing confinement of the welfare state. Herein is the problem, i.e., that the activism of the 1960s came increasingly to reduce the potential for emancipation (and all sense of alternative possibilities) to the welfare state and/or pluralistic politics.

How was one to know, however, that there would come new conservative administration(s) satisfied with the historic social privileges but perceptive about the delicate public-sector engineering necessary to retain them? The conservatism of presidents from Nixon through Carter to Reagan differed mostly (and not insignificantly, of course) in their policies on popular (especially liberal and black) involvement. The Reagan administration in particular, has shown that "big government" is truly "the executive committee of . . . " Alas, matters are never as simple as we wish. Insofar as the welfare state made access to electoral decision-making part of its program, then "participatory" demands found an immediate grounding through which reform ideals were offered up to the same (pluralist?) negotiating principle undergirding the two-party system. Here by cooptation and there by repression, the insurgency was pacified, and expanded participation made room for inclusion of the insurgents!

So what do we fuss about? Merely the persistence of poverty among a minority of the overall American population? In the midst of power and glory? It is measured accurately now by our government's statistical bureaus. Ministrations thereunto are the cherished provinces of helping agencies who use those statistical measurements to explain their requests for incremental budget increases.

Well, there is cause to fuss for two basic reasons. First, the economic hardship among the population continues. It results from a lack of democracy in economic affairs. Strict (shortsighted?) adherence to the principle of profit encourages runaway plants, plant closings, and the organization of meaningless work for trivial wages. Those who try are unpersuasive when they say the lack of opportunity open to individuals in poverty is divorced from the activities of economic elites.

Those who make that argument became prominent during the Reagan era. They are "neoconservatives" who say the central political issue is the role of the public sphere in promoting social well-being. Unlike traditional conservatives, they make negative social conditions the centerpiece of their analysis. Poverty among the people is documented to justify eliminating antipoverty government programs; the push for a color-blind society requires elimination of programs to help blacks and other disadvantaged racial minorities. Neoconservatives emphasize the lack of success we have had in removing social ills. There is a teasing confluence here with the progressivism of the 1960s insofar as this failure is traced to a flaw in modern liberal politics. Indeed, the focus on the statistics of victimization and the attack on liberalism seem to checkmate the voice of "the Sixties." The political thinking of the movement seems exhausted in the critique neoconservatives make of the affirmative state.

The error here is a profound one for which space allows only brief comment. It ignores key aspects of 1960s idealism, particularly the insistence on the salutary role of participation. Growing involvement was the antidote to the lingering effects of isolation. The participatory experience, it was thought, was a precondition for a transformation wherein individuals came to see their well-being in terms of the exercise of choice. In the 1980s, neoconservatives situate the causes for social ills (unemployment) in factors external to and beyond the proper scope of governmental processes (family breakdown, for example). However, they are merely celebrating a bogus choice that remains subordinate to the received sentiments of oppressive traditions. By the expectations of the 1960s, the welfare state—as a humane, if flawed, response to this situation—will inevitably come up short because it fails to generate a kind of participation that is transformative. "Upward" pressure on the political system is eliminated as disadvantaged groups reaccommodate themselves to the prevailing pattern of privilege.

Also, for all its esthetically engaging properties/outrages (i.e., those which tickle our critical faculties), the bottom line is that the cooptation of the personnae and artifacts of the 1960s has come in service of the same commercial motives. Countercultural products of all kinds are promoted materialistically; but aren't "racism" and others forms of bigotry functionally equivalent? What are we to expect when (?) they reacquire marketability? Can't that be done more readily in the absence of a popular and vigilant movement? Isn't it inevitable given the primacy of the commerical motive?

One answer has been out there all along. It results from the logic of movement decline which suggests that, in America, racial minorities and other disadvantaged groups have been assigned quasi-citizenship. They'll see a future sometimes bright with freedom and sometimes dark with prejudice. Each entails the other although the offensive quality will be mollified due to internal stratification within those groups. It is not, of course, the worst of worlds—but is it worthy of allegiance?

An adequate understanding of the 1960s requires some determination as to whether it was a movement against this pattern or an episode in its realization. If, as I contend, there were lively elements of the former, then we are talking about an indispensible source of reflection on the American political system which will challenge us to respond critically and practically to the persistence of injustice.

If it is the latter, then what are we to make of the sacrifices and what are we to tell the children?

Bibliographical Note

Systematic reflection on the movements of the 1960s has clustered roughly into three discernible periods, each of which congeals around a loosely distinguishable project.

The early 1970s saw the first wave of assessment of both black and white activism. Kirkpatrick Sale's *SDS* (New York, 1973) is far and away the most comprehensive and meticulously researched and remains the seminal historical work on that element of the New Left. Greg Calvert and Carol Neiman, in their volume, *A Disrupted History: The New Left and the New Capitalism* (New York, 1971), take a more analytical and political approach that interprets the rise and transmutations of the New Left in relation to a theory of the changing composition of labor in advanced capitalism. James Forman, *The Making of Black Revolutionaries* (New York, 1972), and Cleveland Sellers (with Robert Terrell), *The River of No Return: The Autobiography of a Black Militant and the Life and Death of SNCC* (New York, 1973), provide valuable, albeit clearly partisan, accounts of the natural history of the Student Nonviolent Coordinating Committee and the articulation of its radical elements through Black Power, Pan-Africanism, and Marxism–Leninism.

Forman and Sellers approach their object through a mainly autobiographical medium (bringing the predictable strengths and weaknesses of memoir), while Sale is exhaustively historical, and Calvert and Neiman organize their account around problems of social theory. These volumes nevertheless share an attitude toward 1960s radicalism. Each author, writing just beyond the crest of activism, sees his or her task as documentation and interpretation of phases, perhaps an era, of an extant movement on the verge of confronting new strategic and organizational requirements. Significantly, Sale's *SDS* is dedicated to "Faith in the Future" and Forman's book in part to "All the Unborn Revolutionaries Who Will Accelerate and Intensify the Revolutionary Process." These are the first volumes that discuss the major radical organizations of the 1960s from the standpoint of postmortem examination, but each is optimistic about the movement's ability to metamorphose appropriate forms for the new conditions.

Each book approaches the political movements of the 1960s as having opened avenues for subsequent, cumulative emancipatory activity. Calvert and Neiman seek to develop a political position appropriate to what they perceive as the crossroads facing the Left in the 1970s and are somewhat distinct from the others in that regard. However, the judgment shared by all four books is that the styles of radicalism of the 1960s constituted an appropriate paradigm for political opposition in that period.

After 1975 literature on the 1960s developed a different tenor. By that time the idea of a snowballing movement was no longer tenable, and waning optimism altered the character of reflective writing. Consonant with the drift of popular culture, writing on the 1960s took a turn toward personal memoir. These autobiographies typically exhibit a weariness of spirit, often masked as frenetic motion, and a sense of defeat that turns inward for solace. Dotson Rader's brooding memoir, *Blood Dues* (New York, 1973), might be seen in this regard as a bridge between the two types of literature. Rader somewhat ruefully anticipates and predicts radicalism's disappearance, but the trenchantness of his tone reveals a sense of betrayal that roots his volume more as a response to a moribund but still lingering activism. Later reflections accept the demise of activism as a fait accompli which somehow must be accommodated. Not surprisingly, given the temporal context, accommodation typically takes the form of retreat to personal inventory.

These weary soldiers by and large do not actually repudiate their earlier involvements, however; indeed, they often seem uncertain what exactly to make of their activist pasts. Julius Lester's *All Is Well* (New York, 1976) is a confessional that reconstructs the 1960s as an element, albeit an important one, in the composition of a healthy personality. Jerry Rubin's *Growing (Up) at Thirty-Seven* (Philadelphia, 1976), a cornucopia of psychobabble, depicts the New Left as an arena for acting out his then tacit struggle for self-knowledge and inner peace. Most of Rubin's volume, though, details his experiences in the early 1970s as he moved through one after another of the fads of the burgeoning self-improvement industry. Eldridge Cleaver's *Soul on Fire* (Waco, Texas, 1978) shares the revelation that through all his peregrinations and travail the author's *real* quest all along had been for God and spiritual fulfillment.

By the end of the 1970s reflection on the 1960s moved into a third phase. The varieties of New Left and black activism became a focal point for scholarly reconstruction, often by former participants. Sara Evans's *Personal Politics: The Roots of Women's Liberation in the Civil Rights Movement and the New Left* (New York, 1979) traces the proximate origins of contemporary feminism through the patterns of interaction—and critiques thereof—that developed between movement men and women, particularly in the SNCC and SDS. Todd Gitlin, *The Whole World is Watching!: Mass Media in the Making and Unmaking of the New Left* (Berkeley, 1980), examines the confluence of the New Left's (especially but not exclusively in SDS and the developing antiwar movement) agenda for building a mass movement and the news media's logic of "newsworthiness"; he explores the dialectical interaction of the two imperatives not only to shed light on pressures that articulated 1960s radicalism but also to illuminate the media's structurally constraining impact on political opposition in general in the contemporary United States. The contributions to John Case and Rosemary C. R. Taylor, eds., *Co-ops, Communes, and Collectives: Experiments in Social Change in the 1960s and 1970s* (New York, 1979) seek both to describe various types of mutualist activity that grew out of the New Left and to analyze strengths, limitations, and practical tensions within alternativist experiments; several contributors also consider the ways in which that activity has influenced and been influenced by changes in social structure. Wini Breines's *Community and Organization in the New Left: 1962–1968* (Amherst, Mass., 1982) examines the core political values that undergirded early New Left practice, explicating the normative and pragmatic tensions that shaped the movement's distinctive development. Nigel Young's *An Infantile Disorder?: The Crisis and Decline of the New Left* (Boulder, Colo., 1977) is a critical general history of the British and American New Lefts; Young centers his account on the organizational struggle—reproduced throughout the era's radicalism—between tendencies adhering to ideals of participatory democracy and vanguardism. He argues that this tension, through its ramification into debates over nonviolence, Third Worldism, and other issues, was a major source of the movement's decline. These volumes, all by scholars with roots in the New Left, share an empathetic orientation to the movements they study, and each concludes that New Left era activism laid the basis for subsequent articulation of an oppositional politics.

In addition to the relatively engagé scholarship produced by authors formerly associated with the New Left, other scholars have approached elements of 1960s activism from a more conventionally academic point of view. Clayborne Carson's *In Struggle: SNCC and the Black Awakening of the 1960s* (Cambridge, Mass., 1981) is a rich, impressively thorough history of the Student Non-violent Coordinating Committee that meticulously recounts the actions and debates that defined the SNCC's place in politics from its origin through its exhaustion into Black Power, Pan-Africanist, Marxist, or mainstream politics. Aldon D. Morris, *The Origins of the Civil Rights Movement: Black Communities Organizing for Change* (New York, 1984), examines the organizational and institutional linkages that underlay and defined the specific character of the local movements that constituted the first ten years of popular Civil Rights activism. Doug McAdam's *Political Process and the Development of Black Insurgency, 1930–1970* (Chicago, 1982) explores the extent to which Civil Rights activism was precipitated by broad, structural changes—e.g., changes in the base of the southern economy, urbanization, increasing importance of the black vote outside the South to the Democratic coalition—affecting the black population and race relations both in the South and nationally. Carson does not venture far from his primary subject matter and is given neither to structural generalization nor critical judgment. Morris's volume combines historical reporting with a conceptual apparatus grafted from contemporary sociological theory in an effort to integrate the origins of black activism into the framework of collective behavior research. McAdam's account eschews specific discussion of movement activity altogether in favor of explanation by means of careful description of structural background factors. Unlike the other variant of the new scholarship, Morris's and McAdam's studies—in part because they are not engaged politically—shed virtually no light on the internal dynamics of the movements they address. Carson's study differs from the other two in that regard, but his account's remoteness from the political issues that he records disallows the kind of scholarly critique and analysis that so enrich the more engaged studies.

In addition to these two sets of academic reconstruction, several of which are influenced by a desire to respond to the pattern of self-absorbed reflections that characterized the mid-1970s, two other volumes have sought to counter knee-jerk dismissal of 1960s radicalism. One, Sohnya Sayres and the *Social Text* staff, eds., *The 60s Without Apology* (Minneapolis-St. Paul, 1984), combines historical reconstruction, critical interpretation of various kinds of texts, personal reflection, bibliographical memoir, and theoretical overview to recreate an intellectual and phenomenological appreciation of activism in the 1960s. The other, Dick Cluster, ed., *They Should Have Served That Cup of Coffee: Seven Radicals Remember the Sixties* (Boston, 1979), is a not particularly reflective, self-congratulatory set of tracts that add very little to pedestrian understanding of New Left-era political or cultural activity.

Index

Administration: centralized, 62; and construction of the ego, 221; limitations of administrative state, 77; and negation of desire, 207; and rationality crisis, 23

Adorno, Theodor, 229

Anderson, John, 259

Anti-intellectualism, and the Left, 179

Artificial negativity: age of, 232; as function of massification, 77; and social management, 62

Authenticity, in the past, 245

Baldwin, James, 30

Baraka, Amiri (Le Roi Jones): Black Community Development and, 36; on Gibson, Kenneth, 16; media consciousness of, 42; and philosophical differences with Madhubuti, 48; and poet as spiritual leader, 43; poetry of, 44-47; on politics, 36; and rejection of reason, 44; romanticization of Afro America by, 45-47

Barsky, Edward, 148

Benjamin, Walter, 61, 209

Berman, Dan, 169

Black activism: as catalyst in universalizing one dimensionality, 62; decline of, interpreted, 63; McAdam, Doug on, 5-6; oppositional tendencies in, 5; Piven and Cloward on, 6; and political identity, transformation of, 123; significance of, 76-77

Black aesthetic: definitional problems, 39; Henderson, Stephen on, 39-40; and ideological commitment, 40; Madhubuti, Haki on, 40; and media competition, 42; Rodgers, Carolyn on, 41

Black Americans: culture of, 30-35; and model of selves, lack of, 13; unemployment of, 63

Black church: and black community, 235; and Newton, Huey, 24

Black cultural nationalism: in Afro-American literature, 30-31; as alternative to politics, 38, 74; as artificially constituted otherness, 235; and Black intelligentsia, 32; as conservative force, 31-32; and optation, ease of, 54; and deterioration of American life, 37; and hegemony of over other nationalisms, 38; Karenga, Ron and, 35; as mobilization myth, 74; Pan African, 34; as religion, 43, 47; and revolution, 35; as ritualization of political issues, 48

Black culture: and Black Art, 39, 40; and Black particularity, negation of, 74; and Black Power, 73; and Black social order, 74; Karenga's creation

Black culture (*continued*)
of, 35; nationalists' misunderstand-
ing of, 36; and politics, 36
Black elites: characterization of, 20,
22; and cultural conservatism, 32;
and domination, 64; function of, 15,
17; genesis of, 64; hegemony of, 23;
ideology of, 17; limited mobility of,
68; and management stratum in
South, 67; as neo-colonialist, 20-21;
and primacy in political discourse,
75, 82; relationship of to Black Left,
22; separation of from Black people,
33
Black leadership, generated from outside community, 67
Black Left: political behavior of in future, 25; political obligations of, 21;
relation to Black elites, 22
Black particularity: artificial, 76; and
authenticity, 93 n.49; negation of,
74
Black power, 21, 63; and community
control, 72; genesis of, 72; and popular democratization, 72; and pluralist politics, 75; as reaction against
integrationist ideology, 73
Bloch, Ernst, 252
Bodenheimer, Tom, 167
Brooks, Gwendolyn, 41
Brown, H. Rap, 4, 22, 78
Brown, Sterling, 30, 33
Bureaucratic rationalization: counterproductive tendencies of, 232; and
managing objectification and subjectivity, 210
Button, James, 5, 7

Camus, Albert, 108
Capitalism: capacity to co-opt, 106;
competitive and monopoly sectors
of, 241-42; and objectification, 210;
and separation of work from domesticity, 215; and social activities,
homogenization of, 61; transition
from entrepreneurial to monopoly,
184

Carmichael, Stokely, 23, 78
Chaney, James, 9, 146
Civil Rights Movement: and alliances,
126; anti-imperialist character, 264;
as artificially constituted opposi-
tion, 235; and Democratic party, 69;
development of, 66-71; as homoge-
nization, 234; internal management
perspective on, 66-69
Cleaver, Eldridge, 4, 263
Cloward, Richard, 6, 7
Commoner, Barry, 195
Communism, 239; bureaucratic collec-
tivism in Chinese, 238-39
Communist party, 176
Community control, and Black
power, 72
Connor, Bull, 29
Consensus: cultural challenges to,
122; and dissent, 121
Consumerism: ideology of, 65; and
New Deal, 65
Consumption communities, 188
Cornely, Paul, 147
Cortez, Jayne, 39
Counterculture, 105-11 passim; depol-
iticization of, 110-12; political po-
tential of, 109; and revolutionary
qualities, 114; self-centered, 113; as
state encouraged opposition, 195
Critical theory, and Marxist theory,
228
Croly, Herbert, 185
Crouch, Stanley, 39
Cruse, Harold, 20, 104
Cullen, Phyllis, 169
Cultural revolution: and Black nation-
alism, 35, 104; and character of, 119;
and lifestyle, 104; and real revolution, 106
Cultural subversion, and bureaucratic
intervention, 183
Culture: apparatus, emergence of,
101; clash of, 99; definition of, 99;
experimentation, 103; in 19th-cen-
tury American, 99; and status quo,
108
Cunningham, Phyllis, 150

Dandridge, Dorothy, 70
Davis, Angela, 22
Davis, Rennie, 4, 263
Debray, Regis, 108
Dent, Tom, 39
Domination: of Black community, 66-68; and Black elites, 64; and mass culture industry, 78
DuBois, W.E.B., 4
DuBoisian protest, co-opted by liberalism, 17
Dunbar, Paul Laurence, 30
Dylan, Bob, 4

Ellison, Ralph, 30
Energy policy, 240
Eurocommunism, 240

Falk, Les, 148
Falwell, Jerry, 195
Family, 207-25; and capitalist society, 215; and severing of work and domesticity, 216; substructure for domination in, 211
Fanon, Frantz, 14, 108; and African rejection of white culture, 35; on the blues, 32; and decolonization, conceptualization of, 15
Feminism: emergence of, 122, 236; and one-dimensionality, 236
Finer, June, 150
Fontaine, William T., 18
Ford, Henry, 186
Forman, James, 148
Free clinics, and alienation, 157
Freud, Sigmund, 218-19; and instincts, 219; and Oedipus complex, 218
Friese, Dr. Connie, 149
Fuller, Hoyt, 39

Gardner, John, 195
Garland, Ann, 166
Gibson, Kenneth, 48
Giovanni, Nikki, 42
Godwin, William, 260
Goldsmith, Frank, 167, 175
Gompers, Samuel, 190

Goodman, Andrew, 146
Goodman, Mitchell, 103
Goodman, Paul, 4, 108
Goodrich, Charles, 147
Great Society, 192-93; and transfer payments, 192

Habermas, Jürgen, 229
Haight-Ashbury Free Clinic, 156
Hall, Gus, 260
Hamer, Fannie Lou, 9
Hampton, Fred, 161
Hampton's Family Paper, ambiguities of, 162
Hance, Felicia, 166
Hart, Gary, 82, 259
Hausknecht, Richard, 148
Health care: complexity of, 194; political economy of, 178; politicization of, 157
Henderson, David, 39
Henderson, Stephen, 39
Hendrix, Jimi, 261
Hernton, Calvin, 39
Heydebrand, Wolf, 209
Hill, Tanganyika, 166
Hill-Burton Act, and segregation in South, 148
Hoffman, Abbie, 4, 103
Holloman, John, 147
Homogenization, cultural program of, 71
Hooker, John Lee, 32
Horkheimer, Max, 229
Hughes, Langston, 30, 33
Humphrey, Hubert, 127
Huntington, Samuel, 81
Hurwitz, Elliot, 148

Ideology: and Black uniqueness, construction of, 76; of civil rights movement, 70-71; and New Left, environment of, 134; and New Left, split in, 131; and philosophic constraint, 18-19; and revolutionary agency, 133; scientific, 19; and social theory, 18-20; transitional, 140, 142

Individuality: accidental, 123; corporate designed, 188

Jackson, Jesse, 259
Jacoby, Russell, 3, 160
Jones, LeRoi, 30, 33. *See also* Baraka, Amiri

Kafka, Franz, 207; and necessity, notion of, 210-11, 222
Karenga, Ron, 35
Kennedy, Edward, 167
Kenniston, Kenneth, 102
Kgositsile, Kereopetse, 41
Kilson, Martin, 22
King, Martin Luther, 4
Klonsky, Mike, 4

Lear, Walter, 147
Legitimacy crisis, 201
Levin, Tom, 147
Liberalism, corporate, 69
Liehm, Antonin J., 38, 43
Lifestyle: as a commodity, 105; limitations of as agent of social change, 104-5
Liuzzo, Viola, 9
Lomax, Pearl Cleage, 41
Lukács, George, 229

McAdam, Doug, 5, 7
McLuhan, Marshall, 105
Madhubuti, Haki (Don L. Lee); 37; and Africa, 51; and Black Aesthetic, 40; and Black life, deprecation of, 48-50; and capitalism, 51; influence of on alternative schools, 52; isolationism of, 52; media consciousness, 42; philosophical differences with Baraka, 48
Maggani, Barbara, 166
Managerial capitalism, 183; and expansion of state control, 189; political opposition of, 195
Marcuse, Herbert, 4, 61, 108
Martin, Peter, 103

Marxism, 211; and critical theory, 228; and psychoanalytic turn, 228
Means, Gardiner C., 189
Medical Committee for Human Rights (MCHR): and anti-war protest, 156; and Black Power, 152, 155; broadened constituency of, 164-65; and Communist Party, 173; and counterculture movement, 156; debate over purpose, 149; dissidents of, 172; goals of, 150; and Hampton's Family Paper, 162; local chapters of, 151; National Health Crusade of, 167-69; and National Health Insurance, 167; and politics of guilt, 159; and racism, 175, 176; and sectarianism, 175-76; and shift to the left, 153; and task forces, 169; and women's movement, 164
Mills, C. Wright, 19, 101, 108
Mitchell, Juliet, 219
Moses, Bob, 148
Muhammad, Elijah, 29, 48
Murchie, Pat, 166
Myrdal, Gunnar, 18

Nader, Ralph, 195
Neal, Larry, 30
Neo-colonialism: Baraka on, 16; dominance of Black elite in, 16
Neo-conservatism, 272; Marxist, 246
New Deal, 189-92, 255; and resource creation, 192
New Deal Coalition, and one dimensionality, 77
New Left: and alliances with blacks and women, 138; contradictory impact of, 124; and emphasis on cultural change, 120; failure of, 207; heroic character of, 119; ideological environment of, 134; politics of, 122; rationalizing function of, 234; as 'shock troops of mass culture,' 249; universalizing motion of, 265; weakness of, 143
Newton, Huey, 4, 24, 104

Oedipal phases, 213-14, 218-20; and mediation of domination, 214; and patriarchy, 218-19

Old Left, 256, 269; source of ideological clarity, 270

One dimensionality: age of, 227-32; and disruptive element in domination of South, 68; and New Deal coalition, 77; and transition between entrepreneurial and monopoly capitalism, 230

Opposition: artificially constituted, 234-35; and black activism, tendencies in, 5; in black community, 62; deauthorization of principle of, 3; demise of (of blacks), 75-76; possibilities for, 79; repression and, 61

Page, Thomas Nelson, 31

Parham, John, 149

Perkins, George W., 184

Phillips, Howard J., 195

Physicians Forum, 146

Piven, Frances Fox, 6, 7

Pluralism: and black activism, 5; Robert Smith and, 6-7

Poitier, Sidney, 70

Politics: poeticization of, 110; of subjectivity, 160; working-class 133

Port Huron Statement, 109

Pouissant, Dr. Alvin, 150

Pound, Roscoe, 185

Progrowth coalition: contradictions of, 80; as integrative mechanism, 79; and Reagan, 80

Racism, political significance of, 90-91 n.46

Radicalism: and crisis of New Deal social management model, 259; failure of as emancipatory politics, 8-9; normative vision of, 246; transvaluation of, 120

Rationality crisis, 201; and Habermas, 229

Reagan, Ronald: militarism of, 238; and new growth coalition, 81; and

rerationalization of service state, 197

Reddick, L. D., 18

Reflexivity, and revolutionary consciousness, 124

Reich, Charles, 103

Ricks, Willie, 23

Robeson, Paul, 20

Rodgers, Carolyn, 41

Roosevelt, Franklin, 185

Roosevelt, Theodore, 184, 186

Rossman, Michael, 103

Roszak, Theodore, 103

Rubin, Jerry, 4, 103, 252, 263

Russia, 237

Rustin, Bayard, 6

Sadaukai, Owusu, 23

Sale, Kirkpatrick, 136

Sartre, Jean Paul, 4

Schwerner, Michael, 146

Seale, Bobby, 4

Sectarianism, 124-31; and cultural action, 125

Service state, 183-202; delegation of state power in, 189; dismantling of community in, 191; foundations of, 185; as integrative mechanism, 7; oppositional mechanisms built in, 196; Pound, Roscoe on, 185; rerationalization of, 197

Sinnett, Calvin, 175

Skinner, B. F., 52

Smith, Bob, 149

Smith, Robert, 6, 7

Social amnesia: and alienation, 62; as collapsing of intentions and outcomes of activism, 5; as hypostasization of social movements, 4

Social theory, and ideology, 18-20

Spriggs, Ed, 261

Subcultures, advent and exploitation of, 100

Toomer, Jean, 33

Touré, Sekou, 37

Troupe, Quincy, 39

Turner, Frederick Jackson, 184
Turner, Irene, 148
Turner, James, 29
Turner, Nat, 34

Unemployment, of Black Americans,
    63, 200

Vietnam: catalytic function of, 232-33;
    and new imperialism, 233

Washington, Booker T., 16, 21
Wells, Aaron, 147, 149
Whorton, Don, 169
Wonder, Stevie, 4
Wright, Richard, 33

X, Malcolm, 23

Young, Quentin, 148, 153, 166

About the Contributors

ANDREW FEENBERG is Professor of Philosophy at San Diego State University, and does research on computers and communications at the Western Behavioral Sciences Institute in La Jolla, California. He is the author of *Lukács, Marx, and the Sources of Critical Theory*, (1981) and co-editor of *On Marcuse* (1985). His articles on social and political theory have appeared in *The Philosophical Forum, Theory and Society, Telos, Socialist Review*, and many other publications. In his student days, Dr. Feenberg worked with the student movement at the University of California, San Diego and Duke University. He was in France during the May Events of 1968.

DAVID GROSS spent much of the '60s at the University of Wisconsin in Madison. He received his Ph.D. there in the field of European Intellectual History, and has since taught at the University of Colorado in Boulder. He is an associate editor of *Telos* and has written extensively on modern cultural criticism and social theory. At present he is completing a book on the impact of remembering and forgetting in 20th century culture.

JENNIFER JORDAN participated in the student and cultural nationalist movements of the Sixties at Howard University in Washington, D.C. and received her B.A. (1967) and M.A. (1969) at that institution. Her doctoral work on the influence of aestheticism and decadence on the novels of the twenties was completed at Emory University in 1984 after which she returned to the Howard English faculty.

RHONDA KOTELCHUK was active in the civil rights movement, working with the Southern Student Organizing Committee in Nashville, Tennessee, from 1965 to 1967. She then completed a graduate degree in planning and for the next eight years worked with the Health Policy Advisory Committee (Health-PAC), a research group concerned with critical analysis of the American health care system. She has worked also with the Health Systems Agency of Greater Boston. She is presently on the staff of the New York City Health and Hospitals Corporation, and continues her association with Health-PAC.

JOEL KOVEL became a psychiatrist and psychoanalyst in the Sixties, and has used the latter capacity to frame certain questions about society and the radical project. Among his works have been *White Racism, The Age of Desire,* and *Against the State of Nuclear Terror.* He is currently doing work on Central America, liberation theology, anticommunism, and the theory of human nature.

HOWARD LEVY entered the U.S. Army in 1965. In 1967 he was court-martialed for refusing a direct order to train green beret soldiers (among sundry other charges). After spending more than two years in prison he joined the staff of Health-PAC. He is now director of the Department of Dermatology at Lincoln Hospital in the South Bronx and is an Associate Professor at New York Medical College.

TIMOTHY W. LUKE teaches political science at Virginia Polytechnic Institute and State University at Blacksburg, Virginia. As a college undergraduate from 1969 to 1972, he willingly and unwillingly participated in many aspects of the 'sixties' counter-cultures. And, with the other editors of *Telos*, he works to keep some of the spirit of the 'sixties' alive, while leaving most if its forms behind.

PAUL PICCONE has been editor of *Telos* since its founding in the late 1960s. He was involved in activist politics during that period and has been involved in the attempt to formulate a critical theoretical approach to contemporary American society, as well as in bringing American audiences into contact with the intellectual tradition of "western Marxism." He holds a doctorate in philosophy and has taught sociology and political science at various universities, including several years at Washington University. He presently lives in New York, where he publishes *Telos*.

ADOLPH REED, JR. worked in student, antiwar, GI and poor people's movements during the late 1960s and early 1970s. Like so many others, he went to graduate school to try to make sense of it all and to try to determine the conditions for a critical politics in the aftermath of widespread activism. He is a *Telos* editor and since 1981 has been on the political science and Afro-American studies faculties at Yale University.

ALEX WILLINGHAM has been an engaged observer of the modern protest movement ever since his own college undergraduate days at the beginning of the campus militancy in the early 1960s. He has done research on the rise and consolidation of civil rights protest ideology and reviewed the prospects and pitfalls in the attempted radicalization of the movement. Willingham earned a doctorate in political science from the University of North Carolina and during the 1970s taught courses in political theory, black politics and southern politics at Atlanta University. Today his research centers on issues of participation raised by the politics of the anti-welfare state including assessing the role of the new electoral involvement and the extent to which full access to the political process will be affected by government policy in voting rights. He is a member of the organizing committee, Community Empowerment Project, Highlander Center, New Market, Tennessee, and is Research Associate, Southern Regional Council, Atlanta, Georgia.